THE CRIMINAL COURTS

STRUCTURES, PERSONNEL, AND PROCESSES

THE CRIMINAL COURTS

STRUCTURES, PERSONNEL, AND PROCESSES

N. Gary Holten, Ph.D.
Associate Professor of Criminal Justice
University of Central Florida

and

Lawson L. Lamar, J.D.
State Attorney
Ninth Judicial Circuit of Florida

McGraw-Hill, Inc.
New York St. Louis San Francisco Auckland Bogotá
Caracas Lisbon London Madrid Mexico City Milan
Montreal New Delhi San Juan Singapore
Sydney Tokyo Toronto

This book was set in Times Roman by the College Composition Unit
in cooperation with Ruttle Shaw & Wetherill, Inc.
The editor was Phillip A. Butcher.
The cover was designed by Rafael Hernandez.
R. R. Donnelley & Sons Company was printer and binder.

THE CRIMINAL COURTS
Structures, Personnel, and Processes

5 6 7 8 9 0 DOC DOC 9 5 4

ISBN 0-07-029636-7

Library of Congress Cataloging-in-Publication Data

Holten, N. Gary.
    The criminal courts: structures, personnel, and processes / N.
Gary Holten and Lawson L. Lamar.
    p.   cm.
    ISBN 0-07-029636-7
        1. Criminal courts—United States.   2. Criminal procedure—United
    States.   I. Lamar, Lawson L.   II. Title
    KF9223.H65   1991
    345.73′01—dc20   90-5548
    [347.3051]

ABOUT
THE AUTHORS

N. GARY HOLTEN is chairman of the Department of Criminal Justice and Legal Studies at the University of Central Florida. He holds a B.A. in economics from the University of Connecticut (1961) and an M.A. (1964) and a Ph.D. (1972) in government from the University of Massachusetts. He taught political science and history at Windham College in Putney, Vermont, from 1964 to 1972 and has been on the faculty of U.C.F. since 1972, initially as a member of the Political Science Department. He served as chairman of the Department of Public Service Administration from 1978 to 1984.

In serving a faculty internship in the state attorney's office in Orange County, Florida, in 1975, Dr. Holten began a long-term association with Lawson L. Lamar, the co-author of *The Criminal Courts*. While on leave from the university and working as a court information officer for the Ninth Judicial Circuit, Dr. Holten performed a number of research projects and wrote a citizen's guide to the criminal court process. He has also conducted extensive research into sentencing policies and procedures. Together with Prof. Roger Handberg, in 1985 he undertook a major research project on Florida's sentencing guidelines; and, with Dr. Melvin Jones, he is co-author of a basic text, *The Criminal Justice System*. He is currently engaged with several colleagues in a project studying prison utilization under a grant from the Florida legislature.

Dr. Holten is married to Carol Lighthall Holten and has two boys, Scott and Jameson.

LAWSON L. LAMAR is the state attorney for the Ninth Judicial Circuit of Florida, prosecuting in and for the counties of Orange and Osceola, which include the cities of Orlando, Winter Park, Maitland, and Kissimmee as well as Walt Disney World and Universal Studios, Florida. He supervises 82 trial lawyers who prosecute all levels of offenses in the state courts. He received his J.D. degree from the University of Florida, College of Law, where he graduated with honors.

He previously held the office of sheriff of Orange County, supervising over 2,000 employees in all phases of local law enforcement. Prior to taking office as sheriff, he served as a military intelligence officer in the United States, Europe, and Viet Nam, and later was the chief assistant state attorney of the Ninth Circuit.

He has published articles and commentaries on Florida law and practice, and has been an instructor at the University of Central Florida, Valencia Community College in Orlando, and the University of Louisville.

Mr. Lamar is married, has three children, and lives in Winter Park, Florida.

To Carol and Jo Ann.

This small token is for their love,
encouragement, and participation
in our lives and work.

CONTENTS

PREFACE

This text is for sophomore- and junior-level criminal justice courses that deal with the criminal courts and for related courses in the fields of public administration, political science, and sociology that deal with court organization, policy making, and judicial process and behavior.

It is written by a professor of criminal justice at the University of Central Florida and a long-time prosecuting attorney who served two terms as the sheriff of Orange County, Florida, and is now the state attorney for the Ninth Judicial Circuit. Our collaboration on this project has spanned several years, and we have attempted to produce a highly readable and informative text that covers all important aspects of criminal courts.

As the Table of Contents indicates, the text covers arguments over the nature of justice; a brief history of the development of the Anglo-American legal system; basic tenets of American criminal law and procedure; the organization of courts; the powers, selection, training, and professional orientations of key court personnel; all the steps in the criminal process from arrest through appeal; current developments in court technology and administration; and issues related to the discretion of court officials and attempts to limit that discretion in order to reduce disparities.

What is provided here is the most complete text in adult criminal court process available. The text makes use of a unifying theme throughout: Packer's Crime Control versus Due Process models of the criminal justice process. Having introduced the models in the first chapter, which deals with concepts of justice, we recall them at several points to show their applicability to many different aspects of the operation of the system. Use of the Packer models is hardly new or unique to this text; it is our belief that they remain the most useful conceptualization of the major issues for undergraduate students.

Special features are included throughout to enhance the value of this text to students. Short news articles illustrate the points being discussed. In addition, excerpts from some leading constitutional law cases present pressing issues as dealt with at the Supreme Court level and show the dynamic interpretations of our Constitution with respect to the criminal process and the rights of accused persons.

The writing is, by the way, sometimes informal and even wry in style. As authors, we have no particular ideological commitment but to strip away some of the posturing often characteristic of legalistic or sociological treatments. It is college students we are addressing. While readers are not coddled in terms of level, we do try to maintain interest by occasionally telling a story or giving an inside view of the decision-making process at work. We hope readers find the time spent with this book rewarding.

McGraw-Hill and the authors would like to thank the following reviewers for their many helpful comments and suggestions: Terry C. Cox, Eastern Kentucky University; James A. Fagin, Wichita State University; and Dean J. Spader, University of South Dakota.

N. Gary Holten
Lawson L. Lamar

CHAPTER 1

THE CONCEPT OF JUSTICE

After reading this chapter, students should be able to define and explain the importance of each of the following terms or phrases:

Crime Control Model
Due Process Model
substantive justice
decriminalization
procedural justice
white-collar crimes
victimless crimes
retribution
rehabilitation
psychological therapies
environmental therapies
deterrence
incapacitation

"equal" justice
"individualized" justice
justice of dispensation
adversarial system
inquisitorial system
accusatorial method
burden of proof
reasonable basis test
probable cause
prima facie case
proof beyond a reasonable doubt
constitutional law
selective incorporation

The concept of justice, which is central to an understanding of the criminal courts, is constantly evolving in response to social change and political pressures. What was just yesterday may not be thought of as just tomorrow. Or today! Consider, if you will, the following real-life example.

On May 3, 1978, the police department of Bloomingdale, Illinois, received an anonymous letter stating that a certain married couple was engaged in selling drugs; that the wife would drive the couple's car to Florida on May 3 to be loaded with drugs and that the husband would fly down a few days later to drive the car back; that the car's trunk would be loaded with drugs; and that the couple currently had over $100,000 worth of drugs in their basement. Acting on the tip, a police officer determined the couple's address and learned that the husband had a reservation on a May 5 flight to Florida. Arrangements for surveillance of the flight were made with an agent of the Drug Enforcement Administration (DEA). The surveillance disclosed that the husband took the flight, stayed overnight in a motel room registered in his wife's name, and on the following morning left with a woman in a car bearing an Illinois license plate issued to himself, heading north on an interstate highway used by travelers to the Bloomingdale area. On the basis of the anonymous letter and the Bloomingdale police officer's affidavit setting forth the foregoing facts, a search warrant for the couple's residence and automobile was obtained from an Illinois state court judge. When the man and woman arrived at their home, the police were waiting and discovered marijuana and other contraband in the car trunk and house.

Prior to the couple's trial on charges of violating state drug laws, the trial court ordered suppression of all the items seized, effectively destroying the prosecution's case since suppression of the evidence made proof of violation of state drug laws impossible. The prosecutor appealed the suppression through the appellate courts, losing at every step short of the U.S. Supreme Court because of a rule of case law commonly known as the Aguilar-Spinelli test. That test, established on two Supreme Court cases decided in the 1960s, required that, in order to obtain a warrant based on evidence given by an informant, the police must verify that the informant was a reliable person and must provide a full statement of facts such as would lead the magistrate to conclude independently that the evidence would indeed be found in the place cited in the search warrant.[1] A practical result of the first part of this rule is that it requires the police to *know* the informant; an anonymous person obviously cannot be known to be reliable. In all similar cases decided since the Aguilar-Spinelli rule was adopted, the evidence obtained as a result of anonymous tips had been suppressed, and so it was in this case.

Would justice be better served by upholding the established rule, suppressing the evidence and preventing prosecution of the accused? Or would justice be better served by changing the rule and permitting the prosecution to use the evidence seized as a result of the anonymous tip? Think about this question. It is not merely an academic or theoretical exercise. It is a question that was presented to the Supreme Court in 1982. That Court, which had issued the Aguilar-Spinelli rule in the first place, reversed itself and overturned the decisions of lower courts, thus permitting the evidence to be used.

In discarding the formal rule of *Aguilar* and *Spinelli* the Court set forth a new rule that considers the totality of the circumstances in the case and doesn't require independent proof of the informant's *personal* reliability.[2] This decision represents a shift in the thinking of the Court—and actually reflects the change in its membership—from a due process emphasis to a crime control emphasis.

Another, even more important example of this shift of the Court is the 1984 case of *United States v. Leon*, in which a significant change was made to the exclusionary rule. The Court ruled 6 to 3 that evidence seized with a defective search warrant need not be excluded from use at trial. The ruling created what is called a *good-faith exception* to the exclusionary rule. The Court said that the rule should not apply when the police act with "objectively reasonable reliance" on a warrant that is apparently valid when used but is later ruled defective by a higher court.[3] This case will be discussed again later in this text. Suffice it to say here that it has proved to be one of the most important cases in recent years and that it clearly represents the shift of the Supreme Court from emphasis on due process to a crime control orientation.

TWO MODELS OF JUSTICE

It was Herbert Packer who identified and described the two models or "value systems that compete for priority in the operation of the criminal process." He labeled these the *Crime Control Model* and the *Due Process Model*. He recognized that such polarized models are "distortions of reality" but noted that they are useful in clarifying the terms of discussion by isolating the assumptions that underlie competing points of view about criminal justice policy.[4]

The Crime Control Model

Packer begins his discussion of the models with a statement of the most fundamental proposition of the Crime Control Model: The repression of criminal conduct is by far the most important function to be performed by the criminal process. According to this model, the failure of law enforcement to bring criminal conduct under tight control can lead to the breakdown of public order and hence to the disappearance of an important condition of human freedom. If the laws go unenforced—which is to say, if it is perceived that there is a high percentage of failure to apprehend and convict in the criminal process—a general disregard for legal controls tends to develop. Law-abiding citizens then become the victims of all sorts of unjustifiable invasions of interest. Their security of person and property is sharply diminished and, therefore, so is their liberty to function as members of society. The claim ultimately is that the criminal process is a positive guarantor of social freedom. In order to achieve this high purpose, the Crime Control Model requires that primary attention be paid to the efficiency with which the criminal process operates to screen suspects, determine guilt, and secure appropriate dispositions of persons convicted of crime.[5]

Packer goes on to point out that several things are necessary for this approach to be successful: (1) there must be a high rate of apprehension and conviction; (2) there must be "a premium on speed and finality"; (3) there must be recognition of the fact that speed depends on informality and uniformity, while finality depends upon minimizing opportunities for challenge; and (4) "the process must not be cluttered up with ceremonious rituals that do not advance the progress of a case." Thus the ideal process, according to this model, would emphasize extrajudicial rather than judicial procedures, prefer informal operations to formal ones, use routine procedures, and become, therefore, a managerial model. Packer comments: "The image that comes to mind is an assembly line conveyor belt down which moves an endless stream of cases, never stopping, carrying the cases to workers who stand at fixed stations and who perform on each case as it comes by the same small but essential operation that brings it one step closer to being a finished product, or, to exchange the metaphor for the reality, a closed file."[6]

Packer points out that this approach sees the criminal process as being essentially one of screening the cases at each stage to filter out those involving persons who are likely innocent of the accusation and passing along those involving persons who are probably guilty of the crime. This approach, therefore, involves a presumption of guilt, a presumption, Packer argues, that is not really the opposite of the legal doctrine of presumption of innocence. This presumption of guilt is a practical and predictive one—that is, one that counts on the screening process to catch and filter out those accused persons who are either truly innocent or against whom the evidence is poor. The presumption of innocence is a different rather than a contrasting idea. It holds that, even where the evidence is overwhelming, a person should be treated and processed as though he or she is innocent until there is "an adjudication of guilt by an authority legally competent to make such an adjudication." Thus the presumption of innocence is "a direction to officials about how they are to proceed, not a prediction of outcome," while the presumption of guilt is "purely and simply a prediction of outcome."[7]

The Due Process Model

If the Crime Control Model resembles an assembly line, Packer observes, the Due Process Model looks very much like an obstacle course.

It is based on an ideology that is not the converse of that underlying the Crime Control Model, since it also assumes that repression of crime is a socially desirable goal. Rather, the ideology behind the Due Process Model is "composed of a complex of ideas" involving both the efficacy of crime control and a number of quite different considerations. Packer explains:

> The Due Process Model encounters its rival on the Crime Control Model's own ground in respect to the reliability of fact-finding processes. The Crime Control Model, as we have suggested, places heavy reliance on the ability of investigative and prosecutorial officers, acting in an informal setting in which their distinctive skills are given full sway, to elicit and reconstruct a tolerably accurate account of what actually took place in an alleged criminal event. The Due Process Model rejects this premise and substitutes for it a view of informal, nonadjudicative fact-finding that stresses the possibility of error. People are notoriously poor observers of disturbing events—the more emotion-arousing the context the greater the possibility that recollection will be incorrect; confessions and admissions by persons in police custody may be induced by physical or psychological coercion so that the police end up hearing what the subject thinks they want to hear rather than the truth; witnesses may be animated by a bias or interest that no one would trouble to discover except one specially charged with protecting the interests of the accused (as the police are not). Considerations of this kind all lead to a rejection of formal fact-finding processes as definitive of factual guilt and to an insistence on formal, adjudicative adversary fact-finding processes in which the factual case against the accused is publicly heard by an impartial tribunal and is evaluated only after the accused has had a full opportunity to discredit the case against him. Even then, the distrust of fact-finding processes that animates the Due Process Model is not dissipated. The possibilities of human error being what they are, further scrutiny is necessary, or at least must be available, in case facts have been overlooked or suppressed in the heat of battle. How far this subsequent scrutiny must be available is a hotly controverted issue today. In the pure Due Process Model the answer would be: at least as long as there is an allegation of factual error that has not received an adjudicative hearing in a fact-finding context. The demand for finality is thus very low in the Due Process Model.[8]

Packer points out that the two models disagree on the relationship between efficiency and reliability. The Crime Control Model treats efficiency and reliability as complementary attributes and argues that the more efficient the system is, the more reliable it is in its mission to repress crime; the Due Process Model treats these attributes as competing goals and argues that reliability is a quality-control measure that necessarily cuts down on output and thus hampers the achievement of efficiency. The Crime Control definition of reliability thus relates to the system's overall performance, while the Due Process adherents define reliability in terms of the system not making mistakes in imposing sanctions in individual cases.[9]

The two models also differ on which meaning of guilt should receive emphasis. Whereas the Crime Control Model asserts that factual guilt is the important consideration, the Due Process Model emphasizes the doctrine of legal guilt. *Legal guilt* is that which is determined "in a procedurally regular fashion by authorities acting with competencies duly allocated to them." An accused is thus "not to be held guilty, even though the factual determination is or might be adverse to him, if various rules designed to protect him and to safeguard the integrity of the process are not given effect."[10] A factually guilty person should be found legally innocent, therefore, if the rules are ignored or violated by those administering the law.

This brings us to one other important point of clear difference between the two models. Packer points out that the Crime Control Model can tolerate rules about illegal arrests or searches, coercive interrogations, and so on; what it cannot tolerate is the enforcement of those rules by throwing out the evidence or confessions and reversing the convictions of those found guilty. The Due Process Model insists that law enforcers can be effectively kept in line and deterred from disobeying the rules only by setting free those against whom illegal or incorrect procedures were used.[11]

The Due Process Model is firmly based on an attitude of equality. Packer points out, in fact, that the model is stated most starkly as an attack on the notion that defendants get the kind of justice they can afford. Equal justice, due process adherents point out, demands that the wealth (or power) of defendants have nothing to do with the outcome of their cases. Since as a practical matter most cases are settled prior to trial, and since the financial means of defendants is obviously a factor in representation by counsel, then the due process insistence on equality of treatment results in the requirement that counsel be appointed to represent indigent defendants immediately upon initiation of criminal process.[12]

Finally, Packer notes that there is an underlying skepticism among adherents of the Due Process Model about the very morality, or even the utility, of all or some of the sanctions imposed by the criminal justice system. One observes this particularly in arguments about whether incarceration in prisons as they are today is justifiable or even practicable from a crime control standpoint. Thus there are attempts to strengthen checks on the process by which these sanctions are imposed. Packer writes: "In short, doubts about the ends for which power is being exercised create pressure to limit the discretion with which that power is exercised."[13]

A chart that compares the Due Process Model and Crime Control Model point for point is found in Table 1.1. We shall be returning to

TABLE 1.1
PACKER'S DUE PROCESS AND CRIME CONTROL MODELS: A COMPARISON

Due Process Model	Crime Control Model
Criminal process is slower; fewer persons are processed; fewer antisocial actions are regulated against.	Criminal process is efficient; more persons are processed; more antisocial actions are regulated against.
Personal autonomy is more highly valued than overall societal freedoms; personal privacy rights are paramount; certain criminal violations (e.g., victimless crimes) are more difficult to detect.	Overall societal freedoms are more highly valued than personal autonomy; there is less attention paid to personal privacy rights; all criminal violations (including victimless crimes) are more easily detected.
The adversarial aspect of the criminal justice system is central.	The adversarial aspect of the criminal justice system is deemphasized.
Presumption of innocence is attached to all persons involved in the system.	Presumption of guilt is attached to those persons not screened out of the system.
The central importance of fact finding attaches to the formal, adjudicative, adversarial fact-finding process in which the factual case against the defendant is publicly heard by an impartial tribunal and is decided only after the accused has full opportunity to discredit the charges.	The central importance of fact finding attaches to informal, pretrial, administrative, fact-finding processes, which lead to exoneration of the suspect or entry of a guilty plea. The criminal process is characterized by routinized operations designed to screen out the innocent and convict the guilty as quickly as possible.
There is distrust of any fact-finding process, with a corresponding deemphasis on speed and finality.	There is a basic trust in the fact-finding process, with a corresponding premium placed on speed and finality.
Mistakes in the process are to be prevented at all cost.	The probability of mistakes is accepted to a level where such mistakes interfere with the goal of repressing crime.
Legal guilt is paramount.	Factual guilt is paramount.
As a negative model, it asserts limits on the nature of official power and how it is exercised; the validating authority is the judicial branch.	As an affirmative model, it emphasizes the existence and exercise of official power; the validating authority is the legislative branch.
It sees the criminal process as an obstacle course.	It sees the criminal process as an assembly line.
Emphasis is placed on the individual, on preventing victimization of the defendant by the system, and on protecting the factually *and* legally innocent.	Emphasis is placed on the group, society, or the system, on preventing victimization of the public by criminals, and on convicting the factually guilty.

Source: An unpublished work of Dean Spader, University of South Dakota.

Packer's two models throughout the rest of this text. While they are, as Packer himself points out, oversimplifications, they serve to illuminate most of the points of controversy that will be taken up as the criminal process is examined. It is especially clear, as Packer notes, that the expressions and policies of police and prosecutors closely adhere to many principles of the Crime Control Model, while the Due Process Model is generally represented in the actions and expressions of the defense bar and the judiciary, especially the appellate judiciary.

SUBSTANTIVE VERSUS PROCEDURAL JUSTICE

The discussion of Packer's models raises some basic points that must be examined carefully. We have to make some key distinctions here. One is the distinction between substantive and procedural aspects of justice. This distinction is particularly important to an understanding of the criminal law and process.

Substantive Justice Defined

Substantive justice is that which concerns how best to allocate or distribute the substantive values of society, those values including power, wealth, status, and whatever other "goods" society cherishes. Decisions as to the allocation of these goods can be based on standards that are moral, religious, ideological, practical, or materialistic, depending on the prevailing philosophy or interests of those making the judgments.

The laws that govern these decisions can be said to be "just" or "unjust" depending upon the extent to which the values they reflect and the interests they protect are the same as or different from those of the critic. People who adhere to a belief in the basic right to hold private property, and those who hold it, are likely to label as "just" those laws that uphold the rights of property owners and to label as "unjust" or "subversive" those laws that seek to redistribute wealth or collectivize control over property. People who adhere to collectivist ideologies are likely to label laws that protect private property "unjust" and to call for laws aimed at achieving social and economic justice.

People who are strongly conservative or traditional in their moral and religious views generally attack laws that permit behavior they consider sinful or degenerate as "unjust" laws. Those who consider themselves very liberal or individualistic in their views about morality can be expected to attack laws limiting or controlling sexual behavior or other forms of social conduct as "unjust" intrusions into private matters. These examples serve to illustrate what is meant by issues of substantive justice.

In terms of criminal justice, the substantive issues focus on what acts are to be considered threatening or damaging enough to the safety and welfare of citizens to be prohibited and what sanctions should be provided for such offenses.

At the present time there is much debate over the possible *decriminalization* or even full legalization of some behaviors commonly defined heretofore as crimes in most states. Some fundamental questions are raised in this debate: Should only those acts with direct and identifiable victims be prohibited? Or should criminal law encompass acts that victimize people only indirectly, as members of a class perhaps? What about behavior that may have no apparent victims or seems to victimize only the person engaging in that behavior? We shall return to these questions later.

As far as sanctions are concerned, is justice best served by having the state impose retribution on behalf of the victim? Or is incapacitation of the offender the goal we should seek? Does justice demand simply that the offender be deterred from other criminal acts, or does justice demand that an example be made of the offender in order to deter others from crime? (The former is known as special deterrence, the latter as general deterrence; we shall discuss these terms later.) Or is the only "just" treatment one that seeks to rehabilitate the offender? Does justice require some mix of these goals, with sanctions individualized to fit the needs of each offender, or should "the punishment fit the crime," thus requiring similar sanctions for similar offenses?

These questions are not merely academic. They are at the heart not only of much research and literature but also of the efforts being made by many states and the federal government to reform penal codes and to make the system more responsive to the demands of citizens. We shall shortly examine this matter more closely. For now let us note that the efforts at reform are aimed at making the law conform to some notion of the obligations of justice.

Most of us do not accept the proposition that justice is defined solely by existing law. We tend to believe that laws can be changed in order to better achieve "justice," whether it is defined in terms of the social good or as each person's due.

Procedural Justice Defined

Procedural justice concerns itself with the mechanisms and processes by which society enforces its substantive law and deals with those who violate that law. It refers to how decisions are reached in dealing with accused lawbreakers. Procedural justice is established through the codes of evidence and the rules of procedure used by the courts and other quasi-judicial bodies such as review boards and panels of administrative agencies. The U.S. Constitution spells out certain rights of citizens in connection with the authority of government to enforce the law and adjudicate cases. Virtually all of these rights are procedural in nature. Taken together, they constitute the basis of what is called *due process of law*—in other words, that process that treats accused persons in a just manner.

Many persons complain that only criminals seem to have rights, that the victim and the law-abiding citizen are relatively unprotected and often ignored. This complaint is based on the fact that the rights spelled out in the Constitution are those of citizens against government, and thus are useful to anyone being investigated, arrested, prosecuted, or sentenced by government. The Constitution, to be sure, does not provide for the rights of victims or of citizens in terms of their treatment by other citizens. We shall examine some of the specific provisions of the Constitution and major decisions of the U.S. Supreme Court later in this chapter.

SUBSTANTIVE JUSTICE:
WHAT SHOULD THE LAW PROHIBIT?

As has already been mentioned, substantive issues related to criminal justice revolve around what actions ought to be prohibited and what sanctions are appropriate for specific offenses and offenders, and we have alluded to the continuing controversies in these areas. Let us look now more closely at some fundamental questions and opinions on these matters.

In their text on criminal law, Wells and Weston review the "limitations on lawmaking" and state that lawmakers have "the obligation . . . to exercise the government's police power only in the public's interest: to promote safety, health and general welfare.[14] The problem, of course, is that these terms are extremely vague, especially the term "general welfare." What is the degree of "safety" and "health" to which we are entitled to governmental protection? From what sources of threats to our safety can or should the government protect us? Should we be protected even from ourselves? Or can laws forbidding gambling, use of drugs, and riding motorcycles without helmets be justified on the basis that they protect others—especially our families—from our individual stupidities and carelessness?

Wells and Weston point out that a related fundamental requirement of criminal law is that it give "fair notice" to potential violators. This means that the code containing the prohibitions must be "visible" and "not buried in the mass of case law."[15] Ignorance of the law may not be a legal defense, but justice requires that criminal laws be accessible.

Two areas of criminal law give rise to the greatest difficulties: so-called white-collar crimes and what have been called victimless crimes.

In both of these areas there is controversy as to whether it is appropriate for the behavior to be labeled "criminal" and the "offender" prosecuted and punished by the state. The question arises because there can be difficulty in perceiving that any specific person is victimized in a manner requiring criminal proceedings. Despite their similar aspects, however, there are substantial differences between white-collar crime and victimless crime.

White-Collar Crimes

White-collar crime can be loosely defined as crime that rises out of corruption in the conduct of government and business affairs. It consists of embezzlement, bribery, fraud, the sale of influence, and other such illegalities.

Diffusion of Victimization A pervasive problem with most white-collar, or economic, offenses is the diffusion of victimization among many persons, such as all the stockholders of a corporation or all the customers of a public utility. The target is hardly perceived as "victim" by the offender. An executive who absconds may conclude that since so many persons are "victimized," and each in such a limited or unnoticeable way, that "no one is really hurt." And individual employees or customers who rip off insurance or utility companies generally feel that these rich corporations can afford it—perhaps even deserve it.

Public Wrongs versus Private Wrongs Another related difficulty in white-collar crime is that many of the acts covered by criminal law as public wrongs are also subject to civil actions as private wrongs against individuals or select groups. Private parties can sue for damages for offenses committed by businesses in the marketplace or seek other civil redress; and government can choose to press charges through criminal prosecution, civil action in court, or administrative action through a regulatory agency. This situation suggests that we haven't quite decided whether white-collar crime constitutes a public wrong or a private wrong. In fact, many wrongs, such as a bad-check charge, are often prosecuted as criminal matters even while restitution is sought in the civil courts.

Corporations as "Persons" Another issue in white-collar crime is that corporations long ago won legal status as "persons" under the law for purposes of gaining due process protections. This raises the problem of whether to prosecute the corporation as an entity or to file charges against particular officials or employees who ordered or carried out the criminal acts. The law permits both. But when a corporation is convicted, how is it punished? Since it cannot be incarcerated, it is generally fined. Who winds up paying the fines? Generally this "cost of doing business" is passed along to customers through higher prices.

Criminal Responsibility   When individual executives or other officials or employees of a company (or any other organization such as a union) are singled out for prosecution for acts that benefited the organization, they often offer the defense of duress. They claim they were compelled to act by orders from higher-ups or by conditions created by others that made illegal acts necessary to financial survival or employment security. These claims are usually weak defenses, but they do raise the question as to how to pin down the real responsibility for crimes committed by or in the name of an organization.

Criminal Intent   A final difficulty is that of having to prove that not only did the accused commit a criminal act but knew at the time the act was criminal. Wells and Weston point out that the vast majority of crimes designated by Title 18 of the U.S. Code carry the words "knowingly," "maliciously," "willfully," "with the purpose of," "with intent to," or combinations of these words.[16] They thus require the separate proof of intent, or *mens rea*—the guilty mind. Some offenses do not require this. They are so-called strict liability offenses— those so dangerous or in which proof of intent is so difficult that it would be unreasonable to require such proof. Interestingly enough, some white-collar offenses, such as selling adulterated food, are among these cases.

The upshot of all this is that creating or expanding the list of white-collar crimes places a terrible burden on the criminal justice system. Edwin Sutherland, the criminologist who coined the term "white-collar crime," often criticized the tendency of government to deal administratively or through civil actions with white-collar offenders. He claimed that due to "differential enforcement" many criminals were escaping their just desserts because they were businesspeople or professionals with high status in their communities.[17]

An argument can be made that administrative or civil approaches to many white-collar crimes are more appropriate and effective than criminal prosecution. Not only are the rule of evidence and procedure less demanding on the government, but the remedies available may do more to curb these offenses than the fines and the probationary sentences usually handed out. Companies, unions, and other offending organizations may be forced to compensate victims, submit to tighter government controls (as when the U.S. government placed the Teamsters Union pension fund

under trustees it selected), or shut down or clean up offending operations; they might even be forced out of business altogether.

On the other hand, most white-collar crimes are forms of theft, and an
argument can be made that criminal sanctions have hardly been given a
fair chance to be proved effective. Sentencing in most white-collar crime
cases has amounted to "wrist slapping," and very few offenders have
been sent to jail or prison. Most businesspeople, professionals, union officers, and employees may be more susceptible to deterrence than professional or violent criminals. Subjecting some to prison terms may do
wonders in curbing illegal activities.

Victimless Crimes

The debate over what should and should not be criminalized is especially
intense (and seemingly never-ending) with respect to a collection of behaviors usually referred to as *victimless crimes*. There is no generally accepted
definition of the victimless crime. Edwin Schur suggests the following:

> Victimless crimes are created when we attempt to ban through criminal legis-
> lation the exchange between willing partners of strongly desired goods or ser-
> vices. The "offense" in such a situation, then, consists of a consensual trans-
> action—one person gives or sells another person something he or she wants.[18]

What of the assertion that persons are nevertheless harmed, or "victimized," by these acts? Schur says, in effect, harm or victimization is a
subjective matter, and he argues that the important thing is that the "persons involved in exchanging [illicit] goods and services *do not see themselves* as victims."[19] The key is their unwillingness to report offenses to
authorities.

Hugo Adam Bedau points out that two major problems exist with this
definition: (1) It doesn't cover some important crimes normally discussed
by advocates of decriminalization (vagrancy and drunkenness, for example), and (2) unwillingness to report crimes is hardly an adequate measure of their "harmlessness." Bedau observes that participants may not
be in the best position to judge the harmfulness of an act and that persons
other than the participants may be victimized, and thus conceivably have
a basis for seeking prohibition and penal sanctions.[20]

Social Costs of Criminalization   Schur focuses on four social costs of
criminalization of these behaviors: (1) their enforcement imposes a disproportionate burden on law enforcement, in terms not only of the
cost of resources but of the tactics needed to make a case; (2) they
have the effect of driving up the price of the affected goods and services for all, while the poor receive the brunt of enforcement efforts;

(3) they create criminals not only by definition but also by causing some to steal in order to be able to afford their vices; and (4) they breed corruption in law enforcement as suppliers seek insulation from the law and foster a resultant disrespect for law and law enforcement by members of the public.[21]

Support for Decriminalization   Bedau happens to agree with Schur that laws governing victimless crime ought to be repealed, but he bases his argument not on the concept of social evil as Schur does but on the notion of individual rights. Bedau believes that criminal law should protect such rights that cannot be violated by "deliberate and malicious acts of others" without personal injury.[22] He argues that most victimless crimes do not meet this test. For Bedau, the chief arguments in support of criminalization are (1) that harm is caused to persons other than participants; (2) that the behavior of some persons requires interference for their own physical or moral good; and (3) that the law has a duty to uphold certain moral standards even where harm is not at issue. Having set forth these arguments, he rejects each of them as a justification for criminal law, and would have us rely instead on "the extra-legal institutions in society" to protect individual rights that don't meet his stringent "personal-injury" standard.

Support for Criminalization   Dallin H. Oaks writes as a supporter of criminalization of at least drug- and sex-related offenses. He argues that "there really is no such thing as a victimless crime."[23] Loved ones and/or all society suffers for these offenses, if only in having to provide for rehabilitation of the offender. Even adultery, fornication, and other consensual sex offenses are legitimate crimes because "they pose a threat to the integrity of the family structure, which is the basic supportive institution in our society."[24]

Oaks also believes strongly in the educative and standard-setting functions of the law, functions that become even more important as the extralegal institutions (such as schools and churches) "seem to be progressively less effective."[25] He cites civil rights laws as a prime example of this function. In contrast to the proposition that widely disobeyed laws bring disrespect for all law, Oaks submits that "the law will be discredited if it attempts to *decriminalize* conduct condemned under collective morality."[26]

The debate over victimless crimes thus serves to illustrate the deep division that exists over the purpose of criminal law and the requirements of substantive justice. Some argue for a rather limited protection of lives, health, and safety and for maximum freedom of individuals to decide what acts are harmful and to be avoided. Oaks speaks for many, however, in his assertion that the law properly preserves "public health, safety and *morality*" and that these concepts are subject to community standards and collective decision.

SUBSTANTIVE JUSTICE:
WHAT SANCTIONS SHOULD BE IMPOSED?

Lon Fuller puts it this way: "The ills and disorders of a legal system—at least those that come about despite reasonably good intentions—can all be attributed to the fact that those concerned with the law are not clear as to what it is they are trying to do." The need for clear purpose toward which all efforts of lawmakers and law enforcers can be focused is especially acute in the criminal law, he writes, since "this branch of the law is notoriously afflicted by disputes as to what it is for."[27]

Fuller notes that there are four different theories of the purpose of criminal law and quotes Norbert Wiener's observations about the distress this situation creates:

> Where the law of Western countries is at present least satisfactory is on the criminal side. Law seems to consider punishment, now as a threat to discourage other possible criminals, now as a ritual act of expiation on the part of the guilty man, now as a device for removing him from society and for protecting the latter from the danger of repeated misconduct, and now as an agency for the social and moral reform of the individual. These are four different tasks, to be accomplished by four different methods; and unless we know an accurate way of proportioning them, our whole attitude to the criminal will be at cross purposes. At present, the criminal law speaks now in one language, and now in another. Until we in the community have made up our minds, that what we really want is expiation, or removal, or reform, or the discouragement of potential criminals, we shall get none of these, but only a confusion in which crime breeds more crime. Any code which is made, one-fourth on the eighteenth century British prejudice in favor of hanging, one-fourth on the removal of the criminal from society, one-fourth on a halfhearted policy of hanging up a dead crow to scare away the rest, is going to get us nowhere.
>
> Let us put it this way: the first duty of the law, whatever the second and third ones are, is to know what it wants.[28]

Retribution

Fuller offers the following arguments in support of the theory of *retribution:*

1. It permits the state to exact a regularized and controlled vengeance upon offenders rather than the "unregulated and private vengeance" that would surely occur in its absence. This is due to a "deep impulse of human nature that if not given legitimate expression is bound to find disruptive outlets."

2. It permits the restoration of a sense of guilt in some offenders (particularly the white-collar variety) and supports the fact that some acts are fundamentally wrong even if they don't give rise to instincts of personal revenge. Fuller points out, however, that "the ritual of expiation loses its whole point if those who perform it do so with unclean hands." Corrupt agencies cannot be expected to "reanimate the public sense of sin."

3. It permits honest individuals, those who obey the law, to see that "crime doesn't pay" and, conversely, that lawful behavior does. Since we cannot offer prizes for obeying the law, we accomplish the effect indirectly by punishing lawbreakers. Fuller observes: "Unless this is done the scales of justice will weigh out short measure to the man willing to abide by the rules."[29]

Rehabilitation

There are those, of course, who argue that civilized society should not permit vengeance, much less involve the state in such a primitive and barbaric business. These persons usually argue that rehabilitation should be made the central, it not the exclusive, purpose of the criminal law.

Rehabilitation has been defined as the *restoration of a criminal to a state of physical, mental, and moral health through treatment and training.*[30] It is based on the assumption that an offender's character or behavior can be changed—that the offender can be cured of, or turned away, from criminal tendencies.

Those who support this approach often argue that the effect of punishment, particularly if it consists of a term in prison, is either short-lived or negative. They point out that institutional confinement and conditions are generally dehumanizing and that the released criminal is often hardened in attitude and even more skilled in criminal behavior. Sue Titus Reid writes: "There is little, if any, social value or moral justification in controlling a man's antisocial behavior for a number of years ... and then turning him back into society unprepared to live a law-abiding life."[31] The argument, then, is that retribution not only is morally objectionable, but self-defeating from a practical standpoint.

Lon Fuller argues that "there are good grounds for believing" that purging the system of punishment and replacing it with rehabilitation "cannot be done and should not be attempted."

In the first place, there exists nothing at present that can be called a science of rehabilitation. The place such a science would occupy is today a battlefield for continuing schools of thought. On this field meet protagonists of behaviouristic, psychoanalytic, mechanistic, and moralistic theories, as well as those who humbly ask only a chance to apply intuitive kindness.[32]

Reid surveys the "typology of treatment forms" used in dealing with criminals, grouping them into two broad categories: psychological therapies and environmental therapies. The former concentrate on the condition of the individual offender, the latter on the relationship of the offender to others, to social norms, and to conditions surrounding the individual.[33]

Psychological Therapies   The therapies aimed at treating the offender alone include at least four. *Psychotherapy* aims at developing "a process of growth in a patient"—the development of internal controls over his or her own behavior—through counseling designed to help the patient deal with emotions, especially those of self-esteem, guilt, and anxiety.

Reality therapy rejects psychotherapy's delving into the past and examines the conscious self and behavior rather than the unconscious motivations. It concentrates on developing in the clients a sense of responsibility for their own actions and a sense of what is moral and what is not.

Behavior modification, the third approach, assumes that deviant behavior, like all behavior, is learned and that, through a system of rewards and punishment, criminals can be taught to behave lawfully. The rewards can be tangible, such as money, and the punishments can range from the denial of a valued privilege (such as watching television) to the infliction of actual pain (such as electric shock). An extreme form of behavior modification is physiological behavior control. The methods of control include the use of mind-altering drugs; implantation of electrodes in the brain; and psychosurgery, or surgery to alter or remove brain tissue. All behavior-modification therapies are controversial, but the latter techniques have been under intense attack and have fallen into general disfavor.

Finally, there is *transactional analysis,* an approach that uses games, psychodrama, and role playing. It assumes that there are three personalities within each person: parent, adult, and child. The purpose is to help patients understand themselves and their interaction and to develop "spontaneity and a capacity for intimacy."

Environmental Therapies   The other group of therapies, the environmental, includes group therapy and milieu management. *Group therapy* seeks to alter the behavior of individuals through socialization into a group in the hope of developing a cohesiveness and a sense of useful purpose. It assumes that peer pressure can be used to reform criminals and to provide them with lawful values and goals. *Milieu management* goes further by providing a highly structured and directed environment usually closed to outside influences. It is a technique used by religious cults such as the "Moonies" and by some drug treatment programs. It has been attacked as "programming" and "brainwashing" by critics. There are legitimate questions as to whether this approach merely substitutes dependence on the group or program for the previous dependence on drugs or a deviant subculture.

Levine, Musheno, and Palumbo point out that whatever approach is taken, it is useful only with criminals who do not consider themselves to be professionals. Professional criminals "engage in crime because they believe the benefits exceed the costs, not because they hate society or because they have an uncontrollable impulse to do something violent."[34] Only offenders who have emotional problems seem susceptible to rehabilitation and then, many argue, only those who can freely choose treatment.

Stanley E. Samenow and the late Samuel Yochelson shocked many criminologists and stirred a raging debate among experts and practitioners alike with their even more negative conclusions. Habitual criminals—those usually found in prisons—are distinguishable from law-abiding citizens, wrote Samenow and Yochelson, by their lack of any capacity for love or friendship, their contempt for social norms and the rights of others, their proclivity to lie and deceive at every opportunity, and an inflated sense of their own worth and rights. It is not mental illness or society which is to blame, they assert, but the criminal's own cruelty. Institutions or programs are able to do little or nothing for or to the vast majority of these offenders.[35] The conclusion appears to be that society is wasting its time and resources on attempts to rehabilitate prison populations.

Lon Fuller observes that rehabilitative efforts are directed at persons "(1) branded with the stigma of a crime and (2) selected by standards that do not reliably reflect either the need for curative measures or their prospective success."[36] The rehabilitative approach would work best applied to those contemplating a crime or with a tendency toward violence, not those who have already committed a very serious offense. Thus it may be appropriate for most juvenile offenders or those arrested for relatively minor offenses and not yet subjected to the vagaries of the formal criminal process or the hardening effects of imprisonment.

Deterrence

The object of *deterrence*—discouraging people from committing crimes by making examples of those caught—is compatible with that of retribution. Both call for a measure of pain or deprivation to be imposed on convicted offenders. There is a good deal of debate, however, about whether inflicting punishment on those caught really deters either those being punished—the object of special deterrence—or others for whom the punished offender is being made an example—the object of general deterrence.

Deterrence theory assumes a certain degree of rationality; that is, it assumes that offenders choose to commit crimes after some assessment of the potential benefits and the costs involved. Costs include both the severity or extent of punishment and the chances of its actually being imposed. No doubt some offenders, especially professional and white-collar criminals, actually perform such a cost-benefit calculation. Many experts agree that these offenders are the most likely to be deterred by the possibility of a prison term or punishing loss of property. But most experts assert that such punishments are hardly sure or swift enough to have this desired result. In other words, the risks do not outweigh the potential rewards.

As for so-called crimes of passion, crimes committed out of an irrational impulse to satisfy some need that overwhelms the offender's ability to reason, these are surely not deterrable crimes anyway. No matter how swift, certain, or horrible the punishment, some offenders will not be deterred, even after they have already been punished themselves.

The crime of murder is, of course, the focus of the debate about the deterrent value of capital punishment. Many who advocate the death penalty no longer make claims about deterrence, but now rest their case on retribution and/or incapacitation. At best, the deterrent value of the death penalty may be limited to cases in which robbers or rapists consider the consequences of killing their victims. Virtually everyone agrees that death would have to be far more swift and certain a punishment for any general deterrent effect to be noticed. Some critics of capital punishment recall that in "merry old England" there were over a hundred offenses punishable by death. Picking pockets was one such offense, but pickpockets would still work the crowds that gathered to witness the hangings.

Incapacitation

The last of the four goals, the *incapacitation* of offenders, is also compatible with punishment. Older forms of punishment, such as cutting off the hands of thieves (a practice still followed in some parts of the world), had a direct and permanent result. Incarceration has the effect of incapacitating offenders for at least the term of imprisonment, in the sense that inmates are prevented from victimizing ordinary citizens even if they do continue to commit crimes against one another or members of the prison staff.

Like deterrence, incapacitation is basically a spin-off of punishment, though its more direct purpose is protection of society. There are some situations in which incapacitation is the sole purpose of punishment—as, for example, in permanently putting away psychopaths and in prescribing the psychological therapies mentioned above under "Rehabilitation." Psychosurgery, for example, seeks to alter permanently the behavior of persons by making it virtually impossible for them to commit further violent acts.

Of the four different theories concerning the goal, or goals, of criminal law, which is most in keeping with our concept of justice? A likely response is that it depends on the offense and the offender, that no one goal or compatible combination of them—retribution, rehabilitation, deterrence, incapacitation—suffices. To this we might all agree. How, then, shall we differentiate among the cases and decide which offenders should be punished (and how severely) and which should be rehabilitated (and by which methods)? Should the punishment fit the crime and all those who commit offenses within certain categories be given identical and equal justice? Or should we fit the sanction to the offender, thus individualizing justice case by case?

"EQUAL" VERSUS "INDIVIDUALIZED" JUSTICE

"Equal" Justice

On the face of the U.S. Supreme Court building is chiseled the phrase "Equal Justice under the Law." But does "equal" justice mean identical treatment? Obviously not everyone who breaks the law should receive identical punishment. We would hardly support the idea of sentencing every offender from a pickpocket to a murderer to the same length of prison term. But many agree that penalties should be fixed for each offense in terms of its seriousness and that all robbers should get one penalty and all shoplifters another. Even then we have difficulty, since not all robberies are of equal seriousness and most codes recognize a difference between armed and unarmed (or strong-armed) robberies and between those in which victims are injured and those in which they are not. Still, some demand equal justice for all those guilty of offenses with related characteristics and insist that we assign relative values or weights to each offense. Then we must decide on a scheme of penalties which provides ever stiffer punishments for offenses of increasing seriousness. The system would be flawed, however, unless we sentence every offender to the precise penalty provided for the particular crime he or she committed.

This approach requires not only consistency in sentencing but depends on consistency in the enforcement of the laws by police, in the filing of charges by prosecutors, and in the verdicts of juries. The characteristics of those accused should have nothing to do with their processing or sentence. This kind of justice is what Lon Fuller refers to as "legal justice." It is, he explains, a "justice which demands that we stick by the announced rules and not make exceptions in favor of particular individuals, a justice which conceives that men should live under the same 'rule of law' and be equally bound by its terms."[37]

Dean Spader refers to this approach as one emphasizing the "Rule of Law" as opposed to the "Rule of Man." The latter is marked by the maximization of discretion on the part of criminal justice officials, while the notion of the Rule of Law requires that discretion be tightly restricted or eliminated entirely. The Rule of Law emphasizes the values of even-handedness, uniformity, consistency, visibility, and predictability; its drawbacks include the potential inflexibility, harshness, rigidity, complexity, formalism, and, ironically, inequality.[38]

A system of justice based solely on equality would be mechanistic. Its officials would do nothing more or less than apply the terms of statutes to the evidence before them. It the terms fit, the appropriate charges would be filed, and, if the defendant were found guilty, the appropriate predetermined sentence would be pronounced. The only room for judgment would be that given juries in determining guilt or innocence. Except for the trial, virtually the whole process could be computerized.

Obviously we have carried this argument to its logical—and ridiculous—extreme. No state operates along these lines. But let's look at the other extreme: absolute individualization of justice.

"Individualized" Justice

Suppose we decide that each offender is a person who requires treatment in order to assume a lawful role in society. No matter what the crime, the offender's sentence should be to undergo whatever treatment officials decide will accomplish either the rehabilitation or the special deterrence of this offender. And the treatment would continue for whatever length of time necessary. In some cases, offenders might be released almost immediately. Even persons who have committed murder might undergo little or no treatment if they were deemed to be of no further risk to anyone. This is often the case where persons have murdered a spouse or relative who has been the source and/or the target of all the anger of the offender.

Such an approach would require expertise in evaluating the psychological needs of those who have committed crimes and in predicting their probable future behavior. But does such expertise exist? Is it even possible to infallibly evaluate and predict in such cases? Levin, Musheno, and Palumbo point out that psychiatric therapy has not been successful in attacking the personality disorders of serious offenders and that psychiatrists often differ dramatically in their diagnoses of offenders and in their predictions of future behavior.[39]

Even if such expertise were developed, is it appropriate to abandon completely the retributive aspect of the criminal law and process? Total individualization of justice would seem to require just that. Broaden the application of this approach beyond deciding what sentence to impose to include the operation of the entire process and one gets maximization of discretion, presumably in the hands of experts, in charging, adjudication, sentencing, and release decisions. Spader refers to this as the Rule of Man approach and says it emphasizes the values of flexibility, mercy, compassion, informality, and efficiency. Its obvious drawbacks include the potential for unequal treatment, inconsistency, arbitrariness, capricious abuse of discretion, uncertainty, and uncontrolled provincialism.[40] Table 1.2 contains Spader's illustration of the differences between the two approaches represented by the Rule of Law and the Rule of Man.

A Justice Based on Fairness

What has been generally agreed to is a middle ground that Lon Fuller calls *the justice of dispensation,* a justice ready to make exceptions when the established rules work unexpected hardship in particular cases, a justice ready to bend the letter of the law to accomplish a fair result.[41] In other words, we expect the offender to be treated in accordance with the seriousness of the offense, but also in keeping with individualized characteristics such as his or her previous criminal record, the circumstances of the offense (including the possible role of the victim in precipitating the crime), and other so-called mitigating and aggravating factors.

It is worth noting here, however, that the pendulum, which had swung high in favor of individualization, has begun to swing back in favor of equalization. It accompanies the trend away from rehabilitation to a new emphasis on retribution and incapacitation and is marked particularly by attempts to restrict the discretion of judges in sentencing. It addresses the question: What is *fair?* The attempts to answer this question can come either from the position of what best serves the social good or from the perspective of what is due the offender, the victim, and those in society who wish the law upheld.

TABLE 1.2
RULE OF LAW AND RULE OF MAN: A COMPARISON

		In-kind opposites		
Rule of Law (no discretion)	More law, less discretion	Roughly equal mixture of law and discretion	More discretion, less law	Rule of Man (no law or rules)

Positive values (arguments for)

Theme: "We are a Government of laws and not of men." "No one is above the law."

1. More equal protection, evenhandedness, uniformity, consistency possible
2. More due process, fairness, rationality possible
3. More notice, visibility, continuity, predictability, structure, certainty possible
4. More centralized limits on governmental powers, generality, universality possible

Theme: "Discretion is the handmaiden of justice." "Discretion is the principal source of creativity in government."

1. More individualization and flexibility possible
2. More mercy, compassion, equity possible
3. More creativity and adaptability possible
4. More informality and efficiency possible

Negative values (arguments against)

Theme: "The law and justice are sometimes at odds." "Rigorous law is rigorous injury."

1. More inflexibility, harshness, rigidity; mandatory legalism
2. More rigidity, pigeon holing, technicality, mechanization, inequity
3. More complexity and red tape
4. More blind formalism, unnecessary judicialization, and inefficiency

Theme: "Where the law ends, tyranny begins." "Yes, I'd give the Devil benefit of the law, for my own safety's sake."

1. More unequal treatment (disparity), inconsistency, nonuniformity
2. More arbitrary and capricious abuse of discretion, irrationality
3. More uncertainty, invisibility, unpredictability, lack of structure and continuity
4. More unlimited and uncontrolled provincialism

Source: Adapted from Dean Spader, "Rule of Law vs. Rule of Man," *Journal of Criminal Justice*, vol. 12, no. 4, 1984, pp. 381 and 385.

PROCEDURAL JUSTICE: BASIC STANDARDS

We move now to a consideration of the other major aspect of justice: the procedural. This aspect concerns the means by which society enforces its laws and judges those accused of crimes. In Anglo-American law, procedural justice consists primarily of establishing the obstacles the state must overcome in order to impose sanctions on an offender and, conversely, providing the accused with protection of his or her rights.

There are two basic questions of procedural justice in our legal system: How shall the state "process" those accused of crimes? What burden of proof must the state bear when it seeks to impose penal sanctions on the accused?

The Adversarial versus the Inquisitorial System

There are essentially two approaches to the question of how best to establish the facts of a particular case and determine whether an accused shall be held liable for alleged criminal acts. The two methods are the *adversarial method* and the *inquisitorial method*.

The Adversarial System Anglo-American law long ago settled on the adversary system. This approach, which borrows at least its format from the old trial by battle, has four fundamental features. First, a case consists of two parties with contesting interests and views of what happened. Second, each party gets its "day in court," a full hearing of its side of the dispute. Third, the judge or jury sits as a passive and neutral evaluator of the evidence presented by each side. (It must be noted that in jury trials the judge is called upon to decide what evidence it is proper for the jury to hear and consider.) Fourth, the decision of the court is based only upon the evidence heard and not upon extraneous matters.

In criminal procedures, especially in the United States, courts are supposed to decide whether the accused is to be held guilty of the charges or acquitted by evaluating only those facts that pertain to the particular case at hand. Thus the character of the defendant, even a criminal record of monumental proportions, is not usually relevant. Only if the defendant takes the stand and alleges he or she has no criminal past can the state enter evidence of previous crimes into the record. The point is that the court decides the narrow question: Did the accused commit this particular act or not? It does not pass judgment on the character of the accused at the adjudication stage of the process. The defendant's character becomes an issue only following a conviction and for purposes of sentencing.

The Inquisitorial System The inquisitorial system is the approach used on the European continent. It has three major features. First, the process consists of an active inquiry by the magistrate or court. Second, all parties, including the defendant, are bound to assist the court in its inquiry. Third, the facts leading the court to judgment include the character and history of the accused.

There are many in this country who would prefer such a system to the adversarial method. It appears to be less artificial and ritualistic. It also affords defendants far less protection since it seems to align the court with the state and compels many defendants to overcome more evidence than is permitted in American courts. Some critics in this country allege that our system already acts like an inquisitorial one in many respects. Only in those cases involving a full jury trial does the adversarial process come into play. We shall return to this issue when we discuss plea bargaining in later chapters.

Burden of Proof

In the Anglo-American system, the method of proof is the *accusatorial method,* in which the accuser (the state) bears the entire burden of proving each and every one of its charges. This complete *burden of proof* is backed up by the doctrine of the *presumption of innocence,* which holds that the accused is presumed innocent unless and until the state can prove that he or she is guilty.

On the European continent the burden of proof is shifted somewhat so that the defendant must explain away the state's case. It is not correct to say, however, that the defendant is considered guilty until proven innocent. That attitude may characterize some Communist and other dictatorial systems, but not those of western Europe.

There are several standards, or levels, of proof required at different stages of the criminal process. Four of them can be delineated.

Reasonable Basis   Police are permitted to stop persons on the street and ask questions about their comings and goings if they have a *reasonable basis* for temporarily detaining a person. The "reasonable basis" is supposed to be more than mere suspicion. It should be based upon facts and circumstances that to the police officer provide a significant level of probability that a crime was committed and that the person stopped was party to the crime.

Probable Cause   In order to carry out an arrest or a search of persons or premises, the standard of proof is that of *probable cause.* J. Shane Creamer explains the basic meaning of this phrase:

> Probable cause for an arrest is defined as a combination of facts or apparent facts, viewed through the eyes of an experienced police officer, which would lead a man of reasonable caution to believe that a crime is being or has been committed. Probable cause for the issuance of a search warrant is defined as facts or apparent facts as viewed through the eyes of an experienced police officer which would lead a man of reasonable caution to believe that there is something connected with a violation of law on the premises to be searched.[42]

This standard is similar to that of reasonable basis, but the officer's belief in the probable guilt of the suspect must be stronger to justify the act of arrest. The judge before whom the suspect makes his or her initial appearance following arrest and booking must review the facts of the situation and decide whether the arresting officer had sufficient probable cause to make the arrest. If the judge doesn't believe the standard has been met, the suspect is released from custody.

Police officers may search the suspect at the time of arrest and may search the immediate vicinity of the premises in which an arrest is made. But a thorough search of a premises requires a search warrant issued by a judge or magistrate. Such a warrant is issued only if the officer applying for it convinces the judge that there is sufficient probable cause to perform the search. More on this subject will be provided in subsequent chapters.

In some states the standard of probable cause also serves as the one by which prosecutors and grand juries decide whether to file formal criminal charges against suspects. But even where this is the standard on which formal charges can be based, prosecutors usually act on, and advise grand jurors to act on, the basis of a slightly tougher standard, which we discuss next.

Prima Facie Case The higher standard that prosecutors prefer to use, and the legal standard in some states, is that of a *prima facie case*. This means that the case should be "sufficient on first disclosure" or "reasonably sufficient" to meet the trial standard. Here prosecutors and grand jurors must ask themselves if the evidence presented by the state would, if not contradicted by the defense, justify a verdict of guilty from the trial jury.[43]

Proof beyond a Reasonable Doubt The toughest standard of procedural justice is that used in criminal trials. It requires that the guilt of the defendant be established *beyond and to the exclusion of every reasonable doubt*. This standard goes considerably beyond that used in civil trials, which is based on the *preponderance of evidence*. Whereas civil trials assume the burden of proof is equal between plaintiff and defendant, criminal trials require the state to overcome the presumption of innocence and erase reasonable doubt about the defendant's guilt.

Imagine the scales of justice as evenly balanced at the beginning of a civil trial. The jury need only find that the scales have been tipped visibly in one direction or the other. Imagine the scales being tipped almost entirely in the defendant's behalf at the beginning of a criminal trial. The state is required to produce evidence of such weight as to tip the scales almost completely in the other direction. That is illustrative of the effect of the doctrines of burden of proof and presumption of innocence. To be sure, not every *possible* doubt needs to be overcome. The burden on the state falls short of so absolute a requirement. But some states define the standard as "beyond a reasonable doubt and to a moral certainty," and that is about as close to an absolute standard as one can get.

The elements of procedural criminal justice we have so far discussed are so fundamental a part of the common law and the Anglo-American tradition that they have hardly ever been challenged in the 200 years of our history, despite the fact that they are not stated in the Constitution. We turn now to the so-called constitutional rights of accused persons.

PROCEDURAL JUSTICE: CONSTITUTIONAL STANDARDS

The Constitution is the fundamental legal document of this nation. It is, in its own words, "the Supreme Law of the Land." Yet its original provisions contained little related to criminal justice. This is due largely to the fact that the Founding Fathers intended that police powers (those aimed at protecting the health, safety, and welfare of citizens) be left to state governments. When in 1791 the first ten amendments, which are known collectively as the Bill of Rights, were ratified, they protected citizens against the actions of the federal government but were useless in controlling or regulating the law enforcement processes of the states. Unless the states put similar limitations on their own criminal justice systems, the citizens of those states enjoyed few of the protections or rights we now all take for granted.

Constitutional Provisions

Original Text   As proposed by the Constitutional Convention in 1787 and ratified the following year, the U.S. Constitution provided the following limitations on the powers of Congress in Article I, Section 9:

1. There can be no suspension of the writ of habeas corpus—a writ protecting citizens from imprisonment without trial on specified charges—except in cases of rebellion or invasion that threaten public safety.

2. Bills of attainder—punishment of citizens by legislative act—are illegal.

3. Ex post facto laws—laws that create retroactive criminality and subject the citizens who committed then-legal acts to possible sanctions—are illegal.

The Bill of Rights   Having promised many persons that the first act of the new Congress would be to propose a series of amendments to the

Constitution spelling out the rights and liberties of citizens under the new national government, James Madison delivered sixteen items to the First Congress. Twelve were adopted by that body and sent out for ratification by the states. Ten were ratified and became effective in 1791.

Only those that relate to procedural justice concern us here. The rights they guarantee are as follows:

Amendment IV
• The right of the people to be secure in their persons, houses, papers, and effects against unreasonable searches and seizures
• The requirement that search warrants shall (1) be based on probable cause, (2) be supported by an oath of affirmation, and (3) particularly describe the place to be searched and the persons or things to be seized

Amendment V
• The requirement that charges on "capital or other infamous crime" shall be by grand jury indictment
• Protection against double jeopardy, or being tried twice for the same crime
• The right of persons to refuse to be witnesses against themselves, that is, the protection against self-incrimination
• Protection against being deprived of life, liberty, or property, without due process of law

Amendment VI
• The right to a speedy and public trial
• The right to be tried by an impartial jury of the state and district where the crime was committed
• The right to be informed of the nature and cause of the accusation
• The right to be confronted with the witnesses against oneself
• The right to have compulsory process for obtaining witnesses in one's favor
• The right to have the assistance of counsel in one's defense

Amendment VIII
• Protection against excessive bail and excessive fines
• Protection against cruel and unusual punishment

It is difficult to imagine today how unimpressed many people were with these guarantees. Since they applied only to federal actions, and since federal criminal laws were limited to a few narrowly defined offenses, a leading legal scholar could, as late as 1886, write that the Bill of Rights was "a certain number of amendments on comparatively unimportant points."[44]

The Fourteenth Amendment During the so-called Reconstruction period following the Civil War, Amendments XIII through XV were added to the Constitution. The Fourteenth Amendment contains the following language:

> No state shall . . . deprive any person of life, liberty or property without due process of law.

This clearly applies at least part of the Fifth Amendment to the states. The question became: Does this language incorporate all of the protection of the Fourth, Fifth, Sixth, and Eighth Amendments and thus mean that states must now provide the same protections to the procedural rights of persons that the federal government is required to provide? The definitive answer to such a question could come only from the Supreme Court of the United States.

Constitutional Law and the Supreme Court

When the highest court rules on a case in which someone is seeking to have a statute or a government action nullified on the grounds that it violates the Constitution, the result is *constitutional law*. The authority of the U.S. Supreme Court to examine and, if necessary, overturn laws and executive acts is called *judicial review*. Judicial review may be used to scrutinize the behavior of either the states or the federal government, and the Supreme Court may thus uphold or overturn the ruling of any other court in the nation.

The Period of "Ordered Liberty" As to the question of whether the due process clause of the Fourteenth Amendment meant that states were henceforth responsible for upholding the entire Bill of Rights in their own criminal proceedings, the answer from the Supreme Court has been "no." At first the Court adopted a position that due process was a vague principle of natural law with little specific content. Not until 1937 (almost forty years after the adoption of Amendment XIV) did the Court really try to address the question of the meaning of its due process clause relative to criminal justice in the states.

In *Palko v. Connecticut* the Court refused to apply the Fifth Amendment prohibition against double jeopardy to the states. Justice Benjamin Cardozo wrote that the meaning of the due process clause in the Fourteenth Amendment was that states were required to protect those rights "essential to a scheme of ordered liberty."[45] In 1941 the words of the Court were that the states must provide the "fundamental fairness essential to the very concept of justice."[46] And then in 1948 the Court ruled that the jailing of a man for contempt of court when the court session consisted of a secret hearing in the judge's chambers was a violation of the Sixth Amendment right to a public trial, a right so basic that it applies to the states through the Fourteenth Amendment.[47]

The Period of "Selective Incorporation" As early as 1925 the Supreme Court had ruled that freedom of speech, a First Amendment right, was one of the fundamental rights protected from state abridgment.[48] This began a period of what is called the *selective incorporation* of specific rights within the meaning of the due process clause of Amendment XIV. It was not until 1949 that the Court ruled that one of the procedural rights was "specifically incorporated." That right was the protection against illegal search and seizure found in Amendment IV. The Court declined, however, to put teeth in its ruling—that is, it did not exclude the use of illegally seized evidence from criminal trials.[49]

It was the Warren Court that, in 1961, began what is called the *criminal law revolution* with its ruling in *Mapp v. Ohio* that illegally seized evidence could no longer be used in state criminal trials.[50] Before the decade of the sixties was over, the Supreme Court had ruled that each of the specific procedural rights mentioned in the Bill of Rights was incorporated within the meaning of the Fourteenth Amendment's due process clause, except for two. The Fifth Amendment's requirement that charges on "capital or other infamous crimes" be by grand jury indictment has never been applied, nor has the Eighth Amendment prohibition of "excessive bail" or "excessive fines." Table 1.3 illustrates the present situation and points out the rapidity with which many decades of precedent were reversed under Chief Justice Earl Warren.

Of course, the most famous case in the long list of those decided in the sixties was *Miranda v. Arizona*.[51] It was that case which resulted in the *Miranda warning* that police must apprise suspects of their rights. The real importance of the case was its shaping of rules by which confessions could be evaluated for their "voluntariness" and thus either admitted into evidence or suppressed by trial judges. It brought the Fifth Amendment protection against self-incrimination and the Fourth Amendment right to a defense attorney into full union. Before any custodial interrogation, a suspect must be told that he or she has a right to remain silent, that anything he or she says can and will be used in court, that he or she has the right to an attorney who can be present at any interrogation, and that an attorney will be appointed if the suspect cannot afford one. A suspect may sign a waiver of these rights and confess to a crime, but the absence of a defense attorney at the point at which the waiver is signed often results in attempts to suppress the confession on the grounds that it was not truly voluntary—that some sort of duress was employed by the police.

TABLE 1.3
INCORPORATION OF SPECIFIC RIGHTS BY THE SUPREME COURT

Amendment	Applicable to states?	Case
IV Unreasonable searches and seizures	Yes	*Wolf v. Colorado*, 338 U.S. 25 (1949); *Mapp v. Ohio*, 367 U.S. 643 (1961)
V Grand jury indictment	No	*Hurtado v. California*, 110 U.S. 516 (1884)
Double jeopardy	Yes	*Benton v. Maryland*, 395 U.S. 784 (1969)
Privilege against self-incrimination	Yes	*Malloy v. Hogan*, 378 U.S. 1 (1964)
VI Speedy trial	Yes	*Klopfer v. North Carolina*, 386 U.S. 213 (1967)
Public trial	Yes	*In re Oliver*, 330 U.S. 257 (1948)
Jury trial	Yes	*Duncan v. Louisiana*, 391 U.S. 145 (1968)
Confrontation of witnesses	Yes	*Pointer v. Texas*, 380 U.S. 400 (1965)
Compulsory process	Yes	*Washington v. Texas*, 388 U.S. 14 (1967)
Right to counsel	Yes	*Gideon v. Wainwright*, 372 U.S. 335 (1963) (felonies); *Argersinger v. Hamlin*, 407 U.S. 25 (1972) (all offenses, before imprisonment may be imposed)
VIII Excessive bail and fines	No	None
Cruel and unusual punishment	Yes	*Robinson v. California*, 370 U.S. 660 (1962)

Source: Peter W. Lewis and Kenneth D. Peoples, *The Supreme Court and the Criminal Process*, Saunders, Philadelphia, 1978, p. 63.

This, case, together with *Mapp* and its extension of the exclusionary rule, has given rise to more appeals, more rulings, and increased Court involvement in setting forth detailed guidelines for the conduct of criminal investigations. The exclusionary rule (which we will discuss in Chapter 7) and the Miranda warning are seen as essential to procedural justice by some—and as procedural obstacles to more substantive justice by others. Civil libertarians (those adhering to the Due Process Model) point out that such rules are necessary to protect all citizens against the excesses of law enforcement. Police and their supporters are divided between those who believe these rules have led to better, more professional law enforcement and those Crime Control adherents who believe that police have been handcuffed and that the real impact of these rulings is that ordinary citizens have fewer rights than criminals.

The Period of "New Incorporation" Robert L. Cord suggests that under Chief Justice Warren Burger the Supreme Court entered a period of *neo-incorporation* by holding that, while the Bill of Rights guarantees are applicable to states through the Fourteenth Amendment, they need not be observed in the same way at the state level as at the federal.

Examples of this approach are found in the rulings that uphold the states' use of juries of less than twelve members and the validity of nonunanimous jury verdicts in criminal trials.[52] Cord characterizes this neo-incorporation as "a 'half-way' house between the substance of ordered liberty and that of traditional incorporation" and comments that "the thrust for congruency in federal and state criminal procedures . . . is being decreased."[53]

The Burger Court in Perspective   Despite the swing back toward the fundamental fairness test of the 1940s, the so-called Burger Court was not reactionary. It not only kept intact the major decisions of the Warren Court, it made some clear advances of its own. Perhaps the most important was its 1972 ruling extending the right of indigents to court-appointed counsel in most misdemeanor cases.[54] This decision did much to inspire the trend toward the establishment of the office of public defender in many states and localities.

It was also the Burger Court that tackled the issue of capital punishment in the United States. It first struck down all existing capital punishment statutes as violative of the Eighth Amendment prohibition against "cruel and unusual punishments."[55] Then, in a series of divided opinions, the Court established procedural guidelines under which constitutional death penalties could be imposed. Its position was that death is not necessarily substantively cruel or unusual, but that procedural justice requires that great care be taken that the death penalty not be imposed arbitrarily or capriciously.[56] The Court ruled, for example, that the death penalty is substantively "excessive" in the case of rape of an adult woman.[57]

There are those who point out that, while it is true that no major Warren Court decision was reversed under Burger, restrictive interpretation of doctrines laid down by the earlier Court "narrowed the scope" of the rights extended previously. One observer wrote over a decade ago that "the Supreme Court has become more conservative and more willing to side with prosecutors" and that this has led to a decline of appeals from defendants who have lost at lower levels of the courts.[58] This trend has been strengthened over the past decade and has become especially pronounced since President Ronald Reagan appointed four members of the Court—Justices Sandra Day O'Connor, William Rehnquist, Anthony Kennedy, and Antonin Scalia—and subsequently elevated William Rehnquist to chief justice upon the retirement of Warren Burger in 1986.

We shall have the opportunity in later chapters to refer to specific cases and doctrines of constitutional law as they relate to specific steps in the criminal process. But what is clear even here is that standards as to what procedural justice requires under the terms of the U.S. Constitution are greatly different from what they were forty or even twenty years ago. Students should be aware of the fact that states are free to set standards that are more protective of a defendant's rights (that is, more due process oriented) than those required by the U.S. Supreme Court. It has become clear that the supreme courts of several states have invoked provisions of their own state constitutions to do just that. Justice William Brennan praised this trend and called it "probably the most important development in constitutional jurisprudence today."[59]

In order for state justices to set standards more demanding of police and prosecutors than those set by the Supreme Court, they must find an adequate and independent basis in their own constitutions. Of course, states may not set standards that are narrower or weaker than those required by the U.S. Supreme Court. Justice Brennan, a true liberal and an advocate of the Due Process Model, has said, however, that those standards have become "too narrow and niggardly" to suit him. So he, along with other judges and lawyers, welcomes what is called a "new federalism" under which states are building on the principles of the Warren Court rather than echoing the emphasis placed on crime control by the Supreme Court over the past twenty years.

SUMMARY AND CONCLUSION

This has been a long chapter and one with a very broad scope. We have examined the idea of justice from the perspectives of two competing models—the Due Process Model and the Crime Control Model, as delineated by Herbert Packer. An analysis of the essential difference between substantive and procedural aspects of justice was followed by an examination of key issues related to substantive criminal justice. These focus on what acts require prohibition and punishment by the state and what sanctions or goals of the penal law are appropriate. We then discussed the procedural aspect of justice, distinguishing between the basic rules or standards inherited from common law and the rules laid down in the U.S. Constitution. Attention was paid to the importance of the Supreme Court in the interpretation and application of the procedural guarantees of the Bill of Rights.

This brief survey of the subject of justice does not, of course, do justice to the subject. We have illustrated only some of the key issues involved. But the student should by now be able at least to listen to a speech or debate or read articles or books dealing with criminal justice in a discriminate manner, detect the approach of the speaker or author, and comment on the aspects of justice that are covered and not covered. If we have helped the student to clarify issues and identify biases—including our own—this chapter has served its purpose.

QUESTIONS FOR DISCUSSION

1. (*a*) What would you expect a layperson to say if asked the question: What is the primary goal of the criminal justice system? (*b*) How would you expect a police officer to answer this same question? (*c*) A defense lawyer? (*d*) The victim of a crime? (*e*) A defendant?
2. If your community were surveyed, how would you expect it to split in aligning itself with either the Crime Control Model or the Due Process Model of criminal justice?
3. If you were a judge sentencing persons convicted in your court, would you be more likely to apply the "equal" justice (or Rule of Law) approach, or would you be inclined to "individualize" justice and apply the Rule of Man approach? Why?

NOTES

1. *Aguilar v. Texas,* 378 U.S. 108, 12 L. Ed. 2d 723 (1964), and *Spinelli v. United States,* 393 U.S. 410, 21 L. Ed. 2d 637 (1969).
2. *Illinois v. Gates,* 76 L. Ed. 527 (1982).
3. *United States v. Leon,* 82 L. Ed. 2d 677 (1984).
4. Herbert J. Packer, *The Limits of the Criminal Sanction,* Stanford University Press, Palo Alto, Calif., 1968.
5. Ibid., p. 158.
6. Ibid., p. 159.
7. Ibid., p. 161.
8. Ibid., pp. 163–164.
9. Ibid., p. 165.
10. Ibid., p. 166.
11. Ibid., pp. 167–168.
12. Ibid., pp. 168–170.
13. Ibid., p. 171.
14. Kenneth M. Wells and Paul B. Weston, *Criminal Law,* Goodyear, Santa Monica, Calif., 1978, p. 53.
15. Ibid., p. 54.
16. Ibid., p. 108.
17. Edwin Sutherland, "Is 'White Collar Crime' Crime?" in Bruce J. Cohen (ed.), *Crime in America,* Peacock, Ithaca, N.Y., 1970, pp. 227–235.
18. Edwin M. Schur and Hugo Adam Bedau, *Victimless Crimes: Two Sides of a Controversy,* Prentice-Hall, Englewood Cliffs, N.J., 1974, p. 6.
19. Ibid., p. 7.
20. Ibid., pp. 73–75.

21. Ibid., pp. 11–37.
22. Ibid., p. 64.
23. Dallin Oaks, "The Popular Myth of the Victimless Crime," in Glenn K. Winters and Edward J. Schoenbaum (eds.), *American Courts and Justice,* American Judicature Society, Williamsburg, Va., 1976, pp. 131–150.
24. Ibid., p. 136.
25. Ibid., p. 139.
26. Ibid., p. 142.
27. Lon L. Fuller, *Anatomy of the Law,* Praeger, New York, 1968, p. 26.
28. Norbert Weiner, as quoted in Fuller, pp. 26–27.
29. Ibid., pp. 26–28.
30. James P. Levine, Michael C. Musheno, and Dennis J. Palumbo, *Criminal Justice: A Public Police Approach,* Harcourt Brace Jovanovich, New York, 1980, p. 420.
31. Sue Titus Reid, *Crime and Criminology,* Holt, Rinehart & Winston, New York, 1976, p. 550.
32. Fuller, p. 30.
33. The following discussion is based largely on Reid, pp. 551–559.
34. Levine, Musheno, and Palumbo, p. 406.
35. Ibid., pp. 408–409.
36. Fuller, p. 32.
37. Ibid., p. 38.
38. Dean Spader, "Rule of Law vs. Rule of Man: The Search for the Golden Zigzag between Conflicting Fundamental Values," *Journal of Criminal Justice,* vol. 12, no. 4, 1984, pp. 379–394.
39. Levine, Musheno, and Palumbo, p. 409.
40. Spader, p. 385.
41. Fuller, p. 38.
42. J. Shane Creamer, *The Law of Arrest, Search and Seizure,* Saunders, Philadelphia, 1975, p. 11.
43. Hazel B. Kerper, *Introduction to the Criminal Justice System,* 2d ed., rev. by Jerold H. Israel, West, St. Paul, Minn., 1979, pp. 214–215.
44. Sir Henry Maine, as quoted in Bernard Schwartz, *The Law in America,* American Heritage, New York, 1974, p. 47.
45. *Palko v. Connecticut,* 302 U.S. 319 (1937).
46. *Lisenba v. California,* 314 U.S. 219 (1941).
47. *In re Oliver,* 330 U.S. 257 (1948).
48. *Gitlow v. New York,* 268 U.S. 652 (1925).
49. *Wolf v. Colorado,* 338 U.S. 25 (1949).
50. *Mapp v. Ohio,* 367 U.S. 643 (1961).
51. *Miranda v. Arizona,* 384 U.S. 436 (1966).
52. *Williams v. Florida,* 406 U.S. 356 (1972) and *Apodaca v. Oregon,* 406 U.S. 404 (1972).
53. Robert L. Cord, "Neo-Incorporation: The Burger Court and the Due Process Clause of the Fourteenth Amendment," as reprinted in Peter W. Lewis and Kenneth D. Peoples, *The Supreme Court and the Criminal Process,* Saunders, Philadelphia, 1978, pp. 71–72.

54. *Argersinger v. Hamlin,* 407 U.S. 25 (1972).

55. *Furman v. Georgia,* 408 U.S. 238 (1972).

56. *Gregg v. Georgia,* 428 U.S. 153 (1976); *Proffitt v. Florida,* 428 U.S. 242 (1976).

57. *Cocker v. Georgia,* 433 U.S. 584 (1977).

58. Nathan Lewin, "Avoiding the Supreme Court," *The New York Times Magazine,* October 1, 1976, pp. 31, 90–100.

59. Robert Pear, "State Courts Move Beyond U.S. Bench in Rights Rulings," *The New York Times,* May 3, 1986, pp. 1 and 16.

CHAPTER 2

THE EVOLUTION OF LAW AND COURTS

After reading this chapter, students should be able to define and explain the importance of each of the following terms or phrases:

Draconian Code
Saxon law
bots
the Norman murder fine
felonies
misdemeanors
torts
trial by ordeal
trial by compurgation
trial by battle
presentment jury
justice of the peace
common law courts
Court of King's Bench
Court of Common Pleas

writ system
precedents
stare decisis
equity
Star Chamber
canon law
ecclesiastical courts
benefit of clergy
sanctuary
federal court system
state courts
dual court system
Supreme Law of the Land
mens rea

It is often said that you cannot understand where you are or where you are going without an understanding of where you have been. It is considered obligatory, therefore, for almost any text that deals with social institutions and processes to contain a brief history of the development of those institutions and processes. We consider this especially important in dealing with law and the courts. One reason for this is that perhaps no component of the criminal justice system is more bound by tradition and historical precedents than the courts. Another reason is that students often ask why things are done the way they are since common sense or logic would seem to support doing them quite differently. Sometimes the reply must be that this is simply the way these things have been done since the days of . . . whenever. On many matters, however, one can say that people of vision and wisdom have struggled with the possibilities and problems of alternatives and that experience has taught us that this is the best way.

The law embodies principles and procedures passed on from generation to generation. In the Anglo-American tradition, the law has been continually altered, reshaped, amended, twisted, and sometimes contorted to fit new conditions and serve new social groups and purposes. Under the basic rule of the common law system we inherited from England, history—in the form of previously decided cases—is binding. Decisions in current cases cannot be made in ignorance of precedents established in earlier cases within the same jurisdiction. Established rules and doctrines can be reinterpreted, even consciously reversed, but they cannot be completely ignored.

This is as true of criminal law as it is of civil law. The criminal law of this nation is loaded with rules, definitions, and principles that have evolved over decades and even centuries. The criminal court system—its organization, offices, procedures, and styles—is also the product of gradual, even tortured, evolution. It can be argued that there have been more changes in criminal law and courts in the past thirty years than in all the preceding years of our republic. We may be participating in the most complete overhaul since the Revolution, but there will be no total break with the past.

ORIGINS OF CRIMINAL LAW

Every human society has the need to prohibit acts that are viewed as being so harmful they cannot be tolerated if social order is to be maintained. *Crimes* are those acts which are prohibited and for which perpetrators will be punished. *Criminal law* is made up of those coercive orders of prohibition issued by governing authorities as well as the orders concerning the process by which offenders are brought to justice and the prescribed sanctions that governments impose upon those found guilty of committing violations.

The Draconian Code

In ancient times the notion first appeared that some acts constituted attacks on society, or the state, in addition to whatever harm they did to their direct victims. The Greek lawgiver Draco believed that the violation of society's commands was more important than the harm done to the individual victim. Since both theft and murder were violations of the express will of society, both were to be punished by death. This extreme view was incorporated in what became the Draconian Code.[1] It did not long survive in Greece, but around 1800 England's penal code came very close to the Draconian idea when some 1,700 offenses were punishable by death.

Saxon Law

During the period known as the Dark Ages, there was no distinguishable criminal law. In England attacks upon the lives and limbs of persons were generally punishable by *bots,* mere fines. The amount was determined by what part of the body was injured and to what degree. Some fingers were even valued more than others because of the kinds of weapons used.[2]

About 700 A.D. the first "boteless" offenses—those punishable by loss of life or liberty—evolved; they were apparently limited to treason and violence against the king. It was not for another 250 or 300 years, however, that Alfred, king of the West Saxons, proclaimed that treason was an offense against the law—the first true crime.[3] A parallel development was the notion of "the King's Peace," the idea that the highways used by the king and his agents were under direct royal protection and law enforcement. Gradually the King's Peace was extended to private property so that the king could protect or enforce the law against anyone in the realm. But this did not result in a system of criminal law. Charles Herman Kinnane writes:

> Imagine, as late as just prior to the Norman conquest, having this trifling consolation that if someone murdered you, he need only pay your family the usual monetary fine. Not much protection was to be looked for in the criminal law if the murderer happened to be a powerful enemy who could well afford the luxury of cutting your throat.[4]

The Norman Murder Fine

Even with the invasion of England by the Normans and the many changes wrought by William the Conqueror and his successors, a system of criminal law recognizable to modern observers was very slow and tortuous in developing. William did at least provide for a so-called murder fine. Since Saxons persisted in picking off hated Normans and witnesses were not forthcoming, William proclaimed that entire communities, or "hundreds," would be heavily fined if any Norman was killed therein. This deterred the murder of Normans, and later the protection was extended to all persons. The murder fine caused English people to consider murder a very serious matter and to develop a sense of responsibility toward the law. Kinnane observes that "by one simple, crude rule, a tremendous step in the direction of decent law was taken."[5]

Felonies, Misdemeanors, and Torts

During medieval times, the law began to make a distinction between two kinds of wrongs against a person. *Felonies* came to include any offenses which could be punished by death, dismemberment, escheat (the seizure of all real estate), or "outlawry" of the offender. These offenses included murder, assault with serious injuries, and theft. Other less serious offenses were called *trespasses* or *transgressions*. It was some time before this latter array of offenses was clearly divided into those considered at least somewhat criminal—*misdemeanors*—and those which remained private and noncriminal in nature—*torts*.[6]

ORIGINS OF CRIMINAL PROCEDURES

Since the English common law was essentially court-made or judge-made law, the history of law is the history of court activity. We shall not attempt to examine the entire scope of English development, but touch only on those developments most important to the administration of criminal justice.

Saxon Courts and Methods

The Saxons had developed a series of courts before the Norman conquest. Villages, or hundreds, had hundred courts, and counties, or shires, had shire courts. Each was composed of laypersons known as *suitors* and presided over by a *reeve*. ("Shire reeves" became the modern sheriffs.) Minor wrongs were judged by the hundred courts; more serious matters were turned over to the shire courts. After the Norman conquest, both courts lost jurisdiction over criminal offenses.

Alongside these courts were the *seignorial courts,* a system of courts presided over by lords to settle disputes among their tenants. This system provided the foundation for a pyramidal hierarchy of courts developed by William after the conquest. There were also *borough courts,* which were very important to the development of the law of commerce, but they never had jurisdiction over criminal matters.[7]

The Saxons had two methods for dealing with criminal complaints: trial by ordeal and trial by compurgation. The courts lacked power to enforce the appearance of the offender or adherence to their judgments and relied on the plaintiff to bring the accused in and to enforce the decision. If the defendant could be persuaded or forced to trial at all, he or she was tried by persons relying on signs from a supernatural power as to guilt or innocence. *Trial by ordeal* consisted of such procedures as requiring the accused to hold red-hot irons, plunge an arm into boiling water, or swim with rocks tied to the body. The idea was that an innocent person would not be killed or maimed in the process. *Trial by compurgation,* on the other hand, required defendants to purge themselves of guilt by swearing their innocence and supporting their testimony with testimony sworn to by a number of "oath helpers," usually twelve persons. A liar ("purgeror") would presumably be punished by God either in this world or the next.[8] It should be noted that these trials were presided over by the clergy, and ordeals often took place during the mass.

Norman Innovations

To these rather quaint means of litigation, the conquering Normans added one more appealing to gentlemen of honor: *trial by battle.* The challenger (plaintiff or accuser) and the challenged (defendant or accused) would agree on the place and the weapon—battle-axes were popular—and settle their differences. This at least had the effect of limiting the fighting to two combatants and thus of saving the lives, limbs, and property of those who might have otherwise been required to fight in a private war.[9] It also had the effect of establishing a purely secular means of settling a case and of setting forth the notion that litigation involved the "adversary" process.

Eventually, of course, trial by battle lost its appeal. But another Norman innovation began a development that has culminated in our system of juries. Initially persons were accused of crimes before the local court by men drawn from the hundred. What was essentially a voluntary process of jury service became mandatory with the Assize of Clarendon in 1166. (An *assize* is a session of a court or judges to decide cases put before them.) The new rule was that criminal charges were to come from "presenting juries" of men chosen for this purpose. Those accused by the *presentment jury*—the predecessor of the grand jury—were then subjected to trial by ordeal or compurgation.[10]

The Appearance of Trial Juries

In 1215 priests were forbidden by the Fourth Lateran Council to participate in trials by ordeal. The judges then turned to the presenting juries in many instances to render a verdict of guilt or innocence. But defendants were quite naturally reluctant to be judged by the very men who had accused them and frequently refused to submit themselves to such a trial.

In 1275 the Statute of Westminster provided that persons who declined to be tried would either be imprisoned or would have rocks piled on their chests until they were crushed to death or agreed to trial. Some accepted death rather than risk conviction, since the latter usually resulted in escheat, or forfeiture of all property, and destitution for the accused person's family.[11]

In the 1350s it was decided that presenting jurors could be barred from serving in the trial if the defendant wished them excluded, laying the basis for a distinct trial jury. However, trial juries and presenting juries alike decided matters on their own personal knowledge of persons and events. There were no witnesses or any bother with presentation of evidence. It was another hundred years before these elements were introduced.[12]

THE DEVELOPMENT OF ENGLAND'S COURT SYSTEM

The developments discussed above paralleled and were linked to the development of governmental bodies called courts that eventually came to exercise judicial powers as distinguished from advisory or administrative functions. The Anglo-Saxon general assembly of notables (the Witenagemot) evolved under the Normans into the Great Council of the King, a body with authority in making law, administering it, and litigating cases. This body was in turn replaced by successor agencies ever smaller in membership until the council became a few key advisors and secretaries collectively called the *curia regis,* or court of the king. This agency spun off numerous committees to which were assigned judicial authority, and the committees developed into what we would recognize today as judicial courts. This trend was joined with the gradual appearance of judicial specialists as a group of permanent personnel under the control of the *curia regis.*[13]

The King's Justices

It should be noted that these developments were part of a pattern of centralizing power and authority in the king. The king's justices traveled throughout the kingdom, overseeing the collection of taxes, presiding over local tribunals, and trying and punishing persons accused of offenses against the Crown. These justices came to be divided into justices of gaol (jail) delivery, who had authority over small criminal matters; commissioners of oyer and terminer, who had authority over important criminal cases; and justices in eyre, who were investigators and inspectors of shire administration.

One observer has noted that it was in the "justices' hands that the preservation of the peace rested, at any rate outside London."[14] These officials were generally country gentlemen of substantial means who may have been ignorant of the law and often arbitrary in their actions, but who were also usually motivated by a sense of duty and possessed of considerable common sense.

The office of justice combined judicial and administrative functions, including the power to call out troops to suppress riots. Judicial power grew from that implied in being merely a custodian of persons awaiting trial to one of trier of fact in cases involving minor offenses. In the latter role, the justice was supervised by the Court of King's Bench—a body described in the next section.[15] Before leaving the subject of justices, we must point out that an early decision to involve local citizens in the administration of justice led, through stages covering almost 200 years, to the eventual establishment of the office of justice of the peace.

Common Law Courts

During the reign of Henry II (1154–1189), two distinct judicial courts were split off the *curia regis:* the *Court of the Exchequer,* which dealt with suits involving royal revenues, and the *Court of Common Pleas,* which heard cases between private citizens in what we would refer to as civil litigation. These courts were staffed with professional judges appointed by the king. They had the authority to hear virtually all litigation. Thus royal, centralized courts grew at the expense of local public and private courts of the towns and the lords.

It is a third distinct court in which we are most interested, however: the *Court of the King's Bench.* This court was so named because originally the king himself sat on a bench in judgment of those who came before the bar—a wooden barrier that separated the parties to the case from the king. This court made ample use of the expanding doctrine of the King's Peace to eventually assert jurisdiction over all major crimes, whether committed against the Crown or against citizens of the realm. The king later appointed justices to this bench and delegated to them his royal authority to rule on the cases presented. This court remained tied to the *curia regis* longer than the other two, but by the fourteenth century it was recognized as a separate court with unique original jurisdiction.

The King's Bench also came to have appellate jurisdiction over civil cases tried before Common Pleas. This was rationalized on the basis that most crimes against persons or their property involved injuries for which victims could sue the offenders. Thus if a case was being prosecuted before the King's Bench for such a crime, it made sense to allow that court to drop the criminal case and try the civil aspect instead.[16]

By 1400, the three distinct royal courts had been firmly established. These courts provided the institutional framework through which the great body of the common law was developed. This common law was based on two fundamental features: the writ system and adherence to precedent.

The Writ System

The writ was originally an order from the king to an official to perform (or cease performing) a specific act. Complaints of offenses and injustices directed to the king resulted in his issuance of writs ordering sheriffs to bring defendants to trial before the appropriate justice or court. These writs also contained a formula for resolving the complaint. Each new situation resulted in the creation of a new writ until there was a vast number of them. Plaintiffs could then apply for the writ appropriate to their particular complaint or case. This required the recording and cataloging of the available writs, and a Registry of Writs eventually appeared. Still, unique situations required new writs or formulas for resolving disputes, and the law grew in bulk and complexity.

Adherence to Precedent

The system of established writs was coupled with another development: the practice of recording the decision made by courts in the cases before them, and the eventual adherence to these previously established resolutions by subsequent courts faced with similar cases involving the same writs. By the thirteenth century, *lawyers* (those who knew how to read the law and advise "clients") were utilizing the Year Books, or reports of court proceedings, as a guide to preparing their cases and, eventually, quoting them in their briefs and arguments. Lawyers and judges alike, then, contributed to the adherence to precedent that characterizes the common law system. The principle that courts should adhere to rules laid down in previous cases is called the doctrine of *stare decisis*.

Equity Courts and the Star Chamber

The growth in writs ceased by statute in 1285, and judicial conservatism eventually led to slavish adherence to precedent at the expense of justice. The king and his council therefore exercised their residue of judicial authority to provide for relief from the excesses or narrowness of common law decisions. Kinnane writes that this granting of "super-legal justice" was seen as well within the law rather than as a means of contradicting it.[17]

The result of the repeated grants of relief or extraordinary remedies was the development of the system of equity. "Equity" in general means a spirit of fairness in dealing with one another. It is best expressed as the "golden rule"—treating others as you would have them treat you. In its legal context, *equity* refers to a body of rules or principles developed by courts in keeping with the spirit of fairness.

The chancellor, to whom equity matters were directed, was the most important member of the council, and he gradually referred fewer and fewer of the cases to the council. In 1474 it was decided that the chancellor could act on his own rather than as a representative of the council, and a Court of Chancery was established. The purpose of this court was to produce results that were "equitable," as distinct from "legal." The chancery soon ventured into areas not covered in common law—fraud, for example—and invented many useful remedies. Among these were (1) the *injunction,* a writ ordering someone to refrain from some particular act; (2) the *order of specific performance,* an order to fulfill a contract within a specified period of time; and (3) the *writ of prohibition,* an order to a lower court to cease handling a case because it belongs within the jurisdiction of another court. These judicial orders had the general purpose of stopping harmful acts before they occurred or commanding the fulfillment of contracts and other pledges rather than awarding monetary damages after the harm was done.[18]

The *Star Chamber* was an equity court that appeared during the late fifteenth century—apparently as a remnant of the old council. It became a purely judicial body in the 1530s. Its case load included charges against persons powerful enough to defy common law courts and, writes Kempin, "matters which threaten the security of the realm, such as criminal libel, conspiracy, forgery, and later, fraud and the punishment of judges."[19]

In the seventeenth century, the Star Chamber became synonymous with secrecy, torture, inhumane punishment, and other devices of a cruel monarchy, and it was abolished by Parliament in 1641. This was one of the times during which the emphasis shifted from a crime control model—however extreme or distorted—to a due process model that gave at least some recognition of individual rights. Even after the Star Chamber ceased to exist, some of its creations in substantive criminal law lived on.

Canon Law

No review of historical antecedents of our criminal court system would be complete without at least a reference to the legal system developed by the church. Initially intended to govern internal affairs, the body of canon law developed by the church was soon applied to ordinary citizens and secular affairs. This was largely due to the fact that much of Europe suffered—or enjoyed—the absence of effective secular government. Anglo-Saxon England saw no real distinction between secular and canon law, and we have already noted that it was under the Normans that the clergy came to be banned from a well-established role in the hundred courts.

Our interest in canon law is, in part, due to the fact that, because it had jurisdiction over sin, it therefore dealt with matters of sex crimes and immoral conduct. Thus the modern crimes of incest, fornication, adultery, and "unnatural" sex acts originated in English canon law.[20]

An entire class of persons known collectively as *clergy* were exempt from treatment under secular law; hence all the crimes of priests, nuns, members of various orders, and a number of others covered by a broad definition of clergy were handled under canon law. This concept of *benefit of clergy* was a means by which canon law protected many persons from abuse by secular authorities, but it also became a means of permitting powerful church officials and their allies to act as if they were "above the law." The 1530s saw the abolition of this doctrine.

The concept of *sanctuary* extended the protection of a consecrated place to those fleeing from the law. Many escaped oppression and harassment by hiding in—but also becoming virtual prisoners of—the church and its monasteries and nunneries. Others escaped just applications of the law under the protection of sanctuary. The concept was gradually whittled away and eventually abolished in the 1600s.

When Henry VIII proclaimed himself head of the church in 1531, canon law lost its connection with Rome and withered. The church was from then on subservient to secular law and power; the final blow came in 1857 when *ecclesiastical*, or church-operated, *courts* lost jurisdiction over domestic relations and probate (the proof of wills) to new secular courts.[21] Since that time, canon law has concerned itself solely with the governance of the church.

By the time colonization of North America became a primary goal of British policy, the legal and court system of the mother country was firmly established. It therefore provided the foundation for the American system, if only because it was the only system with which most colonists were familiar.

COURTS IN THE AMERICAN COLONIES

Courts in colonial America had varied and nebulous beginnings. They came into being in an assortment of ways, including specific authorization by the king in royal charters, acts of governors exercising royal prerogative, and legislation by colonial assemblies. The English government permitted a range of experiments, insisting only that colonial law not controvert English law. Judicial bodies in the form of governor and council acted as a court of general jurisdiction. They in turn generally appointed local magistrates or justices of the peace, creating the basis for the two levels of trial courts we have today. Eventually a chief justice and some associates were appointed to hold court. The general trial jurisdiction of these courts covered serious felonies, including those which became known as "capital offenses."[22]

Glick and Vines have pointed out that there was little need for formal court systems in the small settlements that made up most of the colonies. But as towns and cities grew in size and complexity, so did the need for courts to resolve the growing number of disputes.[23] The judicial systems that emerged differed from colony to colony, depending on local customs and beliefs, including religious practices.

There were few lawyers in colonial times, partly because few came here from Europe and partly because few Americans wanted to become lawyers. Most courts were therefore operated by laymen, with businessmen, landowners, and merchants acting as magistrates.[24]

Toward the end of the seventeenth century some states, especially in the more populous northeast, created formal judicial systems. The General Court of Massachusetts began delegating the authority to try cases to county magistrates in 1685. Eventually the General Court created a separate judicial system and limited its own functions to those of a legislature. Connecticut in 1698 created probate courts, perhaps the first such specialized court in the colonies.[25] It would be a while, however, before the idea of separating judicial from legislative functions would develop into separate branches of government.

Justice of the Peace Courts

The lower courts of limited jurisdiction presided over by the justices of the peace were the busiest courts. They certainly disposed of the vast majority of cases, especially criminal. Edwin Surrency comments that the office of justice of the peace, with its "long and honorable history in England," was "the only logical alternative" to a full-time judiciary, which was unsupportable in the colonies.[26] In keeping with tradition, the original inhabitants of the office were usually selected from among the country gentlemen of property and influence who were more than willing to assume a position of such prestige in the community.

Pennsylvania's Courts

Pennsylvania was one colony that went beyond the simple model so far described. To the county Court of Quarter Sessions, which heard most civil and criminal cases, William Penn and the general assembly added the Provincial Circuit Court in 1684. This court rode the circuit to hear the most important cases and to hear appeals from the lower quarter sessions courts.[27] The City of Philadelphia was also permitted by a charter from Governor Penn to establish its own Mayors Court within city limits. This began a trend toward a complex—even mystifying—court structure. Some states today retain court systems that resemble Pennsylvania's early model.

Weaknesses of Colonial Courts

Edwin Surrency documents deficiencies of the colonial courts. He cites complaints pointing to irregular procedures, delays in holding sessions, the lack of lawyers, the arbitrariness or corruption of judges, and unnecessary complexities and duplications of organization.[28]

Yet while some petitioned London for redress of grievances, others later protested the king's interference with the judicial systems of the colonies. The Declaration of Independence contained some specific charges against the king:

> He has obstructed the Administration of Justice by refusing to Assent to Laws establishing Judiciary powers.—He has made Judges dependent on his Will alone for the tenure of their offices, and the amount of payment of their salaries.— ... For depriving us, in many cases, of the benefits of Trial by Jury.

The feeling was widespread among American leaders that England was denying the colonies the chief benefits of English common law and withholding the right of the American judiciary to adapt it to American conditions. The English position was that England alone would decide what law and court system would prevail in the colonies. There was a widespread feeling on the part of colonists that their rights to due process were being abrogated by a Crown desperate to maintain control over colonial behavior. To the colonists, the Crown was more interested in having profitable colonies than it was in the rights of those who inhabited them. William Swindler writes: "Essentially this was the impasse in which the hope of avoiding revolution ultimately perished."[29]

AMERICAN COURTS AFTER INDEPENDENCE

By the summer of 1776, the royal courts had been shut down in most colonies. The courts were reopened by acts of assemblies in most places shortly after the Declaration of Independence, and their structure remained virtually unchanged. But independence raised three key issues: (1) Was the common law to remain in force by acts of the colonial assemblies? (2) Were the courts to continue to be seen as an extension of the executive power or as a distinct branch in keeping with the increasing popularity of the concept of separation of powers? (3) What, if any, role would the electorate play in the judicial system?[30] The answers varied among the thirteen states.

State Courts

The court systems of the new states differed in several respects: in whether courts were created by new constitutions or were continued from old charters; in the length of terms of judges; and in whether governors, legislatures, or both controlled appointment to the bench. However, all the states generally preserved the old organizational principles. Thus there were courts of general trial jurisdiction with civil, criminal, and chancery functions. And in most states there were limited jurisdiction and special jurisdiction courts. All states had at least one court of appellate jurisdiction, and all states accepted the separation of powers doctrine and provided some measure of independence of the judiciary from other branches. This was a break with the past in an attempt to ensure protection of the individual right to due process. On the other hand, procedures were basically unchanged, with the common law remaining in effect or being readopted by legislative acts. Thus what we appeared to have was an attempt to promote new political purposes through courts that in name and function were unchanged from the colonial period.[31]

There was one large, unanswered question: To whom or to what would final appeal be made from state court judgments? What would replace the Privy Council as the final determiner of interstate conflicts? It took several years of confusion and frustration over congressional efforts to resolve territorial disputes among states before there was general agreement on the need for a national judiciary. The only agreement was that a national court would act as a court of first instance in disputes between states. Few could imagine a full-blown federal court system that would parallel the state court systems.

The Federal Judiciary

The Constitutional Convention in 1787 wrestled with two major questions regarding a federal judiciary:

1. Should federal courts have their own original jurisdiction in addition to that of hearing cases involving disputes between states?

2. Should a national court have the power to review—and reverse—decisions made in the states' highest courts?

Those advocating a strong national court system carried the convention and the answer to both questions became "yes." National issues, such as those involving maritime commerce, required a single national body of law applied by federal courts. And since the Constitution—and laws and treaties made under it—was the *Supreme Law of the Land* to which state as well as federal officials were obligated, conflicting interpretations or case law from the states' highest courts could hardly be permitted to stand uncorrected.

Article III of the Constitution established only the Supreme Court of the United States, but it anticipated a *federal court system* in its distinction between appellate and original jurisdiction and its grant to Congress of the power to create other courts. Article III also provided for lifetime tenure for federal judges and protected them from salary reductions by the Congress. It anticipated a criminal jurisdiction by providing for jury trials in criminal cases; such trials were to be held in the state in which the crimes were committed.

The judicial article drew little attention in the states' ratification debates—certainly nothing like the uproar that occurred over the legislative and executive powers of the proposed government. Still there was strong opposition in some quarters. In Virginia John Marshall assured a hostile Patrick Henry that states would be protected by federal judges from a seizure of power by the new federal government. The judges of the federal courts, he declared, would void any law passed by Congress that was not warranted under the powers enumerated in the Constitution for that body. Thus Marshall sold a sweeping concept of judicial review by the national courts over presumably coequal branches of the federal government as a device that would guarantee states' rights.[32]

The First Congress passed the Judiciary Act of 1789, which fleshed out the first true national court system. It provided for four circuit and thirteen district courts. The former were essentially general trial courts. They had appellate jurisdiction over the latter, which were limited trial courts. Serious federal crimes were to be tried by circuit judges. District judges had jurisdiction over offenses for which punishment could not exceed a fine of $100, six months in jail, or a whipping of thirty stripes.[33]

Circuit courts had no judges but were staffed by circuit-riding Supreme Court judges and some district court judges. Some districts were not within circuits and circuit courts in those districts were held by the district judges alone. The requirement that justices travel thousands of miles riding circuit resulted in hardship, delayed justice, and the refusal of distinguished persons to accept appointment.

The Judiciary Act of 1801 sought to overcome this by creating circuit judgeships, but when Thomas Jefferson, a National Republican, was elected in 1800, outgoing Federalist John Adams appointed Federalists to all the new posts before the end of his term. The new administration convinced Congress to repeal the act in 1802. The original circuit riding was reinstated and lasted another eighty-nine years—a long delay in establishing a rational and effective system of federal trial courts.[34]

In 1891 circuit courts of appeal were created. It was not until 1911, however, that circuit and district trial functions were combined into the current U.S. district courts, and the three-tiered structure we know today was established.

The American System vis-à-vis the British

The fact that the United States developed a *dual court system*—that is, separate court systems in each of its states plus a complete federal system of trial and appellate courts—has clearly set it apart from its English origins in one sense. That these courts were created by statute or constitution is also different from the executive origins of the English courts. At the same time, the courts we created and the law and procedures they use—with the exception of the French-based Louisiana system—are firmly rooted in the English common law and equity traditions. Some states, in fact, maintained a clear distinction between common law and equity for many years.

Then in the middle of the last century, a New York lawyer, David Dudley Field, who had studied the English court system and others, headed a New York state commission that overhauled the codes of procedure for that state. The results were felt even in Great Britain. Field's work led to a new civil code for New York in 1848 and to a criminal code in 1857. The Field codes merged law and equity proceedings into one form of civil action and set a pattern in both civil and criminal law that was copied by many other states. His civil code was even the basis for the British Judicature Act of 1873.[35]

While the Field codes were legislatively enacted, further changes have come largely through legislative grants of authority to courts to make and revise their own rules. Thus the Supreme Court of the United States has considerable federal rule-making authority, and the highest courts in many states are the sources of their rules of court.

TOWARD MODERN CRIMINAL LAW

Even with the invasion by the Normans and the many changes wrought by William and his successors, including the development of common law, it was not until the nineteenth century that various concepts of criminal law were brought together in a system that would be recognizable to today's students.

Substantive Law

As discussed in Chapter 1, criminal law is divisible into its substantive and procedural aspects. The substantive aspect deals with what acts are classified as crimes, as opposed to being either civil wrongs or perfectly legal acts. Substantive law includes the concept *mens rea,* or the "guilty mind"—that is, the intent to commit a crime. This concept was borrowed from ancient Roman law and is based on the assumption that a person is in control of his or her own behavior and can rationally choose among alternative courses of conduct. It gives rise to the entire business of determining criminal responsibility and the defenses of infancy, insanity, justification, self-defense, entrapment, and others.[36]

Substantive criminal law also deals with the all-important question of what sanction or penalty to impose for each act or on each guilty offender. A fundamental concept is "no crime without punishment, no punishment without crime." In other words, crimes are those acts defined in a state's penal code, acts for which the law prescribes punishments to be imposed by the state. At the same time, the state cannot punish persons who have not been convicted of a crime, a violation of a criminal law.

Procedural Law

As to procedural aspects, Berman and Grenier have nicely summarized the six basic distinctions that have evolved between the civil and criminal process. They enumerate certain characteristics of the criminal process; that is, it encompasses:

1. An action brought by the government on behalf of the people of a state, not by a private person and not on behalf of only the victim
2. Reference to the action as a "prosecution" and to the government agent who brings it as a "prosecutor"
3. Rules that protect the defendant to a far greater degree than is the case in civil actions, rules that are based on the presumption of innocence of the accused
4. A verdict that is announced as a finding that the defendant is either guilty or not guilty as opposed to a finding for or against the plaintiff (the person who files a civil suit)

5. A judgment by the court that follows the verdict and that results in either an acquittal or a conviction of the defendant

6. The imposition of a sentence upon the convicted that states the penalty that person must bear for his or her crimes.[37]

SUMMARY AND CONCLUSION

This chapter has presented a brief overview of the origins of our criminal law and the courts through which it is administered. Our point has been not to provide a comprehensive history but only to indicate that our court system and our approach to dealing with crime have roots in the distant past. The system and the approach are also obviously subject to continual—if slow—change. The change is often driven by the constant struggle between those seeking the most efficient means of controlling crime and those championing the rights of individuals to full due process of law and specific protection of those rights.

We have ignored many topics of an historical nature in this chapter because we intend to take them up in subsequent chapters. Among these are changes in the selection, training, and discipline of judges, the development of offices of public prosecution and—more recently—of public defense, the trends in court administration and management, and, of course, the major steps in the evolution of constitutional law as it relates to the rights of defendants and the processing of criminal cases.

The student should now be prepared to move on, aware that our notions about crime are rooted in antiquity, with the Greeks, Romans, and Normans making major contributions. The court system through which we operate is the product of a series of ad hoc decisions and almost accidental occurrences as much as it is a product of rational planning. Old forms have been adapted to new ideas and purposes. And we anticipate that contemporary American commissions and studies will prompt major changes in the same time-honored manner.

QUESTIONS FOR DISCUSSION

1. How much does our legal system owe to the English common law as it existed on July 3, 1776?
2. If you had been one of the Founding Fathers, how would you have proposed establishing the framework of the American legal system, considering this was an obvious opportunity to make a complete break with the past?
3. What grievances against the British Crown were fresh in the minds of the drafters of the Declaration of Independence, the Constitution, and the Bill of

Rights and led to the establishment of such safeguards as are found in the Fourth, Fifth, and Sixth Amendments? How do these safeguards provide the foundation for Packer's Due Process Model?

NOTES

1. Robert W. Fergusson and Allan H. Stokke, *Concepts of Criminal Law,* Holbrook, Boston, 1976, p. 27.
2. Charles Herman Kinnane, *A First Book on Anglo-American Law,* 2d ed., Bobbs-Merrill, Indianapolis, 1952, p. 215.
3. Ibid., pp. 216–217 and 220.
4. Ibid., pp. 229–230.
5. Ibid., p. 244.
6. Ibid., p. 230, and see Frederick G. Kempin, Jr., *Historical Introduction to Anglo-American Law in a Nutshell,* 2d ed., West, St. Paul, Minn., 1973, p. 165.
7. Kempin, pp. 23–27.
8. Kinnane, pp. 232–233.
9. Ibid., p.. 244–245.
10. Kempin, pp. 50–51.
11. Ibid., p. 56.
12. Ibid., p. 57.
13. Kinnane, pp. 262–264.
14. George W. Keeton, "The Courts and Judiciary in England on the Eve of the War of Independence," in Glenn R. Winters and Edward V. Schoenbaum (eds.), *American Courts and Justice,* American Judicature Society, Chicago, 1976, p. 20.
15. Ibid., p. 20.
16. Kempin, pp. 31–35, and Kinnane, pp. 264–269.
17. Kinnane, p. 295.
18. Ibid., pp. 295–301, and Kempin, pp. 36–39.
19. Kempin, p. 41.
20. Kinnane, pp. 338 and 343.
21. Ibid., pp. 345–346.
22. Edwin C. Surrency, "The Courts in the American Colonies," *American Journal of Legal History,* vol. 11, 1967, p. 348.
23. Henry R. Glick and Kenneth N. Vines, *State Court Systems,* Prentice-Hall, Englewood Cliffs, N.J., 1973, p. 19.
24. Francis Aumann, *The Changing American Legal System,* Ohio State University Press, Columbus, 1940, pp. 8 and 35.
25. Glick and Vines, p. 21.
26. Ibid., p. 348.
27. Edwin Bronner, "Philadelphia County Court of Quarter Sessions, and Common Pleas," *American Journal of Legal History,* vol. I, 1957, p. 79.
28. Surrency, pp. 254–256.
29. William F. Swindler, "Seedtime of the American Judiciary, 1775–1800," in Winters and Schoenbaum, p. 29.

30. Ibid., p. 30.
31. Ibid., p. 33.
32. Ibid., pp. 42–43.
33. Edwin C. Surrency, "The Judiciary Act of 1801," *American Journal of Legal History*, vol. II, 1958, p. 57.
34. Ibid., pp. 53 and 62–64.
35. Glenn R. Winters, "Two Centuries of Judicial Progress in America," in Winters and Schoenbaum, *American Courts and Justice*, pp. 52–53.
36. Paul B. Weston and Kenneth M. Wells, *Criminal Law*, Goodyear, Santa Monica, Calif., 1978, Ch. 7.
37. Harold J. Berman and William R. Grenier, *The Nature and Functions of Law*, 3d ed., Foundation Press, Mineola, N.Y., 1972, pp. 115–116.

3

COURT SYSTEMS OF THE UNITED STATES

After reading this chapter, students should be able to define and explain the importance of each of the following terms or phrases:

original jurisdiction
appellate jurisdiction
general trial jurisdiction
superior courts
limited trial jurisdiction
special jurisdiction
inferior courts
trial de novo

courts of last resort
intermediate appellate courts
substantial federal question
U.S. Supreme Court
U.S. courts of appeals
U.S. district courts
U.S. magistrates

Having provided a general history of law and courts, we turn now to an examination of the organization of courts in the United States. This nation boasts an extraordinary system of courts in that there are two separate and distinct court systems: the state courts and the federal courts. We are said to have a *dual court system*. These two court systems coexist side by side with remarkably few difficulties. State courts, or course, administer the laws of the states within which they operate. Federal courts administer federal laws. The two systems are linked at the top by the authority of the U.S. Supreme Court to interpret and enforce the terms of the Constitution—the "Supreme Law of the Land." Conflicts between state and federal laws or actions which pose a threat to constitutional order are thus resolvable.

In order to proceed with a discussion of the two parallel court systems we must first deal with the concept of jurisdiction and its various subcategories. A survey of the structures of state and federal court systems will then follow.

JURISDICTION

In simple terms, *jurisdiction* is the power or authority to hear a case or motion and determine a proper remedy. Courts are often pressed to decide whether or not they have proper jurisdiction to hear a particular matter. Finding the court with the proper jurisdiction to hear their cases used to be a major problem for litigants. It has been much less of a problem since common law and equity were merged in the last half of the nineteenth century. Still, each state distinguishes types of jurisdiction and assigns them to various courts.

There are several ways to divide and allocate jurisdictions to appropriate courts. One way is to separate *original jurisdiction*—the authority to try cases, to be the *court of first instance*—from *appellate jurisdiction*—the authority to correct the legal errors of lower, or inferior, courts and to reverse or amend their judgments. A second way is to divide trial courts into jurisdictional levels based on the importance of the cases they may handle. Thus we have courts of limited trial jurisdiction—inferior courts—and courts of general trial jurisdiction—superior courts. Still another way is to separate trial courts according to the subject matter with which they may deal—thus, for example, the distinction between courts with civil jurisdiction and those with criminal jurisdiction. Yet another way is to distinguish courts' jurisdictions according to what persons may appear before them as parties to a case. Consider the distinction between courts that handle disputes between adults and the so-called juvenile courts, which deal with cases in which children and teenagers are involved.

Original versus Appellate Jurisdiction

All state court systems and the federal court system reflect the clear distinction between trial courts and appellate courts. *Appellate courts* are those that spend all or virtually all their time deciding issues and cases on appeal from lower courts. They are called upon by the party losing the case or the argument on a point of law or procedure to consider whether the lower court judge committed a reversible error. If a trial judge misapplies constitutional or statutory provisions or binding case law in ruling on an issue, the losing party may seek a hearing before the appropriate appellate court. In some cases, the appellate court *must* hear and rule on the appeal. In other cases the appellate court may decline to hear the appeal—an act that has the effect of sustaining the ruling of the court below.

Appellate court decisions are the source of case law in the United States. Under the common law notion of *stare decisis,* subsequent cases involving the same issue are to be decided in the light of principles and rules laid down in prior appellate court opinions. These opinions and the case law they contain guide not only successive cases on appeal, but obviously affect the administration of justice at all levels below. Judges and other court officers are expected from that point on to obey the principles established and directives included in case law. Trial courts do not make law in deciding cases. They may have certain local rule-making authority relative to procedures used, but these local rules are not considered law.

Original jurisdiction, as we have said, is the authority to hear the case or matter at its first instance, render a verdict or judgment, and apply the appropriate remedy. Original jurisdiction includes trial jurisdiction but is not limited to the authority to conduct trials. Many matters of original jurisdiction are petitions or motions for writs or court orders of various kinds. Appellate courts are sometimes called upon to exercise original jurisdiction in these nontrial matters.

Matters brought to courts for trial, of course, make up the vast bulk of original jurisdiction material. But trial courts and their judges and magistrates spend much time in nontrial activities. Not only do they deal with many petitions and motions in matters not brought to the courts for trial, they participate in the disposition of most civil and criminal cases without bringing such cases to formal trial.

General versus Limited and Special Jurisdiction

Trial jurisdiction is divided into two basic levels and consists of three specific types. There are courts of *general trial jurisdiction*—sometimes called superior courts. They represent one level and type: courts able to hear virtually any case at first instance regardless of subject, parties involved, or level of importance. The other level of trial jurisdiction is carried out in courts sometimes called inferior courts and is of two types:

1. Courts of *limited jurisdiction* are those permitted to hear cases within prescribed limits of importance. The laws of states provide that cases be divided into classes based on the seriousness of the offense in criminal matters and the sum involved in civil matters, and that courts of limited trial jurisdiction handle the less important cases. (These courts, however, also usually handle proceedings in all criminal cases up to the point of arraignment—a matter we shall explain later.)

2. So-called *special jurisdiction* refers to that which includes only specified parties to a case or subject matters. Special jurisdiction usually includes matters involving juveniles, dispute between family members, or such specific subjects as tax law and probate claims against the government. An example of a court of special jurisdiction in the federal judiciary system is the U.S. Customs Court.

Just as it is not possible to say that appellate courts have only appellate jurisdiction, it is also not possible to say that trial courts have only original jurisdiction. Trial courts of general jurisdiction are called *superior courts* in part because they have appellate jurisdiction over most of the courts of limited and/or special jurisdiction—the *inferior courts*. This appellate jurisdiction does not generally work the way it would in appellate courts, however, because most inferior courts are courts of nonrecord; thus there is no transcript to review. When superior courts assume jurisdiction over cases appealed from such inferior courts, they conduct a new trial, or *trial de novo*. However, where a record exists of the lower court's conduct, general trial courts use the appellate court process of reviewing the record and briefs submitted by attorneys, rendering decisions on points of law, and remanding the case back to the lower court for further proceedings.

Civil versus Criminal Jurisdiction

A fundamental division of jurisdiction is that made between criminal and civil cases. Criminal cases arise from certain lawsuits brought by agents of government against persons alleged to have committed crimes or offenses as defined in various ordinances, codes, or statutes. All other cases or matters brought before the court are civil.

Criminal cases are filed and pursued by the state rather than by a private party. The process is known as a *prosecution*. Its purpose is to deal with the question of the guilt or innocence of the persons accused and to seek the appropriate disposition of the persons found guilty. Civil cases, on the other hand, are filed by private parties—whether groups or individuals—as well as by state agents. The purpose of civil actions is to satisfy, or "make whole," the alleged victims or plaintiffs by such means as awarding them damages; granting them a divorce or custody of children or of property; or enjoining the offending party from performing some harmful act.

It is possible, of course, for some situations to give rise to both civil and criminal cases. If, for example, one person strikes another, causing the victim to sustain a serious injury, the person committing the assault may become a defendant in both a criminal prosecution and a civil suit. The latter could be filed by the victim-plaintiff seeking damages.

Criminal jurisdiction is further subdivided into three general categories: felonies, misdemeanors, and infractions, so-called noncriminal offenses. In most states, felonies are those crimes considered serious enough to warrant a possible year or more in state prison, while misdemeanors are crimes punishable by up to one year in a local jail. *Noncriminal offenses* are violations of local ordinances or state statutes; conviction for a noncriminal offense can draw a fine but not the incarceration of the offender.

STATE COURT SYSTEMS

The systems of courts maintained by the fifty states vary widely in complexity. Honors for the most complicated court system may belong to the state of New York, though Georgia, Massachusetts, and Tennessee also continue to support a baffling array of courts. The simplest court systems in the country may be those of our newest states, Alaska and Hawaii.[1] Several other states have streamlined their court organization in recent years, eliminating many courts of limited and special jurisdiction in the process.

In order to appreciate the pattern of court organization in the United States, we return to the concept of jurisdiction and relate it to four layers, or tiers, of courts. Thus we can speak of *courts of last resort,* or *ultimate appeal,* within each of the states; *intermediate courts of appeal*; *courts of general trial jurisdiction* (usually referred to as superior courts); and last—as well as least in terms of stature—the *courts of limited* and/or *special jurisdiction* (or inferior courts).

In Figure 3.1 we provide an overview of state court structure using these four tiers.

Courts of Last Resort

All states and the District of Columbia each have a court of last resort, or ultimate appeal. In most states it is known as the state's supreme court. Maine and Massachusetts call theirs supreme judicial courts; West Virginia calls its the supreme court of appeals; Maryland, New York, and the District of Columbia refer to theirs as courts of appeals; and the states of Oklahoma and Texas boast separate courts of criminal appeals in addition to their so-called supreme courts.

The title *court of last resort* is somewhat misleading, since a case that involves an important federal question may be appealed to the U.S. Su-

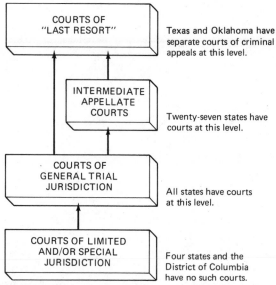

FIGURE 3.1
Structure of State Court Systems
(*Source:* Law Enforcement Assistance Administration,
*National Survey of Court Organization: 1977 Supplement
to State Judicial Systems,* U.S. Government Printing
Office, Washington, D.C., 1977, pp. 4–8.)

preme Court after the appellate process on the state level has been exhausted. Nevertheless, these courts are the last resort *within* their state systems, and they are the ultimate interpreters of state laws and constitutions.

Appellate jurisdiction has been conferred upon the U.S. Supreme Court by various statutes, basically 28 U.S.C. 1251–1258 and various special statutes. Usually one must raise a "substantial federal question," or a matter of interpretation of the Constitution, to warrant a hearing in the nation's highest court.

Intermediate Appellate Courts

As of this writing, twenty-seven states have *intermediate courts of appeal*—appellate courts placed between the state's highest court and its trial courts. These courts tend to be located in states with large populations and resultant heavy case loads. Nineteen of these states maintain only one such court. The other states have divided themselves into appellate districts and have established intermediate appellate courts in each. Texas has fourteen such districts and courts. Ohio claims eleven districts but operates these courts in each of the eighty-eight counties of the state.[2] Other states have between two and five intermediate appellate courts.

New York maintains a two-tiered intermediate appellate system. The entire state is served by appellate divisions of the supreme court (see below for New York's unique use of this term)—four in number. So-called appellate terms of the supreme court, of which there are three, cover the five counties within New York City and the seven counties in its suburban environs. Civil cases from this area must be appealed through both tiers of intermediate appellate courts, but criminal cases are appealed around the appellate division to the highest court, the court of appeals.[3]

Courts of General Trial Jurisdiction

Every state court system boasts courts of general trial jurisdiction—those trial courts that can hear virtually any and all cases. These are the so-called superior courts, though they may also be called district courts, circuit courts, or courts of common pleas. In New York they are called supreme courts. The geographic areas these courts serve are generally either counties or multicounty districts or circuits. There are over 3,500 of these courts in the fifty states, with individual states having anywhere between 4 such courts (Alaska, Hawaii, Delaware, and Rhode Island) and 254 (Texas).[4]

Since these are courts of first instance for the entire range of litigation, they are frequently subdivided by subject matter into departments or divisions specializing in civil cases, criminal cases, probate matters, juvenile cases, and domestic relations cases. These divisions occur in the more populous areas and become quite specialized in urban centers. The judges, however, generally rotate among the divisions, and they are expected to become "generalists" during their tenure on the bench.

In terms of criminal law, the common pattern is for general trial courts to handle all criminal trials and dispositions involving felony charges against defendants. These courts, however, rarely handle the preliminary stages of criminal cases. Courts of limited jurisdiction, usually at the county or municipal level, handle the preliminary matters, even in felony cases.

As mentioned earlier, most general trial courts have appellate jurisdiction over some courts of limited or special jurisdiction. Appellants from lower courts seek to persuade the superior courts to grant them a hearing or trial de novo on the grounds that the lower court denied due process of law.

Courts of Limited and Special Jurisdiction

Courts of limited and special jurisdiction are by far the most numerous and carry the lion's share of the case load in the United States. These courts, often referred to as *inferior courts* or *lower courts,* numbered more than 13,000 over a decade ago and constituted more than three-quarters of all courts in the nation.[5] Over the past few years, however, state after state has reorganized all or part of its judicial system, and many of these courts have been abolished—particularly those courts in which nonlawyers acted as judges or magistrates. In fact, four states and the District of Columbia have no such courts at all. Forty states have courts at the city or town level, thirty-four have county-level courts, and twenty-seven states have limited or special jurisdiction courts as part of their state or district court systems. Seventeen states retain lower courts at three levels of government.

Courts of limited and special jurisdiction come not only in great number but in a bewildering array of sizes and shapes. And they carry a staggering assortment of titles: district courts, county courts, city courts, family courts, probate courts, juvenile courts, justice courts, mayor courts, police courts, orphans' courts, town courts, housing courts, recorders' courts, alderman's courts, surrogate courts, traffic courts, conciliation courts, constitutional county courts, municipal courts, and last—if not least—justice of the peace courts.[6]

Most of the courts named above are strictly limited jurisdiction courts. This again means that they may deal with matters of various kinds, but only up to a legally established level of importance. A typical cutoff for such courts is a $10,000 limit on the value of civil suits and a limit of one year on the length of a jail term the court may impose in a criminal case—the latter meaning that such courts may not dispose of felony cases. Where there are both city or town courts and county or district courts at this level, the former hear cases brought under municipal ordinances, while the latter may hear cases involving state statutes. Thus one could say there are *limited jurisdiction* courts and *petty jurisdiction* courts.

Reviewing the list of courts given above, one notices that many have names that imply they may hear cases involving only certain types of matters—probate, housing, traffic, conciliation—while others deal only with certain parties—family, juveniles, orphans. These are the courts of special jurisdiction. They are not "limited" strictly by the importance of the case; they are "specialized" by the subjects and/or parties they may deal with.

Reform in the Lower Trial Courts

The fact that the array of inferior courts is so bewildering is but one reason why several states have abolished many of them, reorganized and broadened the jurisdiction of others, and generally moved in the direction of consolidation or unification of courts. Organizational reform has also been prompted by the desire to increase efficiency, consolidate budgetary activities, and improve the quality of justice at the level of courts with which most people deal. The goals are generally the elimination of nonlawyers from judicial roles and the ending of "cash register" justice—that is, justice done for a fee.

The most frequent targets for elimination are the justice of the peace courts. They have been abolished in Florida (1972), Iowa (1973), Nebraska (1973), South Dakota (1974), Kansas (1974), Indiana (1976), Alabama (1977), Kentucky (1977), and Georgia (1983). These states were among more than a dozen which structurally reorganized their systems in the years between 1972 and 1984. More will be said about court unification later.

While lower courts have often been defended as vestiges of local rule and common sense and have been championed for their comprehensible procedures and their quick action in disposing of local matters, they have also fallen under severe attack from some quarters. Among the faults found with these courts are their capriciousness, their arbitrariness, their ignorance of the law and of proper procedure, their denial of fundamental rights to some litigants and defendants, their subservience to local political cliques, and their concern with generating fines and fees for themselves and their towns or counties. Certainly the lower courts have not always been gifted with legal talent on the bench, an aspect we shall take up when we deal with the nation's judges.

Still, the inferior court system is absolutely essential in most states. Lower courts must be depended upon to dispose of the vast majority of civil and criminal cases. State reorganization plans have therefore been aimed at strengthening lower courts as a whole, even while eliminating the worst among them. Not all changes are beneficial, however. In Florida, many city officials complain that the county courts cannot (or will not) deal effectively with city ordinance violations. They complain that since "reform" took place, quick resolution of local cases has been replaced by slow, cumbersome, and more expensive litigation—or by no action at all. Certainly this is a danger of reform, and reformers must deal with it in their reorganizational schemes if they are to realize improved justice in the lower courts.

THE FEDERAL COURT SYSTEM

In addition to the court systems of each state and the District of Columbia, there is, of course, the system of federal courts—the third branch of our national government. Its general structure parallels that of judicial structure in most states: a court of last resort, intermediate appellate courts, and general jurisdiction trial courts. There is no level of inferior courts as such in the federal system, but with the expansion of federal jurisdiction has come a body of magistrates working within the general trial courts and performing a growing list of tasks comparable to those assigned to the states' lower courts.

The Supreme Court of the United States

The highest court in the land is the U.S. Supreme Court. It serves as the court of last resort in the federal system and as a possible last resort to litigants appealing from state courts. The Court sits in Washington, D.C., and has for many years consisted of eight associate justices and a chief justice. All are nominated to their respective seats for life terms by the president and confirmed by the Senate.

The fact that the Supreme Court sits atop all other courts in the nation would seem to imply that it is swamped with appeals. It does receive thousands of requests for hearings per year, but chooses only those cases for appellate review that it deems important enough to merit its consideration. If the Supreme Court decides to hear a case, it issues a *writ of certiorari*—an order issued to the lower court demanding its records of the case being considered. There are a few circumstances under which the Supreme Court is compelled to hear a case—when a lower federal court declares a federal law unconstitutional, for example—but these instances are rare. The Court will entertain an appeal in which state laws or state constitutions are at issue only if they are challenged as conflicting with the Constitution, laws, or treaties of the United States. In other words, a *substantial federal question* must be present in such appeals to merit the Court's consideration.

That the U.S. Supreme Court has become a very important participant in the criminal process of the states as well as of the federal government is clear to even the most casual observers. Within the past thirty years a virtual revolution has taken place in the criminal justice system—a revolution largely imposed by the Supreme Court. The momentous decisions of the Warren Court of the 1960s had the effect of bringing the state systems into line with federal interpretations of constitutional provisions regarding the rights of defendants protected under Amendments IV, V, VI, and VIII of the Bill of Rights. The Burger Court of the seventies did little to change the impact of those decisions; rather, it made adjustments, clarifications, and consolidations, as well as some innovations of its own.

The pendulum began to swing in earnest again, however, in the early 1980s, as the Court returned to more conservative principles and came down more often on the side of the state. The relevant case law is examined elsewhere in this volume.

U.S. Courts of Appeals

There are twelve circuit courts of the appeals serving as the intermediate appellate courts in the federal system. Eleven cover the states and one the District of Columbia. These courts take cases appealed from federal trial courts, appeals from regulatory agencies, and interlocutory appeals from both federal and state trial courts. (*Interlocutory appeals* are those that call upon an appellate court to decide a point of law or procedure at issue in a trial, which is suspended until the ruling is made.)

These courts of appeal are staffed by three to fifteen judges, all appointed by the president and confirmed by the Senate. Three-judge panels hear most appeals in these courts, but in rare cases the entire membership of a court may sit. One impact of the Supreme Court's revolutionizing of the criminal process has been an explosion of criminal appeals to the courts of appeals.

U.S. District Courts

There is only one level of trial courts in the federal system; it is composed of the ninety-five U.S. district courts. These general jurisdiction trial courts are located in each state, the District of Columbia, and the six territories of the United States. Each state has between one and four districts within it, and branches of the district courts may exist in several cities within the district. There are over 500 district court judges assigned to these courts. Like their appellate brethren, they are appointed to life terms by the president with the consent of the Senate, but senators from the states in which the vacancies occur have more than a little to do with the actual selection process. The number of judges varies from one in an entire state to over two dozen in a single district of a four-district state.

Within the district courts there are several hundred *U.S. magistrates,* most of them serving on a part-time basis. Under a program initiated in 1969 and fully implemented in 1971, these officials took over the work once done by the U.S. commissioners. They are appointed to eight-year terms by the district court judges whom they serve. They have assumed duties—particularly in criminal matters—that enable us to assert that they constitute a kind of inferior court system within the structure of the general trial courts. These magistrates certainly perform most of the duties that lower courts and magistrates perform within the states' systems: they issue warrants; they conduct initial appearance, probable cause, and preliminary hearings; they determine bail and conditions of pretrial release of accused persons; they review petitions from federal prisoners; and they try cases of petty and minor offenses, which are equivalent of the misdemeanors handled by the judges of courts of limited jurisdiction within the states. (*Petty offenses* are those that can be penalized by up to six months in jail and a $500 fine; *minor offenses* are punishable by up to one year and $1,000.)

The jurisdiction of U.S. district courts is original and exclusive over cases brought under federal law or treaties. There is a good deal of *concurrent jurisdiction*—shared or overlapping jurisdiction—between these courts and the trial courts of states. When a case is brought in a state court and controversies or issues arise involving provisions of the U.S. Constitution, laws, or treaties, a district court may be asked to assume jurisdiction because a federal question has been raised. District courts may, however, decide that the issue does not warrant their involvement.

Other situations in which district courts may be petitioned to "remove" cases from state courts include cases involving diversity of citizenship (that is, citizens of different states or foreign citizens); cases involving U.S. officials or military personnel; and cases in which citizens claim they have been denied fundamental civil rights by state officials acting in accordance with state law. Law enforcement and corrections officials of states are subject to many of these civil suits brought under 42 U.S.C. Section 1983. Through these suits, defendants and prisoners may seek damages—money—and *injunctive relief,* an order to the state official to stop violating a person's rights.

SUMMARY AND CONCLUSION

In this chapter we have provided an overview of the structure of America's dual court system and of how this structure relates to various levels and types of jurisdiction. We have pointed out that the authority to deal with cases and provide judicial remedies is subdivided into appellate and original jurisdiction and that original jurisdiction can be further subdivided into criminal versus civil jurisdiction and general versus limited or special jurisdiction. The court systems of the respective states and of the federal government are each unique in many ways, but they reveal a certain pattern; we can invariably discern courts of ultimate appeal, intermediate appellate courts, general or superior trial courts, and limited or inferior trial courts. This introduction to the structures of the state and federal court systems opens the way for an examination of the judges and the other personnel who operate within the systems.

QUESTIONS FOR DISCUSSION

1. Compare and contrast the court system of your own state with the generic model explained and illustrated in this chapter.

2. Specify the jurisdictional lines drawn between your local trial courts in terms of dollar amounts and classes of crimes and offenses. Do you have any courts of special jurisdiction? If so, what are they?
3. How does your state's appellate court system function in terms of the right to appeal? If your state has the death penalty, what route does an appeal of the death sentence take?
4. Which federal district court hears cases from your community? To what U.S. (circuit) court of appeals would a case tried there be appealed?

NOTES

1. Law Enforcement Assistance Administration, *National Survey of Court Organization,* U.S. Government Printing Office, Washington, D.C., 1973, p. 2.
2. Law Enforcement Assistance Administration, *National Survey of Court Organization, 1977 Supplement to State Judicial Systems,* U.S. Government Printing Office, Washington, D.C., 1977, p. 24.
3. Fannie J. Klein, *Federal and State Court Systems: A Guide,* Ballinger, Cambridge, Mass., 1977, pp. 124–127.
4. LEAA, *Survey, 1977 Supplement,* p. 5.
5. LEAA, *Survey,* 1973, pp. 4 and 5.
6. LEAA, *Survey, 1977 Supplement,* pp. 6–8.

CHAPTER 4

POLITICS, LAW, AND THE COURTS

After reading this chapter, students should be able to define and explain the importance of each of the following terms or phrases:

political environment
legislative bodies
rule making
executives
inherent powers doctrine
superintending authority
writ of mandamus

writ of prohibition
writ of habeas corpus
political parties
balancing the ticket
bar associations
the press
free press versus fair trial

Criminal courts are both political organizations and legal institutions. They operate within an environment in which political influences and considerations are often as important as the requirements of law and the principles of justice. Law itself is a product of the political process. Principles of justice do not evolve by some magic through the passage of time. They are debated, fought over, altered, and clarified (or further muddled) in the political arena. It is equally true that political decision making is guided and limited by long-established notions of what justice demands of a civilized people and society. Therefore, it is to politics that we now turn our attention.

THE POLITICAL ENVIRONMENT

The political environment has a direct and very fundamental impact on at least two matters of criminal law: the selection of judicial personnel (especially prosecutors and judges) and the funding of the court system. But there are any number of other, less direct but often very significant, points of interaction between the judicial and political arenas.

The political environment of which we speak includes legislative bodies, executive and administrative agencies, and the appellate courts. It also encompasses political parties, interest groups of every character and size, and the press. Any agency or group engaged in political activity that has an impact on a trial court is part of the court's political environment. For instance, imagine a judge passing sentence on a person convicted of vehicular manslaughter while under the influence of alcohol—in a courtroom packed with members of MADD (Mothers against Drunk Drivers).

LEGISLATIVE BODIES AND CRIMINAL LAW

Legislative bodies include the two houses of Congress, the various state houses, and the councils and commissions at the county and municipal level that have some measure of lawmaking authority through their power to enact ordinances. The most direct impact these bodies have on trial courts is through their authority to enact statutes or ordinances defining the acts that are to be considered criminal and setting forth the penalties that may be imposed on offenders. To continue with our example from above, MADD lobbies heavily for changes in laws concerning driving under the influence, and the impact of that group has been dramatic in producing substantive changes in the laws of many states.

Substantive Criminal Law

The authority to enact substantive criminal law has been vested in legislative bodies for centuries. It has been only recently, however, that legislatures have engaged in more than piecemeal modifications of established law. In the last two decades, legislatures in many states have undertaken or completed thorough revisions of their penal codes with the common goal of bringing the definitions of crimes and the schedule of penalties into a cohesive package. Some have decriminalized such matters as possession of small amounts of marijuana, certain sexual acts between consenting adults, and various traffic violations. Others have adopted sweeping changes in the structure of penalties, usually in the direction of what is called *determinate sentencing,* with terms that are more fixed or inflexible in length. Still others, such as New York and Florida, have made significant changes in laws related to juvenile justice.

These changes have the effect of making it easier to prosecute in adult criminal courts those juveniles who commit serious or repeated offenses.

These changes in the substantive law have direct and obvious consequences for the criminal courts. They raise or reduce case loads, or at least increase or decrease the discretion of prosecutors as to what is brought before the courts.

Court Structures and Jurisdiction

Legislatures also largely dictate the structures of the court system and define the jurisdictions of most courts, including the authority of court officials. Court reorganization plans have been or are before many state legislatures. For example, in the period between the end of 1974 and 1977 thirteen states reorganized their court systems.[1] In five of these states the changes were accomplished by statute alone. In eight states there were constitutional amendments to effect the changes, but legislative bodies played leading roles in drafting the proposals that were submitted to the voters for ratification.

Even without overhauling court structures, legislative bodies can create new courts and judgeships. Congress authorizes new judgeships for federal courts as the need develops. In 1987 a total of 571 federal district judges were serving in 91 district courts, and 156 court of appeals judges were sitting on the benches of the twelve appellate circuits.[2]

An example of how legislation can change the authority of court officials is contained in the act of Congress that expanded the role of U.S. magistrates. These officials—who replaced U.S. commissioners several years ago—had been performing many pretrial functions for the district courts. Now they may also, with the consent of the parties, hear and dispose of many civil cases, cases involving federal misdemeanor charges, and some federal cases involving juvenile defendants.[3] This relieved a substantial part of the burden of district court judges. Together with an increase in the number of these judges, the act of Congress made it possible for district courts to expedite criminal cases and to hear civil cases that had previously been ignored in these districts.

Rule Making

In addition to the enactment of substantive law and of statutes delineating court structures and assigning jurisdiction, legislatures are also involved in the business of making rules that govern judicial procedure. Charles Grau has found that while courts—generally the highest courts—in forty-seven states may promulgate rules of procedure, the legislatures of all fifty states may do so.[4]

The relative authority of courts and legislatures in rule making varies from state to state. Table 4.1 presents a picture of the variations. Grau points out, however, that states are moving toward a doctrine of *concurrent authority* over rule making; this doctrine grants full authority to courts to adopt procedural rules, while allowing legislatures to veto such rules and adopt procedural statutes.[5]

Procedural rules determine the manner in which claims and rights are asserted, thus affecting the outcome of cases. *Administrative rules* determine when and how the courts are open for business, thus affecting whether some persons have access to them.

An example of administrative rule making by legislation is the 1975 California statute that eliminated all specific exemptions from jury service in that state. Among those previously exempted were lawyers, police officers, firefighters, post office and telephone company employees, various medical professionals, ministers and priests, railroad employees, and even local government officials. The statute now provides that exemptions will be given only to those whose jury service would create "undue hardship on the person or public served by the person."[6] This statute has the obvious potential to change the makeup of trial juries and to affect the outcome of trials.

TABLE 4.1
THE ROLES OF THE COURT AND THE LEGISLATURE
IN RULE MAKING

Role	No. of states
Court:	
May adopt rules under constitutional authority	34
May adopt rules under statutory authority	13
Legislature:	
May disapprove rules	3
May refuse approval	2
May repeal rules	10
May amend rules	13
May adopt procedural rules	50
When rules conflict:	
Court rule governs	25
Legislative statute governs	7

Source: Charles W. Grau, "Who Rules the Court?" *Judicature,* vol. 62, no. 9, April 1979, p. 431.

Don W. Brown studied the impact of this statute in one community (Riverside) by analyzing the change in the occupational makeup of juries and the acquittal rates in criminal trials between 1974 and 1976. He found that juries did change in important ways and that acquittals went from 21 to 24 percent of criminal trial verdicts. He observed, however, that factors other than jury composition could have accounted for the shift in acquittal rate.[7]

The following example will illustrate the difficulty of drawing a line between substantive law and procedural rule making. In one statutory change the Michigan legislature redefined forcible rape within a broader category of "criminal sexual conduct," specified that males could be victims and females could be offenders, included homosexual rapes, and permitted husbands to be charged with raping wives from whom they are legally separated. The same act also dropped the traditional requirement of corroborative evidence for the prosecution and forbade defense cross-examination of victims about their own sexual histories except where the trial judge ruled that such evidence was particularly relevant.[8] These procedural changes, by the way, reflect a trend toward the Crime Control Model—at least with respect to rape—and away from emphasis on the Due Process Model.

Such rule making has clear potential for affecting the processing and thus the outcome of criminal cases in the courts. Some observers have long attacked legislatures for interfering in what they see as the courts' traditional right to make their own rules and have criticized the judges for tolerating it. Others believe just as strongly that both history and the principle of accountability require that legislatures involve themselves in rule making, at least as a check on and corrective for judicial attempts to promote secrecy and limit access to judicial process. Whatever the merits of the argument, rules of procedure and administrative rules, which are products of a political environment, are frequently imposed on courts by legislative bodies.

EXECUTIVE AGENCIES AND CRIMINAL LAW

When we refer to *executives,* in the following discussion, we mean the president and attorney general of the United States, the governors of the fifty states, and the mayors of our cities. These officials can affect the trial courts of this land in many ways. Some of these ways are wholly improper—such as when an executive pressures a judge into a decision favorable to a friend or supporter—but we shall concern ourselves here with the legitimate exercise of executive authority.

Appointments to the Bench

Perhaps the most direct role played by the chief executives of the nation and the states is that of appointing judges to the bench. Of course, the president and the governors do not operate in a vacuum. They are subject to varying degrees of influence and even to outright control in making their judicial appointments.

All federal judges and justices throughout the entire federal court system are appointed by the president. The politics varies for each court to which appointments are made. In general, the president has control over Supreme Court appointments, but nominees' names are submitted to both the American Bar Association and to the attorney general for their evaluation, and the consent of the Senate must be obtained in the form of ratification of the appointment. Appointments to the courts of appeals and district trial courts are largely controlled by the U.S. senators in whose states the vacancies exist. In this process the rule of *senatorial courtesy* prevails. If a senator objects to an appointment within his or her state, all senators are bound by custom to reject the appointment.

Governors appoint most judges to positions on the states' appellate and trial benches, even in states with electoral systems for judges. Because vacancies frequently occur because of midterm resignations, retirements, or deaths, governors have many opportunities to make interim appointments, and the electorate is usually presented with an incumbent judge who was named to the bench by executive appointment. Gubernatorial appointments are subject to varying degrees of legislative influence and generally require the consent of the upper house of the state legislature. In states with merit plans, governors must select from lists of a few (usually three) persons nominated by commissions. Governors are thus somewhat restricted, if not almost dictated to, in making their choices. Still, it behooves those who seek judicial posts not to alienate a governor.

Lawmaking and Budgets

The president and the governors play an important role in lawmaking and in budget making. Insofar as these executives initiate legislative and budgetary proposals and exercise their power to veto acts and appropriations of which they do not approve, they can obviously influence the judiciary. Much substantive criminal law is suggested by or worked on by attorneys general whose staffs often research the need for, and the probable effects of, changes in the criminal and penal codes. Attorneys general are usually then called upon to testify before legislative committees as to pending bills.

Another role played by an attorney general that affects trial courts is that of handling the state's case in any criminal appeal. The decisions of trial court judges are thus either supported or attacked by the attorney general or a representative of that office before the appellate court.

THE FUNDING OF COURTS

Mention has been made of the dependence of courts on legislative and executive agents for money and other resources. This subject requires special attention because it is viewed by some observers as the most serious threat to the existence of a judiciary truly independent of outside political influences.

The Source of Funds

Courts everywhere must compete with every other agency of government and recipient of public funds for their share of the taxpayers' largess. The decisions as to who gets what are made by legislative bodies with input from executives and administrators. The U.S. court system depends upon the will of the president, the Office of Management and Budget, and the Congress. State courts go to their state legislatures. County courts receive money appropriated by county commissions. City courts exist generally within the bounty provided by city councils.

These arrangements are not always so clear-cut, however. While federal courts are entirely dependent on Congress and many state courts rely completely on state legislatures, most courts in this country receive funds from mixed sources. Several years ago a study revealed that state courts of last resort (usually referred to as the state supreme court) were entirely state-funded, but that a few states called upon local governments to help pay for intermediate courts of appeal, and that counties bore the "major fiscal burden" of trial courts. The study reported:

> In half the states autonomous local governments control at least two-thirds of the expenditures of the entire court system. In such states, there may be budgetary authorities in addition to counties; and there is little systematic coordination of authority or responsibility among them.[9]

The fragmentation is compounded, the study continued, by the funding of various court services such as the clerks' offices and probation services "through a multiplicity of non-judicial budgets as well as through the judicial budget."[10]

More recent articles discuss unification trends, including state assumption of court funding in several states. New Hampshire, Michigan, Wyoming, and North Dakota took over or increased state contributions to court budgets in the early 1980s; Michigan was scheduled to achieve full state funding by October 1988.[11]

The problems courts have with obtaining sufficient funds are severe enough for those dealing with only one legislative funding authority. Courts having to depend upon more than one source often find themselves in the middle of quarrels between those bodies over which should pay for what. In Florida, for example, a "unified" court system features state funding of judges' and other staff salaries, furniture, equipment, supplies, and most "expense" items. But counties must provide court-houses and other space, telephone service, and postage and must cover some travel expenses. Recently a minor battle erupted in one Florida county over whether the county should be required to supply water tum-blers for jury rooms or these should be paid for out of the state's allow-ance for expenses.

Judges' Salaries

Not only are the courts politically dependent on other branches for funds with which to operate, the very salaries of the judges are set by law. This power to determine their income is a potentially useful weapon with which to "punish" the judges for unpopular decisions. In 1964 Congress specifically failed to include the Supreme Court justices in a substantial pay raise granted to other high federal officials.[12] In 1977 the new chief justice, Warren Burger, pointed out that over the eight years since 1969 judicial salaries had risen only 5 percent while the cost of living had increased by 60 percent.[13] This state of affairs obviously encourages judges to leave the bench and discourages qualified candidates from applying—all of which has the effect of diminishing the quality of jus-tice.

In 1976 140 federal judges took the unprecedented step of joining a suit before the U.S. Court of Claims over the salary issue. Their argument was that the gap between inflation and their wage increases was a viola-tion of Article III, Section 1, of the Constitution. That section provides that judges' compensation "shall not be diminished during their continu-ance in office." The Court of Claims in May 1977 rejected the argument, ruling that the Constitution "affords no protection from such an indirect, nondiscriminatory lowering of judicial compensation."[14] The point seems to be that the other branches of government retain a powerful weapon through the "power of the purse" which can be used to send a message if not to attack particular judges or courts.

The Doctrine of Inherent Powers

Courts have created a potentially powerful counter weapon that can be used to command that certain resources be made available. The *doctrine of inherent powers* reserves to the judiciary "all powers reasonably re-quired to enable a court to perform efficiently its judicial functions, to protect its dignity, independence, and integrity and to make its lawful ac-tions effective."[15] Jim R. Carrigan writes that these power are inherent in that they exist because the court exists and has the powers "reasonably required to act as an efficient court."

Carrigan examines case law developed from attempts by trial courts to use writs, judgments, orders, and even citations for contempt of court to command local officials (county and city councils) to appropriate funds for additional personnel, such as probations officers, or for equipment and supplies. He asserts that courts "have inherent powers to require reasonable physical facilities adequately furnished, repaired and maintained," including air conditioners, elevators that work during court hours, and new courthouses.[16]

Naturally these powers are rarely used since they create a political firestorm. Still we recall one television newscast which told of an entire city council being jailed by a local judge for refusing to approve funds for something she deemed necessary for her court's operation.

Rather than resort to drastic judicial remedies, most trial courts as well as appellate courts are adjusting to the political reality of their situation by one or both of two means. The judges are becoming more active in lobbying, usually through associations of judges or judicial officials organized at the state level. They are also hiring court administrators and assigning them the tasks of drafting budgets and acting as liaison with funding authorities. This development will be discussed in detail in Chapter 14 when we examine the whole trend toward court management.

APPELLATE COURTS AND THE POLITICAL ENVIRONMENT

In much of the above discussion we have included appellate courts with trial courts in surveying the relationship of the judiciary with other branches of government. We now focus on the relationship that exists between trial courts and appellate courts. Thus we can show that appellate courts are a part of the political—as well as the legal—environment of courts that dispose of criminal cases.

Deciding Cases on Appeal

Appellate courts have their most obvious impact on trial courts through their decision-making power in cases and issues appealed from the lower courts. Appellate courts, asserts Herbert Jacob, "create new norms through conscious policymaking."[17] He continues:

> When they make policy, the courts do not exercise more discretion than when they enforce community norms. The difference lies in the intended impact of the decision. Policy decisions are intended to be guideposts for future actions;

norm-enforcement decisions are aimed at the particular case at hand. Policy-making decisions are usually accompanied by published opinions to which other lawyers can refer in other courts. Appellate courts most frequently make policy decisions. Trial courts set policy only occasionally.[18]

Opportunities for judicial policy making arise whenever appellate courts are called upon to interpret a vague or ambiguous statute or provision of the state constitution or, in the case of federal courts, the U.S. Constitution. When they decide upon the constitutionality of a government action in a criminal case, appellate courts often make new policy regarding what is permissible conduct for law enforcement agencies. At the same time, of course, they either affirm the decision of the lower trial court or reverse it. Thus they express approval or disapproval of what the trial judge did and in effect inform that judge, and all others within their jurisdiction, as to what may and may not be done in the future.

This power to decide cases on appeal means justices can set policies and precedents, then revise or reverse them later. This enables appellate courts to determine the balance that exists at any given time between the Crime Control and Due Process Models of criminal justice. Appellate justices thus have potentially vast power, particularly as it impacts on the behavior of trial court judges and their orientation toward crime control or due process.

Trial judges are human beings who, like others of the species, seek approval from their colleagues and superiors. Most trial judges are highly desirous of a record of having no rulings—or as few as possible—overturned on appeal. Thus most trial judges adhere to appellate rulings (or even try to anticipate them) not only because such rulings are "law," but because they do not wish to be seen by appellate judges—or by other officials or the public, for that matter—as incompetents or troublemakers. A trial judge's record before appellate courts is a widely used measure of his or her qualification for appointment to a higher bench. A few judges have even been denied reelection largely on the basis of the publicity surrounding a large number of reversals on appeal.

Rule-Making, Administrative, and Superintending Roles

In addition to rendering decisions on cases appealed to them, appellate courts perform several other functions that have a direct effect on trial courts.

In forty-seven states (see Table 4.1), courts may adopt their own procedural rules. In most of these states this means that the state's highest court issues the basic rules of criminal, civil, and appellate procedure. These rules are usually published annually. There is generally an allowance made for local rules—that is, rules dealing with procedural details and some administrative rules—which may be made by trial judges and which pertain to practices within their particular jurisdiction. Thus, for example, whether initial appearances of those arrested are all to be held at 9:00 A.M. or 1:00 P.M. the day following arrest may be subject to local rules. But that the initial appearance is to be held before a judge of the county court within twenty-four or forty-eight hours of arrest is the sort of rule set at the state level. The content and detail of state rules pronounced by the appellate court thus prescribe the behavior of trial courts and determine the degree to which trial courts are able to establish local rules.

The administrative role of appellate courts over trial courts depends upon a number of factors. How organizationally independent are trial courts from appellate courts? Are they part of a statewide unified court structure or creatures of county and municipal governments? Are they funded separately from local sources or included in a statewide budget for the judiciary? Does the state's highest court have a court administrator (virtually all do now), and what is his or her role with regard to trial court administrators (where they exist) or other administrative support personnel? What bodies of judges exist for making policy decisions on administrative matters? Is there a statewide judicial council, or are there separate councils within intermediate appellate districts, or are there only judicial conferences with no policy-making authority? These are matters which will be taken up in the last chapters of this book. Suffice it to say here that the extent of administrative authority vested in appellate courts ranges from virtually none to quite considerable.

The superintending authority of appellate courts over trial courts also varies, but it is more clearly a matter of settled law than the rule-making and administrative powers. The *superintending authority* refers to the ability of appellate courts to issue writs that command trial courts to do— or not do—various things. A *writ of mandamus* is a command to take a positive act of some kind, say to set bail on an accused who has been denied bail. A *writ of prohibition* orders that something *not* be done—for instance, that a local judge *not* jail a person ruled in contempt of the judge's court. A *writ of habeas corpus* is perhaps the best known of these writs. It commands that the local authorities bring forth the accused and justify to the court issuing the writ why the accused is being held. Like appellate reversals, these writs are undesirable entries in the record of a trial judge who cares about his or her reputation and future political or judicial career.

OTHER POLITICAL AGENTS

Apart from government agencies and officials, there are several other important elements or agents in the political environment of criminal trial courts. While the impact of legislative and executive bodies is direct and varies somewhat from place to place, the influence of these other agents can range from minimal and quite indirect to virtually controlling. The three major agencies we shall discuss are political parties, the bar associations, and the press. These agencies may check each other as countervailing powers; one or two may be so strong as to negate the impact of the others; or they may be essentially unified in promoting and protecting common interests.

Political Parties

Some urban areas and states—and, at times, the federal government—are dominated by a single political party that is well organized and wins virtually all important elections over a considerable number of years. Republicans in Kansas and Democrats in Chicago come to mind. In situations like these, the judges, prosecutors, and public defenders are subject to partisan election or party control of the appointment process, since the trial courts tend to be operated like other units of government—as arms of the party organization.

The justice that such courts mete out naturally tends to conform to the ideology or interests of the party leaders. This is not to say that these courts are inevitably unjust or corrupt, but there is substantial evidence that these courts are staffed by persons who are loyal to the party first, the public second—or who simply equate the interests of the party and its leaders with that of the public.

Many judicial officials are clearly political "hacks" whose chief qualification for office is a record of service to the party. On the other hand, some party organizations serve as effective screening devices and keep blatantly unqualified or otherwise unsuitable people off the bench. They also usually attempt to ensure representation of all numerically significant ethnic groups in judicial positions through the device of *balancing the ticket*. This practice is especially prominent in big-city Democratic politics. While the judges, prosecutors, and public defenders may all be loyal Democrats, they are a mix of Italians, Jews, blacks, Hispanics, Polish, Irish, and WASPs in terms of ethnic origins.

Martin Levin has conducted a classic study of the criminal courts and judges of two American cities, Pittsburgh and Minneapolis, in which he delineates clearly the differences that emerge between those who are part of a traditional party-dominated system and those in a system in which parties play little or no role.[19] Pittsburgh's courts, like other government offices, are filled with party professionals who are in line for positions in order to maintain ethnic and religious balance. Judges are elected (or appointed in cases of midterm vacancies) from among the ranks of equally partisan prosecutors or from the legislative ranks. The criminal process that results is one emphasizing administrative settlement—that is, plea bargaining. Its product is generally one of leniency in the sentencing of defendants—especially those whose economic plight and family ties evoke the sympathy of the judge. This process and product contrast markedly with those of Minneapolis, where political parties are not involved. We shall take up that city's system when we discuss the role of bar associations.

We noted in Chapter 1 that John Adams's attempt to establish a federal trial judiciary staffed by entrenched Federalist party judges led the victorious Jeffersonian Republicans to scuttle the court structure itself. That did not, of course, put an end to party influence in the federal judiciary. Since its beginnings, each federal court bench has been the object of political patronage. The president inevitably chooses most if not all judges from among the ranks of his own party's members. In the late nineteenth and early twentieth centuries, reformers in many states and cities sought to rid the judiciary of partisan domination. Where they gained power, these reformers pushed through legislation or amendments to constitutions abolishing partisan election or appointment of judges and substituting nonpartisan elections. The hope was that through open primaries the people would select the most qualified judges, regardless of party.

It has not quite turned out that way. What has emerged is a system which, in most places, permits even unqualified persons to win judgeships. The seats tend to go to those with the most campaign funds or the most recognizable names. The capacity to screen out unqualified candidates and to assure ethnic and religious balance on the bench has been eliminated. While the justice meted out in these courts may no longer be partisan, it can instead be totally unpredictable. What one gets depends on the will or whim of the particular judge.

Bar Associations

No political agency has more clout in the courts of this land than the bar association of each state and the American Bar Association. Of the role and importance of these entities Herbert Jacob has written:

> To improve the legal profession and its image, lawyers have organized themselves into bar associations so that they could foster better law schools, eliminate the actual shysters in the profession, and improve legal services to the public. Bar associations have been equally energetic in seeking to raise the economic status of lawyers by restricting entry into the profession, eliminating competition from nonlawyers, and imposing schedules on lawyers and clients. Such activities have made bar associations influential in molding the role of lawyers in the American judicial process.[20]

We shall later take up the role of the bar association in the education and entry of attorneys into practice. For now we wish to focus on the role of the associations in influencing the organization and operation of the courts.

Bar associations include members who are involved in a variety of types of practice and who bring diverse views on what constitutes justice to any debate over changes in the court system. Bar associations have not spoken with a clear voice, therefore, on specific proposals for reorganization of courts or on major changes in substantive law and rules.[21] Some lawyers fight for the status quo from which they derive their daily bread. Thus lawyers who specialize in representing clients in personal negligence suits consistently oppose so-called no-fault insurance plans. Others, however, fight for changes that, they argue, will result in greater justice—or, perhaps, improve their own opportunities. Thus lawyers specializing in criminal defense work almost all favor changes in the law to permit persons subpoenaed before grand juries to be represented by counsel inside the grand jury room.

Jacobs points out that members of the bar band together on some matters in which they all share common interest, such as abolishing the office of justice of the peace.[22] Another example of a proposal sure to elicit the virtually unanimous support of the bar is that to eliminate nonlawyers from the other lower trial courts.

The impact of the bar is most clearly seen in the judicial selection process. The American Bar Association has long played a semiofficial role in the initial screening of potential nominees for positions in the federal system. The ABA rates the nominees as being exceptionally well qualified, well qualified, qualified, or unqualified. Presidents rarely attempt to appoint someone rated as unqualified by the ABA. In states with appointive processes, state bar associations perform much the same task, though some governors and legislatures ignore the advice. Even where judges are elected, the state or local bar association may evaluate the candidates by polling their members and publishing the results in an advertisement taken in the newspapers.

Bar associations invariably support the merit plan for judicial selection. This is in part due to the belief of many attorneys that this plan results in a better class of judges than any other. Of some importance, however, is the fact that merit plans require nominating commissions, which are generally dominated by attorneys selected by the bar association. What replaces the politics of party nominations or legislative-executive patronage allocations is often the politics of the bar association. Those who desire positions on the bench in merit-plan states must have good relations with, or at least an acceptable reputation among, the most powerful members or factions in the bar association.

Jacob observes that, with respect to selecting judges, the legal profession is not always united in its support of bar association candidates. Lawyers whose firms represent banks, insurance companies, and corporations have one set of qualifications and candidates; those lawyers who generally represent plaintiffs who sue these companies have another set.[23] The members of the bar who specialize in a criminal case load are likewise divided between prosecutors and their supporters and those on the defense side. It is likely that bar associations that are essentially united or dominated by a clique will have more influence over the judicial selection process than a bar association that is split into two or more fluid or balanced factions.

We return now to the study performed by Martin Levin. The City of Minneapolis has a nonpartisan election system in which political parties play almost no role, but the "local bar association plays a major role." The bar polls its members and publishes the results; the winner (or at times, the second or third highest candidate) is virtually assured of victory in the municipal election. The bar also dominates interim appointments. When vacancies occur, Minnesota governors almost always appoint the person who wins the special poll conducted among bar members.

The judges selected in Minneapolis, either by election or by interim appointment, are drawn from private law practice rather than political or governmental posts.[24] The justice they produce is much more prosecution- and punishment-oriented than that of the party-selected judges of Pittsburgh. The middle- and upper-middle-class judges of Minneapolis rely much more on judicial (adversary) proceedings than on the administrative (bargaining) approach favored in Pittsburgh. Their reasoning is more legalistic and the treatment they dispense is more related to the offense than to the qualities or needs of the offenders. More and longer terms of incarceration are the rule in Minneapolis.[25]

It appears then that trial courts and their output are affected by political environments. And a bar-dominated environment results in a quite different court and output than one gets from an environment dominated by a traditional party system. Levin, however, warns against drawing the conclusion that "political influences shape the behavior of the Pittsburgh and Minneapolis judges in criminal courts." He stresses the point that the influence is indirect. The two political environments result in the differential socialization and recruitment of judges. It is the judges' own backgrounds, primarily their prior careers in either politics or law practice, that tend to determine the differences in their behavior. Levin comments: "The crucial intervening variable is the city's political system: judges with a particular social and career background that may affect their decisions are recruited by the city's political and judicial selection systems."[26]

The Press

A subject about which there is very little literature is the impact of the press on the functioning of America's criminal justice system. There is, to be sure, a raging debate about the First Amendment rights of reporters versus the Sixth Amendment rights of defendants to a fair trial. There have been some very significant decisions by the Supreme Court on this subject, and we shall survey some of the issues in this controversy. On the other hand, there has been little attention paid to the overall day-to-day relationship between the press and the courts, particularly with regard to the ways in which news coverage of court proceedings and outcomes becomes a feedback mechanism affecting the behavior of court officials.

Free Press versus Fair Trial   The Constitution provides for the protection of freedom of the press in the First Amendment, and that provision has been interpreted as permitting the publication of anything short of that which is libelous or obscene. If the media libel a person, he or she may sue in a civil action. Obscenity is criminal, of course, and the history of attempts to control or suppress pornographic literature is a fascinating subject in itself. In any case, the law provides for postpublication suit in the case of certain materials. It has never permitted prepublication censorship or prior restraint of the press. Thus the press has been quite free to print, and television has been equally free to show, pretty much whatever they decide to present.

The other side of the coin is found in the Sixth Amendment provision that defendants shall have a "speedy and public trial" before "an impartial jury of the State and district wherein the crime shall have been committed." This is the essence of the "fair trial." The ability of the press to influence the outcome of a particular case through coverage of the crime, its investigation, the accused, and pretrial proceedings is well known and documented. It is the most common reason for *changes in venue*—that is, removal of the trial from one place to another—in the search for an impartial jury. Increasingly, this means one whose members have not seen or read a lot of news coverage of the case.

The state as well as the press enjoys the duty of investigating allegations of crime, and police and prosecutors have had their battles with the press over such matters as whether reporters can be compelled by police to provide the names of confidential sources of evidence related to a crime.[27] The press, for its part, has used laws and legal procedures to gain access to information that government officers—including police, prosecutors, and judges—would just as soon keep from the public. The federal Freedom of Information Act was largely a response to efforts by the press and citizens' groups to penetrate what they saw as an unwarranted veil of secrecy behind which government agencies hid policies and actions the citizens had a right to know about.

The battles between the press on the one hand and the government or the criminal defense on the other have been classic confrontations of conflicting rights and perceptions of duty. The press claims to represent the people's right to know what government is doing. The government claims to represent the people's right to effective protection of their safety and welfare. Defense attorneys claim to represent the interest of all citizens in the fair trial of any one citizen in the criminal courts of this land.

A related matter is that of the kind of news-gathering techniques that are allowable in court proceedings. Many years ago, following the sensationalized coverage of the Lindbergh kidnapping case, the ABA led the fight to keep cameras of all sorts out of courtrooms. Canon 3A(7) of the bar association's Code of Judicial Ethics includes a prohibition of television, radio, and photographic coverage of all judicial proceedings. This rule was adopted by virtually every state. Reporters could write about and artists could draw what was going on, but no recording equipment of any kind was permitted. This rule is being relaxed in many states and has been virtually abandoned in a few. Colorado was the first state to make the change in rule permanent. Some states allow such coverage with the permission of all parties, but Florida, Idaho, Minnesota, and Wisconsin require no permission from the parties.[28] It must be added that technology has only recently made possible the miniaturized television camera that can televise in color using available light, thus giving the media access to a generally unobtrusive piece of equipment.

Perhaps the most direct confrontation between judicial officials and the press over news coverage of the criminal process arose from a case in which a New York judge barred reporters and the public from a pretrial hearing on a motion to suppress certain evidence—a gun used in a murder case. The judge feared the publicity generated by the hearing would jeopardize the defendant's right to a fair trial. On July 2, 1979, the U.S. Supreme Court in a 5 to 4 decision upheld the action of the trial judge.[29] In its opinion, the majority said the Sixth Amendment right to a public trial belonged to the defendant, not to the press, and that defendants could ask that the press and public be barred from proceedings, especially where resulting publicity could affect potential jurors. The opinion left unclear whether the authority to bar the press extended only to pretrial hearings or included trials themselves. As a result, judges in several states variously barred the public and the press, or the press but not members of the public, from attending trials. The press, of course, sought legal action to either clarify or reverse the earlier decision of the

Supreme Court. For its part, the press argued that the First Amendment was being violated and that the right of citizens "to observe, in person or through the press, how their judges, prosecutors, police officers perform," was being ignored. One reporter observed:

> Much of [judicial] performance already is hidden from view. The grand jury proceedings, and the plea bargaining which ends an estimated 85 percent of them, are secret aspects of the criminal justice system now.
>
> If most pretrial hearings and some trials are also closed to public and press scrutiny, it will be even more difficult for them to assess how well the system works.[30]

In 1980 the Supreme Court took up a case involving the barring of the public—and, of course, the press along with it—from a criminal trial. The action was taken by a Virginia trial judge in a murder case being tried for the fourth time (the first trial result had been overturned on appeal and two mistrials had followed) upon agreement by prosecution to a defense motion for closure of the trial. The appeal resulted from an attack on the judge's action by Richmond newspapers. The Supreme Court, in a 7 to 1 decision, held that both press and public have an independent right to attend criminal trials and cannot be excluded merely because the judge and both attorneys agree to do so. Chief Justice Burger wrote for the majority and stated that "we are bound to conclude that a presumption of openness inheres in the very nature of a criminal trial under our system of justice." This presumption could be overcome by an "overriding interest" in fairness that could not be served other than by closing a trial. This case, however, presented no findings that such an interest required such drastic means. The sequestering of jurors and witnesses (a subject to be taken up later) was among alternative means suggested.[31]

So the court ruled that while the First Amendment does not provide the public and press with an absolute right to attend criminal trials, they can be barred only if trial courts determine there is an overriding interest in justice that cannot be otherwise accommodated. The Supreme Court reinforced this position in 1982 when it ruled on a case wherein a trial court in Massachusetts closed a rape trial during the testimony of three minor girls who were victims. The Court held 6 to 3 (the chief justice was a dissenter) that neither protecting minor victims from further trauma and embarrassment nor encouraging such victims to come forward was a compelling enough reason to bar coverage of testimony in all cases. Trial judges could, the Court ruled, consider the first claim on a case-by-case basis. The second claim was dismissed by the justices on the grounds that the press can always print the testimony and identities of witnesses as revealed in official transcripts.[32]

Burger's dissent was based on the distinction he made between processes and places (criminal trial courtrooms) traditionally open and proceedings such as the testimony of minor witnesses in sex offense cases traditionally closed.[33] It is now clear, however, that the overriding interest that leads a judge to close any part of a criminal trial will have to be shown to be very compelling and that closing be the only reasonable and effective way to protect that interest.

The Impact of the Press   Legal issues and battles aside, what is the impact of the press on day-to-day administration of justice in America's criminal courts? Eisenstein and Jacob addressed themselves, however briefly, to this question in their study of the felony courts of Baltimore, Chicago, and Detroit. They found that the answer varies from place to place, depending largely on the role the press chooses to play.

In Baltimore, Eisenstein and Jacob write:

> The newspapers played an important role in structuring the environment of courtroom participants. . . . Baltimore's assistant state's attorneys worried that their decisions would come back to haunt them in the press, and they modified their behavior accordingly. The papers reflected (and helped maintain) a generally unfavorable community attitude toward plea bargaining. A relatively experienced assistant for Baltimore (two years in the office) traced his reluctance to plea bargain to his aversion to the responsibility it entailed. When pressed, he revealed that this responsibility included the fear that he would read on back page of the *Baltimore Sun* that a person recently convicted of an offense has committed another crime, and that he, as the assistant prosecutor in the first case, had recommended probation or a short sentence. "I have to protect my reputation."[34]

The authors found that major participants in the felony process "both feared and used" the newspapers for "political intrigues." Leaks of information that would damage or pressure another official or put oneself in a favorable light were very common. Prosecutors even fed reporters with the outcomes of cases the reporters were not able to cover.

Eisenstein and Jacob note that Baltimore's general circulation papers were both conservative on crime issues, with the Hearst *News-American* being somewhat more hard-line than the *Sun*.[35] They observed that the "perspectives of the defendants or the black community" were not portrayed, not even by the black-owned *Afro-American*. "Furthermore, few among judges, prosecutors, or defense counsel adhered to a liberal or strongly pro-defendant position."[36] Thus the impact of the press was, if anything, to reinforce a prevailing set of values and to encourage trials in cases that received substantial publicity.

In Detroit the press played a large but different role from that played in Baltimore. Outcomes of individual cases and publicity for trial prosecutors were rarely seen in print—with good cause, for prosecutors feared adverse publicity from cases that "blew up," cases in which persons previously let off lightly later committed a serious, well-publicized crime.[37] The press in Detroit, in any event, was generally focused on reporting matters other than specific cases. It allied itself with liberal attorneys who sued Wayne County over overcrowding and other poor conditions in the jail. Television documentaries and entire pages of the *Free Press* were devoted to these conditions and the related backlog of court cases.[38] The media joined nearly all major officials in pushing the goal of disposing of cases. *The Detroit News* compared the efficiency of trial court judges in terms of "work output," or cases disposed, commenting that "some judges work harder and faster than others."[39] While the press pushed efficiency and speed, there was disagreement over the goal of justice. The bench and bar were also divided sharply over liberal versus conservative views about criminal justice.[40] Again, the officials reflected the press—or vice versa.

In Chicago Eisenstein and Jacob found a court system "insulated" by the Democratic party organization from outside influences, and a press that played "an ambiguous role."[41] Sensational trials received attention, but there was little or no attempt to cover daily activities of the court. There were no crusades, either. Publicity was unsolicited, because "notoriety was clearly more dangerous for officials' careers than anonymity."[42] Impact was thus minimized.

The jurisdiction with which the present authors are most familiar has one daily newspaper (one of the most profitable in the nation), three major television stations, and four radio stations with new departments—one of the latter aimed at the black audience. Substantial attention is paid to court proceedings here in Orange County, Florida, partly because cameras are allowed in courtrooms. The sensational cases receive extensive coverage in print and on the air, with videotape excerpts of testimony often making the six and eleven o'clock news on each channel. In addition, considerable media attention is given to matters of administration of the judicial system and related components. A certain amount of investigative reporting is done by the paper and all three television stations. They are keenly interested in any legal or political trouble that the sheriff, the state attorney, or any police chief gets into, and a few reporters seem to be preoccupied with uncovering "scandals." The state attorney or one of his top assistants is frequently interviewed in connection with either a specific case or a general problem. Private defense attorneys also comment on cases on trial. Judges and public defenders are rarely interviewed, however.

There is no question but that the media are both courted and feared in this area. The rapid growth of Orange County's population, with its influx of out-of-staters and the dramatic changes in virtually every aspect of its life, has resulted in the undermining of the old power structure and the development of a media-oriented political system. Political parties are not strong here, and officials depend largely on media images as well as on interest-group financing to get elected. Furthermore, the judicial system is organizationally simplified and contained within a few buildings in Orlando, making coverage easier. Thus the press is a vital and influential part of the environment within which the courts operate.

SUMMARY AND CONCLUSION

This chapter has attempted to provide the student with an appreciation of how politics affects the criminal judiciary in this nation. We surveyed the important roles played by government agencies—including legislative bodies, executive agencies, and appellate courts—in the operation of trial courts. We saw how these agencies control the structure of courts, establish substantive and procedural law, allocate the funds to operate trial courts, and control or influence the selection of trial court judges. We also examined the important role played by other political bodies—political parties, bar associations, and the press—indicating ways in which each of these entities has its impact on the trial courts.

All this has not been with the purpose of disparaging the courts or arguing that they are altogether subservient to narrow political interests and pressures. Some judges and courts are, of course, deserving of harsh criticism on these counts. The point is, however, that the independence of the judiciary is a principle that is, at best, qualified by certain realities. As we saw in our brief look at the history of our judicial system in an earlier chapter, courts had political origins and served political (royal) purposes from the very beginning. American independence brought about new bases of court authority—statutes and constitutions—but these, too, are products of political decision making.

QUESTIONS FOR DISCUSSION

1. Determine the roles played by your state's legislature and its court of last resort in establishing the rules of court.
2. Who must approve the funding for your local trial courts? How "political" is this process? Who influences the determination of need?
3. What does your local bar association actually accomplish? Does it reach out beyond being a lawyers' society and provide services that benefit the public?
4. How broadly and accurately do your local media cover your courts? Contrast the various media outlets (newspaper and radio and television stations) as to thoroughness and perceived bias.

5. Does media coverage of crime and court proceedings in your community tend to stir public feelings regarding the negative impact of the Due Process Model on Crime Control Model objectives? Discuss examples.

NOTES

1. National Criminal Justice Information and Statistics Service, *National Survey of Court Organization,* 1975 and 1977 additions of *Supplement to State Judicial Systems,* U.S. Government Printing Office, Washington, D.C.: page 1 of each report.
2. General Services Administration, Office of the Federal Register, *The United States Government Manual, 1983/84,* U.S. Government Printing Office, Washington, D.C., 1983, pp. 67–69.
3. *The Federal Magistrate System: Report to Congress by the Judicial Conference of the United States,* U.S. Government Printing Office, Washington, D.C., 1981, pp. 7 and 12.
4. Charles W. Grau, "Who Rules the Courts? The Issue of Access to the Rulemaking Process," *Judicature,* vol. 62, no. 9, April 1979, p. 431.
5. Ibid., p. 430.
6. Don W. Brown, "Eliminating Exemptions from Jury Duty: What Impact Will it Have?" *Judicature,* vol. 62, no. 9, April 1979, p. 436.
7. Ibid., pp. 440–446.
8. Peter Bonventre, with John L. Dotson, Jr., "Rape Alert," *Newsweek,* November 10, 1975, pp. 72 and 77.
9. Geoffrey C. Hazard, Jr., Martin B. McNamara, and Irwin F. Sentilles, "Court Finance and Unitary Budgeting," in Larry C. Berkson, Steven W. Hays, and Susan J. Carbon (eds.), *Managing the State Courts: Text and Readings,* West, St. Paul, Minn., 1977, p. 263.
10. Ibid., p. 263.
11. Harry O. Lawson, "State Court System Unification," *The American University Law Review,* vol. 31, no. 2, Winter 1982, p. 278; and "Governor Signs HB 200," *New Hampshire Law Weekly,* vol. 10, no. 2, July 6, 1983, p. 13.
12. Herbert Jacob, *Justice in America,* 3d ed., Little, Brown, Boston, 1978, p. 17.
13. Mary Costello, "Politics and the Federal Courts," in Editorial Research Reports, *Crime and Justice,* Congressional Quarterly, Washington, D.C., p. 117.
14. Ibid.
15. Jim R. Carrigan, "Inherent Powers and Finance," in Berkson et al., *Managing the State Courts,* p. 75.
16. Ibid., p. 80.
17. Jacob, p. 32.
18. Ibid., pp. 33–34.
19. Martin A. Levin, "The Politics of Lower Courts," in John A. Robertson (ed.), *Rough Justice: Perspectives on the Lower Criminal Courts,* Little, Brown, Boston, 1974, pp. 192–205.
20. Jacob, p. 44.

21. Ibid., p. 57.
22. Ibid., p. 57.
23. Ibid., pp. 58–59.
24. Levin, p. 195.
25. Ibid., pp. 196–197 and 200–201.
26. Ibid., pp. 209–210.
27. See *Branzburg v. Hayes, in re Pappas,* and *United States v. Caldwell,* 408 U.S. 665, 11 Cr. L. 3333 (1972) on the rights of newsmen called upon to testify before grand juries, and *Zurcher v. Stanford Daily,* No. 76-1600, 3 Med. L. Rptr. 2377–2392 (1978) regarding the authority of police to search newsrooms.
28. David Graves, "Cameras in the Courts: The Situation Today," *Judicature,* vol. 63, no. 1, June–July 1979, pp. 25–27.
29. *Gannet Co., Inc. v. DePasquale,* 435 U.S. 1006, 56 L. Ed. 2d 387 (1979).
30. Aaron Epstein, "Secret Trial May Prevail as Judges Misread Ruling," *Orlando Sentinel Star,* August 26, 1979, p. 2-D.
31. *Richmond Newspapers, Inc., et al. v. Virginia et al.,* No. 79-243, 449 U.S. 894 (1980).
32. *Globe Newspaper v. Superior Court* No. 81-611, 8 Med. L. Rptr. 1689–1696.
33. Ibid., pp. 1696–1700.
34. James Eisenstein and Herbert Jacob, *Felony Justice: An Organizational Analysis of Criminal Courts,* Little, Brown, Boston, 1977, p. 93.
35. Ibid., p. 92.
36. Ibid., pp. 94–95.
37. Ibid., pp. 166–167.
38. Ibid., p. 165.
39. Ibid., pp. 163–164.
40. Ibid., p. 164.
41. Ibid., p. 122.
42. Ibid., p. 132.

CHAPTER 5

JUDGES AND
OTHER COURT OFFICIALS

After reading this chapter, students should be able to define and explain the importance of each of the following terms or phrases:

formal selection systems
partisan election
nonpartisan election
gubernatorial appointment
merit selection system
senatorial courtesy
impeachment
recall elections

judicial qualifications commission
Federal Judicial Discipline Act
clerk of court
bailiff
process server
court reporter
court administrator

To many, the court is the judge. That office is synonymous with what is meant by "the court." Attorneys refer to the judge as the court in such expressions as "if it please the court" and "we move that the court take under advisement."

Judges are certainly used to thinking of themselves as the embodiment of the court and of the courtrooms they serve in as territories over which they are virtually sovereign. They speak of "my courtroom" and of what will or will not be permitted in *this* court. Certainly, in terms of authority, the judge is supreme relative to all others who appear or practice within the courts.

THE POWER OF JUDGES

To most observers, the judge is the most powerful official in the criminal justice system. But not all agree with this assertion. Many, including these authors, believe the prosecutor is really the most powerful in terms of the control he or she has over defendants and cases. Nonetheless, the judge is the most visible and announces key decisions in a public forum. The judge's control of sentencing is usually cited by those who consider him or her the most powerful official. Even this power, however, is limited by the extent to which plea bargaining involves assurances of lenient sentences. It also is being whittled away by legislation enacting mandatory minimum sentences and other attempts to impose "determinate sentencing." We shall have more to say about each of these matters in subsequent chapters.

By suggesting that the judge is not necessarily the most powerful of officials, we do not mean to imply that he or she is without great power. A judge can terminate a criminal case at virtually any point in the proceedings by granting a motion for dismissal, for suppression of key evidence, or for a judicial acquittal. A judge also possesses the ultimate weapon, the power of finding persons in contempt of court and ordering them to jail. Many a brash attorney has been escorted to a jail cell after provoking a judge's anger, and some judges are far more easily provoked than others.

THE CHARACTER OF JUDGES

Americans have a general tendency to idealize the people on the bench. As Donald Dale Jackson observes, "We expect them to be honest, wise, patient, tolerant, compassionate, strong, decisive, articulate, courageous—the list of virtues stretches on with the dogged unreality of a Boy Scout handbook." He continues:

> Every few years a new attempt is made to define the essential qualities of a good judge, and each time the fantasy is spun anew. . . . Yet the impulse to lift judges above the ordinary run of mankind persists even after its fantasy content is conceded. Try as I may, I confess, I cannot put down the notion that a good judge, a truly good judge, is something beautiful, something beyond the normal attainment of men, something one feels an almost pathetic urge to venerate. And so the corollary: a bad judge is worse than a bad anything else. A bad judge enters another dimension of evil, another circle of hell. The bad judge has betrayed our innocent trust, and such betrayal permits no forgiveness.[1]

To say that development of purely objective standards and criteria is impossible is not, however, to say that we must abandon attempts to agree on basic, if ambiguous, measures of judicial ability and quality. Columbia law professor Harry Jones once stated some essential qualities of a trial judge, and Jackson summarized his assertions as follows:

> The demands and strains of his courtroom task require unusual emotional stability, exceptional firmness and serenity of temperament, and . . . great intellectual and psychic endurance. He must have unusual talents of communications. He needs to be "empathetic and endlessly patient" with jurors and witnesses, "compassionate without being mush-headed" in sentencing, "at once sensitive and austere."[2]

Jones admits that, by these criteria, no lawyer has even been *fully* qualified to become a judge, but he writes that every lawyer knows a few judges who are "wonderfully close to the ideal." At the same time, Jackson notes, every lawyer knows alcoholic judges, senile judges, and judges who are psychotic. He continues:

> There are bigots on the bench and arrogant martinets. There are the dull-witted, the narrow-minded, the harsh, and the lazy. There are those who are merely weak, mediocre, the "grey mice" of the judiciary. And there are the callous and insensitive, judges whose exposure to human pride and folly has encrusted their own humanity.[3]

It seems it is easier to label bad judges—or bad qualities of judges—than good ones. Howard James managed to delineate eleven categories of judicial incompetence or weakness:

1. *The Hacks.* Those who sit on the bench as a reward for political favors or services
2. *The Retirees.* Those who treat the bench as a place in which to go into semiretirement from active practice of law
3. *The Failures.* Those who seek the bench because they cannot earn a living in the practice of law
4. *The Inattentive.* Those who are bored by the duties of judgeship and court proceedings
5. *The Misfits.* Those with serious personality disorders
6. *The Informal.* Those who conduct most important business in chambers (off the record) and treat their decisions as political favors
7. *The Incapacitated.* Those who are feeble or in ill health
8. *The Inexperienced.* Those who cannot abandon the partisanship of law practice and adopt the impartiality of judgeships
9. *The Lazy.* Those who "wing it" from the bench instead of learning the law and applying what they learn
10. *The Weak.* Those who are fearful of conducting trials and who let lawyers or other court personnel run their courtrooms

11. *The Prejudiced*. Those who cannot leave behind their economic, religious, ethnic, and other biases when they reach the bench

Of course, any given judge may combine several of these weaknesses and fit into more than one category.[4]

Howard James has stated the opinion that over half of the trial court judges have had no business sitting on the bench, and that only one in ten of lower court magistrates is "really qualified to dispense justice." This indictment was based on his personal observations of courts in several large cities in the late 1960s. Donald Dale Jackson, whose observations were made in the early 1970s, says his estimates are more generous than James's and attributes part of the reason to subsequent reforms in the selection, training, and disciplining of judges. He writes: "My impression is that between 30 and 40 percent of state trial court judges are unfit to sit. On the federal trial bench I would estimate the figure to be about 10 percent. At the magistrate level, perhaps two-thirds are unqualified for the responsibilities they hold."[5]

What is disturbing about these estimates is that both authors agree that the lower courts, the ones that deal with infractions of ordinances and criminal misdemeanors, the ones that therefore handle between 75 and 90 percent of the criminal case business, are staffed largely with persons who should not be on the bench. These are the only judges most citizens ever see in operation—and the ones who dispose of the bulk of criminal cases and sentence the vast majority of defendants. In other words, it is not entirely unfair to say that the poorest-quality judges are in those positions where they can do the most harm.

SELECTION OF JUDGES

Many observers believe that the quality of judges is, at least in part, related to the ways in which we select them. On this matter Americans have been torn between two goals. Should judges be professionals appointed from among other professionals on the basis of background, preparation, and experience—that is, should they be an elitist corps? Or should they be representative of the people who elect them from among candidates who meet minimum qualifications? There are some who have studied the results of various selection schemes and found no direct connection between methods of selection and the quality of the bench.

Formal Systems of Selection

There are four methods currently used for formal selection of judges, regardless of the level of court on which they are to serve. *Partisan elec-*

tions are the rule in thirteen states. Judges are selected exactly as mayors, council members, legislators, and governors are. They obtain the nomination of a political party—whether by primary election, nominating convention, or caucus—then run in the general election against other parties' nominees.

Sixteen states use *nonpartisan election*. Candidates for judge wear no party labels, but compete in primaries and/or general elections according to how many candidates are seeking a given seat. Party organizations have little or nothing to say, therefore, about who the candidates are.

Eight states rely on *gubernatorial appointment* in which the political connections of the potential judge are important, and seats go generally to those who have contributed loyally to the governor's political efforts. Two states use a variation on this political appointment process—vesting the power to dispense the favors in the legislative rather than the executive branch.

Eight states now rely on the so-called *merit selection system*. Under this system nominating commissions—usually composed of politically appointed representatives of the bar association and lay citizens—review the qualifications of prospective candidates and submit a list of three or more names to the governor. The governor then must appoint from the list or reject the package. After one year, or the completion of a term, judges must submit to a "retention" election in which voters decide whether to keep or turn out the incumbents. When vacancies occur, the process starts anew.

Several states use some mixture of two or more of these four systems to fill the benches on various levels of courts. Florida, for example, currently uses a merit plan for appellate judges, but holds nonpartisan elections for trial court judges.

Interim Selections

Whatever the formal method of selection, many judges actually attain the bench through interim appointments. Ryan et al. point out, for example, that in California, a nonpartisan election state, 88 percent of trial court judges were placed on the bench initially by gubernatorial appointments to fill vacancies. They observe that "in states utilizing nonpartisan election only 43 percent of the judges were initially elected; the majority were appointed by the governor or through merit selection. . . . In the partisan election states, however, fully 70 percent of the judges were initially elected."[6]

It is not uncommon in many states for judges to time their resignations or retirements so as to ensure their replacement by an appointed judge. This stems from the belief held by many judges that election, but especially nonpartisan election, is the worst way to select judges, and they use their resignation to create a situation in which the electorate must vote out an incumbent judge—something voters rarely do—or perhaps face no choice at all since incumbents are rarely even challenged.

Selection of Federal Trial Judges and Magistrates

Some attention needs to be given here to the selection of federal district court judges and magistrates. Federal judges at every level are formally appointed by the president of the United States and serve for life, or until they resign, retire, or are removed at the conclusion of an impeachment process. The selection of district court judges, of whom there are currently over 500, is largely controlled by U.S. senators from the states in which the districts are located, especially where at least one of the two senators is of the same party as the president. The president retains real control over these selections only in states where both senators are members of the opposition party.

Senators are given this power of selection through the doctrine of *senatorial courtesy*—a doctrine that calls upon senators from the party that occupies the White House to band together and support each others' selections for various governmental offices within their respective states. Thus if the president nominates a candidate for federal judge, U.S. attorney, or other office requiring the advice and consent of the Senate, and the senator or senators of the affected state object to the appointment, they need only announce that the nominee is objectionable to them and senatorial courtesy requires the other senators to join the objectors in rejecting the appointment and forcing the president to select again. Presidents have learned to consult with their party's senators before selecting candidates. This is the source of some very important patronage for U.S. senators. It also ensures that, to some extent at least, federal district court judges reflect the political culture of the states in which their services are performed. Thus northern federal district judges have tended to be more liberal in their views and southern judges more conservative, though there are notable exceptions to this very broad generalization.

When Jimmy Carter came to office, he pushed for broader adoption of some features of the merit selection system. He created nominating commissions in each of the eleven federal appellate circuits and picked a mix of lawyers and laypeople to serve on the commissions. These groups recommended several candidates for each vacancy on their respective courts of appeals to the U.S. attorney general; the attorney general then forwarded the lists with his own recommendations to the president, who picked the nominee for Senate approval. As for the district judgeships, Carter urged senators to create their own nominating commissions to recommend candidates to the senators themselves or directly to the White House. Senators in thirty states set up commissions of one sort or another, mostly made up of a mix of lawyers and laypersons, and most were instructed to forward their recommendations to the senator's office.[7]

The extent to which these commissions could have attained merit selection was limited in the first place by the voluntary nature of the process (many senators ignored Carter's call) and by the fact that other features of merit selection, especially retention election by the voters, could not be adapted to the federal system. Whether the commissions even improved the quality of candidates selected and whether the process was any less political than before has been questioned. Some lawyers who were interviewed for district judgeship vacancies have asserted that the commissions were just as political and just as partisan in their politics as senators' offices had been in screening candidates. Many critics have pointed out that Democrats dominated the commissions and were predominant among the candidates selected: 94 percent of district court appointments and over 90 percent of courts of appeals slots went to Democrats.[8]

As for the quality of judges selected, there was an overall improvement in the percentage of those rated either "exceptionally well qualified" or "well qualified" by the American Bar Association. While 46 percent of Nixon and Ford appointees were so rated, 51 percent of Carter's received such ratings. On the other hand, under the new system there were four nominees rated "not qualified," two of whom were confirmed anyway and two of whom were withdrawn from consideration.[9]

Two other aspects of Carter's impact on federal judicial selection require attention. One is that by virtue of the Federal Judgeship Act of 1978, Carter appointed more judges to the federal bench than any president before him: 202 to district courts and 56 to courts of appeals. Of those numbers, 117 of the district judgeships and 35 of the appellate positions had been created by the statute; the rest were vacancies that would have occurred anyway. Almost 40 percent of the entire federal bench was thus Carter-appointed.[10] Ironically, President Carter had no opportunity to place a single nominee on the U.S. Supreme Court.

The other aspect is the emphasis Carter placed on appointment of minorities and women. He appointed 41 women, 38 blacks, and 16 Hispanics—more than had previously served on the federal bench in the whole history of the country. Of these judges, 29 of the women (six of whom are black), 28 blacks and 14 Hispanics went on to serve in district courts.[11]

President Reagan abolished the nominating commissions for the courts of appeal, and the fate of states' nominating commissions for district judgeships was mixed. Some Republican senators appointed their own commissions to replace the ones set up by Democrats, some did not.

But President Reagan's major changes in the selection process came within the Justice Department and the White House. At Justice the president gave responsibility for recommending candidates for judicial positions to the Office of Legal Policy and created within it a special counsel for judicial selection. The attorney general, the deputy attorney general, the assistant attorney general in charge of the Office of Legal Policy, and the new special counsel met to recommend candidates to another group, the Committee on Federal Judicial Selection. This body was made up of top-ranked White House staffers and the people from Justice, and its role was explained in these terms by Sheldon Goldman:

> The Committee does not merely react to the Justice Department's recommendations; it is also a source of names of potential candidates and a vehicle for the exchange of relevant information. Furthermore, the president's personnel office conducts an investigation of prospective nominees *independent* of the Justice Department's investigation. It is perhaps not an overstatement to observe that the formal mechanism of the committee has resulted in the most consistent ideological or policy-oriented screening of judicial candidates since the first term of Franklin Roosevelt.[12]

What did this approach produce? In his two terms President Reagan appointed 290 district court judges and 78 appeals court judges who were confirmed by the Senate, and a few others who were not. In total, Reagan filled 372 of 736 positions on the federal bench, but included in that were 18 appellate judges he originally placed on trial benches and one Supreme Court judge he had earlier placed on a court of appeals. Of the total, almost three-quarters had previous judicial or prosecutorial experience, they tended to come from higher socioeconomic status than Carter's appointees, and they included far fewer women and minorities. Only 22 district court appointees (7.6 percent) were nonwhite (14 of those were Hispanic) and 24 were female. Only two appellate appointees were nonwhite, and two were women.[13]

Goldman comments that Reagan's record was second only to that of Carter in appointing women and Hispanics, but his record regarding blacks "was the worst since the Eisenhower administration."[14] Of course, that must be seen in the context of the overall focus of the administration's effort to find young, aggressive, very conservative judges—criteria very few black judges would fit.

As for ABA ratings, about 5 percent of the total appointees were "exceptionally well qualified," and well over half were "well qualified." On the district court level, despite the fact that some candidates received split "qualified/not qualified" ratings, Goldman asserts that Reagan's "appointees can be seen on the whole as the most professionally qualified group of appointees in the past 25 years."[15] The appellate court appointees had a much larger share of split ratings, however, and Goldman comments that one could conclude "the Reagan legacy may be one of lowering of the quality of the appeals bench." However, if one doesn't take ABA ratings that seriously, "such a conclusion is not warranted."[16]

In terms of party membership only thirteen, or 4.5 percent, of his district court appointees were Democrats. This is about the same as Carter's record in appointing Republicans.[17] No Democrats were appointed to appellate benches.

As of this writing, President Bush's approach to judicial selection is unknown.

Federal magistrates, whose authority has been broadened in recent years to include virtually everything judges do in the limited jurisdiction courts of the states, are selected by the district court judges for whom they work. A majority of judges in each district appoint magistrates for either full eight-year terms, or part-time terms of four years.[18] There are over 450 U.S. magistrates.[19]

TRAINING OF JUDGES

Judges all too often ascend to the bench with little or no formal training for the job they are expected to perform. Some, in courts of limited jurisdiction, have no law degrees or even legal training. These nonlawyer judges are disappearing from the scene in most states, but even the judges who are products of the finest law schools have received no preparation from those institutions for the role they are to assume. It is common knowledge among members of the bar and courthouse employees that new judges have to be "broken in" by the attorneys, clerks, bailiffs, and even court reporters who at least have a grasp on how things are done in a given courtroom or proceeding. There is a story, perhaps apocryphal, about a new judge who ascended the bench in a misdemeanor court and found before him a prosecuting attorney and a public defense attorney who also were spending their first day on the job. The task that morning was to pronounce sentences on a number of offenders who had already entered pleas of guilty. The only person in the room with appreciable judicial experience was the court reporter, so she was called upon to go through the case files and indicate what the usual sentence—or "going rate"—was for each type of case before the court. The judge then pronounced the sentences the court reporter recommended.

Formal Training

To be sure, this state of affairs has alarmed many observers as well as participants in the courts, so efforts have been made to provide training sessions of various sorts for new judges. A few states began seminars for trial judges in the early 1960s; and in 1961, in a joint project, the American Bar Association, the American Judicature Society, and the Institute for Judicial Administration organized a series of seminars for trial judges from around the country. This series evolved into the National College of the State Judiciary, which opened its doors in 1964, and is currently headquartered in Reno, Nevada. That college now operates training sessions not only at its headquarters but at various locations throughout the United States. Meanwhile, the National Council of Juvenile Court Judges began training programs for judges appointed to the federal bench, and judges of courts of limited jurisdiction began receiving training offered by various university-related schools or judicial conferences in their respective states.[20] Many states now require newly elected or appointed judges to go through training sessions, generally lasting a week or two, and many sessions are now offered to, if not required for, incumbent judges wishing to update their knowledge and skills. Many of these programs are managed by the respective state court administrator's offices and utilize faculties and facilities of universities and law schools. The effectiveness of these programs obviously varies considerably from place to place, but they at least fill what had been a total void and give judges an opportunity to share their experiences and their views.

Informal "Socialization" of Judges

Formal training programs have not supplanted completely the oldest form of judicial training, the socialization of judges by their peers. Lenore Alpert has identified five states of judicial socialization:

1. *Professional socialization.* The prebench stage of formal legal education and informal training in the practice of law.

2. *Initiation.* A period of "rapid initial adjustment to the bench during the first year, characterized by role definition and reality shock as the judge realizes judging may not be all that he expected."

3. *Resolution.* A two- or three-year period of "intensive learning" that ends when a judge is "comfortable with all aspects of trial judging."

4. *Establishment.* The settling-in period during which a judge tries to cope with judicial life and its conflicting demands and considers whether this time-consuming and isolated lifestyle is what he or she wishes to continue. Most do, and emerge after their ninth or so year on the bench as committed to the career.

5. *Commitment.* The final stage, in which most judges find serenity and a sense of accomplishment.[21]

The first three of these stages involve training of sorts. Alpert studied Florida judges in particular and found that "in contrast to help from those within the court organization, few judges mentioned formal training as aiding their adjustment to trial judging." Judges who did mention formal training programs did so in the context of later in-service sessions rather than preservice sessions and stated that the usefulness of the program was in perfecting techniques and sharing ideas or approaches rather than in learning basic tools.[22]

Alpert divided the substance of what judges need to learn into three categories: legal issues, administrative issues (managing dockets and handling court staffs), and personal issues (coping with the social and political isolation and handling the authority of the office). Of Florida judges who responded to her questionnaire, nearly 70 percent reported substantial learning about legal issues throughout their careers, while about 30 to 40 percent reported continuous on-the-bench learning about administrative or personal matters.[23] This may be surprising, since we assume judges come to the bench knowing a good deal about the law but knowing little if anything about how to manage court business or coping with the personal demands of the office. On the other hand, the results may reflect the fact that law is constantly changing, whereas administrative and personal issues and their resolutions remain fairly constant.

JUDICIAL ACCOUNTABILITY AND DISCIPLINE

It is widely believed that judges are virtually all-powerful and accountable to no one but themselves for their conduct. Much popular literature focuses on the power of courts, calling it "judicial tyranny" and the product of an "imperial judiciary." Though much of this is addressed to the substance of judicial decisions and the increasing tendency of courts to deal with what were once considered "political" issues, some of the criticism is aimed at the behavior of judges on and off the bench. The central issue seems to boil down to how the revered and essential principle of the independence of the judiciary from other branches of government and the prejudices of citizens can be reconciled with the need to hold judges accountable for the professionalism and ethical character of their conduct.

The Appellate Process

The major device for ensuring that the decisions of trial court judges conform to the dictates of law and constitutional provisions is the appellate process. If a judge has committed "reversible error" in the conduct of proceedings, the defendant who loses at trial can seek a judgment from an appellate court to overturn the results and order a retrial or discharge of the case. We treat criminal appeals in a later chapter. Suffice it to say here that appeals, whether of criminal or civil cases, are expensive and time-consuming. Many outrageous acts or decisions by trial judges, especially those of the courts of limited jurisdiction with whom most citizens come into contact, are not appealed. The means of enforcing certain standards through appeal is thus limited in its application. Besides, there are ways of keeping inappropriate acts and decisions off the record and thus not subject to appeal. What is one to do if every time a judge utters a remark that is prejudicial to the case, he or she orders the remark struck from the record? What about cases that are determined in chambers, with the record reflecting only the official outcome?

To be sure, most judges are honest about how they conduct their business and genuinely care about how their decisions are viewed by their superiors. But too many are not honest and do not care. Appellate courts are relatively powerless to deal with them, at least via the appellate process itself.

Traditional Removal Methods

There are two traditional means by which judges whose behavior is sufficiently corrupt may be removed from the bench and stripped of their power to do further harm. These are impeachment and the recall election.

Impeachment If charges of judicial misconduct are serious and weighty enough, they may result in the impeachment of the judge by the legislative branch of government. Generally the lower house holds hearings to determine the facts and make a recommendation to the entire body. If that body agrees that the judge should be subject to removal, it issues articles of impeachment, a document not unlike a grand jury indictment. To be *impeached* is to be charged with offenses that are subject to trial in the upper body of the legislature, or the senate. The senators act as members of the jury in deciding whether the accused judge is guilty of the charges and whether the penalty should be removal.

Obviously such proceedings are very rare. Generally only judges who have been found guilty of crimes in a formal prosecution have been impeached and removed. Judges who are merely unfit have little or nothing to fear from the impeachment process.

Recall Elections Any official who is elected to office is subject to a recall election, that is, one called for the specific purpose of removing him or her from office, and usually selecting a replacement. Depending on provisions in various states, recall elections are held after petitions with a required number of voter signatures have been filed. Thus to be subject to recall, a judge has to have outraged a large number of citizens. This is possible only where a judge has persistently acted in an unpopular or unethical manner, or where his or her treatment of a particular case has caused a storm of controversy. Several years ago, a trial judge in Wisconsin was recalled after he dismissed a rape case on the grounds that the female victim had dressed in a provocative manner, and his decision was major news across the entire country.

Recalls are about as rare as removals following impeachment. Furthermore, judges who are appointed are not subject to recall, and this covers most appellate judges and the entire federal bench.

Judicial Qualifications Commissions

Over two decades ago the state of California pioneered a totally new approach to the matter of disciplining judges. It created an independent commission with a permanent staff whose function was to investigate complaints of judicial misconduct, hold hearings in those cases where the complaints were deemed justified, and make recommendations to the state supreme court as to how judges should be disciplined. The state's constitution provides that the grounds for action are a "disability that seriously interferes with the performance of (a judge's) duties or is likely to become permanent" and "wilful misconduct in office, wilful and persistent failure to perform his duties, habitual intemperance, or conduct prejudicial to the administration of justice that brings the judicial office into disrepute."[24]

In the spring of 1982, the nine-person California commission voted 6 to 3 to recommend the removal of a Los Angeles municipal judge who was found to have:

- Conducted "bargain days" during which defendants received one-half the customary sentence in return for guilty pleas
- Held hearings with neither prosecuting nor defense attorneys present
- Left the bench during criminal trials, instructing attorneys to record their objections to testimony in writing so he could rule on them later
- Sexually harassed a court interpreter
- Told a Mexican-American defendant in a wife-beating case that his conduct might be tolerated in Mexico or Africa, but not in America
- Asked a potential juror, who was Asian-American, about inflation, then commented that he did not know why he was speaking to a Japanese about inflation because "what do fish heads and rice cost?"[25]

The California Supreme Court subsequently removed the judge, only the fifth to have been removed in the history of the commission system. Seven others have been publicly censored, and seventy have resigned when the commission opened investigations into their conduct. Former California Chief Justice Roger Traynor referred to this phenomenon when he said the commission's chief asset was its "prophylactic value."[26]

Other states have copied California's system, and all fifty states now operate under some variation of it. Florida's thirteen-member commission was created in 1966. It is made up of six judges, two each representing and elected by the district courts of appeal, the circuit courts, and the county courts; two attorneys appointed by the Florida bar; and five lay citizens appointed by the governor. They serve staggered six-year terms and are empowered to deal with charges of willful or persistent failure to perform judicial duties; conduct, on or off the bench, "unbecoming a member of the judiciary"; and permanent disability that interferes with performance of duties. A vote of nine members is necessary to recommend the imposition of any discipline, and the options available include private or public censure, forced retirement, and outright dismissal. The state's supreme court takes action on the commission's recommendations.[27]

The Federal Judicial Discipline Act

On October 1, 1981, a federal statute took effect that attempts to apply the principles of state discipline systems and thus to provide an alternative to impeachment, heretofore the only tool available for dealing with the misconduct of federal judges holding appointment "during good behavior." The law established a complex, essentially administrative process involving a series of steps. Complaints may be filed by any person with the clerk of the court of appeals for the circuit in which the judge holds office. The chief judge can dispose of the complaint by taking "appropriate corrective action," or appoint a special investigative committee consisting of himself and an equal number of district (trial) judges and circuit (appellate) judges. The committee's findings and recommendations are referred to the circuit's judicial council, a body representing a mix of other district and circuit judges. The council may impose any of several disciplines short of removal (except in cases dealing with magistrates or bankruptcy judges who may be removed). The judge may appeal the council's actions to the larger judicial conference or one of its standing committees. In fact, the council may kick the matter up to that level itself. The recommendation of either level for removal of a judge requires the conference to transmit the record to the U.S. House of Representa-

News of Note

HASTINGS REMOVED AS FEDERAL JUDGE BY SENATE'S VOTE

GUILTY ON EIGHT ARTICLES

He Calls Vote Unfair but Says He's Upbeat and Will Run for Florida Governor

By David Johnston

WASHINGTON, Oct. 20—In a solemn two-hour proceeding, the Senate today removed Federal District Judge Alcee L. Hastings from the bench by convicting him of eight impeachment articles, including one charging that he had conspired to obtain a $150,000 bribe.

Judge Hastings sat silently facing the senators as Robert C. Byrd of West Virginia called out on the first article, accusing the judge of conspiracy, "Senators, how say you, Is the respondent guilty or not guilty?"

The vote was 69 to 26, providing five votes more than the two-thirds of those present that was needed to convict. Conviction on any single article was enough to remove the judge from office, and he departed shortly after the vote on the conspiracy charge.

Hastings assails verdict

On the Capitol steps, the 53-year-old judge, who served in the Southern District of Florida, pronounced the trial unfair, asserting, "In my opinion, their opinion is void of the wisdom of the forefathers' teachings regarding impeachment." But the judge said he was "upbeat," and he announced he would return to Florida to run for governor.

The conviction was only the sixth time that the Senate has removed a judge from office in an impeachment trial.

In a series of roll-call votes, the senators convicted Judge Hastings on eight of the 17 articles of impeachment. They found him not guilty of three charges, voting unanimously to acquit him of an accusation that he had disclosed sensitive information. The senators decided not to vote on six lesser charges.

Many charges on which Judge Hastings was convicted by the Senate accused him of making false statements and producing false documents in a 1983 criminal trial accusing him of seeking the $150,000 bribe. He was acquitted in the criminal trial.

At the session, the Senate chamber, which on many occasions is sparsely filled, was near capacity, and the senators sat quietly at their leather and wood desks, rising only to cast their votes.

There was no debate.

At the close of the session, Mr. Byrd, a Democrat, presiding as President pro tem, said, "It is therefore ordered that the said Alcee L. Hastings be and is hereby removed." The action forced the judge from an office that paid him $89,500 a year. There was no question of denying him retirement benefits because he had not yet qualified for a pension.

The removal of the judge, who had been on the bench for nearly 10 years since his appointment by President Jimmy Carter, came three years after the Senate ousted Judge Harry E. Claiborne of Nevada. The Senate is nearing final action on impeachment charges against Judge Walter Nixon of Mississippi.

An eight-year ordeal

The Senate action concluded an eight-year ordeal for Judge Hastings. The articles of impeachment accused Judge Hastings of conspiring with a lawyer friend in 1981 to impose a sentence on two criminal defendants that would not include prison time. In return, the charges said, Judge Hastings and the friend, William A. Borders, sought $150,000 from the two defendants who had been convicted of racketeering.

The impeachment charges followed a Federal criminal trial in Miami on the conspiracy charges in 1983 in which the judge was acquitted. Despite the acquittal, a Federal judicial panel concluded in 1987 that there was sufficient evidence that he did conspire to obtain the bribe.

The first phase of the impeachment proceedings took place last year when the House voted 17 articles of impeachment alleging misconduct by the Florida jurist. A committee of 12 senators then reviewed the case and presented their summary to the full Senate last week. They did not recommend any action.

On Thursday, the full Senate debated in a closed session for more than seven hours, with some members clearly uncomfortable, in part because of the judge's acquittal in 1983.

Hastings' friend convicted

Mr. Borders was convicted of the conspiracy charges in a separate trial in 1982 and served a prison term. He has been jailed since last month for refusing to testify before the Senate panel in the Hastings case, but several senators said he would be released after the Senate vote.

The votes today were narrowly sufficient to convict, crossing ideological, re-gional and party lines. They came after the chairman and co-chairman of the special Senate committee that investigated the charges said they would not vote to convict.

Two-thirds of the 95 members who were present today were required to convict the Judge, so 64 votes were needed to find him guilty. The narrowest vote for conviction was by three votes.

Several senators said the outcome reflected the deep divisions among them over the case. "This was a difficult, close call," said Senator Patrick J. Leahy, Democrat of Vermont, who voted to convict the judge on only one count. "Most of the evidence was circumstantial."

Senator Jeff Bingaman, Democrat of New Mexico, chairman of the Senate committee that reviewed the charges, announced before the session that he would vote not guilty on each charge.

Mr. Bingaman's announcement followed a similar move on Thursday by Senator Arlen Specter, Republican of Pennsylvania, vice chairman of the committee, who urged fellow senators to reject the charges.

Proof said to be lacking

Mr. Bingaman and other senators said the evidence presented failed to provide adequate proof that Judge Hastings was guilty. "The proof did not carry me to the necessary degree of certainty," said Mr. Bingaman.

Source: *The New York Times*, October 21, 1989, p.1

tives for possible impeachment action.[28] This complicated system has many questionable features, and the statute is vague on many key points regarding the makeup and selection of committees and councils (one per circuit) and regarding the rules of procedure.[29]

Whatever the faults of this approach, it was used in the case of Judge Alcee Hastings of the Southern District of Florida. On February 4, 1983, Judge Hastings was acquitted on federal criminal charges of conspiracy to commit bribery. Six weeks after the jury's verdict, two other federal judges filed a formal complaint charging that Hastings obstructed justice and lied under oath. In April a five-judge panel began a three-year investigation, and on August 29, 1986, the panel recommended impeachment. That recommendation was endorsed in March 1987 by the Judicial Conference of the United States and the findings were forwarded to the House of Representatives. After its own investigation, the House on August 3, 1988, voted 413 to 3 to impeach Judge Hastings. His trial by the Senate resulted in his conviction and removal on October 20, 1989, thus completing a 5½-year process.[30]

Weaknesses in the Discipline Process

The rarity with which impeachment and recall have been used was alluded to earlier. The new commissions, with their ability to use sanctions short of removal, have much potential to fill the void, since they are standing bodies whose sole activity is the investigation of complaints against judges. Nevertheless, many observers point out that very few investigations lead to any action against judges, and they cite a fundamental weakness built into the system: Laypersons and attorneys alike are generally intimidated by the power of judges and have no desire to become involved in a fight they may well lose. To rephrase a cliché, hell hath no fury like a judge complained against, and a judge who has been investigated, censured, or reprimanded can hardly be counted on to be solicitous toward an attorney who was a complainant. Since most attorneys work before the same judges in case after case over a period of years, they are reluctant to endanger their careers or the interests of their future clients. Complaints are usually forthcoming, therefore, only from the most courageous of attorneys or in situations where a number of attorneys band together against a particularly bad judge. In addition to fear, however, there is the even stronger sense of camaraderie among members of the legal profession with a concomitant tendency to put up with each other's quirks or to deal with problems informally so as not to embarrass a colleague.

COURT SUPPORT PERSONNEL

If judges are the so-called line personnel in the criminal courts, there are several other people performing absolutely essential staff, or supporting, functions. It goes without saying that courts could not operate without the offices of prosecution and defense, but these are separate and distinct line agencies to be taken up in the following chapter. By "support personnel" here, we mean officials whose duties are generally limited to direct staff support services to the trial courts. Among these are the clerk of court, the bailiff, the process-server, the court reporter, and the court administrator.

The Clerk of Court

The *clerk of court* is the official records keeper, that is, the custodian of all legal documents and records of judicial proceedings. At the appellate level and for the entire federal system, the clerks are appointed, but most states provide for election of clerks for the trial courts, generally at the county level. Elected clerks tend to be more independent than appointed clerks, and some who remain in office for many years, watching judges come and go, become the virtual masters of the courts.

The specific duties of the clerk of court vary considerably from place to place, but beyond merely keeping records, clerks may be custodians of evidence being used in cases not yet disposed, issuers of subpoenas for jury service, administrators of the jury selection system, and administrators of the funds collected in fines and fees and paid out to jurors, witnesses, and others. Some places give clerks the powers of magistrates in the issuance of warrants for arrest. Clerks are often the officials who are responsible for monitoring the whereabouts or treatment of all offenders sentenced by the court and for bringing to the court's attention any failure on the part of such persons to pay fines, make restitution payments, or whatever other obligations they have been assigned. The office of clerk has traditionally also been in charge of court docketing, calendar management, and the gathering of statistics for official reports on court business. In recent years some of these duties have been shifted to a relatively new official, the court administrator, whom we shall discuss shortly.

Bailiffs and Process Servers

Persons with security and enforcement functions attached to the court are the bailiffs and process servers. Both are commonly employees, even sworn deputies, of the county sheriff's office. In some places, in fact, sheriffs do little except provide these court services and maintain jails.

The *bailiff,* or court deputy, is the court's security personnel. The bailiff carries out the judge's orders in maintaining decorum in the courthouse, keeping custody of and protecting defendants, summoning witnesses, and providing various services for jurors. It is the bailiff who keeps jurors who have been sequestered—in effect, locked up—housed, fed, and untainted by outside contacts or news accounts of the case they are hearing or deliberating. In many respects the bailiff is a uniformed "go-fer" for the judge and jury, but his or her responsibilities are vital to maintaining the integrity of the process by preventing harm to anyone involved or the escape of defendants.

The *process server* is the official who goes into the community to give notice of official court action to persons named. The process server may typically serve warrants for arrest, subpoenas to testify, summonses to appear for any of several purposes, and orders of the court to either do something or cease from doing something. The spectrum obviously covers civil as well as criminal matters, but in criminal matters at least the servers are usually sworn law enforcement personnel, generally sheriff's deputies or investigators working for the prosecuting attorney. In the federal system, U.S. marshals carry out these duties.

The Court Reporter

The *court reporter* is the person responsible for recording all official proceedings and producing an exact transcript of what takes place in court or in attorneys' offices where witnesses are being deposed, that is, interviewed under oath to preserve testimony. The court reporter is a highly trained and skilled person whose contribution is crucial to the creation of an official record.

Court reporters have traditionally been private entrepreneurs who charge fees for their services and who charge by the page for transcripts. Increasingly, however, courts are putting court reporters on salary, often under the supervision of the court administrator.

Any of several methods may be used to record testimony. In the traditional method, a stenotype machine that enables the reporter to type symbols as rapidly as people talk is used. In recent years audiovisual technology has been increasingly employed. Some courts have employed audiotaping of proceedings, generally using a multitrack system that permits speakers to be identified by the microphone that picks up their voices. Other courts have experimented with videotaping proceedings. Still another technique has the court reporter using a stenomask—a mask containing a microphone held up to the mouth into which the reporter repeats what he or she hears.

Finally there is computer-assisted transcribing, or CAT, a technique by which the stenographer records signals on computer tape as well as on traditional paper. The tape is then fed into a word processor to produce a rough draft of the transcript at considerable savings of time. Only corrections then need to be entered before printing.

In the use of audiotaping and/or videotaping, court reporters may be operators of the recording equipment—which is radically different, of course, from the conventional stenotype and stenomask machines. The skills needed in equipment operation are obviously quite different; and traditional court reporters claim that so too are the results.

Tests comparing audio-based systems with traditional stenographic systems have produced conflicting results. Utah and New Jersey studies resulted in conclusions favoring traditional methods, especially in terms of the accuracy of transcripts.[31] But studies performed in federal courts concluded that audio-based systems are not only faster and cheaper, but more accurate as well. The study done by the Federal Judicial Center concluded that an electronic system costs less than half the comparable stenographic system, and a General Accounting Office study asserted that after initial capital investments of between $7.5 and $14.3 million in equipment, the courts could save $10 million a year using audio-based reporting.[32]

The Court Administrator

In the 1950s a new court official first appeared on the scene: the *court administrator*. The office was widely adopted through the 1970s, and every state now has a state court administrator who reports to the chief justice of the highest court of appeals, and trial court administrators are working for the chief or presiding judges in most of the major trial court systems throughout the country. Court administrators come from varied backgrounds and have widely disparate training and experience. Their duties and responsibilities are as large or as narrow in scope and their authority is as commanding or as limited as the judges for whom they work desire them to be. Generally the larger the system, the more important the administrator in the scheme of things, but invariably a chief judge is the administrator's immediate superior, and the success of the operation depends heavily on the cooperation of the two.

The tasks assigned to a court administrator generally include the following:

- Drafting budgets and their justifications
- Supervising court expenditures
- Managing court assets, including furniture, equipment, and space in the courthouse
- Managing court personnel, who may include court reporters, bailiffs, probation officers, and other staff persons
- Compiling statistics and preparing reports on court operations
- Managing the calendaring and docketing systems and monitoring the flow of cases
- Acting as liaison between the court and other agencies, especially the clerk's office and criminal justice agencies
- Acting as spokesperson for the court to the press and public
- Analyzing the work load and the processing of cases and making recommendations regarding procedures, judicial assignments, and even statutory provisions

Given the above, it is increasingly obvious that court administrators require training in public administration and management. Programs are even emerging in graduate schools of public administration aimed at judicial administration and policy making so that prospective or in-service court administrators may prepare for or perfect their skills in dealing with the demands of this unique and challenging enterprise.

SUMMARY AND CONCLUSION

In this chapter the position of judge has been examined from several perspectives. The demands in terms of character, and the many ways judges can fail to meet the test, have led us to considerations of the means by which judges are selected. Special attention has been paid to so-called merit plans of selection and how President Carter attempted to employ some of their features in his selection of an unusually large number of federal judges. We looked at the training of judges, with some focus on the informal on-the-bench training that predominates. We also presented material on judicial accountability and, in particular, on efforts at both the state and federal levels to provide alternatives more useful than impeachment and recall elections.

We also took brief looks at supporting personnel in the court system. The roles of clerks of court, bailiffs and process servers, court reporters, and the relatively new court administrators were all examined. Judges may "embody" the court, but they would be ineffective without these officials to carry out essential tasks within the overall judicial operations.

Any institution is, to reuse on old cliché, only as good as the persons who staff it and keep it going. The judicial system of this nation depends utterly on the qualities and dedication of the judges and the other professional people at whom we have looked.

QUESTIONS FOR DISCUSSION

1. Why would a lawyer in your community wish to become a judge?
2. How would that lawyer attain the post if he or she wanted to? To what degree does old-fashioned politics play a role in this process?
3. What qualities and credentials would you like to see required of candidates for judicial office? Would these qualities and credentials differ depending on the level of court? If so, how? What qualities do you think should disqualify a person from a judgeship?
4. What is the mechanism in your community or state for unseating a judge who is simply doing a poor job? How about a corrupt judge? How difficult would it be to unseat the former? The latter?

5. What changes would you make in the procedures by which your judges are selected for office? How about the procedures by which they are disciplined or removed from office?

NOTES

1. Donald Dale Jackson, *Judges,* Atheneum, New York, 1974, pp. 7 and 8.
2. Ibid., p. 9.
3. Ibid., p. 10.
4. Howard James, *Crisis in the Courts,* rev. ed., McKay, New York, 1977, pp. 6–10.
5. Jackson, p. 379.
6. John Paul Ryan et al., *American Trial Judges: Their Work Styles and Performance,* Free Press, New York, 1980, p. 122.
7. Alan Neff, "Breaking with Tradition: A Study of the U.S. District Judge Nominating Commissions," *Judicature,* vol. 64, no. 6, December–January 1981, pp. 256–268.
8. Sheldon Goldman, "Carter's Judicial Appointments: A Lasting Legacy," *Judicature,* vol. 64, no. 8, March 1981, pp. 348 and 350.
9. Ibid., p. 350.
10. Ibid., p. 345.
11. Ibid., p. 349.
12. Sheldon Goldman, "Reorganizing the Judiciary: The First Term Appointments," *Judicature,* vol. 68, nos. 9–10, April–May 1985, pp. 315–316.
13. Sheldon Goldman, "Reagan's Judicial Legacy: Completing the Puzzle and Summing Up," *Judicature,* vol. 72, no. 6, April–May 1989, pp. 318, 322, and 324–325.
14. Ibid., p. 322.
15. Ibid., p. 322.
16. Ibid., p. 325.
17. Ibid., p. 322.
18. Steven Puro, Roger L. Goldman, and Alice M. Padawer-Singer, "The Evolving Role of U.S. Magistrates in the District Courts," *Judicature,* vol. 64, no. 10, May 1981, p. 438.
19. *Annual Report of the Director of the Administrative Office of the United States Courts, 1982,* U.S. Government Printing Office, Washington, D.C., 1983, p. 3.
20. Glenn R. Winters, "Two Centuries of Judicial Progress in America," in Glenn Winters and Edward J. Schoenbaum (eds.), *American Courts and Justice,* American Judicature Society, Chicago, 1976, p. 58.
21. Lenore Alpert, "Learning About Trial Judging: The Socialization of State Trial Judges," in James A. Cramer (eds.), *Courts and Judges,* Sage, Beverly Hills, Calif. 1981, pp. 107–109.
22. Ibid., p. 115.
23. Ibid., p. 128.
24. Jackson, p. 393.

25. Wallace Turner, "Coast Panel Urges Removal of Judge," *The New York Times,* May 8, 1982, p. 24.

26. Jackson, p. 393.

27. Mark Hulsey, "Unfit to Hold Office?" *The Florida Bar,* July–August 1981, pp. 534–535.

28. Eric Neisser, "The New Federal Judicial Discipline Act: Some Questions Congress Didn't Answer," *Judicature,* vol. 65, no. 3, September 1981, pp. 144–145.

29. Ibid., pp. 147–160.

30. R. A. Zaldivar, "Senate Finds Hastings Guilty," *The Miami Herald,* October 21, 1989, pp. 1 and 22A.

31. John J. Prout, Jr., "Letter to the Editor," *The New York Times,* January 21, 1983, p. 16.

32. David Lauter, "Tape Recorders Still Top Reporters," *The National Law Journal,* July 18, 1983, p. 12.

CHAPTER 6

ATTORNEYS
AND THE BAR

*After reading this chapter, students should be able to define and explain
the importance of each of the following terms or phrases:*

integrated bar	inner ring of firms
canons	middle ring of partnerships
ethical considerations	outer ring of solo practitioners
disciplinary rules	courthouse regulars
rule of confidentiality	lawyer as double agent
quasi-judicial functions	indigency standard
prosecutorial discretion	assigned-counsel system
general practitioners	public defender's office
solo practitioners	contract system

Lawyers control most of the administration of justice. They conduct the
tasks of prosecution, defense, and almost all judging. Lawyers in the
United States have formally organized themselves into groups known as
bar associations, in order to protect the integrity and image of the profession.

BAR ASSOCIATIONS AND THEIR ROLE

In the early days of bar associations in the late nineteenth century, membership was extended to any who desired to join, and one could easily
practice law without being a member of the bar.[1] But twentieth-century
legal reformers were impressed that the medical profession usually re-

quired membership in a medical association, with its attendant standards and discipline, before a physician could utilize the local hospital. The reformers saw the desirability of imposing a similar standard on lawyers.

The American Judicature Society was formed in 1913 to improve the court system and the bar. It quickly began to work toward the goal of requiring bar membership as a prerequisite to doing legal work both in and out of court. The concept is similar to that of a "closed shop" in which only union members can be employed, but in order to avoid anti-union sentiment, a "closed bar" was and still is referred to as an *integrated bar* rather than a closed shop.[2]

The term "bar" itself is derived from the name of the partition running across a courtroom that separates the general public from the space occupied by the counsel, judges, and laypeople involved with the trial, including the jury and parties to the suit. In old England, court was often conducted outdoors, or perhaps indoors, under improvised conditions, with merely a wooden bar set up to keep the participants from the spectators.

Most states of the union today have integrated bars, and the trend has been to establish them by means of a court order. Integration by order of the state supreme court allows state bar associations to function without interference from legislative and executive branches. In this situation, only the supreme court can create rules for the bar association, and the doctrine of separation of powers is maintained.

A Lawyer's Education and Admission into Practice

The American Bar Association, itself formed in 1878, assisted in forming the American Association of Law Schools in 1900, an accrediting association managed by the member law schools.[3] The AALS sets standards in such areas as admittance, libraries, and curricula and prescribes the equivalent of a three-year course of study for graduation.

The ordinary standard for admittance to the bar today is not merely the possession of a degree in law but the successful completion of a comprehensive set of rigorous examinations. This was not always the case. In the nineteenth century the local judge would orally examine the candidates and allow them to be sworn. Obviously this led to a set of standards that varied widely from jurisdiction to jurisdiction and enabled many weak lawyers to practice law. Once sworn in before one court, an attorney would be allowed to practice in other courts because most other judges would honor the decision of their fellow judge. Today's system also typically looks into the background of the person seeking admittance in order to determine if that person is of sufficiently good character for admittance. Bar membership has been deemed to be a privilege the bar can deny for good cause. This authority to deny membership has helped to keep potentially embarrassing applicants from becoming lawyers.

Even with formalized standards and tests for admission, some lawyers commit unethical or illegal acts, and therefore mechanisms exist for removal from the bar, suspension from practice, and other lesser sanctions.

Ethics of the Profession

All lawyers are subject to their state's published code of professional responsibility. The state codes closely follow the American Bar Association's Code of Professional Responsibility, which was adopted in 1970 and has been since amended. The codes typically consist of three types of rules: canons, ethical considerations, and disciplinary rules.

The *canons* are general and conceptual. The preamble of a fairly typical code of professional responsibility, that of the Florida bar, describes canons as "statements of axiomatic norms, expressing in general terms the standards of professional conduct expected of lawyers in their relationship with the public, with the legal system, and with the legal profession. They embody the general concepts from which the ethical considerations and disciplinary rules are derived." As an example, consider Canon 4 of the Florida code: "A lawyer should preserve the confidences and secrets of a client."[4]

The same preamble, in describing *ethical considerations,* states that they should be "aspirational in character and represent the objectives toward which every member of the profession should strive." The preamble goes on to state that ethical considerations "constitute a body of principles upon which the lawyer can rely for guidance in many specific situations." So it is obvious that the ethical considerations are not presented as hard and fast, enforceable rules per se. The general nature of an ethical consideration is apparent in one example from the Florida code: "Maintaining the integrity and improving the competence of the bar to meet the highest standards is the ethical responsibility of every lawyer."[5]

In rather stark contrast to the ethical considerations, which are admittedly "aspirational in character," are the *disciplinary rules,* which are mandatory in character and punishable if breached. The preamble and preliminary statement of the code of professional responsibility of the Florida bar describes disciplinary rules as follows:

> The disciplinary rules, unlike the ethical considerations, are mandatory in character. The disciplinary rules state the minimum level of conduct below which no lawyer can fall without being subject to disciplinary action. Within the framework of fair trial, the disciplinary rules should be uniformly applied to all lawyers, regardless of the nature of their professional activities. The

code makes no attempt to prescribe either disciplinary procedures or penalties for violation of a disciplinary rule, nor does it undertake to define standards for civil liability of lawyers for professional conduct.... An enforcing agency, in applying the disciplinary rules, may find interpretive guidance in the basic principles embodied in the canons and reflected in the ethical considerations.[6]

Causes for potential discipline include conviction of crime and acts constituting contempt of court. The bar can discipline its members in many ways, depending upon the severity of the offense. Discipline measures include but are not limited to censure, suspension from practice, and actual disbarment.

CRITICISM OF THE PROFESSION

As most readers know, the legal profession has been under a barrage of criticism—from members of the profession itself as well as from the general public. The bar has been referred to as a kind of semisecret society more interested in enriching itself than in serving its clients or the public. The profession has been chastised for caring more about mutual protection against outside attacks than about cleansing itself of its unethical members. The most common criticism of the profession is that it has turned away from the role of assisting people in resolving disputes to one of creating and exacerbating disputes so that lawyers' services are required on an ever-increasing scale. Charles Halpern, a public interest lawyer, blames this phenomenon on "the way lawyers are trained to approach (social) problems." Another attorney from a large Washington firm, however, blamed it on the simple fact that "there are too many lawyers generally and too little business."[7]

Another constant criticism of the profession is that the parties who have the most money usually win legal battles, regardless of what justice requires. We have grown used to seeing news reports about poor souls who are about to lose or have lost their shirts because their opponents utilized "batteries" of "high-powered" lawyers. We see an ever-increasing number of incidents in which two powerful adversaries—perhaps one a government agency—conclude a long-fought legal struggle with what amounts to a draw (the settlement of the federal antitrust suit against AT&T comes to mind), and the press comments that the only true winners are the trial lawyers, who stand to collect enormous fees.

An increasing theme of critical articles and commentaries is that the canons of ethics are themselves unethical from a broader social perspective. The canon that generally causes the greatest uproar is the *rule of confidentiality*, which urges an attorney to keep conversations with his or her clients confidential even where such conversations reveal client guilt for heinous unsolved crimes or, even more startlingly, where clients reveal they are about to commit crimes. (The canon does make exception in the case in which breaking a client's confidence will save lives or prevent great bodily harm to intended victims.) Such rules speak to the larger issue of where a lawyer's final obligation lies: to the client, to society, or to the client's victims? The canons urge lawyers to remember that they are "officers of the court" and thus obligated to serve justice. But the tension between this obligation and the interests of a client are usually resolved by a lawyer in favor of the client.

It is only fair to point out that attorneys make the case that weakening the rule of confidentiality would make their professional job impossible, since it depends on a client's trust that what is told the lawyer will go no further. If a client cannot count on that, he or she will tell the lawyer as little as possible, making defense of the case an unpredictable venture at best.

When a defendant tells his attorney that he intends to commit perjury in his own defense, the attorney has an obligation to try to dissuade the client from doing so. Should that effort fail, the attorney may seek to be removed from the case. But the court can, at its discretion, deny permission for the withdrawal.

We do not intend to leave the impression that most lawyers are cads and that the profession is without social merit. Neither is the case. We seek to point out, however, that the profession is under some attack and that there are legitimate concerns about its rules and its role.

THE PROSECUTOR

The office of the prosecutor, by whatever name it might be known from jurisdiction to jurisdiction, is cloaked in a mantle of images based partly in truth, partly in fiction, and dependent as much on television drama as on hard fact. The prosecutor's image as an officer of the court, impartially enforcing all the laws with a goal of balancing all the equities and clearing the innocent as well as convicting the guilty, is usually somewhat accurate. Wide variations in the performance of the prosecutorial function do, however, exist, not only from jurisdiction to jurisdiction but from prosecutor to prosecutor.

The prosecutor has a very special role in relation to local law enforcement. Especially in the case of small or less sophisticated law enforcement agencies, the prosecutor or an assistant will often serve as legal advisor to sheriff's deputies and police officers. Prosecutors often guide case development from the very beginning of a complex criminal investigation, drafting search warrants, preparing wiretaps, bringing witnesses before grand juries, compelling testimony, and ultimately making the decision as to whether to proceed to court. The practice on the part of law enforcement officers of seeking counsel from prosecutors prior to arrest is growing across the country. This reliance on the prosecutor's advice is rooted in the increasing complexity of criminal practice; alert police officers recognize the fact that the chances of winning a conviction are enhanced through the use of the prosecutor as counsel during investigation.

The ideal prosecutor would be totally neutral and dispassionate in considering all the evidence. He or she would search just as arduously for facts and law that would clear the innocent as for the means to charge and convict the guilty. Yet in a very real and practical sense, such ideal impartiality is limited by the prosecutor's role in devising the criminal charges and often the final plea bargain that decides the case's outcome. The function of the prosecutor is often described, in part, as being *quasi-judicial*. "Quasi" is a misleading prefix to a degree, since prosecutors often make more "judicial" decisions than the judges before whom they appear. Judges in criminal cases are primarily passive in their trial roles, and prosecutors have the ability to be proactive, deciding whether a criminal lawsuit should even be brought in the first place. Judges usually have much less latitude to act than the prosecutors who appear before them. The judge runs the court, but the prosecutor decides what will come within the court's jurisdiction and how it will be charged.

The power and office of the prosecutor is created by state legislation or constitution and is limited to the grants of power contained therein. The prosecutor is the chief attorney for the public in the area of criminal law. He or she has virtually unreviewable power in deciding whether to proceed with prosecution or to decline to take criminal action. This power is probably the greatest discretionary power in the criminal justice system and is known as *prosecutorial discretion*.

Selection of Prosecutors

On the local and state levels, most prosecutors are elected for terms of four years by the electorate whom they serve, and the elections are usually partisan in nature. United States attorneys are appointed by the president with the consent of the Senate. The usual case involves an initial recommendation by the senators of the state where the federal prosecutor is to serve. In most cases, the U.S. attorneys are of the president's political persuasion, and new appointments are generally made when a president of another party is elected. The process is much like that described earlier regarding the appointment of federal judges, but no commissions were ever created to assist senators in their selection of candidates.

Many prosecutors do not consider their positions to be career positions; they are primarily interested in using the office to make a name for themselves before going back into private practice or to help their chances of election to higher office. Many, if not most, prosecutors leave office voluntarily rather than by defeat at election. Some prosecutors do make the position a career, though they represent only a small proportion of the 2,600 chief prosecutors nationwide.

Assistant prosecutors are generally selected at the sole and often political discretion of the prosecuting attorney. In some offices a change of prosecuting attorney, especially to one of an opposing political party, leads to a sweeping termination of existing assistants and a wholesale hiring of replacements. But a growing number of offices are now being governed by merit, and some job security is available for assistants, especially lower-ranking assistants, during political change. In a few places assistant prosecutors are even unionized.

The prosecutor's office has been traditionally regarded as a starting point for a newly graduated lawyer who desires to prepare for trial practice and build a reputation while not yet requiring a very high salary. This causes a relatively rapid turnover of assistant prosecutors, with attendant beginner's errors and failures at trial, especially early in the learning curve of each fledgling prosecutor. Law enforcement officers and judges are frequently heard to complain that by the time an assistant has learned the job he or she moves on to private practice, usually as a criminal defense lawyer who knows all the tactics and vulnerabilities of the state's officials.

Normally the only prerequisite to becoming a prosecutor is being a member of the bar and impressing the elected or appointed chief prosecutor, who hires the assistants. The new assistant will normally begin with less important cases, often in traffic or misdemeanor court. He or she then usually works up to prosecuting felony offenses. Senior assistants, in larger offices, supervise junior assistants and handle the most serious cases and sometimes conduct grand jury proceedings.

Most colleges of law do not place emphasis on preparation for the practice of criminal law, and prosecutors have to develop these skills themselves. The traditional training method in a prosecutor's office is on-the-job training with supervising attorneys giving some guidance. One of the present authors recalls more than a few experiences when, as a beginning prosecutor, he walked into the office and was assigned a case file by a supervisor who didn't even know if witnesses had yet been placed under subpoena for a trial that was to begin in a few minutes! One thinks of the baby bird being kicked out of the nest, having equal odds of flying or crashing.

Exercise of Prosecutorial Discretion

Earlier we spoke of the fact that the prosecutor has the authority to see that prosecution is either initiated or dropped. That is the essence of prosecutorial discretion. A criminal lawsuit begins with the preparation of an accusation of crime. The grand jury may vote to bring an indictment, or the prosecutor, in many jurisdictions, may file an information. Chapter 9 details the process of initiation of prosecution. Suffice it to say at this point that the prosecutor holds great sway over the grand jury and total discretion over the filing of accusative informations.

Day-to-Day Prosecutorial Duties and Realities

Prosecutors represent the state at every stage of a criminal proceeding. They appear at arraignment and defend motions to suppress evidence and dismiss the prosecution. They attempt to obtain a favorable plea and, if unsuccessful, take the case to a jury or nonjury trial. They develop trial skills at the expense of the state and at a rate usually much faster than contemporaries engaged in civil litigation. Prosecution is often considered the very best means of gaining a great deal of trial experience in a short time. Much of that trial experience will certainly be gained by going up against vastly more experienced attorneys who are often "graduates" of the prosecutor's office. Experience comes quickly to a new prosecutor who is not afraid to try cases and does not seek to make life easy by accepting less-than-favorable plea bargains. Trying cases is hard work and is fraught with the potential for both loss of reputation and ego damage if success does not come often enough! Some young prosecutors find out that they just do not have what it takes and leave the office to seek out the branches of law that do not require much trial work.

But for those who stay, the duties require such concentrated and continued effort that prosecutors should ideally devote themselves full-time to the office and should not engage in private practice. Still, in many small jurisdictions the prosecutor is forced to serve only as a part-time representative of the people and part-time as a private practitioner. This situation usually flows from the fact that the jurisdiction cannot afford a full-time prosecutor or that the duties simply do not require that many hours of dedicated effort.

A major concern in regard to part-time prosecutors is that conflicts of interest may arise between the duties of prosecutor and those of private attorney. Direct conflicts of interest are easily discernible and are obviously unethical and illegal. But less direct conflicts are inherent in the reality that the prosecutor has to deal as a private attorney in informal and cooperative ways with the very same attorneys who defend the cases under prosecution. This system encourages accommodation that may be less than totally desirable to the ends of justice. The National District Attorneys Association does, however, encourage prosecutors to participate in private endeavors in legal education, commission, and consultant work, as these activities are not likely to produce conflicts of interest and *are* likely to produce benefits to the criminal justice system.

The National District Attorneys Association also believes that the office of prosecutor should be approached as a career position. The NDAA cites James N. Johnson: "The advantages of career prosecutors are fairly obvious. Longevity should breed commitment to the tasks of a prosecuting career. Experience should develop the expertise necessary to avoid trial error and appeals, which are costly to the district attorney's office in time, money and efficiency."[8]

Unfortunately, turnover of prosecuting attorneys has usually been quite high; all too often chief prosecutors and their assistants consider the office to be a stepping-stone to higher political office or to a more financially lucrative position as a private practitioner, with a reputation and name recognition garnered as a prosecutor trying "headline" cases.

THE DEFENSE ATTORNEY

The very term "defense attorney" tends to conjure various images in the minds of most Americans. In the lay imagination, these images rest upon impressions gained from the media. This, of course, means that the images are often inaccurate, since the media do not always understand what they report so often—the proceedings of criminal courts. Even lawyers in civil practice and new criminal legal practitioners frequently do not understand the role of the so-called criminal lawyer. We shall try to offer some insight.

It is probably fair to say that a criminal defense attorney is a person who either specializes in or handles a substantial number of criminal cases. Many lawyers are *general practitioners,* who handle an occasional criminal case because they tend to take most cases that come their way. Some of these attorneys may call themselves criminal defense lawyers, but many criminal law specialists feel that anything more than a casual defense of a simple criminal case requires special experience. Many other attorneys practice almost exclusively outside the area of criminal law and will only take criminal cases if a good client insists.

Preparation and Qualities

Since few colleges of law place any emphasis on preparation to practice criminal law, most practitioners acquire whatever specialized skills and polish they have in the field.

Actual on-the-job training in a public defender's office or a civilian law office typically constitutes the bulk of initial post-law-college skill development. Many public defender's offices offer in-service training or even an "apprenticeship" in which the new lawyer goes to court with an experienced attorney and is allowed to begin trial practice with some supervision. Because of somewhat limited funding and staffing in most public defender's offices, however, new lawyers are quickly thrust into trial on their own. Typically, they either learn fairly quickly or do rather poorly; in the latter case, they then often seek a mode of practice that will keep them out of the trial courtroom, or "pit," as it is sometimes known.

The beginning lawyer in a private firm is usually brought along rather more slowly and will often "carry the briefcase" for a senior attorney in the firm. Many such firms receive rather high fees from the defendants that they represent and a good deal of investigation, research, discovery, and preparation will be done in the average case. The new lawyer in such a firm will often learn how to do such preparatory work first, and trial experience will come much more slowly than for the average public defender.

Formal advanced courses and seminars are available through a myriad of sources, including but not limited to public defender associations and offices; national, state, and local bar associations; trial lawyer associations; and various private educational firms. Many practitioners keep growing professionally through continuing education, but human nature being as it is, some of those who most need continuing education are the least likely to seek it.

Private Practice of Defense Law

As with any other field of law practice—or any other human endeavor—the practice of defense law is engaged in by lawyers of various skill levels and with varying degrees of economic success. The field does seem to attract more than its share of marginal practitioners. Some observers speculate that a marginal practitioner, who, by the very definition of the term, is not very successful, is comfortable around that element of society that requires criminal defense. Others believe that the relative simplicity of some of the more mundane criminal matters makes this an easy area in which to practice if care is taken to avoid complex cases. Some defense lawyers are attracted by the feeling that society oppresses certain classes and individuals for invidious reasons and that defense of these persons is somehow the "right" thing to do.

Perhaps a better explanation of the unsavory reputation of criminal law is not that it attracts a particular kind of lawyer so much as it keeps the others away. Herbert Jacob puts it into the context of the increasing specialization in the practice of law, the expanding role of larger and larger law firms (some called megafirms), and the fact that more and more lawyers never see the inside of a courtroom. He comments:

> As in other fields, criminal law has become a specialty of its own. Whereas becoming a tax specialist in a large firm gives a lawyer prestige, becoming a criminal lawyer is likely to cost the attorney whatever prestige he has acquired. A criminal law practice requires close contact with the seamy side of life. In many cases the work does not pay very well, for the clients are not wealthy. If the lawyer defends a notorious criminal, the community may misunderstand and associate the lawyer with his client. For these reasons, relatively few lawyers desire criminal cases; where at all possible they avoid taking them.[9]

The bulk of private criminal defense work is done by *solo practitioners* whose backgrounds and skills are markedly different from those of firm attorneys. Whereas firm attorneys are drawn from the upper and middle classes and attend the more prestigious law schools, solo practitioners tend to come from groups lower on the socioeconomic scale and have probably received their law degrees from middle-level or even standard law schools. Jack Ladinski once categorized lawyers in large urban areas into three rings: the *inner ring* of large firms, a *middle ring* of smaller firms and partnerships that conduct a general law practice, and an *outer ring* of the solo practitioners who hang around the courthouse "in hopes of picking up crumbs from the judicial table."[10]

Abraham S. Blumberg studied the criminal courts of a major American city some years ago and found that *courthouse "regulars"* include some lawyers who found office-based practices a bore and whose incomes were "well above the national average for lawyers."[11] He observed, however, that these regulars practice a kind of confidence game with most of their clients. Since legal services are intangible in nature, a lawyer can pretend to be doing more for a client than is actually being done.

The various canons of legal ethics prohibit attorneys from practicing criminal law on a contingent-fee basis, so various fee arrangements are used. The most successful lawyers are apt to be able not only to command the highest fees but to demand and, more importantly, to receive prepayment of fees—that is, prior to trial. It is obvious that the typical defendant is going to be hard to collect from if convicted and sent to prison. Less successful practitioners often resort to time payments, and in some states it is possible to pay attorney's fees by credit card.

Blumberg asserts that there is a type of attorney who insists on collecting the fee in advance, letting the client know that the potential success of the legal effort depends on the amount and timing of the payment.

Then the attorney prepares the client for the likely conviction that is coming and makes a deal with the prosecutor for a plea bargain. The plea bargain enables the prosecutor to record another conviction, enables the court to dispose of the case rapidly, and enables the defense attorney to tell the client that this deal was made possible through the use of considerable skills, well-placed contacts, and great effort. Blumberg alleges that in the sense that the lawyer assists the prosecutor and the court more than the client, that lawyer acts as a *double agent*.[12]

This highly unflattering picture of the private defense attorney is hardly fair to the thousands who are honest and earnest in their efforts on behalf of their clients. And even in those cases where the defendant's overwhelming guilt leads to a conviction, despite the defense attorney's admirable performance, the defendant often blames not himself or herself but the attorney. Few incarcerated persons have much good to say of their counsel, even if a fine job was actually done. This factor sometimes leads to the disillusionment of those practitioners motivated primarily by a desire to right the wrongs of society and causes them to seek other fields of legal practice where the clients are more grateful or at least not so ungrateful. After all, some defendants really are not very pleasant people. The lawyers who come from middle-class, liberal backgrounds usually learn about the wide range of human behavior only after practicing criminal law. And some attorneys never expose themselves to this sometimes socially unacceptable and often sordid endeavor and never learn about other classes and behavior patterns at all.

Right to Free Counsel under the Sixth Amendment

We all remember that the Sixth Amendment states in a pertinent part, "In all criminal prosecutions, the accused shall enjoy the right . . . to have the assistance of counsel for his defense." Exactly what this means has been a topic of considerable debate and appeal. As late as 1942 the Supreme Court of the United States in *Betts v. Brady* said that the states were not obligated to furnish free counsel in every serious case.[13]

In 1963 the Supreme Court in *Gideon v. Wainwright* changed its position and said once and for all that persons charged with serious crimes are entitled to counsel even if they cannot afford a lawyer.[14] This case is so important to the development of constitutional law and the rights of persons accused of crimes that excerpts from the opinion by Justice Hugo Black, who had been a dissenter in the *Betts* case, are presented here for the student's examination.

In 1972 the Supreme Court again addressed the issue of free counsel for the indigent, this time in minor cases, in its decision in *Argersinger v. Hamlin*.[15] The *Argersinger* Court ruled "absent a knowing and intelligent

Gideon v. Wainwright

372 U.S. 335, 83 S. Ct. 792, 9 L. Ed. 2d 799 (1963)

FROM THE OPINION

By Justice Black

Petitioner was charged in a Florida state court with having broken and entered a poolroom with intent to commit a misdemeanor. This offense is a felony under Florida law. Appearing in court without funds and without a lawyer, petitioner asked the court to appoint counsel for him, whereupon the following colloquy took place:

> The COURT: Mr. Gideon, I am sorry, but I cannot appoint Counsel to represent you in this case. Under the laws of the State of Florida, the only time the Court can appoint Counsel to represent a Defendant is when that person is charged with a capital offense. I am sorry, but I will have to deny your request to appoint Counsel to defend you in this case.
>
> The DEFENDANT: The United States Supreme Court says I am entitled to be represented by Counsel.

Put to trial before a jury, Gideon conducted his defense about as well as could be expected from a layman. He made an opening statement to the jury, cross-examined the State's witnesses, presented witnesses in his own defense, declined to testify himself, and made a short argument "emphasizing his innocence to the charge contained in the Information filed in this case." The jury returned a verdict of guilty, and petitioner was sentenced to serve five years in the state prison. Later, petitioner filed in the Florida Supreme Court this habeas corpus petition attacking his conviction and sentence on the ground that the trial court's refusal to appoint counsel for him denied him rights "guaranteed by the Constitution and the Bill of Rights by the United States Government." Treating the petition for habeas corpus as properly before it, the State Supreme Court, "upon consideration thereof" but without an opinion, denied all relief. Since 1942, when Betts v. Brady, 316 U.S. 455, was decided by a divided Court, the problem of a defendant's federal constitutional right to counsel in a state court has been a continuing source of controversy and litigation in both state and federal courts. To give this problem another review here, we granted certiorari....

The Sixth Amendment provides, "In all criminal prosecutions, the accused shall enjoy the right... to have the Assistance of Counsel for his defence." We have construed this to mean that in federal courts counsel must be provided for defendants unable to employ counsel unless the right is competently and intelligently waived. Betts argued that this right is extended to indigent defendants in state courts by the Fourteenth Amendment. In response the Court stated that, while the Sixth Amendment laid down "no rule for the conduct of the states, the question recurs whether the constraint laid by the amendment upon the national courts expresses a rule so fundamental and essential to a fair trial, and so, to due process of law, that it is made obligatory upon the states by the Fourteenth

Amendment." In order to decide whether the Sixth Amendment's guarantee of counsel is of this fundamental nature, the Court in Betts set out and considered "[r]elevant data on the subject . . . afforded by constitutional and statutory provisions subsisting in the colonies and the states prior to the inclusion of the Bill of Rights in the national Constitution, and in the constitutional, legislative, and judicial history of the states to the present date." On the basis of this historical data the Court concluded that "appointment of counsel is not a fundamental right essential to a fair trial." It was for this reason the Betts Court refused to accept the contention that the Sixth Amendment's guarantee of counsel for indigent federal defendants was extended to or, in the words of that Court, "made obligatory upon the states by the Fourteenth Amendment." Plainly, had the Court concluded that appointment of counsel for an indigent criminal defendant was "a fundamental right, essential to a fair trial," it would have held that the Fourteenth Amendment requires appointment of counsel in a state court, just as the Sixth Amendment requires in a federal court. . . .

We accept Betts v. Brady's assumption, based as it was on our prior cases, that a provision of the Bill of Rights which is "fundamental and essential to a fair trial" is made obligatory upon the States by the Fourteenth Amendment. We think the Court in Betts was wrong, however, in concluding that the Sixth Amendment's guarantee of counsel is not one of these fundamental rights. . . .

Governments, both state and federal, quite properly spend vast sums of money to establish machinery to try defendants accused of crime. Lawyers to prosecute are everywhere deemed essential to protect the public's interest in an orderly society. Similarly, there are few defendants charged with crime, few indeed, who fail to hire the best lawyers they can get to prepare and present their defenses. That government hires lawyers to prosecute and defendants who have the money hire lawyers to defend are the strongest indications of the widespread belief that lawyers in criminal courts are necessities, not luxuries. The right of one charged with crime to counsel may not be deemed fundamental and essential to fair trials in some countries, but it is in ours. From the very beginning, our state and national constitutions and laws have laid great emphasis on procedural and substantive safeguards designed to assure fair trials before impartial tribunals in which every defendant stands equal before the law. This noble ideal cannot be realized if the poor man charged with crime has to face his accusers without a lawyer to assist him. A defendant's need for a lawyer is nowhere better stated than in the moving words of Mr. Justice Sutherland in Powell v. Alabama:

> The right to be heard would be, in many cases, of little avail if it did not comprehend the right to be heard by counsel. Even the intelligent and educated layman has small and sometimes no skill in the science of law. If charged with crime, he is incapable, generally, of determining for himself whether the indictment is good or bad. He is unfamiliar with the rules of evidence. Left without the aid of counsel he may be put on trial without a proper charge, and convicted upon incompetent evidence, or evidence irrelevant to the issue or otherwise inadmissible. He lacks both the skill and knowledge adequately to prepare his defense, even though he have a perfect one. He requires the guiding

hand of counsel at every step in the proceedings against him. Without it, though he be not guilty, he faces the danger of conviction because he does not know how to establish his innocence. 287 U.S., at 68–69.

The Court in Betts v. Brady departed form the sound wisdom upon which the Court's holding in Powell v. Alabama rested. Florida, supported by two other States, has asked that Betts v. Brady by [sic] left intact. Twenty-two States, as friends of the Court, argue that Betts was "an anachronism when handed down" and that it should now be overruled. We agree.

The judgment is reversed and the cause is remanded to the Supreme Court of Florida for further action not inconsistent with this opinion.

Reversed.

---

waiver, no person may be imprisoned for any offense, whether classified as petty, misdemeanor, or felony unless he was represented by counsel." The Court went on to say, "we reject, therefore, the premise that since prosecutions for crimes punishable by imprisonment for less than six months may be tried without a jury, the may always be tried without a lawyer." Thus the Court made it clear that, if a person unable to afford a lawyer were to be placed in jeopardy of going to jail, he or she had to have counsel provided free of cost.

Some have argued that a universal right to counsel is needed in all criminal cases, no matter how minor. They note that many judges circumvent the intent of *Argersinger* by announcing at the outset that no jail sentence will be imposed, and thus no attorney is provided.

Many other concerns exist, such as the right to free counsel for appeals, free transcripts for appeals, and the right of public-funded counsel for minor cases where penalties short of jail are available; but these issues are beyond the scope of the present discussion.

The Indigency Standard In the wake of *Gideon* the states reacted by providing free counsel for indigents. The logical threshold question is what standard is to be applied for a determination of indigence? The Supreme Court spoke to this issue in *Adkins v. E. I. Du Pont Co.,* a case involving a related issue, where the opinion stated:

> We cannot agree with the court below that one must be absolutely destitute to enjoy the benefit of the statute. We think an affidavit is sufficient which states that one cannot because of his property pay or give security for costs . . . and still be able to provide himself and dependents with the necessities of life.[16]

In another, more recent, case a U.S. circuit court of appeals held unconstitutional a New Mexico state judge's requirement that a person be a pauper in order to be eligible for free counsel.[17] The American Bar Association has promulgated a standard for the provision of appointed counsel based on a level of eligibility that protects the basic means of a defendant and his or her family. The standard recommends:

> Counsel should be provided to any person who is financially unable to obtain adequate representation without substantial hardship to himself or his family. Counsel should not be denied to any person merely because his friends or relatives have sources adequate to retain counsel or because he has posted or is capable of posting bond.[18]

A common thread among state standards seems to be the "substantial hardship" concept, with some jurisdictions setting out specific standards for earnings and property holdings that would disqualify a defendant from indigency. In all states the court still causes the defendant who requests free representation to be questioned, and the decision is predicated on standards that vary not only from state to state but also from judge to judge.

It should be noted that most jurisdictions—in fact, three-quarters of those counties responding to a Department of Justice survey—require defendants to pay some portion of the costs of their defense.[19] This is commonly done by billing defendants ruled to have some ability to pay. The fees are usually a small fraction of what private counsel would charge for comparable services.

Defense Systems for the Indigent   Attorneys who represent indigent clients come to court under one of two circumstances. Either they are assigned or appointed by the courts and receive compensation in the form of court-approved fees, or they are salaried staff members in the public defender's office. There are three different approaches, however, to structuring the provision of defense services.

One approach is the *assigned-counsel system* that employs private attorneys drawn from lists of those volunteering for such service. This approach is used in almost two-thirds of the counties of this country, though they are predominantly rural counties. (Texas reported using it in 252 of 254 of its counties, and three states use it in all counties.) Counsel can be assigned on either an ad hoc (case-by-case) basis or by using a coordinated assigned-counsel system in which an administrator distributes the case load among several attorneys.[20]

The second approach is a *contract system* whereby the county enters into formal agreements with individual practitioners, a law firm, the local bar association, or a nonprofit legal aid organization for provision of defense services. Only about 6 percent of our counties use this approach.[21]

The third approach, of course, is the establishment of a *public defender's office*. Public defender's offices are organized at either the state or local level. Most statewide systems involve the appointment of a single state public defender who then employs attorneys to work in branch offices in counties or population centers. The most common local model is to have a county public defender appointed by the county commission or board of supervisors.[22] He or she then hires the necessary staff. Among the variations is the Florida model, which provides for twenty public defenders as constitutional officers, each elected in his or her circuit of the state—a mirror image of the model for state attorneys.

Public defenders serve only about a third of all counties, but over two-thirds of the population. Forty-three of the nation's fifty most populous counties have public defender's offices. Most public defenders are full-time in the job themselves and most hire staff attorneys, but three-quarters of the counties have offices with three or fewer staff attorneys.[23]

There is a growing problem in public defender's offices with cases involving codefendants. Since no law firm can represent more than one client with conflicting defenses in any one case, a situation involving such codefendants requires that other means be used to obtain counsel for the codefendant. It is estimated that 25 percent of felony cases involve codefendants and thus require the appointment of additional "outside" attorneys.

There is also a problem of limited resources and the number of cases that any one attorney can handle in even the most rudimentary way. Some public defender's offices have either negotiated or won by litigation a limit to the number of clients or cases that can be assigned to them. Other cases must be assigned, on a contract system, to outside attorneys to be added to the number of cases these attorneys are already handling as conflict-of-interest cases. Thus many counties must support two systems: a public defender's office and an assigned-counsel program.[24]

SUMMARY AND CONCLUSION

This chapter has presented a treatment of the legal profession and of the offices of prosecution and defense. We began with a look at bar associations and discussed their role in training attorneys, in admitting them to the bar, and in providing ethical guidelines and rules for them. We also commented on some criticisms leveled at the legal profession.

The role of the prosecutor was viewed in terms of its demands on lawyers and of the criteria and method of selection for the position. We pointed out that virtually all prosecutors on the local level are elected, but that prosecutors in a few states and in the federal system serve by appointment. We examined the work of the office and career patterns of prosecutors, pointing out that few stay in the job for long, most choosing private practice or higher political office after a short stint as prosecutor. We touched on the problems inherent in part-time work as a prosecutor, particularly in the potential conflicts of interest between carrying out public duties and serving the interests of clients.

The defense bar was also examined—with attention paid to training, which is mostly on the job; the role of the private bar; the impact of the *Gideon* and *Argersinger* cases on providing defense services for indigents; the standards for designating "indigency"; and the structure of defense systems.

The decisions of the Supreme Court that caused the state to assume the costs of the legal defense of the poor have had a great impact, one that is still reverberating through the criminal justice system and the agencies that fund it. The creation of public defender's offices was no doubt long overdue, but there is a fundamental problem with having the state act as the agent that accuses and prosecutes and at the same time provide a defense for those accused. This paradox is not lost on most of those so defended, and the fact they doubt the state can do both is reflected in the use of the slang term "PD," for "prison deliverer." This is unfair to the bulk of hardworking attorneys in public defense offices, and it encourages a phenomenon that plagues both prosecution and defense— the rapid turnover that sees attorneys moving to better paying and less exhausting careers. The task of building professional and career-oriented offices is still before us.

QUESTIONS FOR DISCUSSION

1. How is your community's prosecutor selected and how long has he or she been in office? What prior experience did the person have?
2. How visible is the prosecutor's office? How visible are its activities to the citizens of your community? How does the prosecutor use the media and how do the media treat the prosecutor?
3. To the extent that the prosecutor makes statements to the public or speeches to groups, what position does he or she take regarding Crime Control values versus the principles of the Due Process Model?
4. By whom are most indigent defendants represented in your community's courts? Is the representation adequate in your view? If not, what could be done to improve it, and how should its cost be handled?
5. Find out which private attorneys in your community routinely defend in criminal cases. Is the activity spread around or are there a few "regulars" who do the bulk of it?
6. If your local public defender or prominent defense attorneys make public speeches, how do they appear to stand on the values of the Due Process Model versus those of the Crime Control Model?

NOTES

1. Dayton McKean, as cited in Herbert Jacob, *Justice in America,* 2d ed., Little, Brown, Boston, 1978, pp. 46–47.
2. Ibid., p. 47.

3. M. Louise Rutherford, as cited in McKean, p. 46.
4. *The Florida Bar Journal,* vol. 54, no. 8, September 1980, p. 91.
5. Ibid., p. 91.
6. Ibid., p. 79.
7. *The New York Times,* August 13, 1982.
8. James N. Johnson, "The Influence of Politics upon the Office of the American Prosecutor," *American Journal of Criminal Law,* vol. 2, Summer 1973, pp. 187–193.
9. Herbert Jacob, *Justice in America,* 4th ed., Little, Brown, Boston, 1984, pp. 78–79.
10. Jack Ladinsky, "The Impact of Social Backgrounds of Lawyers on Law Practice and the Law," *Journal of Legal Education,* vol. 16, 1965, p. 128.
11. Abraham S. Blumberg, *Criminal Justice: Issues and Ironies,* 2d ed., New Viewpoints, New York, 1979, p. 242.
12. Ibid., p. 245.
13. *Betts v. Brady,* 316 U.S. 455 (1942).
14. *Gideon v. Wainwright,* 372 U.S. 335 (1963).
15. *Argersinger v. Hamlin,* 407 U.S. 25 (1972).
16. *Adkins v. E. I. Du Pont Co.,* 335 U.S. 331, 339 (1948).
17. *Arroya v. Baker,* 427 F. 2d 73 (10th Circ. 1970).
18. American Bar Association, Project on Standards for Criminal Justice, *Standards Related to Providing Defense Services,* Standard 6.1, Approved Draft, 1968.
19. Bureau of Justice Statistics, *A National Survey: Criminal Defense Systems,* U.S. Government Printing Office, Washington, D.C., 1984, p. 2.
20. Ibid., pp. 4 and 5.
21. Ibid., pp. 5 and 6.
22. Ibid., pp. 3 and 4.
23. Ibid., p. 3.
24. Ibid., p. 4.

CHAPTER 7

EVIDENCE AND ITS ADMISSIBILITY

After reading this chapter, students should be able to define and explain the importance of each of the following terms or phrases:

the exclusionary rule
the "good-faith" exception
actions of private persons
unprotected interests
expectation of privacy
probable cause doctrine
search warrants
confidential informant
reliability of informants
totality of the circumstances
specificity requirement

electronic eavesdropping
minimization
postarrest searches
hot-pursuit searches
vehicular searches
plain-view doctrine
custodial searches
"stop-and-frisk" rule
secret agents
consent searches

The pivotal point in the whole criminal justice process is quite obviously the trial. If the prosecutor cannot prevail in the effort to convict the accused, the process is, in that particular case, forever stopped by the action of the Fifth Amendment to the Constitution, which states, in pertinent part, "nor shall any person be subject for the same offense to be twice put in jeopardy of life or limb." This so-called double jeopardy provision is discussed in detail in Chapter 9 but really boils down to the fact that the prosecutor only has one chance to present the case against the defendant on a specific charge.

THE BURDEN OF PROOF

The prosecutor, with one chance to convict, must meet a burden of proof that is variously defined in different jurisdictions but basically requires overcoming the presumption of innocence that the law gives to every accused, no matter how guilty he or she, in fact, is. The prosecutor must prove, as to each and every material portion of the charge against the defendant, that the defendant did what is stated in the indictment or information. This proof must be of a convincing nature and must establish the defendant's guilt beyond a reasonable doubt or to a moral certainty.

The lawyers in noncriminal or civil cases have an easier burden of proof: There they must prove only that the preponderance of the evidence that exists is enough to tip the scales of justice in the direction of their client. The defendant in a criminal case, however, does not have a duty to come forward with any proof at all. The accused not only has a presumption of innocence that the prosecutor must overcome very convincingly but has as well an absolute right to be silent.

With this heavy burden of proof and the prohibition against seeking a second trial, it is clear that the prosecutor's case must be based upon good evidence. By "good," we mean evidence that is both convincing and legally presentable to the jury. The rules of what a lawyer can and cannot present a jury are constantly evolving and are rooted in the Constitution, common law, statutes, rules of court, and modern case law interpreting all of these sources.

With all of these technical limitations upon what kinds of things a jury may see and hear and with the clear prescription of how conclusive the final proof must be, the modern gatherer of evidence must not only have the talents of Sherlock Holmes but also be skilled in the law and in the rules of evidence. If the facts gathered by the investigator are barred from the courtroom, they are of no use in gaining a conviction.

With these requirements in mind, we can approach the problems of gathering evidence not just from the viewpoint that the police and the prosecutor must be convinced of an individual's guilt but that they must have sufficient admissible evidence to convince an impartial jury of that guilt. We must, therefore, deal with some rules concerning the admissibility of evidence.

THE EXCLUSIONARY RULE

In order to understand the concept of the exclusionary rule, we must examine the constitutional provisions that were so frequently abused as to make the rule necessary. The basic protections against unreasonable search and seizure are contained in the Fourth Amendment (1791): "The right of the people to be secure in their persons, houses, papers, and effects, against unreasonable searches and seizures, shall not be violated, and no warrants shall issue, but upon probable cause, supported by oath or affirmation, and particularly describing the place to be searched, and the persons or things to be seized."

During reconstruction following the Civil War, the Fourteenth Amendment was ratified; it provided, in pertinent part, that "No State shall abridge the privileges or immunities of citizens of the United States nor shall any State deprive any person of life, liberty, or property, without due process of law; nor deny to any person within its jurisdiction the equal protection of the laws."

The *Weeks* Case

The provisions of the Fourth Amendment were often ignored in the years following its ratification, and many unreasonable searches and seizures produced incriminating evidence that was used in trials to obtain convictions that could not have been gained otherwise. The protections of the Fourth Amendment were empty words to persons so convicted. In 1914, the Supreme Court in *Weeks v. United States* decided to make the Fourth Amendment enforceable in the federal courts.[1] This case established the *exclusionary rule,* which prohibits the trial use of evidence secured through illegal search and seizure. This prohibition was designed to keep federal agents from profiting from bad searches. The Court reasoned that the exclusion of such evidence would effectively enforce the Fourth Amendment. This rule is severe in that its operation can and does exclude logical, relevant evidence that is in no way unreliable. It has absolutely nothing to do with truth, other than it can, in fact, keep truth from reaching the jury. It quite simply punishes police misconduct or lack of technical legal expertise. Its action has freed many criminals, but it has also done much to protect our right of privacy by imposing effective sanctions on police misconduct.

The *Wolf* Case

Thirty-five years after the *Weeks* case was handed down, the Supreme Court again considered the exclusionary rule in *Wolf v. Colorado* when it first weighed the wisdom of extending the exclusionary rule to the courts of the then forty-eight states.[2] Justice Felix Frankfurter delivered the opinion of the Court; he began by observing:

> The precise question for consideration is this: Does a conviction by a State court for a State offense deny the "due process of law" required by the Four-

teenth Amendment, solely because evidence that was admitted at the trial was obtained under circumstances which would have rendered it inadmissible in a prosecution for violation of a federal law in a court of the United States because there was deemed to be an infraction of the Fourth Amendment as applied in *Weeks v. United States* . . . ?

Justice Frankfurter was looking to the Fourteenth Amendment that purports to give the rights a citizen finds in the federal system to the citizen in the various state systems. He acknowledged the rights of citizens in the state courts to be secure from unreasonable searches and seizures and went on to discuss the many ways that the states could enforce the Fourth Amendment short of having the Supreme Court mandate the exclusionary rule for the state court systems. The Court decided to leave the states to their own devices to enforce the Fourth Amendment. History would prove that the Court had little cause for optimism in trusting the states to discipline their own police forces. Abuses continued to be widespread and the need for federal court intervention eventually became clear.

The *Mapp* Case

By 1961 the Supreme Court of the United States had doubtless noticed that leaving the enforcement of the Fourth Amendment to each individual jurisdiction was not working very well in many places, despite the Court's clear message urging compliance. The Court utilized a particularly horrendous example of unreasonable search and seizure as the vehicle by which it was to require the states to adopt the exclusionary rule. *Mapp v. Ohio* was a case out of Cleveland, Ohio, where police officers, with no search warrant and on only vaguely stated suspicions, ransacked Miss Mapp's home over her objection, refused to allow her to consult with her attorney, and used the evidence so seized to convict her of possessing lewd and lascivious books, pictures, and photographs.[3]

The *Mapp* court spoke of the Fourth Amendment in the following terms: "Because it is enforceable in the same manner and to like effect as other basic rights secured by the Due Process Clause, we can no longer permit it to be revocable at the whim of any police officer who, in the name of law enforcement itself, chooses to suspend its enjoyment." The Court therefore ruled that states must from that time forward follow the federal practice of excluding illegally seized evidence from criminal trials.

The forced exclusion of evidence gained by unreasonable search and seizure, a practice that often allows the criminal to profit because the police officer erred, has, since 1961, had a major role in guaranteeing the civil liberties of all Americans.

The "Good-Faith" Exception

In 1984 the Supreme Court took very significant action when it narrowed the number of cases wherein the exclusionary rule applied. In *United States v. Leon*[4] and *Massachusetts v. Sheppard,*[5] with majority opinions written by Justice Byron White, the Court held that the exclusionary rule should not apply where a law enforcement officer conducting a search acts with a good-faith, objectively reasonable reliance on a warrant issued by a detached and neutral magistrate, even if the warrant is subsequently found to be invalid. The Court set out prerequisites for the exception to keep it from being abused. First, the majority opinion stated that the deference accorded to the magistrate's finding of probable cause does not preclude inquiry into the knowing or reckless falsity of the affidavit upon which the finding is based. Second, the courts must insist that the magistrate actually perform a "neutral and detached" duty and not merely be a rubber stamp for the police. Third, the appellate courts must not honor a search warrant that is based upon information in an affidavit that does not "provide the magistrate with a substantial basis for determining the existence of probable cause." The Court went on in footnotes 20 and 23 of the *Leon* opinion to state that law enforcement officers should have a reasonable knowledge of what the law prohibits and that an officer should *not* rely on the magistrate's authorization if that officer has cause to know that the search is illegal.

In *Leon* and *Sheppard,* the Court reemphasized its preference for warrants by increasing the "rewards" for prior judicial determination of probable cause. Again, the Burger Court seemed to be leaning toward the Crime Control Model of procedure but did not, it seems, lose sight of the protections afforded by the Due Process Model. Because the *Leon* case broke precedent on the exclusionary rule, on the following pages we excerpt Justice White's majority opinion and include Justice William Brennan's strong dissenting opinion as well.

Only the future will tell if the Court will extend the rationale of the good-faith exception to warrantless searches, an area that addresses a great deal more law enforcement activity than searches with a warrant. Remember, the Fourth Amendment ostensibly holds a preference for warrants. Time will tell.

LIMITS ON FOURTH AMENDMENT RIGHTS

The Fourth Amendment does not protect citizens from any and all searches and seizures they might think are "unreasonable." The Supreme Court has recognized that certain limits exist on the protections implied under the Fourth Amendment.

United States v. Leon

82 L. Ed. 2d 677

FROM THE OPINION

By Justice White

This case presents the question whether the Fourth Amendment exclusionary rule should be modified so as not to bar the use in the prosecution's case-in-chief of evidence obtained by officers acting in reasonable reliance on a search warrant issued by a detached and neutral magistrate but ultimately found to be unsupported by probable cause.

To resolve this question, we must consider once again the tension between the sometimes competing goals of, on the one hand, deterring official misconduct and removing inducements to unreasonable invasions of privacy and, on the other, establishing procedures under which criminal defendants are "acquitted or convicted on the basis of all the evidence which exposes the truth."

A facially valid search warrant was issued in September 1981 by a state superior court judge. The ensuing searches produced large quantities of drugs at the Via Magdalena and Sunset Canyon addresses and a small quantity at the Price Drive residence. Other evidence was discovered at each of the residences and in Stewart's and Del Castillo's automobiles. Respondents were indicted by a grand jury in the District Court for the Central District of California and charged with conspiracy to possess and distribute cocaine and a variety of substantive counts.

The respondents then filed motions to suppress the evidence seized pursuant to the warrant. The District Court held an evidentiary hearing and, while recognizing that the case was a close one, granted the motions to suppress in part. It concluded that the affidavit was insufficient to establish probable cause, but did not suppress all of the evidence as to all of the respondents because none of the respondents had standing to challenge all of the searches. In response to a request from the Government, the court made clear that Officer Rombach had acted in good faith, but it rejected the Government's suggestion that the Fourth Amendment exclusionary rule should not apply where evidence is seized in reasonable, good-faith reliance on a search warrant.

Appeals Court Affirmed It

The District Court denied the Government's motion for reconsideration and a divided panel of the Court of Appeals for the Ninth Circuit affirmed.

We have concluded that, in the Fourth Amendment context, the exclusionary rule can be modified somewhat without jeopardizing its ability to perform its intended functions. Accordingly, we reverse the judgment of the Court of Appeals.

Language in opinions of this Court and of individual Justices has sometimes implied that the exclusionary rule is a necessary corollary of the Fourth Amendment or that the rule is required by the conjunction of the Fourth and Fifth Amendments. These implications need not detain us long. The Fifth Amendment theory has not withstood critical analysis or the test of time, and the Fourth Ammendment "has never been interpreted to proscribe the introduction of illegally seized evidence in all proceedings or against all persons."

The substantial social costs exacted by the exclusionary rule for the vindication of Fourth Amendment rights have long been a source of concern. "Our cases have consistently recognized that unbending application of the exclusionary sanction to enforce ideals of governmental rectitude would impede unacceptably the truth-finding functions of judge and jury."

An objectionable collateral consequence of this interference with the criminal justice system's truth-finding function is that some guilty defendants may go free or receive reduced sentences as a result of favorable plea bargains. Particularly when law enforcement officers have acted in objective good faith or their transgressions have been minor, the magnitude of the benefit conferred on such guilty defendants offends basic concepts of the criminal justice system. Indiscriminate application of the exclusionary rule, therefore, may well "generate disrespect for the law and the administration of justice." Accordingly, "as with any remedial device, the application of the rule has been restricted to those areas where its remedial objectives are thought most efficaciously served."

Remedial Objectives Examined

Close attention to those remedial objectives has characterized our recent decisions concerning the scope of the Fourth Amendment exclusionary rule. The Court has, to be sure, not seriously questioned, "in the absence of a more efficacious sanction, the continued application of the rule to suppress evidence from the [prosecution's] case where a Fourth Amendment violation has been substantial and deliberate." Nevertheless, the balancing approach that has evolved in various contexts—including criminal trials—"forcefully suggests that the exclusionary rule be more generally modified to permit the introduction of evidence obtained in the reasonable good-faith belief that a search or seizure was in accord with the Fourth Amendment."

When considering the use of evidence obtained in violation of the Fourth Amendment in the prosecution's case-in-chief, we have declined to adopt a per se or but for rule that would render inadmissible any evidence that came to light through a chain of causation that began with an illegal arrest. We also have held that a witness's testimony may be admitted even when his identity was discovered in an unconstitutional search.

Balancing Approach Evolves

As yet, we have not recognized any form of good-faith exception to the Fourth Amendment exclusionary rule. But the balancing approach that has evolved during the years of experience with the rule provides strong support for the modification currently urged upon us. As we discuss below, our evaluation of the costs and benefits of suppressing reliable physical evidence seized by officers reasonably relying on a warrant issued by a detached and neutral magistrate leads to the conclusion that such evidence should be admissible in the prosecution's case-in-chief.

Because a search warrant "provides the detached scrutiny of a neutral magistrate, which is a more reliable safeguard against improper searches than the hurried judgment of a law enforcement officer 'engaged in the often competitive enterprise of ferreting out crime,''' we have expressed a strong preference for warrants and declared that "in a doubtful or marginal case a search under a warrant may be sustainable where without one it would fail." Reasonable minds frequently may differ on the question whether a particular affidavit establishes probable cause, and we have thus concluded that the preference for warrants is most appropriately effectuated by according "great deference" to a magistrate's determination.

'Neutral and Detached'

Deference to the magistrate, however, is not boundless. It is clear, first, that the deference accorded to a magistrate's finding of probable cause does not preclude inquiry into the knowing or reckless falsity of the affidavit on which that determination was based.

Second, the courts must also insist that the magistrate purport to "perform his 'neutral and detached' function and not serve merely as a rubber stamp for the police." A magistrate failing to "manifest that neutrality and detachment demanded of a judicial officer when presented with a warrant application" and who acts instead as "an adjunct law enforcement officer" cannot provide valid authorization for an otherwise unconstitutional search.

Third, reviewing courts will not defer to a warrant based on an affidavit that does not "provide the magistrate with a substantial basis for determining the existence of probable cause." Even if the warrant application was supported by more than a "bare bones" affidavit, a reviewing court may properly conclude that, notwithstanding the deference that magistrates deserve, the warrant was invalid because the magistrate's probable-cause determination reflected an improper analysis of the totality of the circumstances, or because the form of the warrant was improper in some respect.

Rational in Some Cases

Only in the first of these three situations, however, has the Court set forth a rationale for suppressing evidence obtained pursuant to a search warrant; in the other areas, it has simply excluded such evidence without considering whether Fourth Amendment interests will be advanced. To the extent that proponents of exclusion rely on its behavioral effects on judges and magistrates in these areas, their reliance is misplaced.

Judges and magistrates are not adjuncts to the law-enforcement team; as neutral judicial officers, they have no stake in the outcome of particular criminal prosecutions. The threat of exclusion thus cannot be expected significantly to deter them.

We have frequently questioned whether the exclusionary rule can have any deterrent effect when the offending officers acted in the objectively reasonable belief that their conduct did not violate the Fourth Amendment. "No empirical researcher, proponent or opponent of the rule, has yet been able to establish with any assurance whether the rule has a deterrent effect." But even assuming that the rule effectively deters some police misconduct and provides incentives for the law enforcement profession as a whole to conduct itself in accord with the Fourth Amendment, it cannot be expected, and should not be applied, to deter objectively reasonable law enforcement activity.

It is the magistrate's responsibility to determine whether the officer's allegations establish probable cause and, if so, to issue a warrant comporting in form with the requirements of the Fourth Amendment.

Cost of Exclusion Noted

We conclude that the marginal or nonexistent benefits produced by suppressing evidence obtained in objectively reasonable reliance on a subsequently invalidated search warrant cannot justify the substantial costs of exclusion.

In so limiting the suppression remedy, we leave untouched the probable-cause standard and the various requirements for a valid warrant. Other objections to the modification of the Fourth Amendment exclusionary rule we consider to be insubstantial. The good-faith exception for searches conducted pursuant to warrants is not intended to signal our unwillingness strictly to enforce the requirements of the Fourth Amendment, and we do not believe that it will have this effect. As we have already suggested, the good-faith exception, turning as it does on objective reasonableness, should not be difficult to apply in practice. When officers have acted pursuant to a warrant, the prosecution should ordinarily be able to establish objective good faith without a substantial expenditure of judicial time.

No Freezing Effect Seen

Nor are we persuaded that application of a good-faith exception to searches conducted pursuant to warrants will preclude review of the constitutionality of the search or seizure, deny needed guidance from the courts, or freeze Fourth Amendment law in its present state. There is no need for courts to adopt the inflexible practice of always deciding whether the officers' conduct manifested objective good faith before turning to the question whether the Fourth Amendment has been violated. Defendants seeking suppression of the fruits of allegedly unconstitutional searches or seizures undoubtedly raise live controversies which Article III empowers Federal courts to adjudicate.

FROM THE DISSENT

By Justice Brennan

Ten years ago, in United States v. Calandra I expressed the fear that the Court's decision "may signal that a majority of my colleagues have positioned themselves to reopen the door (to evidence secured by official lawlessness) still further and abandon altogether the exclusionary rule in search-and-seizure cases." Since then, in case after case, I have witnessed the Court's gradual but determined strangulation of the rule. It now appears that the Court's victory over the Fourth Amendment is complete. That today's decision represents the piece de resistance of the Court's past efforts cannot be doubted, for today the Court sanctions the use in the prosecution's case-in-chief of illegally obtained evidence against the individual whose rights have been violated—a result that had previously been thought to be foreclosed.

The Court seeks to justify this result on the ground that the "costs" of adhering to the exclusionary rule in cases like those before us exceed the "benefits."

But the language of deterrence and of cost/benefit analysis, if used indiscriminately, can have a narcotic effect. It creates an illusion of technical precision and ineluctability. It suggests that not only constitutional principle but also empirical data support the majority's result. When the Court's analysis is examined carefully, however, it is clear that we have not been treated to an honest assessment of the merits of the exclusionary rule, but have instead been drawn into a curious world where the "costs" of excluding illegally obtained evidence loom to exaggerated heights and where the "benefits" of such exclusion are made to disappear with a mere wave of the hand.

The majority ignores the fundamental constitutional importance of what is at stake here. While the machinery of law enforcement and indeed the nature of crime itself have changed dramatically since the Fourth Amendment became part of the Nation's fundamental law in 1791, what the Framers understood then remains true today—that the task of combating crime and convicting the guilty will in every era seem of such critical and pressing concern that we may be lured by the temptations of expediency into forsaking our commitment to protecting individual liberty and privacy. It was for that very reason that the Framers of the Bill of Rights insisted that law enforcement efforts be permanently and unambiguously restricted in order to preserve personal freedoms. In the constitutional scheme they ordained, the sometimes unpopular task of insuring that the government's enforcement efforts remain within the strict boundaries fixed by the Fourth Amendment was entrusted to the courts.

Foundation Is Examined

A proper understanding of the broad purposes sought to be served by the Fourth Amendment demonstrates that the principles embodied in the exclusionary rule rest upon a far firmer constitutional foundation than the shifting sands of the Court's deterrence rationale. But even if I were to accept the Court's chosen method of analyzing the question posed by these cases, I would still conclude that the Court's decision cannot be justified.

Mode of Analysis Scrutinized

But, as troubling and important as today's new doctrine may be for the administration of criminal justice in this country, the mode of analysis used to generate that doctrine also requires critical examination, for it may prove in the long run to pose the greater threat to our civil liberties.

At bottom, the Court's decision turns on the proposition that the exclusionary rule is merely a "judicially created remedy designed to safeguard Fourth Amendment rights generally through its deterrent effect, rather than a personal constitutional right."

This view of the scope of the Amendment relegates the judiciary to the periphery. Because the only constitutionally cognizable injury has already been "fully accomplished" by the police by the time a case comes before the courts, the Constitution is not itself violated if the judge decides to admit the tainted evidence. Indeed, the most the judge can do is wring his hands and hope that perhaps by excluding such evidence he can deter future transgressions by the police.

Reading Is Attacked

Such a reading appears plausible, because, as critics of the exclusionary rule never tire of repeating, the Fourth Amendment makes no express provision for the exclusion of evidence secured in violation of its commands. A short answer to this claim, of course, is that many of the Constitution's most vital imperatives are stated in general terms and the task of giving meaning to these precepts is therefore left to subsequent judicial decision-making in the context of concrete cases.

A more direct answer may be supplied by recognizing that the Amendment, like other provisions of the Bill of Rights, restrains the power of the government as a whole; it does not specify only a particular agency and exempt all others. The judiciary is responsible, no less than the executive, for insuring that constitutional rights are respected.

When the fact is kept in mind, the role of the courts and their possible involvement in the concerns of the Fourth Amendment comes into sharper focus. Because seizures are executed principally to secure evidence, and because such evidence generally has utility in our legal system only in the context of a trial supervised by a judge, it is apparent that the admission of illegally obtained evidence implicates the same constitutional concerns as the initial seizure of that evidence. Indeed, by admitting unlawfully seized evidence, the judiciary becomes a part of what is in fact a single governmental action prohibited by the terms of the Amendment. Once that connection between the evidence-gathering role of the police and the evidence-admitting function of the courts is acknowledged, the plausibility of the Court's interpretation becomes more suspect.

He Says Meaning Is Lost

I submit that such a crabbed reading of the Fourth Amendment casts aside the teaching of those Justices who first formulated the exclusionary rule, and rests ultimately on an impoverished understanding of judicial responsibility in our constitutional scheme. For my part, "the right of the people to be secure in their persons, houses, papers and effects, against unreasonable searches and seizures" comprises a personal right to exclude all evidence secured by means of unreasonable searches and seizures. The right to be free from the initial invasion of privacy and the right of exclusion are coordinate components of the central embracing right to be free from unreasonable searches and seizures.

If the overall educational effect of the exclusionary rule is considered, application of the rule to even those situations in which individual police officers have acted on the basis of a reasonable but mistaken belief that their conduct was authorized can still be expected to have a considerable long-term deterrent effect.

After today's decision, however, that institutional incentive will be lost. Indeed, the Court's "reasonable mistake" exception to the exclusionary rule will tend to put a premium on police ignorance of the law. Armed with the assurance provided by today's decision that evidence will always be admissible whenever an officer has "reasonably" relied upon a warrant, police departments will be encouraged to train officers that if a warrant has simply been signed, it is reasonable, without more, to rely on it.

'Grave Consequences' Seen

Although the Court brushes these concerns aside, a host of grave consequences can be expected to result from its decision to carve this new exception out of the exclusionary rule. A chief consequence of today's decision will be to convey a clear and unambiguous message to magistrates that their decisions to issue warrants are now insulated from subsequent judicial review.

Creation of this new exception for good faith reliance upon a warrant implicitly tells magistrates that they need not take much care in reviewing warrant applications, since their mistakes will from now on have virtually no consequence: If their decision to issue a warrant was correct, the evidence will be admitted; if their decision was incorrect but the police relied in good faith on the warrant, the evidence will also be admitted. Inevitably, the care and attention devoted to such an inconsequential chore will dwindle.

Moreover, the good faith exception will encourage police to provide only the bare minimum of information in future warrant applications. The long-run effect unquestionably will be to undermine the integrity of the warrant process.

Although the Court's decisions are clearly limited to the situation in which police officers reasonably rely upon an apparently valid warrant in conducting a search, I am not at all confident that the exception unleashed today will remain so confined. Indeed, the full impact of the Court's regrettable decision will not be felt until the Court attempts to extend the rule to situations in which the police have conducted a warrantless search solely on the basis of their own judgment about the existence of probable cause and exigent circumstances. When that question is finally posed, I for one will not be surprised if my colleagues decide once again that we simply cannot afford to protect Fourth Amendment rights.

Actions of Private Persons

The rights provided by the Fourth Amendment have only been enforced against governmental intrusion and not against unreasonable searches and seizures by private persons. The case that states this most clearly is the rather interesting case of *Burdeau v. McDowell,* where the Supreme Court stated that the Fourth Amendment acted "as a restraint upon the activities of sovereign authority and . . . not . . . a limitation upon other than governmental agencies."[6] At least one state supreme court has held this to apply in its trial courts, in a decision by which a husband was allowed to use evidence that proved his wife was guilty of adultery, evidence he had gained through a forced entry of her separately maintained apartment. It is likely that *Burdeau* will be followed in other state courts faced with this same problem.

Protected versus Unprotected Interests

Not all citizens' interests and areas are protected from intrusion by the government. An important case, *Katz v. United States,* does a great deal to explain what a citizen has a right to expect the government to leave unsearched if a warrant has not been obtained.[7] The reasoning of *Katz* is seen again and again in search-and-seizure cases handed down by various courts since it was decided in 1967.

Mr. Katz was convicted in federal court of telephoning betting information from Los Angeles to Miami and Boston. The FBI had attached an electronic listening and recording device to the outside of a telephone booth that Katz was in the habit of using. Up to the time of the *Katz* decision the federal courts had generally used a standard for such cases that was based on a trespass, or unlawful entry, theory, and in *Katz* the federal prosecutors argued that, since the telephone booth had not been pierced or entered by the government, all was well.

Both parties to the suit placed great emphasis upon the fact that the booth constituted an "area," one side urging that it was protected and the other that it was not. The Court said such an analysis was misleading. "The Fourth Amendment protects people, not places. What a person knowingly exposes to the public, even in his own home or office, is not a subject of Fourth Amendment protection. . . . But what he seeks to preserve as private, even in an area accessible to the public, may be constitutionally protected."[8]

The *Katz* Court went on to reason that the reach of the Fourth Amendment's protections does not depend upon whether a physical intrusion takes place. A person's rights have more to do with whether he or she had reasonable *expectations of privacy* or, to put it another way, whether the privacy that the government violated was one upon which the citizen "justifiably relied."

The Court stated that what Katz "sought to exclude was not the intruding eye [the booth was glass]—it was the uninvited ear. . . . No less than an individual in a business office, in a friend's apartment, or in a taxicab, a person in a telephone booth may rely upon the protection of the Fourth Amendment."[9] The ruling, however, does not mean that all conversations are protected. Later in this chapter we deal with proper uses of electronic eavesdropping and undercover agents who may, in fact, be "bugged."

Katz made it clear that the Supreme Court of the United States would enforce a person's expectations of privacy if they were *reasonable*. This sounds simple enough to nonlegalists. But what is immediately obvious to the person with an awareness of the law is that in the interpretation of "reasonable" lies the key. Many criminal lawsuits have been won or lost because evidence was or was not excluded, depending upon whether the court thought that a person's expectations of privacy were reasonable or unreasonable. Some of the issues litigated have included whether people have a constitutionally protected expectation of privacy as to their garbage, their desks at work, acts in a public toilet stall, and return addresses on their incoming mail. The complexities are endless, and there are no simple "yes" or "no" answers as to whether any of the above is protected.

PROBABLE CAUSE

When we read the Fourth Amendment, we note the words "And no warrants shall issue, but upon probable cause, supported by oath or affirmation." Warrants generally are either for the arrest of a person, for the search of a place, or for the placement of authorized wiretaps. It is clear that no such warrants will be issued unless a sworn statement, or affidavit, sets out facts that constitute "probable cause," whatever that is. Many kinds of searches can be made without warrant if probable cause is present and circumstances either preclude the timely obtaining of a warrant or other extenuating factors are involved.

What It Has Come to Mean

Until around the time of the American Revolution, the English had established a tradition of using so-called open warrants, which did not even identify who was to be arrested. The responsibility was delegated entirely to the officer, who at that time was often a man of no learning whatsoever. This abuse was assailed in the courts in England just prior to the Revolution when Lord Mansfield held: "It is not fit, that the receiving or judging of the information should be left to the discretion of the officer. The magistrate ought to judge and give certain directions to the officer."[10] It has been said that one of the most important causes of the American Revolution was revolt against arbitrary searches and seizures made under color of law. And the authors of our Bill of Rights had the English abuses clearly in mind when they required that probable cause be presented on oath to an impartial magistrate.

The framers of the Fourth Amendment did not tell us what "probable cause" amounted to. Then-current English law spoke in terms of "probable cause to suspect," but later cases in this country required more than that. Most modern cases have required evidence of a quantity and quality to create "reasonable cause to believe" or "reasonable grounds to believe" that a certain person has committed a certain crime or that certain evidence is in the place to be searched. The present authors believe that a "more likely than not" standard is a good explanation of what probable cause really is.

Why It Is Important

If the defense in a criminal case desires to have evidence excluded, it will make a written motion to the court for a hearing. Such a hearing is known as a *suppression hearing,* and the issue of whether probable cause existed is the most frequently argued point, since probable cause is the most subjective and ill-defined standard. Some students—and law instructors—like to think of the required quantity of proof as a 51 percent probability. While that is an aid to thinking, it is of little help in evaluating a case where circumstantial evidence seems to be in conflict. The real, bottom-line test of whether probable cause existed in a particular case is whether the judge can be persuaded that it existed. Because few persons, including judges, have the wisdom of Solomon to guide them in evaluating such complexities, the losing party in a suppression hearing is often convinced that the court was in error.

SEARCHES WITH A WARRANT

An ordinary *search warrant* is nothing more than an order by a court of competent jurisdiction to a law enforcement agency to conduct a search. It is issued if the police officer or some other person satisfies the court, upon oath or affirmation—an affirmation is used rather than an oath for people who object, most commonly on religious grounds, to swearing an oath—that probable cause exists. This evidence is usually presented in the form of an *affidavit*; the person making the affidavit is known as an *affiant*. Sometimes the language sounds stilted: "Your affiant further says that . . . , etc." The affidavit and search warrant must meet all of the standards of the Fourth Amendment; that is, they must include particular—that means unambiguous—descriptions of places to be searched and be based on probable cause, sworn to by oath. The reason for the requirement of the oath is, of course, to ensure truthfulness. Such are the basic requirements for a warrant, but many other requirements have arisen to complicate matters.

Role of Confidential Informants

The landmark case of *Spinelli v. United States* involved a search warrant procured by the FBI that had two major defects.[11] The first was simple. The affidavit merely stated the conclusions of the agents and did not give the magistrate the facts upon which he could make his own decision as to whether there was probable cause. The Court ruled that the lack of such "underlying circumstances" was intolerable. The issuing magistrate must examine the logic and not rely upon the assessment of the officers. The second defect in the case had to do with the issue of probable cause:

in this case the probable cause had its origin in a person *other than the affiant,* a so-called *confidential informant* ("C.I.") whose identity was to remain secret from the defense. The Court said that the use of a C.I. would have been acceptable if the magistrate had been provided with the information that would have enabled him to decide on his own that the informant was reliable.

This requirement of underlying circumstances and proof of *reliability of the informant* constituted the so-called two-pronged test of *Spinelli.* Much verbiage was subsequently inserted into search warrant affidavits in order to meet that test until the Supreme Court reversed that holding in *Illinois v. Gates* in 1983.[12] As was explained in Chapter 1, the new standard is one of a *totality of the circumstances* and substitutes a standard of reasonableness for the rigid, separate, and independent requirements of *Spinelli.* In short, the recent case shifts the emphasis from a very technical due process approach to one based more on common sense and more in keeping with the Crime Control Model. It is clear that some evidence that was suppressible before the *Gates* decision might now very well be admitted at trial and lead to a conviction.

Specificity Requirements

The Fourth Amendment also requires that the search warrant "particularly describ[e] the place to be searched, and the . . .things to be seized." The issue of whether the place to be searched was or was not described adequately has been frequently litigated, and the cases generally provide a standard of sufficient description to lead the officer to that place and none other. Defects such as an incorrect street number have been held not to invalidate a warrant of otherwise sufficient particularity to describe the proper place to be searched and none other.

The things to be searched for and seized must also be described with specificity. In the case of bootleg whiskey or narcotics, the description can usually be in rather general terms. If stolen property is sought—property composed of otherwise lawful objects and not materials that are contraband by their very nature—a very detailed description is called for so that otherwise inoffensive property will not be mistakenly seized by the police. Such property must (or should) be described by serial number, distinguishing marks, or the like.

Electronic Eavesdropping

The Congress of the United States recognized in Title III of the crime control act of 1968 that criminals, especially organized criminals, use wire and oral communications extensively in the conduct of their crimes and conspiracies to commit crimes. Recognition of this fact was manifested when Congress provided a lawful way to seize such communications through the use of wiretaps and clandestine microphones. Title III sets out very specific guidelines for the use of wiretaps. No evidence obtained by these clandestine means will be admissible in a prosecution unless the requirements of Title III are met. Not only will the evidence be excluded, but the gatherers will be guilty of the crime of unlawful wiretapping or bugging if they are not in compliance. Title III allows the states to enact similar legislation, and many of the states have done so. The state statutes must be at least as restrictive as the federal.

Electronic eavesdropping can only be utilized for specific serious offenses, which are listed in the statute. The technique may only be resorted to whenever conventional means have been tried and failed, or when conventional means cannot be expected to succeed, or when excessive danger to the investigators is present.

This type of investigation requires a detailed, sworn application containing probable cause that communications of the type sought will be obtained—not an easy task. Unless a confidential informant overhears a defendant using the telephone such probable cause must normally be derived from circumstantial evidence. No other search-and-seizure procedure is as complex or technical. It is not uncommon for the documentation to fill from fifty to seventy-five pages of text.

The laws regulating such interceptions of communications require that the agents managing the wiretap or bugging device not listen to conversations other than of the type set out in the application and order. Conversations of a noncriminal nature must not be monitored, and if a wholly new type of crime is detected, the agents must seek permission of the court to listen to that type of conversation. Conversations that are "privileged" under the rules of evidence—such as attorney-client, clergy-parishioner, and the like—are also exempt from electronic eavesdropping. The entire concept of not listening to what is not criminal or proper to hear is called *minimization*. To properly "minimize" their electronic surveillance, investigators must flip their listening device on every few moments, listen to a few words or a sentence, and, if the conversation is still not pertinent, flip the device off. If the conversation has turned to matters under investigation, officers may begin listening and recording.

As a practical matter, it is often difficult to determine whether a particular conversation is criminal in nature because sophisticated criminals sometimes use prearranged codes. The authors are aware of one wiretap in which a rock concert promoter was heard to order narcotics as "board feet" of lumber presumably to be used as bleachers for concert-goers. The types of wood specified (oak, pine, etc.) actually referred to types of drugs being ordered. Without the testimony of informers who are participants, it is often impossible to break such a code.

A person who is the subject of a wiretap or is substantially monitored is required to be notified of the fact within ninety days of the completion of the interception. This provision was designed to ensure that persons subjected to such surveillance are always informed of the fact.

SEARCHES WITHOUT A WARRANT

The Supreme Court has repeatedly expressed its preference for searches by warrant and has even said that searches without warrant are per se unreasonable under the Fourth Amendment unless they fall within a few specific and fairly well delineated exceptions. The number of such exceptions to the need for a warrant has slowly grown in number and complexity, and we shall examine some of the most important.

Postarrest Searches

One exception is search incident to arrest. When an officer performs an arrest, he or she is allowed to search, without a search warrant, within an area where the arrestee might be able to reach out for a concealed weapon that might endanger the officer or where the arrestee might be able to hide or destroy evidence. The court has held that this type of search cannot extend beyond the area from within which the arrestee might gain possession of a weapon or destructible evidence and has suppressed evidence recovered from more distant areas—adjacent rooms and the like. The case of *Chimel v. California* provided this rule, which is sometimes referred to as the *immediate control rule*.[13] More will be said about *Chimel* in the next chapter.

Hot-Pursuit Searches

Another exception to the need for a warrant is known as the "hot-pursuit" exception and allows the search of a premises if "exigent circumstances" justify the entry into and search of a house in the hot pursuit of a fleeing criminal.[14] Such a search must be limited to finding the suspect and weapons that he or she might use against the officers.

Vehicular Searches

Automobiles and other movable vehicles may be searched under the warrantless search provisions laid down by the Supreme Court in *Carroll v. United States*.[15] The rule holds a search warrant unnecessary where there is probable cause to search an automobile stopped on the highway, the car is movable, the occupants are alerted to the police and their interest in the occupants, and the car's contents might never be found again if a warrant must be obtained. The Court's reasoning is that an immediate search of the vehicle is a lesser intrusion than a long detention to write a search warrant and obtain a judge's signature, and so an innocent party is able to continue more rapidly on the way.

The Plain-View Doctrine

The so-called *plain-view doctrine* allows seizure of contraband or evidence by an officer without a warrant if he or she is lawfully in a position to observe the evidence. In the execution of a search warrant, an officer can lawfully seize items not particularly described in the warrant if they are found in the course of a reasonable search. For example, an officer who, in the course of a detailed search of a dwelling for an ounce of heroin, looks inside a grand piano for the narcotic and discovers that the piano is stolen, can legally seize that piano. Conversely, the same officer, if equipped with a warrant for a stolen grand piano, cannot look inside the reservoir of a toilet and lawfully seize a packet of heroin.

Custodial Searches

Yet another exception to the necessity for a search warrant is found in *United States v. Robinson,* where the Supreme Court decided that police officers have a right to search an arrested person who has been taken into custody for objects as small as "a safety pin or razor blade."[16] The Court's reasoning was that a defendant who is to be transported and held in custody has some potential motivation to escape and might harm the custodial officer. This case leaves no doubt that custodially arrested persons may be very thoroughly searched, quite possibly including an examination of body cavities.

The "Stop-and-Frisk" Rule

A contrasting rule is found in the case of *Terry v. Ohio,* which established the so-called *stop-and-frisk* rule.[17] In *Terry* an experienced police officer noticed two men standing in a downtown area who appeared to be "casing" a potential stickup, but the officer had only "reasonable grounds" to believe that the suspects were armed and dangerous and had no "probable cause" to arrest. The *Terry* Court allowed a limited "patdown" of the suspects' outer clothing in the course of a reasonable search for weapons. The big difference between scope of allowable searches in *Terry* and in *Robinson* revolves around the theory that the "street encounter" in a stop-and-frisk case—where an officer is interested in determining if a suspicious person is indeed a lawbreaker—is less threatening to the person searched than a search associated with arrest. Thus the frisk is less likely to cause the suspect to resort to weapons not detectable in a pat-down. This pat-down is only authorized to protect the officer's safety and is not designed to be a search for evidence. If it is appropriately used and it just happens to yield evidential materials, those materials will not be suppressed at trial and can lead to conviction. A proper "Terry stop and frisk" can lead to the seizure of incriminating matter that in turn provides probable cause for arrest that will allow a detailed "Robinson search" of the person and a "Chimel search" of the area within the arrestee's immediate control, both of which could produce additional admissible evidence.

Secret Agents

A great many cases—including the most famous, *Osborn v. United States,* which involved Teamster boss Jimmy Hoffa—have held that the police may send a person to converse with a suspect so that evidence of incriminating conversations might be gathered.[18] This theory is not disturbed by the *Katz* decision that talked in terms of reliance upon justifiable expectations of privacy. The Supreme Court has held since *Katz* that "however strongly a defendant may trust an apparent colleague, his expectations in this respect are not protected by the Fourth Amendment when it turns out that the colleague is a government agent regularly communicating with the authorities."[19] Strong case law also exists to the effect that it does not matter whether the undercover agent is carrying electronic recording or transmitting devices because the conversation is freely given to the primary recipient, the agent. Whether the agent relates it from memory, from notes, or with electronic aids makes no difference.

Consent Searches

There is no doubt that a search conducted with the consent of the person who has standing to object to the search can produce evidence that is not suppressible. It is, however, the prosecutor's burden at trial to show that the consent was obtained freely and voluntarily and without coercion. Consent given by a third party is not valid unless the third party and the person against whom the evidence is to be used share access to the place searched. For example, if A and B share a house and each has a separate and exclusive bedroom, A can consent to the search of common rooms and A's own bedroom but not to B's exclusive bedroom.

SUMMARY AND CONCLUSION

This chapter has provided a brief survey of some principles that govern the collection of evidence. Prosecutors bear a heavy burden of proof to overcome the presumption of innocence, and that burden is made all the more difficult by the rules and principles of constitutional law that are intended to protect our liberties.

The exclusionary rule is of central concern, and its development is traced through key Supreme Court cases, including the one that introduced a very limited "good-faith" exception. Also reviewed are several limits to the protection of the Fourth Amendment, including the uses of electronic eavesdropping techniques. Searches without warrants, which are justified in certain situations, are also discussed.

The authors have attempted to present no more than an overview of some of the more commonly encountered pitfalls to collection and utilization of evidence. To do more would require a text devoted to the topic. The skilled investigator should be able to collect evidence that not only clearly demonstrates the suspect's guilt but is admissible in a court of law. When the evidence gathered reaches the quantity required to provide at least probable cause that the suspect did indeed commit the crime in question, it is time to evaluate the appropriateness of arrest. That is the purview of the next chapter.

QUESTIONS FOR DISCUSSION

1. Explain how the exclusionary rule was applied to state court proceedings. Discuss the rule's impact on state and local law enforcement tactics and training. Is the Due Process Model served too well by this rule, and do Crime Control values suffer excessively because of it?
2. How and why do *Leon* and *Sheppard* depart from the original rule? Can the good-faith exception lead to law enforcement abuse of citizens' rights under the Fourth Amendment?
3. While *Leon* and *Sheppard* apply to searches with warrants, can the new rule be adopted to searches without warrants? If so, how will this expansion of the new rule endanger citizens' due process rights?
4. Do you agree or disagree with the Supreme Court's ruling in the *Carroll* case, in which the Court authorized the warrantless search of movable vehicles? Why?
5. In this day of better-educated, more professional, and better-equipped police officers, do we still need the exclusionary rule? If not, what sanctions could be provided that would safeguard citizens against unreasonable searches and seizures?

NOTES

1. *Weeks v. United States,* 232 U.S. 383, 34 S. Ct. 341, 58 L. Ed. 652 (1914).
2. *Wolf v. Colorado,* 338 U.S. 25, 69 S. Ct. 1359, 93 L. Ed. 1782 (1949).

3. *Mapp v. Ohio,* 367 U.S. 643, 81 S. Ct. 1684, 6 L. Ed. 2d 1081 (1901).
4. *United States v. Leon,* 82 L. Ed. 2d 677 (1984).
5. *Massachusetts v. Sheppard,* 82 L. Ed. 2d 737 (1984).
6. *Burdeau v. McDowell,* 256 U.S. 465, 475, 41 S. Ct. 574, 576, 65 L. Ed. 1048, 1051 (1921).
7. *Katz v. United States,* 389 U.S. 347, 88 S. Ct. 507, 19 L. Ed. 2d 576 (1967).
8. Ibid.
9. Ibid.
10. *Leach v. Three of the King's Messengers,* 19 How. St. TR 1002 (1765).
11. *Spinelli v. United States,* 394 U.S. 410, 89 S. Ct. 584, 21 L. Ed. 2d 637 (1969).
12. *Illinois v. Gates,* 76 L. Ed. 527 (1983).
13. *Chimel v. California,* 395 U.S. 752, 89 S. Ct. 2034, 23 L. Ed. 2d 685 (1969).
14. *Warden v. Hayden,* 387 U.S. 294, 87 S. Ct. 1647, 18 L. Ed. 2d 782 (1967).
15. *Carroll v. United States,* 267 U.S. 132, 45 S. Ct. 280, 69 L. Ed. 543 (1924).
16. *United States v. Robinson,* 414 U.S. 218, 94 S. Ct. 467, 38 L. Ed. 2d 427 (1973).
17. *Terry v. Ohio,* 392 U.S. 1, 88 S. Ct. 1868, 20 L. Ed. 2d 889 (1968).
18. *Osborn v. United States,* 385 U.S. 323, 87 S. Ct. 429, 17 L. Ed. 2d 394 (1966).
19. *United States v. White,* 401 U.S. 745, 91 S. Ct. 1122, 28 L. Ed. 2d 453 (1971).

8

INITIATION OF
THE FORMAL PROCESS

After reading this chapter, students should be able to define and explain the importance of each of the following terms or phrases:

capias
booking
confessions
custodial interrogation
Miranda warning
lineup
initial, or first, appearance
bail

bond
bail bondsman
release on recognizance
summons, or notice to appear
station house release
field citations
preventive detention
habeas corpus

In this chapter we shall deal with the steps that constitute the initiation of the formal processing of a criminal case against a particular suspect. We cover here the procedures involved in arrest, booking, confessions, suspect identification, initial appearance, and the setting of bail or conditions for pretrial release.

ARREST

Arrest invokes the formal criminal process against a particular person. An arrest attracts the public interest and is the source of a great deal of criminal litigation.

The Nature of Arrest

It is generally agreed that an arrest takes place when a person is detained or held without that person's permission—that is, against his or her own will. A criminal arrest contains four distinct elements: (1) the intent of the law enforcement officer to make the arrest; (2) the officer's authority to make the arrest (either real or apparently real); (3) the restraint of the person arrested, either actual or constructive; and (4) the arrestee's realization that he or she has been arrested. A mere holding of a person against that person's will is not an arrest unless it is for the purpose of bringing him or her to the court or some other legal authority in a prosecution. Physical force is not required. The submission to authority, be it real authority or only apparent, is sufficient even if it is a peaceful submission, even if it is totally passive. The control can be by physical contact and overpowering of the arrestee, or it can be by the arrestee's acquiescence to the show of authority.

A particularly helpful definition of arrest is found in the *California State Penal Code* at Sections 834 to 834.2:

> An arrest is taking a person into custody, in a case and in the manner authorized by law. An arrest may be made by a peace officer or by a private person. . . .
> An arrest is made by an actual restraint of the person, or by submission to the custody of an officer. The person arrested may be subjected to such restraint as is reasonable for his arrest and detention.[1]

Court Orders for Arrest

Arrest Warrant   The warrant for arrest commands the seizure of a named (or otherwise described) person for the commission of a specified criminal act. The issuance of the arrest warrant is predicated upon the submission of sufficient sworn testimony in the form of an affidavit to the magistrate to convince the magistrate that probable cause exists. If the magistrate is satisfied, the warrant is issued.

You will note that the issuance of the warrant is in no way dependent upon the filing of formal charges by a prosecutor. Arrest warrants are normally obtained in most jurisdictions by a police officer or even an ordinary citizen making application to a magistrate of some sort. In those states that still have justices of the peace, even they, who perhaps have never seen the inside of a law library much less of a law school, may issue warrants for arrest.

This system of allowing citizens to apply for (or in the vernacular, to "swear out") a warrant has led to many abuses and unfounded arrests. It is not uncommon for cross warrants to be sworn out and issued in cases where two persons each make an affidavit that accuses the other of being the culprit and for the magistrate, without further investigation, to issue arrest warrants for both parties. The injustice of such unregulated warrants is obvious. The practice of issuing warrants upon citizens' complaints directly to magistrates is being sharply curtailed as judicial reform comes to more and more states.

Capias   Another type of court order for a person's arrest is the *capias*. The word "capias" is of Latin origin and translates as "that you take." A capias is issued when a grand jury returns an indictment or a prosecutor files an information against a person who is not in custody. The capias has the same practical result as the arrest warrant: They both order the police to take a person into custody and bring that person before the court.

Importance of Court Orders for Arrest   The Supreme Court of the United States has consistently shown a preference for arrest by warrant (here we include capias in the generic term "warrant") over warrantless arrest. The preference for the warrant stems from the fact that it is issued by a neutral and detached magistrate. The Court has contrasted that judicial objectivity with the zeal of the police officer who is at the same time in the business of ferreting out crime. As an example, in *Aguilar v. Texas,* the Supreme Court stated that probable cause with a warrant could be based on less persuasive evidence than probable cause without a warrant.[2] A prudent law enforcement officer should always seek a warrant if time allows, especially if the case is important.

The affidavit that underlies the warrant must provide the facts from which the magistrate can determine the presence of probable cause; the affidavit cannot provide merely the officer's conclusions as to whether the alleged perpetrator is guilty. The standards discussed in Chapter 6 in relation to the underlying facts and reliability of information to support search warrants apply equally to arrest warrants.

The probable cause that supports the capias is the probable cause that led the grand jury to indict or the prosecutor to file the information. The filing of these formal charges leads to an almost automatic issuance of the capias in a typical jurisdiction. This process will be discussed in detail in Chapter 9.

Probable Cause for Arrest

The validity of every arrest, whether made with a warrant, with a capias, or without a warrant, depends upon whether probable cause existed at the moment of arrest. This standard of probable cause is well defined in federal cases and must be at least as stringent in state courts. Issues other than probable cause arise in determining the validity of an arrest, but the presence or absence of this rather subjective degree of proof is the crux of most disputes involving arrest.

Whether there is probable cause for arrest is probably the most important legal question that street officers face. It is fortunate that one need not be a lawyer to understand probable cause. It is a commonsense rather than a technical legal concept.

From the discussion in Chapter 7, you will recall that the Fourth Amendment requires, but does not define, probable cause. Almost all cases make reference to "reasonable grounds to believe" or "reasonable cause to believe" that the particular person committed the specified criminal act. Even though most cases contain proof that is incapable of being quantified, a standard of "over 50 percent of probability" is helpful in analysis. This standard was discussed in connection with search and seizure in the previous chapter, and the definition is no different when applied to arrest.

Factors in a Lawful Arrest

Police administrators are painfully aware that a great proportion of lawsuits against police officers and their departments stem from arrests where inadequate probable cause existed at the time of arrest and/or excessive force was used and an injury or at least an alleged injury to the arrested person resulted.

Suppressible Evidence The most critical problem that arises from unlawful arrest is not the possibility of a civil suit but the fact that, under the exclusionary rule, evidence derived from such an arrest may be suppressed and made unavailable for use in the trial.

The time of arrest is usually one of great stress for the suspect, and more confessions are obtained at that time than any other. Not only does the stress of arrest induce testimony, but the defendant often has not yet obtained the usually persuasive advice of counsel to exercise his or her right to silence. Persons are often in possession of evidence at the time of their arrest or frequently say something that leads the officers to discover more evidence. All of this evidence will be withheld from the eyes and ears of the jury if the judge decides that the arrest was improper. This can be harmful or even fatal to the case, and a factually guilty defendant may well go free because of legal error on the part of the police.

Forcible Entry Different statutes in most states have modified English common law, which allowed peace officers to break into a building other than a dwelling in any manner necessary, but restricted breaking into a dwelling to "the breach of doors and windows." A 1980 Supreme Court case, *Payton v. New York,* resulted in a ruling that a forced entry into a person's home for the purpose of making a felony arrest may occur only if an arrest warrant has been issued or an emergency exists.[3] This overturned the old common law standard permitting forcible entry without a warrant into a suspect's home for purposes of arrest on felony charges. It can be argued that due process is better served with the intervention of judicial or prosecutorial authority evidenced by the requirement of a warrant. The interest of crime control would, however, seem to be as much jeopardized by this ruling as due process is served by it.

Virtually all jurisdictions require that the officers announce their presence and purpose and allow the occupants adequate time to voluntarily open the door prior to resorting to force to break in. Of course, this requirement can lead to a delay that provides the suspect an opportunity to dispose of evidence. Drug dealers are notorious for flushing drugs down the toilet to avoid conviction.

SEARCH AND SEIZURE DURING ARREST

The question of the scope of an officer's right to search the arrestee and the immediate surrounding in the process of arrest has been richly addressed by courts. The reason for this attention has been the fact that the arrest process often produces much evidence that defendants wish to exclude from the trial.

The question of just how thorough the search of an arrested person may be was answered by the Supreme Court in *United States v. Robinson,* where Robinson was lawfully arrested and the arresting officer conducted a detailed search of his person prior to placing him in the patrol car for a trip to the District of Columbia jail. The detailed search revealed the presence of fourteen gelatin capsules of heroin within a crumpled cigarette package in a coat pocket. Robinson was convicted for possession of heroin and appealed. Justice Rehnquist stated for the Court:

> It is well settled that a search incident to a lawful arrest is a traditional exception to the warrant requirement of the Fourth Amendment. This general exception has historically been formulated into two distinct propositions. The first is that a search may be made of the person of the arrestee by virtue of the lawful arrest. The second is that a search may be made of the area within the control of the arrestee.[4]

The Court went on to reason that a "full custody" arrest places the suspect in close proximity to the arresting officer for an extended period of time and that the arrested person may feed quite threatened by the serious restraint of liberty, factors that present a potential danger to the safety of the police. The opinion allows an officer to search for weapons as small as "a safety pin or razor blade." Obviously, such a ruling allows a very thoroughgoing search; the gelatin capsules in the Robinson case were a by-product of that search and therefore became admissible evidence.

The "Stop-and-Frisk" Rule

Arrest and its resultant authority to search must be distinguished from a process that bears some similarities: stop and frisk. As was revealed in Chapter 7, the Supreme Court of the United States in *Terry v. Ohio* recognized that a trained police officer might be faced with a situation in which he or she does not have probable cause for arrest but does have reasonable grounds to believe a suspect is armed and dangerous. In that situation, the law allows the officer to conduct a limited "pat-down" of outer clothing to reveal the presence of weapons which could endanger the officer while he or she is questioning the suspect.[5]

The search authority for stop and frisk is much more limited than the search authorized incident to custodial arrest. Stop and frisk is less threatening, in the opinion of the Supreme Court, in that the citizen has a shorter period of contact with the officer and the need for detailed search is less.

Search of Immediate Surroundings

In its opinion in *Chimel v. California,* the Supreme Court considered a case in which police arrested a man in his home and used the arrest as a reason to conduct a rather detailed warrantless search of the entire home. Evidence was found and used to convict Chimel, and an appeal was filed. The reasoning of the Court in response to the appeal is interesting:

> [W]hen an arrest is made, it is reasonable for the arresting officer to search the person arrested in order to remove any weapons that the latter might seek to use in order to resist arrest or effect his escape. Otherwise, the officer's safety might well be endangered, and the arrest itself frustrated. In addition, it is entirely reasonable for the arresting officer to search for and seize any evidence on the arrestee's person in order to prevent its concealment or destruction. And the area into which an arrestee might reach in order to grab a weapon or evidentiary items must, of course, be governed by a like rule. A gun on a table or in a drawer in front of one who is arrested can be as dangerous to the arresting officer as one concealed in the clothing of the person arrested. There is ample justification, therefore, for a search of the arrestee's person and the

area "within his immediate control"—construing that phrase to mean the area from within which he might gain possession of a weapon or destructible evidence.

There is no comparable justification, however, for routinely searching rooms other than that in which an arrest occurs—or, for that matter, for searching through all the desk drawers or other closed or concealed areas in that room itself. Such searches in the absence of well-recognized exceptions, may be made only under the authority of a search warrant. The "adherence to judicial processes" mandated by the Fourth Amendment requires no less.[6]

The Court thus overturned the conviction and ordered the trial court to suppress the evidence seized in this search.

BOOKING

Booking, in its most restrictive sense, is merely the making of an administrative record of arrest, and the term has its origin in the old bound book of arrests. Today the term usually means the entire processing of a new prisoner, including not only the making of records but the taking of photographs ("mug shots"), fingerprinting, detailed searches, bathing, and issue of inmate clothing. The booking process often includes lineups and interrogation; it should always allow the arrestee the time and the means to communicate with family and an attorney. In many jurisdictions the booking procedure is long and complex and must be performed by the arresting officer. Such a system actually works to discourage arrest because of the nuisance it presents to the officer. This is especially true in drunk-driving cases, where chemical and other sobriety tests are required at a great expense of time.

Well-administered departments attempt to minimize the officer downtime and inconvenience of the booking process. This allows more productivity by returning the officer to patrol or investigative duties and removes a factor that actually motivates the officer not to arrest. A system that provides for "notices to appear" as an alternative to custodial arrest is of considerable value in these regards. We will take up notices to appear later in this chapter.

The booking of a person who is arrested upon officer-determined probable cause—in other words, in the absence of an arrest warrant or capias—usually includes the preparation of a written formal accusation, called a *complaint,* that is filed with the magistrate. The complaint sets out, usually upon oath, the elements of the offense and typically is sworn to before a notary. The complaint is often prepared during booking.

CONFESSIONS AND POLICE INTERROGATIONS

Moving beyond the arrest and booking of a suspect, we now take up what happens after the suspect is in custody.

Importance of Confessions

It is an absolute fact that, even though Agatha Christie would have you believe otherwise, many criminal cases cannot be solved without a confession or an admission from the suspect. Even though forensic science has progressed greatly in recent times, the police still must be able to obtain self-incriminating statements if they are to solve very many cases and win at trial.

It is also a fact that the persons the police wish to interrogate are often uncooperative and must somehow be convinced to speak the truth. The suspect is often not only reluctant but also "streetwise" and hardened. Many suspects have been through the system before and are quite cool and calculating when confronted by an interrogator. These problems notwithstanding, a confession is often vital to conviction.

The *Miranda* Case

Prior to 1966 a confession was admissible in court in these United States if it was voluntary, that is, not coerced. This standard was met if the confession was obtained under circumstances that did not make the statement "probably untrue," a standard that varied widely from court to court, of course, depending on the attitudes and training (or lack thereof) of the lower court magistrate. A great many abuses took place because the standard gave the police little guidance and suppressed a few confessions except those resulting from "the third degree." It is clear that crime control values predominated during this period, and that due process values received minimum—if any—attention from most lower courts.

In 1966 the Supreme Court squarely faced the problem of continuing abuses, and Chief Justice Earl Warren delivered the Court's opinion in *Miranda v. Arizona*. This is a landmark case that brought due process values into sharp focus and required them to be applied and abided by at all levels. Any police officer in the United States should be able to explain the so-called Miranda rule.

The Court made its analysis of the problem and conceded that most interrogation is psychologically if not physically coercive. It reasoned that either type of stress could result in improperly obtained confessions. At issue was the Fifth Amendment provision: "No person . . . shall be compelled in any criminal case to be a witness against himself." The crux of the question presented by *Miranda* and every other confession case is just how much compulsion must be present in order to violate the Fifth. The *Miranda* Court, prior to summarizing its holding, held quite clearly that freely and voluntarily obtained statements are always going to be admissible:

The fundamental import of the privilege while an individual is in custody is not whether he is allowed to talk to the police without the benefit of warnings and counsel, but whether he can be interrogated. There is no requirement that police stop a person who enters a police station and states that he wishes to confess to a crime, or a person who calls the police to offer a confession or any other statement he desires to make. Volunteered statements of any kind are not barred by the Fifth Amendment and their admissibility is not affected by our holding today.[7]

Briefly, *Miranda* holds that when a person is taken into custody or otherwise deprived of his or her freedom in any significant way and is subjected to questioning—so-called *custodial interrogation*—that person must be advised of certain pertinent facts: (1) The person has a right to be and remain silent; (2) anything the person says can be used against him or her in a court of law; (3) the person has the right to the presence of an attorney; (4) if the person cannot afford counsel but desires one, an attorney will be appointed by the court prior to any questioning; and (5) the person has the opportunity to assert and exercise these rights at any time, even after the interrogation has begun.

The sanction applied for violation of the *Miranda rule* is, of course, the suppression of the confession and all the evidence gathered as a byproduct of the confession. You will note that this sanction may or may not relate to the reliability of the evidence gathered; it is simply a way of enforcing the self-incrimination protections of the Fifth Amendment.

The police, especially the old-timers, raised a great hue and cry at the *Miranda* decision, claiming that efficient law enforcement was forever injured. But a careful analysis after more than two decades of the rule shows us that the police have become more efficient and more fair. From time to time it is very frustrating to hear a guilty defendant assert the constitutional right to remain silent when no evidence, short of a hoped-for confession, will ever allow justice to be done, but in our society of law and balanced rights, a lesser standard would make all of us less free. Americans have a right to protection from excesses of interrogation inflicted upon them by police who may be overly anxious to solve a case in the absence of good evidence.

LINEUPS AND OTHER PRETRIAL IDENTIFICATION PROCEDURES

The so-called *lineup*, where a victim or a witness to a crime views a number of persons in an attempt to identify the perpetrator, is a long-established police procedure. It is a fairly accurate way to find out if a witness will be able to make an identification at a later date when it really matters, in the courtroom. A benefit to the suspect is also inherent in the process, that being the ability to show the prosecutor that identification is impossible and that further pretrial incarceration is not warranted. It is obvious, however, that a lineup can be conducted so as to be improperly suggestive and thus unfair to the suspect. An example would be a lineup in which a thin older suspect stands alone among several obese younger persons.

Legal Complications

An interesting body of case law has developed around some key questions: (1) What particular lineup procedures are prejudicial? (2) Is the absence of defense counsel prejudicial? (3) If it is prejudicial, does the procedure in question taint the identification itself or merely limit the testimony about the lineup identification at the trial?

In deciding pretrial identification cases, the Supreme Court has been careful to explain that standing in a lineup or having one's picture exhibited to a victim or witness has nothing to do with the Fifth Amendment privilege against having to testify against oneself. Being compelled to disclose information that one possesses by testimony is quite different from being compelled to exhibit physical characteristics. Requiring a robber to speak the words uttered during the robbery is not testimonial compulsion; it is merely an exhibition of the voice characteristics of a potential defendant so that a victim has the opportunity to make an identification.

The Right to Have Counsel Present

The Sixth Amendment to the Constitution provides in part: "In all criminal prosecutions, the accused shall . . . have the assistance of Counsel for his defense." In 1967 the Supreme Court in *United States v. Wade* addressed a case where a defendant complained that his right to counsel was violated insofar as he did not have a lawyer present during his appearance (and identification) at a lineup conducted after he was formally charged.[8] The Court noted that a lineup was a "critical stage" of a prosecution, and the presence of a defense lawyer, unless waived by the defendant, was necessary to protect the accused against a lineup that could be suggestive to the witness and "taint" later identification. The Court pointed out that mistaken identification would be fixed in the mind of the witness and could later lead to the same mistake of identity at trial.

Wade asked the court to disallow his subsequent courtroom identification because he did not have a lawyer at his lineup. The Court ruled that in such cases the prosecution should have an opportunity to establish "by clear and convincing evidence that the in-court identifications

were based upon observations of the suspect other than the line-up identification.'' The Court explained:

> Where, as here, the admissibility of evidence of the line-up identification itself
> is not involved, a per se rule of exclusion of courtroom identification would be
> unjustified. . . . A rule limited solely to the exclusion of testimony concerning
> identification at the line-up itself, without regard to admissibility of the court-
> room identification, would render the right to counsel an empty one. The line-
> up is most often used, as in the present case, to crystalize the witnesses' iden-
> tification of the defendant for future reference. We have already noted that the
> line-up identification will have that effect. The State may then rest upon the
> witnesses' unequivocal courtroom identification and not mention the pretrial
> identification as part of the State's case at trial.[9]

The *Wade* Court went on to suggest several factors to be considered in
determining whether the courtroom identification had an origin separate
from the lineup where counsel was denied. The factors include the prior
opportunity to observe the criminal act, the existence of any discrepancies between a pretrial description and the defendant's actual description, any identification prior to lineup by any other person, and the identification of photographs of the defendant prior to lineup. If the court is
satisfied that the lineup identification was independent, in-court identification is not excluded and only testimony as to lineup identification is
disallowed. If, of course, the court is not satisfied of the independent basis for identification, neither the in-court nor the lineup identification is
permitted, which can lead to the acquittal of the defendant.

It is a little difficult to define the role of defense counsel at a lineup.
Counsel is obviously there to spot factors that could unfairly point out
the defendant to the viewer. Is the accused the only man in handcuffs,
the only one in prison garb, the only Oriental, the only one not in a business suit? The factors that could cause improper identification are endless. The defense lawyer should register his or her objections prior to the
viewing. It is obvious that lineups cannot be made of perfectly homoge-
neous groups, but an honest effort to avoid singling out the defendant
should be made.

In 1972 the Court retreated slightly from *Wade* by announcing its holding in *Kirby v. Illinois*[10] *Kirby* involved a case where the victim of a robbery in Chicago viewed the defendant at the police station at a very early
stage in the proceedings, prior to the filing of formal charges by the prosecutor. No lawyer was present, and no right to a lawyer's presence was
explained to Kirby. The Court neatly distinguished between *Wade* and
Kirby, stating that in the former case that formal prosecutorial proceedings had commenced but not in the latter. The opinion in *Kirby* states
that preindictment lineups are not a ''critical stage'' of the prosecution

and that the presence of counsel is not essential. The opinion does, however, concede that such lineups could be improperly suggestive, which could lead to suppression of lineup identification testimony and even later in-court identification, depending upon whether the suggestibility was excessive and an independent source of identification existed.

To most readers the above discussion may seem so technical that it appears that the Supreme Court is engaged in semantic hairsplitting. It is important, however, to keep in mind that the Court is attempting to define the parameters of due process and to provide local and state authorities with guidance as to how the balance should be struck between the interests of crime control and the protection of the due process rights of those accused of crimes. The guidelines offered by the Court as to how to conduct a lineup are relatively clear. The matter of the precise role of defense attorneys at such lineups is, as has been pointed out, not as clear.

INITIAL, OR FIRST, APPEARANCE

Previously we discussed the role that magistrates in the criminal court may play in issuing warrants for arrest. Now we take up their postarrest role.

Every jurisdiction requires that an arrested person be brought before a magistrate within a short period of time after arrest. The time period is described in most states as "without undue delay" or "without unnecessary delay," and some states provide a specific time limit, but all states allow time for necessary booking procedures. Some states allow a delay after arrest of up to twenty-four to forty-eight hours, with extensions available for weekends or holidays.

The magistrate must do certain things at initial appearance. Typically, the magistrate ascertains that the person before the bench is indeed the person charged, reads or explains the charges, explains the defendant's rights to counsel and to silence, and reviews the bail amount.

In the case of *Gerstein v. Pugh,* the Supreme Court ruled that arrests based only upon the officer's probable cause determination must be reviewed by a neutral magistrate to determine if the Fourth Amendment's probable cause requirements have been met.[11] The court reads the sworn complaint to determine the presence of probable cause that the person before the court is the one who did indeed commit the crime charged. If the magistrate agrees with the officer, he or she enters a finding of probable cause for pretrial detention. This lengthens the period of time an accused may be detained without the filing of formal charges by the prosecutor or grand jury or the holding of a more formal preliminary hearing, a process which will be discussed later. If the magistrate disagrees and finds that probable cause is not present, he or she will often allow the police an extra day or so to produce more sworn facts. If no extra time is allowed of if the police still fail to convince the magistrate of probable cause, the defendant is released from custody without any prejudice to ultimate prosecution. Double jeopardy obviously does not come into play here because the ultimate question of guilt or innocence is not decided by the judge, just whether probable cause enough for pretrial detention exists in sworn statements. It should be noted that the proceedings involved at the initial appearance are not necessarily adversarial (involving opposing lawyers) in nature.

The requirement of rapid judicial review of probable cause imposed by the Supreme Court in *Gerstein v. Pugh* is designed as a protection against long periods of incarceration without neutral judicial review. Prior to that case, it was not uncommon in many jurisdictions for a person to be jailed for a long period of time on the say-so of a police officer, not always a neutral party.

Recall from previous discussion that lower court magistrates are occasionally not the cream of the judicial profession. Some are subject to various political or social pressures, and they are incapable of exercising independent judgment or authority in these preliminary steps in the criminal process. Some routinely rubber-stamp the actions of the police; others are inclined to agree with their associates in the defense bar regardless of the facts or the law. Suffice it to say that while neutrality and objectivity are the ideal, they are often missing at this stage of the proceedings.

PRETRIAL STATUS OF THE ACCUSED

If we are to honor the presumption of innocence that, at least in theory and procedure, cloaks every accused until he or she has either entered a plea of guilty or *nolo contendere* or has been found guilty, we must concede that arrest is primarily intended to make the accused available for trial. How, then, is this availability to be ensured?

Bail

The Eighth Amendment has three provisions, the first of which is that "excessive bail shall not be required." No clue as to what constitutes "excessive bail" is to be found anywhere in the document. The courts have helped at the appellate level, generally providing case law that requires bail in a sum that should ensure the defendant's arrival in court for trial. Capital crimes—those subject to the death penalty—are generally not bondable, but bail may be set in those cases in which the state's evidence is not clear.

Bail as a concept dates back to the Norman conquest of England. The first system was known as "frankpledges," where the entire community would be required to pledge its property as security for the appearance of one of its members who was accused of crime. This resulted in great pressure upon the accused to appear. While this system obviously long ago fell into disuse, its descendant—bail—is now in use almost everywhere.

The fairness of bail varies widely from jurisdiction to jurisdiction and, within jurisdictions, from judge to judge. Sometimes the amount set is scrupulously fair. It can, however, be grossly biased, depending upon the crime, the victim, the race or social station of the parties, and the personality and integrity of the judge or magistrate.

The federal government approached the problem of bail with the Bail Reform Act of 1966 that formally gave guidance to federal magistrates an judges as to how accused persons should be admitted to bail. Section 2 of the act states: "The purpose of this Act is to revise the practices relating to bail to assure that all persons, regardless of their financial status, shall not needlessly be detained pending their appearance to answer charges, to testify, or pending appeal, when detention serves neither the ends of justice nor the public interest." The act goes on to urge the judge to use conditions of release that "will reasonably assure the appearance of the person for trial." Means such as enlisting a person to supervise the accused, restricting travel and abode, posting cash or a surety *bond* are suggested. The court is directed to consider "the nature and circumstances of the offense charged, the weight of the evidence against the accused, the accused's family ties, employment, financial resources, character and mental condition, the length of his residence in the community, his record of convictions, and his record of appearance at court proceedings or of flight to avoid prosecution or failure to appear at court proceedings."[12] These standards provide guidance for the federal system; the state systems are guided by local rules and federal and state case law.

Bail has been frequently criticized as being inequitable since it favors those with financial resources over the poor. And the system has led to the appearance of a powerful figure, the *bail bondsman*. Looked down upon by some as being a parasite on the system, the bondsman makes his living by collecting a fee from the accused—usually 10 to 15 percent of the face amount of the bond—to put up the bail on his or her behalf. The bondsman guarantees payment to the government if the defendant fails to show and he, the bondsman, cannot produce the defendant within a reasonable time, usually six months. The practice seems plainly incorrect, making a person with roots sufficient to assure continued presence in the community post monetary bond or pay a nonreturnable fee to a bondsman

News of Note

LONG WAITS CITED ON ARRAIGNMENTS

DELAYS IN NEW YORK CITY CALLED ILLEGAL BY SOME OFFICIALS

By Philip Shenon

Thousands of people arrested in New York City are being held in custody for two days or more awaiting their first court hearings—a situation described by some officials as illegal and inhumane.

A series of Federal court rulings have held that the time between arrest and arraignment can be no longer than 24 hours. Under New York State law, a suspect must be taken into court for arraignment and a bail hearing "without unnecessary delay."

But in Manhattan and the Bronx, where the delays are worst, suspects, some of them teen-agers, are being detained an average of two days in hot, overcrowded, sometimes dangerous facilities.

Defense attorneys argue that the delay is unlawful imprisonment, since the defendants have not been convicted.

The delays, officials say, have grown particularly long in recent months. The chief reason: more arrests for serious crimes.

But it goes beyond that. Ultimately, the delays can be blamed on an antiquated arrest-to-arraignment process that has been likened to an assembly line with too many workers and too little supervision.

A survey of the city's five district attorney's offices indicates that suspects can expect to wait two days for arraignment in Manhattan and the Bronx, and 25 hours in Brooklyn. In Queens, the average wait is about 14 hours; in Staten Island, abut 10 hours.

At arraignment—the first court hearing for a case—suspects are formally notified of the charges against them and make a plea. A bail hearing is usually held during the arraignment.

Until then, suspects have almost no rights. Most will not be appointed a lawyer until they get into the courtroom. Between arrest and the bail hearing, they are usually allowed only one telephone call.

"The system is a complete nightmare," said Richard Emery, a staff counsel with the New York Civil Liberties Union. "People, many of them innocent, are needlessly being deprived of their liberty. They are being held in pens that are not only filthy and noisy, but also unsafe."

The New York Civil Liberties Union and the Legal Aid Society have threatened to take legal action to force the city to cut the backlog.

Rise in felony arrests blamed

Officials blame much of the recent delay on the increased number of felony arrests—the cases that are least likely to be thrown out before arraignment.

While misdemeanor arrests grew only slightly in the first five months of the year, the number of arrests for felonies rose by nearly 10 percent, to 48,000, from the same period last year.

In Manhattan, many of the arrests were made as part of Operation Pressure Point, the Police Department's campaign to curb drug trafficking on the Lower East Side. Those cases often require special handling, prosecutors say, since suspects accused of drug dealing tend to have lengthy criminal records.

Computer problems have also slowed arraignments: Before suspects are brought into a courtroom, information about their criminal records must be transmitted from computers in Albany, and recent technical breakdowns have sometimes delayed the data by several hours.

6 agencies handle each case

But those problems are only part of the procedure that follows the arrest of a suspect.

Each case must be handled by at least six criminal-justice agencies, and those agencies have often had difficulties in cooperating with one another.

Almost no one wants to defend the arrest-to-arraignment system. And most officials acknowledge that the blame for the delays must be shared—by the police, by prosecutors, by defense attorneys, by judges.

Prosecutors complain that many judges are slow in handling arraignments. Judges complain that defense attorneys take too much time interviewing clients. Defense attorneys complain that prosecutors pursue cases that should never have been brought to court.

"What's going on is atrocious," said the supervising judge of Manhattan Criminal Court, William J. Davis. "Everyone should be arraigned within a reasonable time, and a reasonable time is 24 hours."

"The system is like a machine with interconnecting parts," he said. "If one part goes out of whack, it tends to disturb the functioning of the rest of the machine. I think we can turn the system around, but it's going to take rethinking."

After being arrested, suspects are usually taken to a precinct station house, where preliminary arrest reports are filled out. They are then moved to a central booking office, where fingerprints are taken, evidence is logged and information about the crime is fed into a computer.

The delays begin early in the procedure, according to officials. And if one delay occurs, it tends to compound those that come later.

"It's like the price of a gallon of milk," said the Manhattan District Attorney, Robert M. Morgenthau. "When the wholesale price goes up a penny, the consumer ends up paying 10 cents more."

Among the main sources of delay are these:

• The central booking computer sometimes breaks down, which can hold up a defendant for hours.

• While the defendant is being processed, the arresting officer must travel to the district attorney's office to be interviewed about the case.

• The complaint rooms in the Bronx, Manhattan and Staten Island close at night. So in those boroughs, officers who make an arrest late at night must return to the complaint room the following morning.

• Suspects must be transported among central booking, the court and police precincts, and traffic congestion can hold up delivery. If they are held overnight, many defendants must be returned to a precinct cell to sleep.

• When defendants finally get to court, they must be interviewed by their attorneys, who usually work for the Legal Aid Society. The society is paid by the city to represent low-income people.

• There are sometimes too few Legal Aid lawyers in court.

Source: The New York Times, July 11, 1984.

if the cash cannot be raised. This is especially true if the person has dependents and the commitment to the bondsman reduces his or her ability to support them and retain counsel.

Alternatives to Bail

In recent years various alternatives to bail have gained wide usage in response to two factors: the aforementioned unfairness of bail and the overcrowding of jail facilities that is due largely, in most parts of the country, to the incarceration of persons not able to post bail or even to pay the bondsmen's fees.

Release on Recognizance   Release on personal recognizance involves a personal pledge to appear and is not a particularly new system for release. It is appropriate when a person's ties to the community are sufficient to justify releasing that person on his or her word. During the bail reform movement of the 1960s, studies showed that release on personal recognizance (usually referred to as "R.O.R") is a low-risk endeavor if the accused's background is checked for a number of factors. A prime factor to be considered is, of course, the likelihood that the defendant, if found guilty, would receive a substantial sentence. In the authors' jurisdiction, over one-third of the persons arrested are offered R.O.R., and that includes both persons who otherwise would have posted cash or surety bonds and those who would otherwise have had to remain in jail awaiting trial.

Supervised Release   Supervised release places the accused in the custody of another person or organization, including so-called half-way houses; this system is not used in too many jurisdictions. It is designed to take persons who are slightly greater "skip risks" than the ideal R.O.R. candidate and release them under circumstances that tend to ensure their return for court proceedings. These programs typically require the released person to make periodic reports to a counselor and to hold a job.

Release upon Summons or Notice to Appear   A large and growing number of jurisdictions have implemented systems that apply in misdemeanor situations and encourage an officer to evaluate factors that make a person very likely to appear in court. Under this system, if the factors are present to the officer's satisfaction, the offender is not arrested but is issued a *summons,* or *notice to appear,* which is analogous to a traffic ticket. This system is available only for persons who otherwise would be arrested for misdemeanors. Officers do not have the authority to release accused felons. Some jurisdictions require that the offender be first brought to the station and a *station house release* be then effected; others allow *field citations,* with release on the spot.

The Florida system that was reworked by the authors allows release by the officer on the scene or by the jailer after an examination of residency, employment, family, etc. Such a system keeps most local residents from having to post bond—a practice that more than anything else provides professional bondsmen their high profits—and keeps the police officer or deputy sheriff from having to leave the patrol zone to engage in the lengthy procedure of booking the defendant. It should be understood that bail reform, including all of the alternatives mentioned here, is attractive to law enforcement not only for altruistic reasons but for practical ones: Bail reform can help to ease the overcrowded conditions of our jails.

Preventive Detention In 1984 Congress passed yet another bail reform act, which, among other provisions, allows a federal court to detain an arrestee without bail pending trial; the object is to deny a dangerous arrestee access to potential witnesses or other victims and the opportunity to flee justice. This decision represents a clear departure from a due process approach of assuring the presence at trial and serves the Crime Control Model in a very practical way. In order to subject an arrestee to such detention, the judge is required to find that no conditions of release "will reasonably assure the appearance of the person as required and the safety of any other person and the community."

Some states have adopted similar legislation to provide for pretrial detention of dangerous arrestees. In the absence of such legislation, defense attorneys argue with considerable success that bail is for the purpose of assuring the presence of the accused in court and should not be denied on the grounds of the community's or an individual's safety.

Such a challenge was made against the federal Bail Reform Act of 1984 in a New York case involving two defendants charged with racketeering, fraud, extortion, gambling, and conspiracy to commit murder.[13] While several U.S. courts of appeals had upheld these provisions against similar challenges, the Second Circuit Court of Appeals had ruled that the provision was unconstitutional, and U.S. Attorney Rudolph Giuliani took the case to the Supreme Court for a definitive ruling. The Supreme Court ruled in May 1987 that the provisions were constitutional and were employed correctly in the case at hand. The justices split 6 to 3, with Chief Justice Rehnquist writing the majority opinion and Justice Thurgood Marshall writing the major dissenting opinion. Since these conflicting opinions so clearly represent the Crime Control and Due Process Models at work, excerpts are provided here for the reader's examination.

United States v. Salerno

95 L. Ed. 2d 697 (1987)

FROM THE OPINION

By Chief Justice Rehnquist

The Bail Reform Act of 1984 allows a Federal court to detain an arrestee pending trial if the Government demonstrates by clear and convincing evidence after an adversary hearing that no release conditions "will reasonably assure . . . the safety of any other person and the community." The United States Court of Appeals for the Second Circuit struck down this provision of the Act as facially unconstitutional, because, in that court's words, this type of pretrial detention violates "substantive due process." We granted certiorari because of a conflict among the Courts of Appeals regarding the validity of the Act. We hold that, as against the facial attack mounted by these respondents, the Act fully comports with constitutional requirements. We therefore reverse.

Responding to "the alarming problem of crimes committed by persons on release," Congress formulated the Bail Reform Act of 1984, as the solution to a bail crisis in the Federal courts. The Act represents the national legislature's considered response to numerous perceived deficiencies in the Federal bail process. By providing for sweeping changes in both the way Federal courts consider bail applications and the circumstances under which bail is granted, Congress hoped to "give the courts adequate authority to make release decisions that give appropriate recognition to the danger a person may pose to others if released."

To this end, the Act requires a judicial officer to determine whether an arrestee shall be detained. . . . If the judicial officer finds that no conditions of pretrial release can reasonably assure the safety of other persons and the community, he must state his findings of fact in writing, and support his conclusion with "clear and convincing evidence."

Detention Determination

The judicial officer is not given unbridled discretion in making the detention determination. Congress has specified the considerations relevant to that decision. These factors include the nature and seriousness of the charges, the substantiality of the Government's evidence against the arrestee, the arrestee's background and characteristics, and the nature and seriousness of the danger posed by the suspect's release. Should a judicial officer order detention, the detainee is entitled to expedited appellate review of the detention order. . . .

A facial challenge to a legislative Act is, of course, the most difficult challenge to mount successfully, since the challenger must establish that no set of circumstances exists under which the Act would be valid. The fact that the Bail Reform Act might operate unconstitutionally under some conceivable set of circumstances is insufficient to render it wholly invalid, since we have not recognized an "overbreadth" doctrine outside the limited context of the First Amendment. We think respondents have failed to shoulder their heavy burden to demonstrate that the Act is "facially" unconstitutional.

Respondents present two grounds for invalidating the Bail Reform Act's provisions permitting pretrial detention on the basis of future dangerousness. First, they rely upon the Court of Appeals' conclusion that the Act exceeds the limitations placed upon the Federal Government by the Due Process Clause of the Fifth Amendment. Second, they contend that the Act contravenes the Eighth Amendment's proscription against excessive bail. We treat these contentions in turn.

Due Process Clause

The Due Process Clause of the Fifth Amendment provides that "No person shall . . . be deprived of life, liberty, or property, without due process of law. . . . " This Court has held that the Due Process Clause protects individuals against two types of Government action. So-called "substantive due process" prevents the Government from engaging in conduct that "shocks the conscience," or interferes with rights "implicit in the concept of ordered liberty." When Government action depriving a person of life, liberty, or property survives substantive due process scrutiny, it must still be implemented in a fair manner. This requirement has traditionally been referred to as "procedural" due process.

Respondents first argue that the Act violates substantive due process because the pretrial detention it authorizes constitutes impermissible punishment before trial. The Government, however, has never argued that pretrial detention could be upheld if it were "punishment." . . .

As an initial matter, the mere fact that a person is detained does not inexorably lead to the conclusion that the Government has imposed punishment. . . . Unless Congress expressly intended to impose punitive restrictions, the punitive/regulatory distinctions turns on " 'whether an alternative purpose to which [the restriction] may rationally be connected is assignable for it, and whether it appears excessive in relation to the alternative purpose assigned [to it].' "

We conclude that the detention imposed by the Act falls on the regulatory side of the dichotomy. The legislative history of the Bail Reform Act clearly indicates that Congress did not formulate the pretrial detention provisions as punishment for dangerous individuals. Congress instead perceived pretrial detention as a potential solution to a pressing societal problem. There is no doubt that preventing danger to the community is a legitimate regulatory goal.

Bail Reform Act Limits

Nor are the incidents of pretrial detention excessive in relation to the regulatory goal Congress sought to achieve. The Bail Reform Act carefully limits the circumstances under which detention may be sought to the most serious of crimes. . . . The arrestee is entitled to a prompt detention hearing, and the maximum length of pretrial detention is limited by the stringent time limitations of the Speedy Trial Act. . . . We conclude, therefore, that the pretrial detention contemplated by the Bail Reform Act is regulatory in nature, and does not constitute punishment before trial in violation of the Due Process Clause. . . .

We have also held that the Government may detain mentally unstable individuals who present a danger to the public and dangerous defendants who become incompetent to stand trial. We have approved of postarrest regulatory detention of juveniles when they present a continuing danger to the community. Even competent adults may face substantial liberty restrictions as a result of the operation of our criminal justice system. If the police suspect an individual of a crime, they may arrest and hold him until a neutral magistrate determines whether probable cause exists. . . .

Respondents characterize all of these cases as exceptions to the "general rule" of substantive due process that the Government may not detain a person prior to a judgment of guilt in a criminal trial. Such a "general rule" may freely be conceded, but we think that these cases show a sufficient number of exceptions to the rule that the Congressional action challenged here can hardly be characterized as totally novel. Given the well-established authority of the Government, in special circumstances, to restrain individuals' liberty prior to or even without criminal trial and conviction, we think that the present statute providing for pretrial detention on the basis of dangerousness must be evaluated in precisely the same manner that we evaluated the laws in the cases discussed above.

. . .While the Government's general interest in preventing crime is compelling, even this interest is heightened when the Government musters convincing proof that the arrestee, already indicted or held to answer for a serious crime, presents a demonstrable danger to the community. Under these narrow circumstances, society's interest in crime prevention is at its greatest.

On the other side of the scale, of course, is the individual's strong interest in liberty. We do not minimize the importance and fundamental nature of this right. But, as our cases hold, this right may, in circumstances where the Government's interest is sufficiently weighty, be subordinated to the greater needs of society. We think that Congress's careful delineation of the circumstances under which detention will be permitted satisfies this standard. When the Government proves by clear and convincing evidence that an arrestee presents an identified and articulable threat to an individual or the community, we believe that, consistent with the Due Process Clause, a court may disable the arrestee from executing that threat. . . .

Respondents also contend that the Bail Reform Act violates the Excessive Bail Clause of the Eighth Amendment. . . .

The Eighth Amendment addresses pretrial release by providing merely that "Excessive bail shall not be required." This Clause, of course, says nothing about whether bail shall be available at all. Respondents nevertheless contend that this clause grants them a right to bail calculated solely upon considerations of flight. . . . In respondents' view, since the Bail Reform Act allows a court essentially to set bail at an infinite amount for reasons not related to the risk of flight, it violates the Excessive Bail Clause. Respondents concede that the right to bail they have discovered in the Eighth Amendment is not absolute. A court may, for example, refuse bail in capital cases. And, as the Court of Appeals noted and respondents admit, a court may refuse bail when the defendant presents a threat to the judicial process by intimidating witnesses. . . .

For even if we were to conclude that the Eighth Amendment imposes some substantive limitations on the national legislature's powers in this area, we would still hold that the Bail Reform Act is valid. Nothing in the text of the Bail Clause limits permissible Government considerations solely to questions of flight. The only arguable substantive limitation of the Bail Clause is that the Government's proposed conditions of release or detention not be "excessive" in light of the perceived evil. Of course, to determine whether the Government's response is excessive, we must compare that response against the interest the Government seeks to protect by means of that response. Thus, when the Government has admitted that its only interest is in preventing flight, bail must be set by a court at a sum designed to insure that goal, and no more. . . .

In our society liberty is the norm, and detention prior to trial or without trial is the carefully limited exception. We hold that the provisions for pretrial detention in the Bail Reform Act of 1984 fall within that carefully limited exception. The Act authorizes the detention prior to trial of arrestees charged with serious felonies who are found after an adversary hearing to pose a threat to the safety of individuals or to the community which no condition of release can dispel. The numerous procedural safeguards detailed above must attend this adversary hearing. We are unwilling to say that this Congressional determination, based as it is upon that primary concern of every government—a concern for the safety and indeed the lives of its citizens—on its face violates either the Due Process Clause of the Fifth Amendment or the Excessive Bail Clause of the Eighth Amendment.

The judgment of the Court of Appeals is therefore reversed.

FROM THE DISSENT

By Justice Marshall

This case brings before the Court for the first time a statute in which Congress declares that a person innocent of any crime may be jailed indefinitely, pending the trial of allegations which are legally presumed to be untrue, if the Government shows to the satisfaction of a judge that the accused is likely to commit crimes, unrelated to the pending charges, at any time in the future. Such statutes, consistent with the usages of tyranny and the excesses of what bitter experience teaches us to call the police state, have long been thought incompatible with the fundamental human rights protected by our Constitution. Today a majority of this Court holds otherwise. Its decision disregards basic principles of justice established centuries ago and enshrined beyond the reach of governmental interference in the Bill of Rights. . . .

The majority approaches respondents' challenge to the Act by dividing the discussion into two sections, one concerned with the substantive guarantees implicit in the Due Process Clause, and the other concerned with the protection afforded by the Excessive Bail Clause of the Eighth Amendment. This is a sterile formalism, which divides a unitary argument into two independent parts and then professes to demonstrate that the parts are individually inadequate.

On the due process side of this false dichotomy appears an argument concerning the distinction between regulatory and punitive legislation. The majority concludes that the Act is a regulatory rather than a punitive measure. The ease with which the conclusion is reached suggests the worthlessness of the achievement. . . . The majority finds that "Congress did not formulate the pretrial detention provisions as punishment for dangerous individuals," but instead was pursuing the "legitimate regulatory goal" of "preventing danger to the community." Concluding that pretrial detention is not an excessive solution to the problem of preventing danger to the community, the majority thus finds that no substantive element of the guarantee of due process invalidates the statute.

Hypothetical Case Offered

This argument does not demonstrate the conclusion it purports to justify. Let us apply the majority's reasoning to a similar, hypothetical case. After investigation, Congress determines (not unrealistically) that a large proportion of violent crime is perpetrated by persons who are unemployed. It also determines, equally reasonably, that much violent crime is committed at night. From amongst the panoply of "potential solutions," Congress chooses a statute which permits, after judicial proceedings, the imposition of a dusk-to-dawn curfew on anyone who is unemployed. Since this is not a measure enacted for the purpose of punishing the unemployed, and since the majority finds that preventing danger to the community is a legitimate regulatory goal, the curfew statue would, according to the majority's analysis, be a mere "regulatory" detention statute, entirely compatible with the substantive components of the Due Process Clause.

The absurdity of this conclusion arises, of course, from the majority's cramped concept of substantive due process. The majority proceeds as though the only substantive right protected by the Due Process Clause is a right to be free from punishment before conviction. The majority's technique for infringing this right is simple: merely redefine any measure which is claimed to be punishment as "regulation," and, magically, the Constitution no longer prohibits its imposition. Because the Due Process Clause protects other substantive rights which are infringed by this legislation, the majority's argument is merely an exercise in obfuscation.

Issue of Excessive Bail

The logic of the majority's Eighth Amendment analysis is equally unsatisfactory. The Eight Amendment, as the majority notes, states that "excessive bail shall not be required." The majority then declares, as if it were undeniable, that: "This Clause, of course, says nothing about whether bail shall be available at all." If excessive bail is imposed the defendant stays in jail. The same result is achieved if bail is denied altogether.

Whether the magistrate sets bail at $1 billion or refuses to set bail at all, the consequences are indistinguishable. It would be mere sophistry to suggest that the Eighth Amendment protects against the former decision, and not the latter. Indeed, such a result would lead to the conclusion that there was no need for Congress to pass a preventive detention measure of any kind; every Federal magistrate and district judge could simply refuse, despite the absence of any evidence of risk of flight or danger to the community, to set bail. This would be entirely constitutional, since, according to the majority, the Eighth Amendment "says nothing about whether bail shall be available at all." . . .

The essence of this case may be found, ironically enough, in a provision of the Act to which the majority does not refer. Title 18 U.S.C. Sec. 3142(j) provides that "nothing in this section shall be construed as modifying or limiting the presumption of innocence." But the very pith and purpose of this statute is an abhorrent limitation of the presumption of innocence. The majority's untenable conclusion that the present Act is constitutional arises from a specious denial of the role of the Bail Clause and the Due Process Clause in protecting the invaluable guarantee afforded by the presumption of innocence.

Presumption of Innocence

. . .Our society's belief, reinforced over the centuries, that all are innocent until the state has proved them to be guilty, like the companion principle that guilt must be proved beyond a reasonable doubt, is "implicit in the concept of ordered liberty," and is established beyond legislative contravention in the Due Process Clause.

The statute now before us declares that persons who have been indicted may be detained if a judicial officer finds clear and convincing evidence that they pose a danger to individuals or to the community. The statute does not authorize the Government to imprison anyone it has evidence is dangerous; indictment is necessary.

But let us suppose that a defendant is indicted and the Government shows by clear and convincing evidence that he is dangerous and should be detained pending a trial, at which trial the defendant is acquitted. May the Government continue to hold the defendant in detention based upon its showing that he is dangerous? The answer cannot be yes, for that would allow the Government to imprison someone for uncommitted crimes based upon "proof" not beyond a reasonable doubt. The result must therefore be that once the indictment has failed, detention cannot continue.

But our fundamental principles of justice declare that the defendant is as innocent on the day before his trial as he is on the morning after his acquittal. Under this statute an untried indictment somehow acts to permit a detention, based on other charges, which after an acquittal would be unconstitutional. The conclusion is inescapable that the indictment has been turned into evidence, if not that the defendant is guilty of the crime charged, then that left to his own devices he will soon be guilty of something else. . . .

Indictment and Consequences

To be sure, an indictment is not without legal consequences. It establishes that there is probable cause to believe that an offense was committed, and that the defendant committed it. Upon probable cause a warrant for the defendant's arrest may issue; a period of administrative detention may occur before the evidence of probable cause is presented to a neutral magistrate. . . .

The finding of probable cause conveys power to try, and the power to try imports of necessity the power to assure that the processes of justice will not be evaded or obstructed. . . . The detention purportedly authorized by this statute bears no relation to the Government's power to try charges supported by a finding of probable cause, and thus the interests it serves are outside the scope of interests which may be considered in weighing the excessiveness of bail under the Eighth Amendment. . . .

Honoring the presumption of innocence is often difficult; sometimes we must pay substantial social costs as a result of our commitment to the values we espouse. But at the end of the day the presumption of innocence protects the innocent; the shortcuts we take with those whom we believe to be guilty injure only those wrongfully accused and, ultimately, ourselves.

Throughout the world today there are men, women, and children interned indefinitely, awaiting trials which may never come or which may be a mockery of the word, because their governments believe them to be "dangerous." Our Constitution, whose construction began two centuries ago, can shelter us forever from the evils of such unchecked power. Over two hundred years it has slowly, through our efforts, grown more durable, more expansive, and more just. But it cannot protect us if we lack the courage, and the self-restraint, to protect ourselves. Today a majority of the Court applies itself to an ominous exercise in demolition. Theirs is truly a decision which will go forth without authority, and come back without respect. . . .

HABEAS CORPUS

Habeas corpus is treated here because it is a means of securing the release of a person who is unlawfully restrained. Because it is a means of obtaining release from custody, it is placed after our treatment of bail, but do not think that it is in any way similar to the other techniques for obtaining release for incarcerated persons. Habeas corpus is a unique process and only the end product, release from confinement, is in any way comparable with release on bond, release on recognizance, and the other methods typically used for pretrial release.

Definition of Habeas Corpus

Habeas corpus is an ancient common law writ that is designed to effect a speedy release of persons who are *illegally* deprived of their liberty or *illegally* detained in the custody of a person who is not entitled to exercise custody over them. *Habeas corpus* is a Latin term meaning "you have the body." Habeas, as it is sometimes called, is the most effective method of securing the release of a person who is unlawfully jailed. It is not designed to inquire into the ultimate merits of the charge against a person; its sole purpose is to determine if the detention is legal. If the detention is found to be illegal, habeas results in release of the person from custody.

Applications of Habeas Corpus

The writ of habeas corpus is not a lawsuit or action in the normal sense; it is what is known as a *summary remedy*. It is normally used to attempt to effect the release of a person accused of crime, but it is sometimes used for persons committed to mental hospitals or jailed for contempt, which, in a strict sense, is not a crime. Even though it typically is used for criminal cases, it is a civil, not a criminal, action.

In order for a habeas corpus action to even be considered by the court, there must be an actual deprivation of liberty. If a person is out on bond, habeas is not a proper remedy. The restraint in criminal cases is ordinarily jail but can be other types of restraint upon the person's liberty to come and go where and when he or she pleases. A notice to appear does not deprive one of the sort of liberty that habeas corpus is designed to protect.

Generally the writ is limited in its application and should not be granted where relief could be procured by the use of a more ordinary remedy—such as a motion for release upon recognizance, or a motion for bond reduction, or an appeal—unless the judgment or process under which the prisoner is being held is totally invalid. Nor should habeas be used where the defendant is merely asserting that the charge does not constitute a crime; in that case the defendant should instead attempt to quash the information or indictment rather than seek habeas.

Use in Extradition Habeas corpus is frequently used in extradition matters. In order for an extradition to be lawful, certain jurisdictional rules must be scrupulously followed, and habeas corpus is an ideal means to challenge basic jurisdictional matters. Four basic issues are often challenged in habeas actions for interstate extradition of prisoners: (1) whether the prisoner is the identical person wanted by the demanding state, (2) whether the governor of the demanding state has certified that the indictment or information is authentic, (3), whether the prisoner is a fugitive from justice, and (4) whether the prisoner is substantially charged by information or indictment with a crime in the demanding state. The reader will note that whether the petitioner who objects to extradition is guilty is not a matter for habeas corpus to address. That issue can only properly be addressed by a trial on the merits of the case once the prisoner is returned to the demanding state.

Use by Prison Inmates Many convicted state prisoners serving time in state penitentiaries resort to the federal courts for habeas corpus. These courts will hear such petitions only if the petitioner has exhausted all remedies in state courts.[14] And a federal judge will only free a prisoner when he or she determines that the case is one of exceptional circumstances of peculiar urgency involving the violation of rights granted by the Constitution, laws, or treaties of the United States. This resort to federal habeas is so popular in Florida that a courtroom has been set up at the state prison near Starke so that the federal judge can hear the petitions within the prison rather than have the prisoners travel en masse by bus to distant Jacksonville.

Prisoners often prepare their own petitions for the writ of habeas corpus and in the not-too-distant past often used any sort of paper available, such as the back of an unrelated piece of printed matter. Nowadays many prisons have prison lawyer projects that enable inmates to be represented at habeas corpus proceedings, and some institutions without such projects have preprinted or mimeographed fill-in-the-blank petitions for habeas corpus. Suffice it to say that most such petitions are denied because they have no merit at all. But it is difficult to fault a prisoner who has exhausted all other remedies for at least going through the drill of petitioning for federal habeas.

Comment

DON'T SUBVERT HABEUS CORPUS

By Judd Burstein

The Senate and House Judiciary Committees are considering legislation, sent to Capitol Hill by the Reagan Administration, that seeks to reform habeus corpus procedures. In reality, it would radically curtail the right to petition the Federal courts for a writ of habeas corpus. The prospect of such a law's being enacted is profoundly disturbing, for it would devalue vital constitutional protections.

The importance of the writ of habeas corpus can hardly be overemphasized. Its literal translation, from the Latin, is, "You have the body," and originally in English common law it was used to command a jailer to produce a prisoner for a court appearance. Today, convicts in state prisons use it to ask Federal courts to deliver their bodies from what they insist is unlawful incarceration. When a prisoner contends that he has been unconstitutionally convicted in a state court and that his state's appellate courts have refused to redress the claimed wrong, his only remedy is a Federal habeas corpus petition.

If the Reagan Administration's proposal is enacted into law, though, the availability of habeas corpus relief will be severely limited. Federal courts will be barred from hearing habeas corpus cases if a prisoner does not complain of a constitutional violation within one year after all state appeals have failed or if he has unsuccessfully litigated his claim in his state court.

Such limitations will prevent the writ of habeas corpus from fulfilling its most important purpose: giving the Federal courts an opportunity to ensure that the Constitution is uniformly applied throughout the United States.

In the case of Irvin v. Dowd, in 1961, for example, the Indiana courts saw nothing wrong with forcing a murder defendant to be tried, convicted, and sentenced to death by a jury with eight members who, before the trial began, thought the defendant was guilty. If Leslie Irvin had not filed a habeas corpus petition, the United States Supreme Court could not have ruled that the Constitution will not permit trial by such partisan juries Yet, the Reagan Administration's proposed legislation would have required the Federal court to dismiss Mr. Dowd's habeas corpus petition because his claim already had been rejected by the Indiana courts. This would have been a particularly odious result because, although convicted at his second trial, Mr. Dowd's initial death sentence was reduced by the second jury to one of life imprisonment.

Attorney General William French Smith, speaking in January at a conference on the administration of justice, attempted to justify this remarkable dilution of constitutional protections by pointing to the inconvenience caused by a supposed "flood" of habeas corpus petitions. Yet, in the year ended in June 1981, the almost 600 Federal District Court judges were faced with only about 7,800 habeus corpus petitions. On the average, each had to decide just 13 petitions. This seems more like a trickle than a flood.

Most important, though, is that inconvenience to the court system is not a legitimate justification for drastically limiting the availability of habeas corpus relief.

Constitutional rights, by their very nature, are inconvenient. They stand as a buffer between the state and the citizen, assuring the citizen of fair prosecution. Undoubtedly, life for the judges and court aides would be easier if they did not have to be so concerned about a defendant's constitutional rights. Indeed, it is true that most habeas corpus petitions are without merit, for most state prisoners have received fair treatment. But what of those relatively few prisoners—the Leslie Irvins—whose rights are grievously violated? Do we allow them to slip through the cracks of the justice system? Can we justify, for example, a refusal to overturn a conviction based upon prosecutorial pandering to racial prejudice simply because a state court already has rejected an appeal or because the defendant, perhaps through ignorance, did not present his constitutional claim to the Federal courts until a year and day after it had been rejected by the state court? Does the passage of time or an erroneous decision by a state court make this violation of the right to due process any more tolerable?

It is fairness, not convenience, that is the hallmark of our judicial system. Since the enactment, in 1868, of the 14th Amendment, which prohibits the state from depriving anyone of due process of law, there has existed, at least in principle, a commitment to ensure that all criminal trials are conducted in the manner prescribed by the Constitution.

The Reagan Administration's plan reneges upon this commitment by exalting the virtue of efficiency over that of fairness. This result would be unconscionable, one that would convert the reality of a constitutional system of justice into an illusion.

Judd Burstein is a lawyer who specializes in criminal defense.

Source: The New York Times, March 30, 1982.

Comment

LETTERS

HALT THE ABUSE OF HABEAS CORPUS UNLIMITED

To the Editor:

A recent Op-Ed article by Judd Burstein [March 30] described pending Congressional reform of habeas corpus procedures as "radical" and suggested the legislation would devalue constitutional protections. Permit me to offer your readers a legal analysis of the bill, which Mr. Burstein was either unqualified to give or chose not to so as to avoid weakening his premise.

The legislation in question was proposed by the Department of Justice in an effort to end gross abuses of the writ of habeas corpus, abuses which have stalled finality of judgment, undermined the integrity of state court judgments and destroyed public confidence in the criminal-justice system.

Mr. Burstein says the legislation will prevent Federal courts from reviewing state court judgments to be sure the Constitution is being faithfully applied. This, of course, is the central issue in the debate between those who seek to curtail the recent trend of Federal district and circuit courts to second-guess juries, state trial judges and, in many instances, state supreme courts, and those who want an unlimited number of courts to which they can appeal, in the hope that they may find one that will ultimately agree with their position.

The bill would limit Federal review to questions of fundamental unfairness. Under these circumstances, a Federal court could always make a determination of the issue of fairness or rights violations without regard to a state court's conclusion. I believe that "fairness" requires nothing more to be accorded to any individual.

The unspoken premise of Mr. Burstein's position is that state courts cannot be trusted to protect the constitu-tional rights of persons accused of criminal acts. I reject this suspicion as unfounded, and the U.S. Supreme Court has also repeatedly rejected such a contention. As the Court said in Powell v. Stone in 1976, state court judges are obligated to safeguard personal liberties and are as competent as Federal district judges to decide Federal constitutional claims.

Mr. Burstein listed Irvin v. Dowd as an example of the need for broad habeas corpus powers in the district courts. Under the fairness standard in the bill, the Dowd case *could* have been reviewed by a Federal court by petition for habeas corpus. Moreover, even with passage of the bill every defendant can still seek review of his conviction by petitioning for certiorari review to the U.S. Supreme Court.

In the last seven years, the Supreme Court has reviewed three Florida cases involving alleged denial of fair trial because of adverse pretrial publicity. In each case, the judgment of the Florida Supreme Court was upheld, and Irvin v. Dowd was found not applicable.

Mr. Burstein's description of the bill as "radical" indicates a bias toward allowing a case to be forever appealed and re-appealed, even though the state may be unable, because of the passage of time, faded memories and missing witnesses, to retry the defendant.

Moreover, the Constitution and our courts require a defendant be given a speedy trial *because* memories fade, witnesses die or disappear and it may become impossible for the accused to present a defense. The people, as represented by the prosecution, have the same right to a speedy trial.

Legislation similar to that now pending, which I proposed in 1980, was endorsed by the National Association of Attorneys General, the Conference of Chief Justices, the National Governors' Association and the United States Attorney General's Task Force on Violent Crime. It is ridiculous to suggest that these groups would collectively endorse any "radical" legislation.

The attempt to label the legislation a Reagan Administration effort to renege on our commitment to a constitutional system of justice is clearly political rhetoric designed to defeat a bill that enjoys bipartisan support.

Jim Smith
Attorney General of Florida
Tallahassee, Fla., April 15, 1982

Source: *The New York Times*, April 25, 1982.

SUMMARY AND CONCLUSION

In this chapter we have examined the formal procedures that initiate the criminal process. We have explained and examined problems associated with arrest, booking, interrogations, lineups and other identification procedures, initial appearances, and the establishment of conditions that are supposed to ensure the appearance of the accused.

It must be obvious that considerable discretion is involved in each of these steps. Police officers are given ambiguous guidance by courts in how to exercise their powers of arrest and arrest-related searches. The conduct of interrogations and lineups is a matter of increasing court scrutiny, but investigators still exercise their own judgment in instituting these procedures. Magistrates or judges in lower courts have considerable leeway in deciding whether to issue warrants, whether an arrest has met probable cause standards, and what bail or other conditions to place on the pretrial release of an accused person.

If police and judges enjoy considerable discretion and authority over suspects, prosecutors enjoy even more. In our next chapter we consider the role of the prosecutor in the filing of formal charges against the accused.

QUESTIONS FOR DISCUSSION

1. Describe the quality of evidence required for a valid arrest.
2. Miranda rights attach only when two conditions or factors are present. Explain them and discuss the potential gray areas of each one.
3. Edwin Meese, U.S. attorney general under Ronald Reagan, proposed the outright abolition of the Miranda rule. Discuss this proposition from the standpoint of Packer's Due Process Model and his Crime Control Model. In your view, would the abolition of the Miranda rule make a significant contribution to the crime control process?

4. Under common law, only one goal, the assurance of the defendant's presence at trial, was theoretically served by setting bail. Under the federal bail laws, a second major goal was approved. Discuss this second purpose for bail in terms of due process versus crime control values.

5. Arguments about the bail bond system include its reputed economic discrimination against the poor. It can be argued, on the other hand, that the truly indigent really have nothing to lose and that the real discrimination is against those with at least some property and/or income. Discuss. How would you change the system to promote fairness and, at the same time, assure that all those not detained return for trial?

NOTES

1. *California State Penal Code*, Section 834.
2. *Aguilar v. Texas*, 378 U.S. 02 (1964).
3. *Payton v. New York*, 445. U.S. 573 (1980).
4. *United States v. Robinson*, 414 U.S. 218, 94 S. Ct. 467, 38 L. Ed. 2d 427 (1973).
5. *Terry v. Ohio*, 392 U.S. 1, 88 S. Ct. 1868, 20 L. Ed. 2d 889 (1968).
6. *Chimel v. California*, 395 U.S. 752, 89 S. Ct. 2034, 23 L. Ed. 2d 685 (1969).
7. *Miranda v. Arizona*, 348 U.S. 436, 86 S. Ct. 1602, 16 L. Ed. 2d 694 (1966).
8. *United States v. Wade*, 388 U.S. 218, 87 S. Ct. 1926, 18 L. Ed. 2d 1149 (1967).
9. Ibid.
10. *Kirby v. Illinois*, 406 U.S. 682, 92 S. Ct. 1877, 32 L. Ed. 2d 411 (1972).
11. *Gerstein v. Pugh*, 414 U.S. 1062, 94 S. Ct. 567, 38 L. Ed. 2d 467 (1973).
12. Pub. Law 89-465, 89th Cong. S. 1357, 80 Stat. 214.
13. *U.S. v. Salerno*, 95 L. Ed. 2d 697 (1987).
14. *Mooney v. Holohan*, 79 L. Ed. 179 (1934).

CHAPTER 9

INITIATION OF
FORMAL PROSECUTION

After reading this chapter, students should be able to define and explain the importance of each of the following terms or phrases:

discretion	preliminary hearing
screening	bindover decision
information	legal sufficiency standard
in-custody cases	system efficiency standard
PROMIS	overcharging
grand jury	defendant rehabilitation standard
indictment	diversionary programs
transactional immunity	trial sufficiency standard
use immunity	

THE POWER OF THE PROSECUTOR

Many laypeople are surprised to learn that prosecutors are the most powerful officials in the criminal justice system; their power lies in the exercise of their almost unbridled discretion to file or not file criminal charges.

Discretion in Charging

Under common law and through generations of practice, the only legal limit on the prosecutor's decision-making authority is the maximum charge possible under the criminal statutes that fit the acts the accused is alleged to have committed. The prosecutor, however, is under no legal compulsion to bring the highest charge possible. In fact, prosecutors are under no legal compulsion to level any charge at all, and their decision to charge or not charge an accused is not reviewable by any other legal authority. Prosecutors do not formally answer to the courts on this matter; they answer directly only to the electorate who placed them in office.

The decision to charge is based on a combination of a variety of factors. These factors and the process that results in criminal charges will be examined in this chapter.

Central Position in the System

Another aspect of the prosecutor's role that adds to the power of the office is the fact that the prosecutor occupies a central position in the criminal justice system, being placed squarely between the law enforcement or police agencies and the trial courts. Prosecutors deal directly on a day-to-day basis with police officers, defense attorneys, and judges. The district attorney or state attorney is usually referred to—often by statute—as the "chief law enforcement officer" in the jurisdiction; on the other hand, the prosecutor is also an "officer of the court."

Prosecutors may also have direct dealings with corrections programs and officials, especially if their offices are involved in programs that "divert" some offenders from formal prosecution and adjudication into treatment programs operated by these officials. Prosecutors also become involved in probation revocation hearings and are sometimes called upon to give statements to parole boards about whether a prisoner ought to be paroled or a parole violator ought to be returned to prison. In fact, prosecutors often use probation or parole revocations as a means of putting "bad guys" away in lieu of prosecuting them on their new offense.

As we have previously made clear, no other office or agency plays such a crucial and central role in the system as a whole. There is no better vantage point from which to observe and study the entire criminal process than a prosecutor's office.

THE INTAKE FUNCTION

Our attention will now be turned toward the process that results in criminal charges being filed—or not filed—with the trial courts.

Screening of Cases

The examination of cases and the decision as to what, if anything, should be done with the defendant within the criminal legal system (or, in some cases, within alternative nonadjudicative systems) is known as the *screening*, or *intake*, function, and that function is the prosecutor's clearest exercise of power. The prosecutor has the power, sometimes in conjunction with a grand jury, to initiate a criminal lawsuit known as *prosecution*, not to initiate one, or to divert the wrongdoer into an alternative program that may avert the necessity of a prosecution. To initiate the case directly, without involvement of a grand jury, the prosecutor files a charging document known as an *information*.

Cases come to the prosecutor's attention in one of two forms: those in which a suspect has already been arrested and booked—*in-custody cases*—and those in which no arrest has as yet been made—*at-large cases*.

In-Custody Cases   Most arrests are warrantless and are based on an officer's decision as to whether there is probable cause to arrest. This process places the initial decision to invoke the criminal process squarely in the hands of the police. The prosecutor usually becomes aware of the case at the time of the initial appearance of the accused. At this state in the proceedings, the prosecutor generally has a copy of the officer's complaint and little else; the practice then is to wait a few days, hoping to receive a more thorough police report on which to weigh the facts of the case. The prosecutor will also, with luck, receive criminal history information on the defendant that will enable him or her to make a more reasoned choice among the alternative dispositions for the case.

The mere fact that a police officer makes a decision to arrest a person and proceeds to make that arrest without the intervention of a prosecutor or a judge puts the prosecutor in a different posture than if he or she is consulted first. It is fairly easy for a prosecutor to decline to prosecute a case if the police have not yet made an arrest, but if the police initiate the case through arrest, the prosecutor then assumes a higher profile if he or she chooses to dismiss the case or refuses to make a charge after the "brave and public-spirited" police officer has already taken action. Some officers use this fact to good advantage and make direct arrests in those cases that they consider to be marginal but wish to see prosecuted. Prosecutors will refrain from declining a close case more often if it has been preceded by an arrest. The act of the officer leading off with an arrest puts the onus on the prosecutor to be equally and appropriately aggressive in upholding the law.

At-Large Cases   Typically, the case in which the defendant is not already in custody places less pressure on the prosecutor to initiate prosecution. He or she is not then faced with the situation of having to accuse a police officer of a bad arrest, which is implied in a decision that releases a defendant already preliminarily labeled by the police as factually guilty. In at-large cases the decision not to prosecute does not place the prosecutor in such obvious opposition to the police.

When the police come to the prosecutor prior to arresting the defendant, the case quality is often improved. The prosecutor, having legal training and experience with juries, and with detachment from the investigation, is often able to point out deficiencies in the investigation that still can be remedied prior to arrest. The prosecutor can also urge the police not to arrest prematurely.

Many states have speedy-trial rules that require a defendant to be brought to trial within a specific time limit or the case is lost. Premature arrest will start these time limits running, and sometimes the result is a loss in a case that could have been won if it had been properly developed prior to arrest. In the authors' jurisdiction, cases as old as seven years have been won when evidence has finally been developed that was not available at the moment that probable cause ripened out of mere suspicion. Officers must sometimes be reminded that no case is "closed by arrest" and that the standard of proof for trial is not probable cause, which is the arrest standard, but proof beyond a reasonable doubt. Skilled police officers, if they have faith in their prosecutor, will often consult with him or her during the earliest stages of an investigation and follow the advice given. In this role then, the prosecutor functions at least in part as a police executive.

Factors Affecting the Decision to Charge

The weight of the evidence against the accused is not the only factor prosecutors consider when deciding whether to file or seek formal charges against persons. There are a number of considerations that must be taken into account.

Record or "Criminality" of Accused   Statutes generally do not distinguish very well between a crime committed by a young first offender who is influenced by peer pressure and who is unlikely to recidivate, or commit further crimes, and the very same crime perpetrated by a hardened criminal. Statutes define the elements that constitute an offense but do not deal with the source or nature of the criminal conduct. The attachment of a criminal status to the first offender above may label him or her in such a way as to practically ensure recidivism, whereas the imposition of criminal sanctions in the second case may be absolutely necessary to isolate the offender from future potential victims. Some discretion in the decision to impose the criminal code must be exercised, and it is the prosecutor who, in law and in practice, is the person who makes these decisions.

Potential Harm of Prosecution to the Accused   The mere invocation of the criminal process, whether the case is ultimately won or lost, is often destructive of the individual and of his or her chances to continue functioning in society. If the person charged is already suffering from social, educational, or vocational disadvantages, then the initiation of prosecution can be the catalyst of final social failure. The invocation of the process is exceedingly serious.

Character, Role, or Reliability of the Victim   Sometimes the prosecutor is faced with a case in which the complaining victim is at least morally if not legally as blameworthy as the accused. Not only might the prosecutor be unimpressed with the victim's cause, so too, the prosecutor reasons, might a jury. It is generally held, for example, that a prostitute makes a poor complainant as a victim in a case of rape. Juries have been known to acquit habitually battered wives who maimed or even murdered their abusive husbands, even where the evidence is clear that the attack was premeditated and carried out when the victim was asleep or otherwise incapable of defending himself.

Another related problem is that of the victim who is likely to change or has changed his or her story (battered wives all too often fit this category) or is unavailable to testify, as is often the case with migrant workers, tourists, and vagrants.

Availability of Alternatives to Prosecution (Diversion)   The prosecutor may decide to utilize nonjudicial means to deal with certain types of offenses committed by certain types of offenders. For example, a minor property crime by a first offender looking for money to support a drug habit might result in the offender's being offered the choice to engage in a drug rehabilitation program or be prosecuted. Rehabilitative programs, if well administered, can provide a lower rate of recidivism at lower cost than traditional disposition through the courts. Some prosecutor's offices attempt these remedies on an informal basis in communities without any structured program, typically by requiring the offender to enter into a contract with the prosecutor whereby the offender agrees to refrain from unlawful conduct for a period of time, or else be prosecuted. Such unstructured programs may not have the success rate of structured programs but are virtually cost-free and sometimes can yield results much closer to justice than would otherwise occur.

These factors illustrate the expectation that prosecutors—like police officers and judges—will seek to "individualize" justice rather than mechanically apply the appropriate law to the defined act in every instance. Other factors have broader implications for the system of criminal justice.

The Chances of Conviction   A common reason for refusal to prosecute, even when the accused is obviously guilty, is the prosecutor's belief that a jury cannot be convinced either because of the highly circumstantial nature of the evidence or the probability that key evidence will be suppressed by the trial judge. If evidence is gathered by unlawful means, it is foolish to attempt to base a case on it.

Outmoded Statutes   Some criminal laws are foolish or outmoded. The term "desuetudinous" is used to describe statutes that have, for one reason or another, fallen into disuse. Such statutes are usually found in the area of sexual morals. Fornication and adultery and an often ingenious list of "crimes against nature" are proscribed but rarely prosecuted. Legislators decline to abolish such statutes since the moralists in their constituency cry out against such efforts while supporters of repeal too often remain silent. On the other hand, any prosecutor who regularly attempts to enforce these laws in contradiction to the middle-of-the-road morality of most of the constituency is probably doomed to lose office. The safest reaction in these matters by both legislators and prosecutors is inaction.

The Usefulness of the Accused's Testimony against Other Offenders
Another reason for a prosecutor to drop a case against an individual is that the offender has agreed to present testimony for the state—or "turn state's witness"—against another person. This process is referred to as "flipping" a defendant. It is often very useful to prosecute a serious, habitual, professional offender rather than prosecute the person flipped. It can be very distasteful, however, when such a deal is necessitated by the sheer lack of other evidence against the person more deserving of prosecution.

The Limits on Prosecutorial Resources   Prosecutor's offices typically have very limited budgets, and they may not have the number of attorneys (or the quality of attorney) that it takes to pursue every case brought to their attention. The chief prosecutor must set some priorities to deal with a case load that could overwhelm the office. The screening and charging process will (or should) reflect those priorities. Overworked offices sometimes reject cases they would otherwise accept and prosecute for the sheer lack of resources to handle them. Prosecutors who do this argue that they must select those cases that will result in the greatest degree of justice being done with the available personnel.

The Limits on the Capacity of the Courts A factor related to the one just discussed is that of the resources and capacity of the trial courts. Judges will complain—usually directly to the prosecutor and in private—that their dockets are overloaded with trivial cases and that they are being compelled to work too hard or too fast to do justice to the important ones. Judges have subtle ways of enforcing their desire for fewer cases. They do, after all, have the authority, and indeed the duty, to dismiss cases that do not meet standards of provability, to suppress evidence that was obtained by illegal means or is otherwise questionable, and to grant continuances to the defense. These actions can have the effect of wearing down the state and of compelling the prosecutor's office to alter its own priorities in the filing of cases.

The ABA Standards on Charging

The American Bar Association has established sets of standards for the criminal justice system which include standards for prosecutors, defense attorneys, and trial judges. Pertinent to the above discussion is Section 3.9 of the ABA code, which deals with discretion in the charging decision. We reproduce it here since it is a clear statement of the ethical and professional basis for prosecutorial discretion.[1]

Discretion in the Charging Decision

(a) It is unprofessional conduct for a prosecutor to institute or cause to be instituted criminal charges when he knows that the charges are not supported by probable cause.

(b) The prosecutor is not obliged to present all charges which the evidence might support. The prosecutor may in some circumstances and for good cause consistent with the public interest decline to prosecute, notwithstanding that evidence may exist which would support a conviction. Illustrative of the factors which the prosecutor may properly consider in exercising his discretion are:

(i) the prosecutor's reasonable doubt that the accused is in fact guilty;

(ii) the extent of the harm caused by the offense;

(iii) the disproportion of the authorized punishment in relation to the particular offense of the offender;

(iv) possible improper motives of a complainant;

(v) reluctance of the victim to testify;

(vi) cooperation of the accused in the apprehension or conviction of others;

(vii) availability and likelihood of prosecution by another jurisdiction.

(c) In making the decision to prosecute, the prosecutor should give no weight to the personal or political advantages or disadvantages which might be involved or to a desire to enhance his record of convictions.

(d) In cases which involve a serious threat to the community, the prosecutor should not be deterred from prosecution by the fact that in his jurisdiction juries have tended to acquit persons accused of the particular kind of criminal act in question.

(e) The prosecutor should not bring or seek charges greater in number or degree than he can reasonably support with evidence at trial.

Certain factors we have mentioned seem to be brought into question by the bar's code—specifically concern with "political advantages or disadvantages," and with conviction rates. In real life of course, prosecutors must win and hold onto office if they are to put into effect their ideals of justice. On the other hand, it is well to keep in mind that a prosecutor who values a political career to the detriment of doing what he or she senses to be justice is unworthy of the office.

A Case Selection Policy

Most prosecutor's offices do not have a written policy for case selection and charging. In an office with a handful of attorneys, this may present no problem since communication among associates is continuous. Many critics insist, however, that the lack of a clearly articulated policy leads to inconsistency and unfairness.

A great deal of effort has been expended in some quarters to develop systems of standards for prosecution and related devices for coding and scoring cases. A common approach is to create forms on which all important elements of a case can be recorded for analysis. These elements include the characteristics of the offense (the level of misdemeanor or felony involved, the presence or use of a weapon, the seriousness of any injury to the victim, the value of property stolen or destroyed), the characteristics of the alleged offender (any criminal record or history, any ties to the community), and even characteristics of the victim. Each element can be assigned a numerical weight that represents the degree of seriousness with which the office views it. Entry of information on this form is followed by the tabulation of the "score" that this case earns.

The best known of these systems is *PROMIS* (*Prosecutors' Management Information System*). This has many uses as a case-tracking and management information system, but at its heart is its use in scoring criminal cases. (Figure 9.1 illustrates a sample form.) A prosecutor can simply establish a threshold score (a total numerical point value any case must reach to be considered seriously for prosecution) and declare that any case falling below it will be dropped. A more realistic and rea-

crime, the charge is usually known as an *indictment*. So much for presentments.

Composition of the Grand Jury

The English tradition called for twenty-three grand jurors, with a simple majority vote of twelve required to indict. Today the number of grand jurors varies from fifteen to twenty-four among jurisdictions and even varies within a jurisdiction. The number of votes required to indict, however, is still usually twelve.

The composition of grand juries has resulted in challenges to the process utilized to select the members, with such challenges usually going to the racial composition of the jury. The post–Civil War Fourteenth Amendment requires equal protection and generally requires that there be no discrimination on the basis of race, sex, age, or religion.

There are, however, legal qualifications for being able to perform grand jury duty. Typically, jurors must reside in the area in which they serve; be old enough to vote; have no prior felony convictions; and be able to speak, read, and write the English language. Voter registration lists are commonly used as a reservoir of names from which to select at random grand (and for that matter, petit) jurors.

Role of the Grand Jury

The grand jury has been described as being both a sword and a shield. This refers to the dual role of this institution as an aggressive investigator of criminal conduct on the one hand and a protector of the rights of innocent citizens on the other. This body, composed of a cross section of members of the community, is supposed to assess the behavior of other members of the same community and decide who should and who should not be brought before the court to answer criminal charges. But the grand jurors in modern urban society rarely if ever have independent knowledge of the matters or persons being investigated.

There are several tools at the disposal of the grand jury. One tool is the expertise of the local prosecutor, who is by law its legal advisor. He or she advises the grand jurors as to the law relative to matters before them and answers their questions. The prosecutor often distributes copies of appropriate statutes and takes on the role of a teacher in explaining the interrelationships of various elements of the law. Jurors may also ask the judge who impaneled them to answer questions on the law, but this is rarely done.

Another tool is the secrecy of grand jury proceedings. Matters under investigation, the identity and testimony of witnesses, and the advice of the prosecutor are all kept secret by law. This secrecy was originally intended to protect persons not indicted from adverse publicity and community stigmatization. It also, however, serves the purpose of eliciting testimony from witnesses in cases where the danger of violence to witnesses exists. Testimony secured in grand jury hearings may later be introduced at public trials if the witness tries to change his or her story. This is done in a process known as *impeachment* of the witness. Another aspect of this secrecy is the protection it offers to the grand jurors themselves who may question witnesses, deliberate, and render decisions without fear of public attacks on their actions.

Still another tool is the ability to compel testimony. Persons subpoenaed to appear before grand juries may be held in contempt of court if they refuse to appear or to testify. This power to compel testimony carries with it a grant of immunity to the affected witness. This immunity often means that the witness will not be prosecuted for his or her role in the criminal episode being investigated. This is called *transactional immunity*. Some states and the federal government, however, offer only *use immunity*. This means that the individual is not immune from prosecution in connection with the crime, but that the testimony compelled before the grand jury cannot be used in such a prosecution. This rather neat device frequently has the effect of encouraging witnesses to tell grand juries everything they ever wanted to know in the hope that this will negate the possibility of their being prosecuted at all. Of course, other witnesses' testimony about the same matters can still be used against them in a trial. In any case, the power to compel testimony under threat of contempt and to offer use immunity to witnesses is a tool that grand juries find very useful—even essential—in many investigations.

Of course, the power to compel testimony through the offer of immunity has been challenged as a threat to the Fifth Amendment rights of persons under investigation and called as witnesses before grand juries. In 1972 the U.S. Supreme Court upheld the constitutionality of use immunity in a case involving persons who refused to testify before a federal grand jury when offered use immunity instead of complete transactional immunity.[2] Opinions in that case, *Kastiger v. United States,* are excerpted on the following pages.

Criticisms of the Grand Jury

The grand jury is today the object of attack from some quarters. The chief criticism is that this body has become the "prosecutor's darling" and is little more than a "rubber stamp" for any action a prosecutor wishes to take. Studies show that grand juries issue indictments in about 95 percent of the cases brought by the prosecutor. Even the 5 percent

Kastiger v. United States
406 U.S. 441 (1972)

FROM THE OPINION

By Justice Powell

This case presents the question whether the United States Government may compel testimony from an unwilling witness, who invokes the Fifth Amendment privilege against compulsory self-incrimination, by conferring on the witness immunity from use of the compelled testimony in subsequent criminal proceedings, as well as immunity from use of evidence derived from the testimony.

Petitioners were subpoenaed to appear before a United States grand jury in the Central District of California on February 4, 1971. The Government believed that petitioners were likely to assert their Fifth Amendment privilege. Prior to the scheduled appearances, the Government applied to the District Court for an order directing petitioners to answer questions and produce evidence before the grand jury under a grant of immunity conferred pursuant to 18 USC §§ 6002-6003. Petitioners opposed issuance of the order, contending primarily that the scope of the immunity provided by the statute was not coextensive with the scope of the privilege against self-incrimination, and therefore was not sufficient to supplant the privilege and compel their testimony.

The District Court rejected this contention, and ordered petitioners to appear before the grand jury and answer its questions under the grant of immunity.

Petitioners appeared but refused to answer questions, asserting their privilege against compulsory self-incrimination. They were brought before the District Court, and each persisted in his refusal to answer the grand jury's questions, notwithstanding the grant of immunity. The court found both in contempt, and committed them to the custody of the Attorney General until either they answered the grand jury's questions or the term of the grand jury expired. The Court of Appeals for the Ninth Circuit affirmed.... This Court granted certiorari to resolve the important question whether testimony may be compelled by granting immunity from the use of compelled testimony and evidence derived therefrom ("use and derivative use" immunity), or whether it is necessary to grant immunity from prosecution for offenses to which compelled testimony relates ("transactional" immunity)....

I

The power of government to compel persons to testify in court or before grand juries and other governmental agencies is firmly established in Anglo-American jurisprudence. The power with respect to courts was established by statute in England as early as 1562, and Lord Bacon observed in 1612 that all subjects owed the King their "knowledge and discovery." While it is not clear when grand juries first resorted to compulsory process to secure the attendance and testimony of witnesses, the general common-law principle that "the public has a right to every man's evidence" was considered an "indubitable certainty" that "cannot be denied" by 1742. The power to compel testimony, and the corresponding duty to testify, are recognized in the Sixth Amendment requirements that an accused be confronted with the witnesses against him, and have compulsory process for obtaining witnesses in his favor. The first Congress recognized the testimonial duty in the Judiciary Act of 1789, which provided for compulsory attendance of witnesses in the federal courts. . . .

But the power to compel testimony is not absolute. There are a number of exemptions from the testimonial duty, the most important of which is the Fifth Amendment privilege against compulsory self-incrimination. The privilege reflects a complex of our fundamental values and aspirations, and marks an important advance in the development of our liberty. It can be asserted in any proceeding, civil or criminal, administrative or judical, investigatory or adjudicatory; and it protects against any disclosures that the witness reasonably believes could be used in a criminal prosecution or could lead to other evidence that might be so used. This Court has been zealous to safeguard the values that underlie the privilege.

Immunity statutes, which have historical roots deep in Anglo-American jurisprudence, are not incompatible with these values. Rather, they seek a rational accommodation between the imperatives of the privilege and the legitimate demands of government to compel citizens to testify. The existence of these statutes reflects the importance of testimony, and the fact that many offenses are of such a character that the only persons capable of giving useful testimony are those implicated in the crime. . . .

Petitioners contend, first, that the Fifth Amendment's privilege against compulsory self-incrimination, which is that "[n]o person . . . shall be compelled in any criminal case to be a witness against himself," deprives Congress of power to enact laws that compel self-incrimination, even if complete immunity from prosecution is granted prior to the compulsion of the incriminatory testimony. In other words, petitioners assert that no immunity statute, however drawn, can afford a lawful basis for compelling incriminatory testimony. They ask us to reconsider and overrule Brown v Walker, . . . and Ullmann v United States, supra, decisions that uphold the constitutionality of immunity statutes. We find no merit to this contention and reaffirm the decisions in Brown and Ullmann.

III

Petitioners' second contention is that the scope of immunity provided by the federal witness immunity statute, 18 USC § 6002, is not coextensive with the scope of the Fifth Amendment privilege against compulsory self-incrimination, and therefore is not sufficient to supplant the privilege and compel testimony over a claim of the privilege. The statute provides that when a witness is compelled by district court order to testify over a claim of the privilege: "the witness may not refuse to comply with the order on the basis of his privilege against self-incrimination; but no testimony or other information compelled under the order (or any information directly or indirectly derived from such testimony or other information) may be used against the witness in any criminal case, except a prosecution for perjury, giving a false statement, or otherwise failing to comply with the order." . . .

Petitioners draw a distinction between statutes that provide transactional immunity and those that provide, as does the statute before us, immunity from use and derivative use. They contend that a statute must at a minimum grant full transactional immunity in order to be coextensive with the scope of the privilege. . . .

The statute's explicit proscription of the use in any criminal case of "testimony or other information compelled under the order (or any information directly or indirectly derived from such testimony or other information)" is consonant with Fifth Amendment standards. We hold that such immunity from use and derivative use is coextensive with the scope of the privilege against self-incrimination, and therefore is sufficient to compel testimony over a claim of the privilege. While a grant of immunity must afford protection commensurate with that afforded by the privilege, it need not be broader. Transactional immunity, which accords full immunity from prosecution for the offense to which the compelled testimony relates, affords the witness considerably broader protection than does the Fifth Amendment privilege. The privilege has never been construed to mean that one who invokes it cannot subsequently be prosecuted. Its sole concern is to afford protection against being "forced to give testimony leading to the infliction of 'penalties affixed to . . . criminal acts.'" Immunity from the use of compelled testimony, as well as evidence derived directly and indirectly therefrom, affords this protection. It prohibits the prosecutorial authorities from using the compelled testimony in *any* respect, and it therefore insures that the testimony cannot lead to the infliction of criminal penalties on the witness. . . .

Although an analysis of prior decisions and the purpose of the Fifth Amendment privilege indicates that use and derivative-use immunity is coextensive with the privilege, we must consider additional arguments advanced by petitioners against the sufficiency of such immunity. We start from the premise, repeatedly affirmed by this Court, that an appropriately broad immunity grant is compatible with the Constitution.

Petitioners argue that use and derivative-use immunity will not adequately protect a witness from various possible incriminating uses of the compelled testimony: for example, the prosecutor or other law enforcement officials may obtain leads, names of witnesses, or other information not otherwise available that might result in a prosecution. It will be difficult and perhaps impossible, the argument goes, to identify, by testimony or cross-examination, the subtle ways in which the compelled testimony may disadvantage a witness, especially in the jurisdiction granting the immunity. . . .

A person accorded this immunity under 18 USC § 6002, and subsequently prosecuted, is not dependent for the preservation of his rights upon the integrity and good faith of the prosecuting authorities. As stated in Murphy:

> Once a defendant demonstrates that he has testified, under a state grant of immunity, to matters related to the federal prosecution, the federal authorities have the burden of showing that their evidence is not tainted by establishing that they had an independent, legitimate source for the disputed evidence. . . .

This burden of proof, which we reaffirm as appropriate, is not limited to a negation of taint; rather, it imposes on the prosecution the affirmative duty to prove that the evidence it proposes to use is derived from a legitimate source wholly independent of the compelled testimony.

This is very substantial protection, commensurate with that resulting from invoking the privilege itself. The privilege assures that a citizen is not compelled to incriminate himself by his own testimony. It usually operates to allow a citizen to remain silent when asked a question requiring an incriminatory answer. This statute, which operates after a witness has given incriminatory testimony, affords the same protection by assuring that the compelled testimony can in no way lead to the infliction of criminal penalties. The statute, like the Fifth Amendment, grants neither pardon nor amnesty. Both the statute and the Fifth Amendment allow the government to prosecute using evidence from legitimate independent sources. . . .

There can be no justification in reason or policy for holding that the Constitution requires an amnesty grant where, acting pursuant to statute and accompanying safeguards, testimony is compelled in exchange for immunity from use and derivative use when no such amnesty is required where the government, acting without colorable right, coerces a defendant into incriminating himself.

We conclude that the immunity provided by 18 USC § 6002 leaves the witness and the prosecutorial authorities in substantially the same position as if the witness had claimed the Fifth Amendment privilege. The immunity therefore is coextensive with the privilege and suffices to supplant it. The judgment of the Court of Appeals for the Ninth Circuit accordingly is Affirmed.

FROM THE DISSENT

By Justice Douglas

The Self-Incrimination Clause says: "No person . . . shall be compelled in any criminal case to be a witness against himself." I see no answer to the proposition that he is such a witness when only "use" immunity is granted. . . .

If, as some have thought, the Bill of Rights contained only "counsels of moderation" from which courts and legislatures could deviate according to their conscience or discretion, then today's contraction of the Self-Incrimination Clause of the Fifth Amendment would be understandable. But that has not been true, starting with Chief Justice Marshall's opinion in United States v Burr. . . . where he ruled that the reach of the Fifth Amendment was so broad as to make the privilege applicable when there was a mere possibility of a criminal charge being made.

The Court said in Hale v Henkel, that "if the criminality has already been taken away, the Amendment ceases to apply." In other words, the immunity granted is adequate if it operates as a complete pardon for the offense. . . . That is the true measure of the Self-Incrimination Clause. . . .

When we allow the prosecution to offer only "use" immunity we allow it to grant far less than it has taken away. For while the precise testimony that is compelled may not be used, leads from that testimony may be pursued and used to convict the witness. My view is that the framers put it beyond the power of Congress to *compel* anyone to confess his crimes. The Self-Incrimination Clause creates, as I have said before, "the federally protected right of silence," making it unconstitutional to use a law "to pry open one's lips and make him a witness against himself."

By Justice Marshall

Today the Court holds that the United States may compel a witness to give incriminating testimony, and subsequently prosecute him for crimes to which that testimony relates. I cannot believe the Fifth Amendment permits that result.

The Fifth Amendment gives a witness an absolute right to resist interrogation, if the testimony sought would tend to incriminate him. A grant of immunity may strip the witness of the right to refuse to testify, but only if it is broad enough to eliminate all possibility that the testimony will in fact operate to incriminate him. It must put him in precisely the same position, vis-à-vis the government that has compelled his testimony, as he would have been in had he remained silent in reliance on the privilege.

The Court recognizes that an immunity statute must be tested by that standard, that the relevant inquiry is whether it "leaves the witness and the prosecutorial authorities in substantially the same position as if the witness had claimed the Fifth Amendment privilege." . . . I assume, moreover, that in theory that test would be met by a complete ban on the use of the compelled testimony, including all derivative use, however remote and indirect. But I cannot agree that a ban on use will in practice be total, if it remains open for the government to convict the witness on the basis of evidence derived from a legitimate independent source. The Court asserts that the witness is adequately protected by a rule imposing on the government a heavy burden of proof if it would establish the independent character of evidence to be used against the witness. But in light of the inevitable uncertainties of the fact-finding process, see Speiser v Randall, . . . a greater margin of protection is required in order to provide a reliable guarantee that the witness is in exactly the same position as if he had not testified. That margin can be provided only by immunity from prosecution for the offenses to which the testimony relates, i.e., transactional immunity. . . .

The Court today sets out a loose net to trap tainted evidence and prevent its use against the witness, but it accepts an intolerably great risk that tainted evidence will in fact slip through that net.

---

that are rejected by the grand jury may include cases the prosecutor really wanted dropped anyway but didn't want the blame for doing so.

The prosecutor is the dominant force in the jury's proceedings. Other actors, including law enforcement officers, attorneys, evidence technicians, and various other experts, are there by invitation or subpoena only. William J. Campbell, a former prosecutor who became a federal district court judge, has written that:

> . . . the grand jury has ceased to function as an agency independent from prosecutorial influence. It is today but an *alter ego* of the prosecutor. It has outlived its reputation as the bulwark of democracy. Indeed, it is that very pretention that has led some to suggest that the grand jury has instead become

the bulwark of prosecutorial immunity, encouraging abuses by permitting the prosecutor to carry on his work with complete anonymity.[3]

Other critics have pointed to the fact that grand juries have been used to indict persons for political reasons, as seen in the cases of anti-Vietnam war protestors during the Nixon administration. These indictments generally led to acquittals or dismissals in trial courts, but the damage to the defendant's reputation and finances had been done. The public is not necessarily aware that indictment is only the initiation of a formal case and that this accusatory act is not a finding of guilt. Furthermore, grand juries may issue reports highly critical of the "suspicious" or "unethical" acts of a person or even name a person as an "unindicted co-conspirator" in a case. These actions have the effect of attacking persons without providing them an opportunity to formally defend themselves.

Because the potential for abuse is so great, the effectiveness and usefulness of a grand jury depends upon the good faith, talent, and integrity of the prosecutor as well as the quality of citizens who sit on it. The authors' own experience in working with many grand juries leads them to believe that, properly and honestly advised, the grand jury is anything but a rubber stamp, that it still functions as a shield for citizens as well as a sword for the government.

THE PRELIMINARY HEARING

In a great many cases the involvement of the trial court in the determination of probable cause extends beyond its examination of the sworn complaint at the initial appearance. It includes the *preliminary hearing,* a device whose usage and impact have more variation from state to state than almost any other feature of the criminal process. Our attempts to generalize about it without putting the reader on notice to look for local variations would not be of service. We can, however, make one generally valid statement: The preliminary hearing is usually limited to cases in which persons have been arrested on felony charges.

Format of a Preliminary Hearing

The preliminary hearing resembles a nonjury or so-called bench trial in which the judge sits as the trier of fact unaided by a jury. The authors have referred to the proceedings as a "minitrial" when describing the format (not the effect) of a hearing to laypeople. The prosecutor calls witnesses to testify in demonstrating probable cause that the alleged offender actually did perpetrate the crime involved. The quantity of proof required is, again, probable cause and not beyond and to the exclusion of each and every reasonable doubt, as is required at trial. A few jurisdictions merely require the civil law standard: a preponderance of the evidence.

Benefits of a Preliminary Hearing

The defendant has the opportunity to cross-examine the prosecution witnesses in the preliminary hearing. This factor often leads the defendant to demand a hearing in those states and upon those occasions wherein the defendant is not otherwise entitled to "discovery." The defendant has an opportunity to examine the state's or the federal government's case in detail, a chance to "discover" what the prosecutor can produce at trial. On the other hand, those jurisdictions that have broad rules permitting the defendant to find out all about the prosecutor's case through mandatory exchange of information have a low rate of demand for preliminary hearings by the defense.

One good tactical reason for the prosecutor to desire a preliminary hearing is to preserve testimony for trial if it is anticipated that a witness or witnesses may be unavailable at a later time. You will recall that the Sixth Amendment to the Constitution gives a defendant the absolute right to be confronted by the witnesses against him or her. This normally means that the prosecution witnesses have to be personally present at trial to testify and that the defendant has the right to cross-examine them by asking leading questions. If the witness is not present, the Sixth Amendment and the rules of evidence prohibit anyone else from repeating what was said earlier—because of the right of confrontation by cross-examination guaranteed by the Sixth Amendment and because of the rule against "hearsay" testimony. An exception to both mandates pertains, however, if sworn testimony was adduced in prior proceeding where the defendant and the issues were the same, the defendant had the right of cross-examination, and the proceedings were recorded reliably. A preliminary hearing provides all of these things. The authors have been involved in several cases in which the witnesses were not expected to be available for trial because they were not residents in the jurisdiction or because their fear of or affinity for the defendant made them likely to flee. Such witnesses, if the court can be convinced of the need, can be jailed until the preliminary hearing is completed. On a few occasions involving particularly dangerous and powerful defendants, the authors have hidden the witnesses from harm until they were brought to the preliminary hearing and their testimony safely recorded. At that point, the fact that the witness need not appear at trial for a conviction to be gained is made clear to the defendant with the hope of dislodging any further motive to harm the witness.

The Hearing Procedure

One common element throughout the jurisdictions is the right to counsel. In *Coleman v. Alabama,* the Supreme Court held that the preliminary hearing was a "critical stage" in the prosecution and thus the defendant was entitled to free counsel.[4] The court did not say that a preliminary hearing was per se a right but rather said that if the state chose to conduct a preliminary hearing it had to provide a lawyer if the defendant was too poor to afford one.

In many jurisdictions, the rules of evidence for a hearing are not the same as the formal rules encountered for trial. Some states and the federal government allow the use of hearsay testimony to differing degrees. All jurisdictions allow the defense to call witnesses, but in a preliminary hearing the defense usually does not wish to alert the prosecutor to its tactics. If a defendant should opt to tell a lie this early in the proceedings it is easier for the prosecutor to controvert the testimony. Lies that surprise the prosecutor at trial are much harder to field.

Access to a Preliminary Hearing

The right to a preliminary hearing is not an unlimited one. At both federal and state levels a prior indictment by a grand jury almost always nullifies any requirement for, or right to, a preliminary hearing; the hearing is forestalled by the filing of an information within a certain time period, which varies from state to state, after arrest. In Florida, for example, no preliminary hearing is required in such cases if the information or indictment is filed within twenty-one days of arrest. In the majority of states, however, a *bindover decision* at a preliminary hearing is required before prosecution can be initiated through the filing of an information.

Impact of the Bindover Decision

As a rule, grand juries are in no way bound by the bindover or by the lack of a bindover decision. In those states where the prosecutor is limited to direct filing only in those cases preceded by bindover, he or she is usually limited to filing on those charges stipulated by the bindover order. If the grand jury decides to indict on a case where the magistrate has refused to bind over, it obviously has the right to indict.

In a number of states the prosecutor may file despite a magistrate's refusal to bind over. The prosecutor, as a practical matter, will usually do this only where additional evidence is developed after the hearing or where the magistrate has clearly erred. To do otherwise would place the prosecutor in clear opposition to the magistrate, not always a desirable position.

CHARGING PATTERNS

The ABA standards offer a neutral and idealistic point of view for the charging decision, but differing philosophies of prosecutors and local needs and beliefs result in differing prosecutorial styles. Four distinct patterns of charging emerge, according to Joan Jacoby.[5] The typical prosecutor's office will use a weighted blend of these polarized patterns, which are described below.

The Standard of Legal Sufficiency

The *legal sufficiency standard* dictates that a case be filed if it contains all the elements necessary to meet the requirements of the statute. One can apply this standard by reading a summary of the facts of the case and checking them against what the criminal statute says must be present. This represents nothing more than an inventory and does not require the decision maker to have any great skill or experience. It does not take into account other factors or the availability of ameliorative alternatives to traditional prosecution. Let's look at a hypothetical situation to further examine the process.

Daniel Defendant is seen by Willing Witness to enter Virgil Victim's garage by breaking the locked door and is further seen to depart with Virgil's $310 bicycle, riding off into the darkness. We can apply a statute that defines burglary with these words: "The breaking and entering of the structure of another with the intent to commit a felony is a felony punishable by up to thirty years' imprisonment." Or we can apply another statute that defines theft in these words: "The unlawful taking of the property of another with the intent to permanently deprive the true owner of such property is a felony punishable by up to five years' imprisonment if the property is of the value of $300 or more."

Let's analyze our case on the basis of legal sufficiency. Dan (1) did break, (2) did enter, and (3) at least arguably did so with the required *intent* to commit a felony. He (4) did commit a felony because (5) he took property (6) of another (7) worth over $300, (8) arguably with the intent to deprive Virgil forever of the use and benefit of the said bicycle since he rode it away. The case is legally sufficient. If legal sufficiency were our standard, we would make Daniel a felony defendant with a chance of drawing up to thirty years in prison.

The legal sufficiency pattern is most often found in the charging of misdemeanor cases where the stakes are not nearly as high as our example and to which the prosecutor's least skilled lawyers, usually low-paid beginners, are assigned.

The Standard of System Efficiency

The *system efficiency standard* dictates that cases be moved quickly and efficiently even if significant compromises are required. Screening is used to accept those cases that can be readily disposed of, with an emphasis on charging in order to induce pleas. For instance, difficult cases with less than convincing proof will not be charged because they induce the defendant to maintain innocence and demand costly and time-consuming trials. And some defendants are charged with more counts or higher charges than the case would otherwise merit in order to encourage that defendant to plead at the level the prosecutor really wants. Such a defendant is usually assured by the defense attorney that he or she "got a deal" in accepting a plea bargain. This is the so-called *overcharging policy*. A variation of the "overcharging" theme is known as *undercharging*; here the prosecutor calls a serious offense by a less serious name, usually charging what should be a felony as a misdemeanor. This practice also induces pleas because the prosecutor will indicate to the defendant that if he or she does not plead guilty to the lesser offense, that charge will be dismissed in favor of the maximum charge possible, which will expose the defendant to a considerably greater risk than pleading guilty to the lesser charge initially offered.

Under this system of charging, the prosecutor will also strive to make deals with prosecutors from other jurisdictions that also have charges on the defendant in order to consolidate the charges into one plea bargain deal. The object is, of course, to cause the defendant to seize "a good deal" and avoid a trial.

Prosecutors who rely on this system will often seek to justify it by claiming that they are overloaded and must reject the less important cases. This results in screening out those cases that involve offenses of little interest to the community—cases such as consensual sex offenses, minor thefts, trespasses, and violations of regulatory statutes. In an extreme situation, the number of cases dismissed "because of the lack of prosecutorial resources" will increase and will eventually include those that the community perceives as "serious." This can be very effective in raising the public consciousness as to the plight of the prosecutor and can consequently result in an increase in the office budget!

Going back to our hypothetical case and looking at it from the system efficiency viewpoint, we find that the prosecutor might "overcharge" the case against Daniel by adding more counts to the indictment or information than would be necessary to obtain maximum penalties for a defendant of this background. Hence Daniel Defendant would be charged not only with burglary but also with the theft of the bicycle and with riding a bicycle without displaying a light. The hope is that if Daniel sees the opportunity for a "deal" by pleading guilty only to burglary, he will be so grateful that the other charges are dropped that he will eagerly enter his plea.

This approach also encourages assistant prosecutors to offer defendants lower pleas than are appropriate in order to avoid the necessity of trials. It's quite simple. If the defendant does not wish to tender a plea at an appropriate level and instead says, in effect, "Try me," the prosecutor must do so. But the prosecutor wants to avoid trial in order to devote the time it would take to try just one case to striking plea bargains in several cases. But such a practice eventually leads to a deterioration of the system of justice. Prosecutors must at least occasionally back up their bluffs with effective trials. Only in this way can they wield any clout in demanding pleas that approximate just dispositions.

Another application of the system efficiency pattern is for the prosecutor in our hypothetical case to charge Daniel merely with trespassing or petit theft, with the threat of overcharging or correct charging prior to trial if Daniel decides not to plead guilty. Daniel is on the horns of a dilemma: either he pleads guilty to the lesser offense or he exercises his Sixth Amendment right to trial and stands to be sentenced much more severely for more serious offenses if he loses.

There is an important point that must be made clear: The fairness of these approaches is utterly predicated on the fact that Daniel is actually guilty. What if Willing Witness has a grudge against Daniel and, seeing *someone* commit the crime, merely takes advantage of the situation to settle the grudge with Daniel? If poor Dan protests his innocence, he risks being sentenced much more severely.

The Standard of Defendant Rehabilitation

In the authors' judgment, this system—if balanced with stringent treatment of those not deserving of nontraditional rehabilitative alternatives— offers the best service to the offender in terms of an opportunity to be a contributing citizen. It also offers the nonoffending citizens protection from offenders, and it is a very cost-effective system. Let's examine this option with some care.

Although the sociology of criminal behavior is beyond the scope of this text, we doubt that the statement that most multiple offenders are not going to be rehabilitated and will probably commit more crimes will meet much learned opposition. We also believe that we will not be widely contradicted if we assume that some first offenders can be rehabilitated if they are offered that chance and the threat of sufficient penalty if they do not indeed rehabilitate themselves. The pattern of case charging under the *standard of defendant rehabilitation* is generally predicated upon these assumptions.

This standard has as its goal the identification of those offenders who can benefit from rehabilitative programs and the placement of such offenders in effective programs without subjecting them to formal prosecution. We can again make use of the case of Daniel Defendant in explaining a typical approach to this pattern of charging and case disposition.

Let's assume that Dan is guilty in fact and is apprehended. Upon checking, the prosecutor finds that Dan has never been in trouble before. She also determines that Dan was influenced by peer pressure and confessed upon being caught. Dan even retrieved the bicycle from hiding and returned it to Mr. Victim. Upon interview, Dan's pastor, teachers, and neighbors all attested to his good attitude and otherwise good morals.

If all the participants in the program, including the police, prosecutor, counselor, and victim, agree that Dan should have a "second bite at the apple," he will be offered the chance to participate in a *diversionary program*. It is "diversionary" in the sense that Dan is diverted from traditional criminal justice channels and placed under supervision designed to allow him success in a noncriminal lifestyle.

Diversionary programs are usually oriented toward vocational goals, with the belief that if a person is gainfully employed in a job that gives him or her a sense of self-esteem, that person will be less likely to recidivate. Some programs are more sophisticated and emphasize long-term goals requiring more than vocational training; such programs often emphasize higher education at local institutions.

Diversionary programs typically have a much lower recidivism rate than incarceration. It is obviously easier to keep on going to the same job that one had under pretrial diversion than to find skills, tools, and a job after release from prison. It is often as simple as that. Employability, employment, and work habits often are factors that make the difference between continuing criminality and a productive life.

As helpful as rehabilitative programs are for those who can be expected to benefit from them, only a small minority of offenders are appropriate subjects for such programs. In jurisdictions utilizing the defendant rehabilitation pattern of charging, much judicial time and energy is saved whenever a person is diverted. The prosecutor is saved the time of charging, preparing, and trying the case. This, at least in theory, gives the prosecutor the opportunity to place more emphasis on other cases. This charging pattern usually supports a charge of the most serious crimes the evidence will support, a practice that ensures that pleas will more closely resemble the level of charging for those defendants who refuse to plead guilty. Guilty pleas "as charged" are most often induced by prosecutors who can convincingly say that they will proceed to trial and win if defendants refuse to so plead. The defendant rehabilitation pattern allows the prosecutor to do this more frequently than in systems where the court dockets are clogged with cases that otherwise could have been disposed of through diversion.

The Standard of Trial Sufficiency

The *trial sufficiency standard* dictates that only those cases that prosecutors believe they can win in a jury trial will be charged. This system does not depart from the traditional role of the prosecutor as an accusatory rather than a rehabilitative officer. In this system the rehabilitative roles are consigned to the jail keeper, the probation officer, and the parole officer, with the judge saying who will go where upon conviction.

Cases are evaluated on a basis of determining probability of winning, period. Advocates of this system do not grade a case by any other criteria; they do not weigh the record of the defendant, the likelihood of recidivation, the heinousness of the crime, or whether a weapon was used. Critics of this system, including the authors, feel that such practices do little to promote justice and only make the trial prosecutor's job easier and his or her record appear more successful. There is little doubt that factors other than the probability of winning at trial should be considered in the decision to charge, a decision that is the single most important aspect of the prosecution process. The road to justice is decidedly forked at the point of charging.

The trial efficiency pattern of charging puts a great premium on quality police work. If the police work is faulty and the case thereby weakened, the prosecutor will summarily reject the case, which usually leads to a feeling of rejection on the part of the police officer who made the case. This apparent lack of prosecutor support for the police often causes hard feelings in the law enforcement community, which soon spreads to the community at large. Officers are not hesitant to inform victims whose cases are not going to be prosecuted that the lack of prosecution is due to a "soft-on-crime" attitude on the part of the prosecutor or to the prosecutor's preoccupation with his or her conviction rate. This creates a schism between prosecutors and the people they should be serving. The public deserves a prosecutor who is interested in combating crime, and the prosecutor must accept and prosecute some cases where equity requires prosecution even if guilt may be difficult to prove.

The judges in a given jurisdiction may place pressure upon the prosecutor to screen cases for trial sufficiency since this will put less of a work load on the courts. (Judges, like prosecutors and other people, can be lazy.) This method of charging produces the lightest trial case load because all but the strongest cases are rejected. When only the strongest cases remain and are charged, not only is the raw numerical load lessened but the tendency will be for defendants to enter a greater percentage of guilty pleas. A defendant who is clearly guilty according to an analysis of the admissible evidence is much more likely to plead guilty than one who stands a better chance of being acquitted at trial. Thus the actual work load upon the courts is further lessened—it takes only a few minutes to accept a plea of guilty, where it usually takes at least a day to conduct even the simplest felony trial.

Another factor that often leads the senior prosecutor to adopt a policy of trial sufficiency screening is the fact that the assistant prosecutors generally are most comfortable with easy-to-prove cases. Whatever the driving force might be—perhaps lack of desire to do that which is difficult, perhaps the desire to minimize the potential of ego damage that results when an insecure lawyer fails to win a case—it is clear that the average junior prosecutor is apt to prefer a system that gives him or her less to do and a greater chance of success at doing what little there is left to do.

SUMMARY AND CONCLUSION

In this chapter we have examined the steps involved in the initiation of formal prosecution, the factors that determine or influence the decision-making process, and the reasons for and the results of various patterns of charging by prosecutors. We have emphasized the tremendous importance of the decisions that are made at this stage of the criminal process. We have said that the power of the prosecutor to initiate criminal action, to determine the level of seriousness of that action, or to decline to file charges is the most sweeping power given to any official in the criminal justice system.

It is essential to note, however, that prosecutors do not exercise this power in a vacuum. They, like other criminal justice officials, are "checked" by several means and influenced by various people. We have already discussed the political nature of the office—the fact that prosecutors are elected officials and that funds to operate the office are voted by county commissions and state legislatures. We must also note that citizens react to prosecutorial actions as members of grand juries and trial juries. In their decisions as members of these bodies, citizens make known the will and standards of the community regarding crime and the handling of offenders. If citizens routinely acquit defendants in pornography cases, for example, the alert prosecutor will back off and adjust office policy accordingly.

Relations with other members of the criminal justice community are important, too, if the prosecutor wants to maintain any reputation as a professional. The police cannot be rendered a hostile force if the prosecutor expects any cooperation from them or a decent work product out of their departments. Prosecutors, after all, don't generally work "on the street," generate their own case load, or gather the evidence to be used in court—except in some very serious or complex cases. By and large, they depend upon law enforcement to input the material with which they work. Relations with defense attorneys and judges are equally important. Angry judges and defense attorneys who refuse to negotiate can make the lives of prosecuting attorneys quite unhappy.

To summarize, the prosecutor is not a totally free agent; he or she is just one member of a courthouse work group.[6] The group's members must work to establish common norms, and a common environment in order to achieve common tasks. They must interact with each other in ways that keep the system functioning in a manner that is acceptable and achieves, on the whole, something that approximates justice.

QUESTIONS FOR DISCUSSION

1. How much discretion does a prosecutor have in making the decision to charge or not to charge an accused person? Is this discretion excessive in your view? If so, does it most threaten values inherent in Packer's Crime Control Model or the values of the Due Process Model?
2. Is the grand jury really the "prosecutor's darling"? If so, what could be done to alter this status? Would the changes you espouse be more likely to favor the Crime Control or the Due Process Model?
3. How are grand juries used in your community? Could they be employed for new and more beneficial purposes, such as perhaps focusing on protection of the environment?
4. If you were a prosecutor, which of the four patterns of charging discussed in this chapter would you be most likely to employ? Why? Could it differ from case to case?

NOTES

1. American Bar Association, *Standards Related to the Prosecution Function and the Defense Function,* Project on Standards for Criminal Justice, Institute for Judicial Administration, New York, 1971, pp. 33–34.
2. *Kastiger v. United States,* 406 U.S. 441 (1972).
3. William J. Campbell, "Eliminate the Grand Jury," *Journal of Criminal Law and Criminology,* vol. 64, no. 2, 1973, p. 179.
4. *Coleman v. Alabama* 339 U.S. 1, 90 S. Ct. 1999, 26 L. Ed. 2d 387 (1970).
5. Joan E. Jacoby, *Pretrial Screening in Perspective,* National Evaluation Program Phase I Report, U.S. Government Printing Office, Washington, D.C., 1976, pp. 10–16.
6. James Eisenstein and Herbert Jacob, *Felony Justice: An Organizational Analysis of Criminal Courts,* Little, Brown, Boston, 1977, pp. 9 and 10.

CHAPTER 10

ADJUDICATION
BY PLEA

After reading this chapter, students should be able to define and explain the importance of each of the following terms or phrases:

nolo contendere pleas	*nolle prosequi* of charges
zero-sum game	sentence bargain
vertical plea deal	plea-taking checklist
horizontal plea deal	voluntariness
lesser included offense	factual basis

Adjudication is the process of attaining finality in litigation—with the exception, of course, of posttrial appeals. There are two routes to termination of a criminal case: (1) a trial that results in conviction or acquittal and (2) entry of a plea of guilty or *nolo contendere* ("no contest") by the accused. This chapter focuses on the latter of these routes.

PLEAS AT ARRAIGNMENT

Arraignment is the proceeding at which the accused is first brought before the court subsequent to being charged by indictment or information. To be *arraigned* is to be presented with these formal charges. At the conclusion of the reading of the charges, the defendant is asked how he or she pleads. In all states the plea may be "guilty" or "not guilty," but in about half of the states, the plea may also be one of "no contest."

Nolo Contendere Pleas

Nolo contendere is a plea that is, for all practical purposes, a plea of guilty, but it enables the defendant to say that he or she is not admitting guilt. Its legal usefulness pertains mostly to situations in which the crime may also give rise to a civil suit against the defendant. A plea of guilty in criminal court is admissible as evidence in the civil trial. A plea of no contest, on the other hand, cannot be used in a civil case arising out of the same transaction or incident. A defendant who has shot and wounded a victim and who has been sued for damages by that victim is well advised, therefore, not to plead guilty in the criminal case, but to plead *nolo contendere* to avoid both a trial and the admission of guilty. Most states that permit *nolo* pleas, however, also permit judges to decline to accept them in lieu of guilty pleas, so the defendant may not always benefit by pleading *nolo contendere*.

Not Guilty Pleas

While pleas of guilty are common at arraignments on misdemeanor charges—especially where defendants understand that only fines and/or restitution payments are likely to be ordered—pleas of not guilty are the general rule at arraignments on felony charges. On those occasions where defendants refuse to speak out, are obviously incompetent to plead, or are not represented by an attorney, the court will ordinarily enter a plea of not guilty on their behalf.

Guilty Pleas

Occasionally a defendant will try to plead guilty at arraignment under circumstances the court finds unacceptable. As we have noted above, an obviously incompetent or unrepresented defendant who faces serious changes will not be permitted to enter a guilty plea. Later in this chapter we shall examine in greater detail the tests a judge is supposed to apply to guilty pleas. For now let us simply note that such pleas should not be accepted unless given by a defendant in full command of his or her faculties, in full knowledge of the possible consequences, after full consultation with an attorney, and completely voluntarily.

THE PHILOSOPHY OF PLEA BARGAINING

A *plea bargain* is the result of negotiations between the prosecutor and the accused, or, more precisely, between the prosecuting and defense attorneys. The negotiated plea of guilty or of *nolo contendere* is tendered by the defendant at the end of the negotiations. The negotiations can be over the number of counts or charges against the accused—sometimes called a horizontal plea bargain; over the seriousness of the charges, for instance, in establishing whether the offense is a high felony or a low felony—a so-called vertical plea bargain; or over the severity of the sentence—a sentence bargain. In cases involving multiple serious charges against a single defendant, all three of the forms of plea bargains may be discussed and agreed upon. The act of negotiation, however, implies that some benefit (or perceived benefit) is realized by both parties, not just the defendant.

Trials as Zero-Sum Games

A trial can be seen as a classic *zero-sum game*. By that we mean that a trial is like a game in which one side loses and the other side wins. Assuming the stakes are even, one win equals one loss in value. The game produces a net sum for all participants of zero. Thus for any player or team entering such a game, the value of a potential loss is equal to the value of a potential win. This is not to say that the risk of loss is equal to the chances of winning. The risk or chance would depend upon the strengths and weaknesses of the players and/or the degree to which the rules of the game or conditions favor one side or the other. Calculations of the stakes and the relative risks are as common to courtroom work groups as they are to military field commanders and professional gamblers.

Since most cases present a zero-sum game situation, both sides usually have an interest in settling the matter in a manner in which they can each claim to have gained something, thus seeming to achieve a positive rather than a zero-sum outcome. That is, both sides are often willing to give up the chance of a complete victory in order to avoid a possible total loss.

This is especially true where engaging in the battle, or trial, would consume considerably more energy and time than would settling the matter. Time and energy saved seem to add to the net gain enjoyed by both sides. This is not to say that trials always take more time and energy than plea negotiations. Most trials, even at the felony level, take at least a day of everyone's time; often no less is expended in preparing for and conducting negotiations.

Plea Bargains as a Response to Case Loads

This brings us to a consideration of the classic argument offered in support of plea bargaining—that it is the product of heavy case loads and the need to move these loads through the courts as quickly and efficiently as possible. Some studies of the criminal court process indicate this is not the case. Milton Heumann writes that "plea bargaining is not new to the criminal court, nor is it a direct function of case pressure." He continues:

> Recourse to the trial as a mode of case disposition is the exception, not the rule, and this proposition holds even when case volume is controlled. This is true of our courts today and appears to have been true historically. To develop an explanation of plea bargaining and of the incentives of each of the participants to engage in it, and to base that explanation on case-pressure considerations, is to ignore these findings. The guilty plea and the plea bargain are far more central to the local criminal court than the plea bargaining literature suggests. Rather than being simply an expedient dictated by unmanageably large case loads, plea bargaining is integrally and inextricably bound to the "trial" court.[1]

Heumann cites data from 1880 to 1954 indicating that trials have never accounted for more then 20 percent of criminal dispositions and, since 1910, have accounted for 10 percent or less. He also found that low-volume courts were just as and sometimes more likely than high-volume courts to settle cases by plea.[2] Other studies have obtained similar results and most have asserted that the extent to which courts rely on plea agreements is dependent on local values and practices usually long-established among members of the legal community and courtroom work groups.[3]

J. Michael Thompson, on the other hand, developed an elaborate model to test the degree to which case-load pressure might be related to plea rates and studied the relationship in cases selected from five states. He defined case-load pressure as how many cases must result in a guilty plea to complete the processing of every case filed without adding to the backlog of cases. He found that variation in case-load pressure explains about 20 percent, or one-fifth, of the variability in actual plea rates—in other words, case load is only one factor contributing to plea bargaining.[4]

But if case pressure contributes only a small part to plea bargaining, what other factors count? We turn to a consideration of the objectives and motivations of the major actors: prosecutors, defense attorneys, and judges.

The Prosecutor's Objectives

The prosecutor may have any one of a number of reasons, or a combination of reasons, for negotiating for guilty pleas with defendants. The reasons may be grouped into those that relate to the strength of the case against the accused, those that are systemic in character, and those that are political or personal to the prosecutor. We shall look into each of these categories.

Evidence-Related Factors   A reason that is often cited, and with validity in most instances, for accepting pleas to reduced charges is that the state's case is weak. The absence of evidence needed to produce a verdict of guilty, an absence that creates a high risk of losing the case, is a powerful incentive to prosecutors to negotiate for and agree to a plea of guilty. That way the state gets a conviction, even if for something less than what the accused really did.

It is not unusual for witnesses to become unavailable at the time of trial. It happens for a number of reasons, not the least of which are fear and aggravation at the system for dragging them repeatedly to interviews, depositions, hearings, and so on. Many witnesses, including victims, have no roots in their society and are literally "here today, gone tomorrow." When essential witnesses cannot be found, the prosecutor is often left with little choice but to agree to a plea bargain. (An absent witness can still give testimony, however, if that witness's statements are recorded at a preliminary hearing or other hearing where the defense has an opportunity to confront and cross-examine the witness.)

Police officers are sometimes problematic witnesses. They are often not completely objective in presenting their cases, even to the prosecutor at the time of screening. It is embarrassing to the officer to have the prosecutor reject a case at screening; it is less embarrassing, in the minds of many officers, for the prosecutor to lose the case at trial. So officers are inclined to make the case seem stronger than it is, not necessarily by lying, but by presenting only those facts that are incriminating and leaving out facts that are exculpatory in nature. After the prosecutor finds out about the holes in the case as it was presented by the police, he or she may be reluctant to put that officer on the stand. But there are officers who investigate cases with defense positions in mind, and they present both perspectives in their reports. Such officers may have more cases rejected at screening, but they will be used more readily as trial witnesses, and prosecutors are much more likely to win when they are. Justice is definitely better served by this approach.

Victim-Related Considerations   In some cases the victim or the victim's family desires to avoid going to trial. This can be for a variety of reasons; often it is a desire to avoid further traumatization of the victim, especially if the victim is a child or an otherwise sensitive or frail person. It must be remembered that if a case goes to trial, the victim must take the stand and testify in the presence of the defendant, no matter now frightening that confrontation might be. This prospect often causes some parents to avoid trial in order to prevent a child from taking the stand. The prosecutor must then negotiate with counsel for the accused, knowing but not revealing the fact that the victim cannot be called to testify if the case goes to trial.

A recent case in Orange County, Florida, represents a switch on the usual situation. A prosecutor convinced a young woman and her mother to go to trial on a sexual battery case that was several years old, the crime having occurred when the victim was a child. It took many hours of interviewing and counseling to prepare the women for the ordeal and to convince them the case could be won. The day that the trial was to begin, the prosecutor accepted a plea and the defendant was sentenced to twenty years. The victim and her mother were outraged at not being allowed to testify after having relived the crime many times and steeling themselves for the confrontation. They told the press they felt cheated out of their day in court. The prosecutor stated that he agreed to the plea because the sentence was so stiff—though it was not the life sentence the accused might have received—and because in his judgment the victim was still shaky as a witness. The prosecutor expressed surprise and disappointment in the victim's reaction since he had just spared her and her mother the trauma of a trial and had avoided the risk of loss.

Spouse abuse cases are notorious for being dropped when the victim, usually the wife, declines to testify. Because so many victims change their minds, prosecutors have traditionally been reluctant even to file such cases. It is now more common for prosecutors to inform victims before the hearing that charges, once filed, will not be dropped and that if the case goes to trial the victim will be placed on the stand, reluctant or not. Still, faced with a hostile witness, prosecutors will often accept a plea to a lesser charge rather than risk a debacle in trial.

Bargains to Induce Testimony   In an occasional case, a defendant who had a relatively minor role in a crime or who has fewer prior offenses in his background than his codefendants will confess rather than fight the overwhelming evidence of his guilt, while the evidence against his associates may be light or totally lacking. Under that combination of circumstances, prosecutors may offer to reduce charges against the less culpable defendant to induce him to testify against the others. The "wheelman"—who has been recognized as he waits by the curb with the engine running—in a bank robbery in which people are injured or even killed is an example of an individual in this situation. The offer a prosecutor would make to reduce charges against the wheelman is legitimate if the prosecutor is convinced the fellow is telling the truth. Unlike most plea bargains, these deals involve a certain risk—that too much is given away to one defendant in the hope of nailing others. The chances of misidentification or perjury must be guarded against. Certainly the defense counsel for the codefendants will, during cross-examination of the witness, bring out the fact that this testimony was dealt for and hammer away at its credibility. Prosecutors have lost cases in which key testimony came from people in return for deals and juries had reasonable doubt about such bargained-for testimony.

Societal Considerations Considerations of societal interests often influence prosecutorial behavior with respect to plea bargaining. Certain classes of defendants or types of offenses present circumstances under which prosecutors are far less likely to offer a deal, preferring to take their chances in court. In other words, the stakes often become high enough that the risks involved in going for the win are worth it.

Heumann found that the prosecutors he studied drew sharp distinctions between serious and nonserious cases, and that they also drew a related but separate distinction between defendants whose cases would require time and those whose cases would not. He writes that in a nonserious matter:

> [Defendants] are amenable to defense requests for a small fine . . . some short, suspended sentence, or some brief period of probation. . . . The central concern with these nonserious cases is to dispose of them quickly. . . . On the other hand, if the case is serious, the prosecutor . . . [is] likely to be looking for time. The serious case cannot be quickly disposed of by a no-time alternative. These are cases in which we would expect more involved and lengthy plea bargaining.[5]

Heumann goes on to point out that among the factors that determine the relative seriousness of a case are the degree of victim harm, the amount of violence used, the defendant's prior record, the characteristics of both offender and victim, and the defendant's motive—all factors that are independent of the formal charges themselves.

As to the time/no-time distinction, prosecutors consider not only the seriousness of the crime, but other matters as well. One of these is the risk of losing because of a weak case, which prompts a willingness to agree to a no-time disposition even in a relatively serious case. Another consideration is the record of the offenders; a prosecutor may wish to press charges against an offender who, though never committing a really serious offense, has a long string of minor ones. The prosecutor may decide that it is time to achieve a societal goal and teach the accused a lesson, and so no deal is struck.[6]

This desire to achieve societal goals in plea bargaining was also addressed by Rosett and Cressy, who studied the use of plea bargaining by prosecutors and other court officials in tempering the harshness and rigidity of the law. Rosett and Cressy concluded that prosecutors often believe that, by agreeing to plea deals, they are "doing justice."[7] Heumann notes the same effect when he writes about the prosecutor redefining his professional goals:

Possessing more information about the defendant than the judge does, the prosecutor—probably unconsciously—comes to believe that it is his professional responsibility to develop standards that distinguish among defendants and lead to "equitable" dispositions. Over time, the prosecutor comes to feel that if he does not develop these standards, if he does not make these professional judgements, no one else will.[8]

Work Load Reduction   The most frequently cited reason for plea bargaining is that, without it, prosecutors and the courts would not be able to handle all their cases. It is a fact that most prosecutors have more cases than they can physically try. Consider that felony cases can involve several hours or even days of pretrial processing that can include preparation of discovery, attendance at depositions of witnesses, legal research, interviewing and preparing one's own witnesses, representing the state at hearings on various motions, and the drafting of arguments. There are jurisdictions in which, given these duties, a prosecutor cannot try even half the cases that cross his or her desk.

On the other hand, the time and energy required to negotiate a plea deal may also be considerable. If defense attorneys are skilled and experienced, and the stakes are high enough, they will insist that the prosecution satisfy them that the state has a winnable case before they will advise their clients to plead guilty. Defense attorneys sometimes wait to see if the state's key witness is really present, or they wait to examine the makeup of the jury pool. It is a fact that many cases are not settled until the very day or hour of the trial—and sometimes not until the jury has been selected and evidence is being presented. Such last-minute pleas or agreements to plead do little to save time or quicken the disposition of case loads.

As we have already noted, work load reduction is an argument that, when examined empirically, holds little water as an explanation for plea bargaining. The fact is that most cases are settled because of the nature of the cases themselves, not because they must be pushed out of the way to get to the others awaiting disposition. Heumann states that prosecutors "do not view their propensity to plea bargain as a direct outcome of case pressure," but speak instead of "mutually satisfactory outcomes," "fair dispositions," and so on. That a backlog would develop if bargains were eliminated is generally agreed on, but that does not explain why prosecutors engage in the practice. That explanation lies elsewhere. Heumann argues the explanation has more to do with a prosecutor's need to develop a set of standards (or adopt some prevailing ones) about how cases ought to be dealt with, and with a kind of mellowing process the prosecutor undergoes as he or she gains experience.[9]

Considerations of Ego and Public Image   Two factors remain to be discussed: the dictates of the prosecutor's ego and the resultant desire to avoid a loss, and the related matter of public image and the desire to avoid bad publicity. At first most new prosecutors are relatively "gung ho" to press full charges and take cases to trial, but within a few months their attitude has changed to one of avoiding defeat. Besides, as Heumann points out, the prosecutor's authority to plea bargain is a source of power over the lives of people. A prosecutor learns to adjust to and use this power.

As for public image, chief prosecutors generally want to get reelected or move on to bigger and better things, and so are ever mindful of the public's perception of their performance. Assistant prosecutors almost everywhere serve at the pleasure of their bosses, and so are conscious of the need to avoid adverse publicity. Such considerations lead prosecutors to be reluctant to plea bargain in high-visibility cases lest they be criticized for being "soft." Some offenders who commit especially notorious crimes or pick on celebrity victims are thus likely to find getting a deal much more difficult than would otherwise be the case.

The Defense's Objectives

The reader can infer much as to the objectives of defendants from a reading of the prosecutor's objectives discussed above. The defendant always wants out of the system with as little injury as possible. Even those few who are truly innocent of the charges sometimes seek to minimize the damage rather than seek complete vindication and risk a loss at trial.

A defendant's attorney will examine the case, its facts, its players, the character and quality of the prosecutor and the judge to whom the case is assigned, and then confer with the client as to the options, risks, and stakes associated with negotiating. The first and most obvious question is what the prosecutor can prove if the case goes to trial. Sometimes the discovery process will provide answers to that question. Once the defense has enough facts to estimate the probability of a jury verdict of guilty as charged or guilty of some lesser offense, it is ready to test the waters with the prosecutor (and with the judge, where the bench participates in the bargaining process) in order to minimize the consequences for the defendant.

Uncertainty as a Motivator   In trying to estimate the prosecutor's ability to convict, the defense attorney is struck by the fact that it is almost impossible to predict what a jury will do. Too many variables enter into jury behavior to make predictions anything but foolhardy. On top of this concern is the one about what the judge will do at sentencing should the verdict be one of guilty. Some lawyers refer to going to trial as "rolling the dice."

Some accused persons are less apprehensive than others, believing that there is always the chance of prosecutorial error or carelessness or change of heart in a witness. But some defendants who have an excellent chance of acquittal still plead guilty to reduce risk and to minimize the stakes. Their attorneys know about and inform them of the penalty for going to trial—the traditional practice of sentencing jury-convicted defendants to harsher terms than those who throw themselves on the mercy of the court or those who, if in a position to do so, cooperate with authorities in making cases against others. Demonstrations of remorse are generally rewarded by judges, while demonstrations of lack of remorse are generally severely punished.

Work Group Pressures Defense attorneys, too, feel compelled to moderate their own behavior as part of a work group. Heumann spells out the ways in which both prosecutors and judges can communicate their hostility to defense attorneys who consume their time and energy with motions challenging the arrest, the search, the amount of bond set, the jurisdiction of the court, and so on.[10] An attorney can jeopardize the chances of sympathetic treatment for his or her other clients if that attorney makes too much fuss over what is considered a routine case. The attorney can find that access to files and reports becomes severely restricted and cooperation from prosecutors is reduced to that which is absolutely mandated by law or ordered by the judge. In short, defense attorneys learn that to minimize the impact of the system on most of their clients, they must minimize their own impact on the system.

Rosett and Cressy comment on this aspect of the defense attorney's life by pointing out that the very nature of the work isolates him or her from the other system members—that defense attorneys cannot allow themselves to get too close to prosecutors, to judges, or even to their own clients. "There are strong pressures on [the defense attorney] to cooperate, to identify, and his job is lonely because he considers these influences dangerous, even corrupting," Rosett and Cressy write. "He walks a tightrope, maintaining a balance between adversariness on the one hand and cooperation on the other. If he leans too far in either direction, he falls."[11]

Work Load as a Factor This factor is subtle and is obviously related to work group pressures. Defendants are not motivated by their lawyers' work loads; they want the best defense possible in each case. Defense attorneys also generally want to do the best they can for each of their clients. But they live in a real world. In the case of private attorneys, bills must be paid and effort must be related to the fees the client can or will pay. In the case of public defenders, they must keep their large case loads moving along. Pleas generally take less time than trials, and the earlier in the process the defendant decides to plead guilty, the more quickly that case can be disposed of and a new one taken up.

Plea Bargaining and the Maturation Process   Heumann traces defense attorneys' careers through three stages: The first stage is a period of adjustment in which the young, idealistic fighter runs into the reality of plea bargaining and initially resists the pressures. The second stage occurs when the reality of the factual guilt of most clients and the "unwinnability" of most cases become obvious and the sanctions placed by judges and prosecutors on adversarial behavior become painful. The defense attorney then begins to deal out most cases. Heumann comments, "He is satisfied with the results obtained—indeed he is surprised at how lenient the dispositions are—but he is unhappy with the means used to achieve these results."[12] The third and final stage occurs when the attorney's mind-set changes and he or she accepts the presumption of plea bargaining as the guiding principle. The attorney has developed enough confidence and enough rapport with prosecutors that he or she can be an "informal adversary" on cases in which there is good legal or factual basis to go to trial. Behind-the-scenes negotiations can get cases dropped or at least sharply reduced in impact. Actual trials become the last resort only for those cases on which the prosecutor cannot or will not deal.[13]

The Court's Objectives

Obviously the court's mission is to see that justice is done, but how that mission is accomplished is complicated by real-world factors, including crowded dockets that make it impossible to try every case. Judges come to the bench with their own presumptions about what they're going to do, but they are not able to impose their beliefs and values without constraint. Heumann states flatly that the "judge's position is reactive."[14] That is, he or she waits for matters to come before the bench, and most of them come in the form of prearranged agreements between prosecutor and defense counsel.

A judge has personal views on matters of punishment, deterrence, rehabilitation, and so on; a judge also has views on whether emphasis should be placed on equality of sanctions or on individualization of justice to fit the offender and circumstances of the case. As Rosett and Cressy point out, the law usually gives little guidance on how a judge is supposed to rule.[15] (This is not true in a state that has a highly determinate sentencing scheme or rigid sentencing guidelines, but this is a matter to be taken up later.)

Rosett and Cressy spell out the fix judges find themselves in. They have the power to "do justice" and to do in each case what they think is correct.

> At the same time, the judge knows how important the steady rate of guilty pleas is in his court and how crucial his cooperation is in enabling the system to work. It makes no sense for him to sit in court all day deciding cases in which there are no substantive issues. If a case is clear-cut, it should be disposed of by a guilty plea or a dismissal. Otherwise the lawyers are not doing their jobs. But for a guilty plea system to work there must be some reliable expectation of what the sentence will be if the defendant pleads guilty, and this expectation inevitably must come explicitly or implicitly from the judge who will impose sentence. . . . No matter how aloof a judge may think he is and no matter how eccentric others may think he is, he shares in a framework of understandings, expectations and agreements that are relied upon to dispose of most criminal cases.[16]

Quite simply, if judges cannot be predictable, then plea bargains will be tougher to come by. If bargains are difficult to arrange, trials increase. If trials increase, cases can quickly become backlogged. If the docket becomes backlogged, either the court must be in session longer hours, the burden must be shifted to other judges, or cases must be dismissed for lack of "speedy trial." Case-load pressure may have little to do with the settlements arrived at in individual cases, but it certainly contributes to the inclination of judges to encourage settlement.

The basic method many judges use to encourage pleas is to punish those with trial convictions more severely than those who plead, especially if in the judge's opinion the issues contested at trial are "frivolous." The approaches judges use, however, vary. Some remain above the fray, so to speak, and merely accept what is dealt them. These judges are sometimes unhappy with the results, but feel constrained not to overturn them. Other judges involve themselves informally, either by discussing terms with the attorneys or making veiled threats about what they might do if the matter is not settled. Still others institutionalize plea bargains by conducting hearings in the courtrooms or in chambers at which all parties are present and a sort of "pretrial" or "minitrial" takes place. Whatever the mode or motivation for participation, though, the judge is as much a part of plea bargaining as are the attorneys.

THE PROCESS OF PLEA BARGAINING

The actual bargaining process itself is usually informal and may take place during any meeting between the lawyers, even chance meetings in the courthouse hallways. But as has been stated, judges can at times involve themselves, and the process can be formalized into pretrial conferences. It is more common, however, for one lawyer to approach the other and simply say, "Look, the Jones case is coming up soon and I thought we might be able to work something out." Sometimes a certain amount of bluffing or "poker playing" is engaged in, with each lawyer overstating his or her own case and trying to find out exactly how strong a case the other lawyer has and what he or she intends to do with it.

Some negotiations can be protracted and involve several conversations over several days or even weeks. This is not uncommon in high-stakes cases, especially where there is also a close call on the direction in which the evidence points. On the other hand, it is also common for so-called negotiations to be nothing more than an initial offer and its acceptance. This is especially true in low-stakes cases, what are called "junk" or "garbage" cases—cases in which the facts indicate lack of real harm to the victim or lack of real criminal intent on the part of the offender. Such cases often involve personal disputes and drunken acts.

Negotiations are typically carried out without the accused being present. The defense attorney normally approaches the prosecutor first, then relaying to the client the prosecutor's "best" offer. The client is usually unhappy about the bargain until convinced by the attorney that the offer represents the least of several alternative evils—in other words, that the risks are high for refusal. No one wishes to agree to something unpleasant unless he or she is fearful that lack of agreement will bring even more unpleasant consequences. The authors have known defense attorneys to use many different techniques to persuade their clients to plead guilty when they know that will bring some form of punishment. Some lawyers explain calmly, some cajole, and some try to intimidate. Whatever technique the lawyer uses, the accused will invariably wonder what would have happened had he or she insisted on going to trial.

We cannot end this discussion without pointing out a paradox. It has to do with an attorney's skills: Can a lawyer who cannot convince a client of the wisdom of a guilty plea convince a jury of that client's innocence? And is it not possible that a lawyer who is almost always successful at persuading a client to plead might also be the most effective in the courtroom and thus the least in need of plea bargaining for a client?

THE PRODUCT OF THE BARGAIN

Plea deals can occur before charges are filed or after arraignment. They can take several forms. The most common plea bargains are (1) an agreement to reduce the level of charges or take a plea to lesser included offenses—a *vertical plea deal*; (2) an agreement not to prosecute on some charges in response to a plea to others—a *horizontal plea deal*; and (3) an agreement for a plea to the charges as filed in return for the prosecutor's acquiescence in a lenient sentence—a *sentence bargain* for a plea "straight up." In complex multiple-charge cases, these types may be combined.

Pleas to Lesser Charges

The negotiation of a plea to a lesser included offense requires an understanding and agreement on the part of the defendant that he or she will plead guilt to an offense that is less serious and therefore less severely punishable than the one with which the defendant was originally charged. A *lesser included offense* is one that is actually contained within the offense originally filed but lacks one or more of the criminal elements of the original offense.

A good example is provided by first-degree murder, which is a criminal homicide involving premeditation—a calculated intent to kill. Lesser included criminal homicides are second-degree murder, manslaughter, and various aggravated and simple batteries. These are all lesser offenses within the crime of first-degree murder, and each drops an element from the original crime, with premeditation being the first to go. Batteries drop even the element of death of the victim. Much more commonly used lesser included offenses are trespass within the crime of burglary and petty theft within the crime of grand theft.

The plea to a lesser included offense is generally acceptable to those concerned because the evidence is usually very clear as to guilt on the lesser. The lesser offense carries less time, or even a reduced chance of incarceration, for the accused, and this provides the incentive to plead to the lesser.

Prosecutors are often quick to point out that pleas to lessers are intellectually honest and that the task of determining sentence is left to the judge "where it belongs." It is often easier for prosecutors to face disgruntled victims with the explanation that the judge imposed the sentence at his or her own volition based on the "no strings attached" tender of a guilty plea than for prosecutors to admit to victims that they agree with that sentence. Prosecutors do not, as we have already made clear, legally represent victims in criminal proceedings, but they do come under substantial pressure from victims and/or victims' families. Some prosecutors feel as though victims are, in effect, their "clients" and that they must be answered to when deals are made that may anger them.

Dropped Charges or Cases

In many cases involving multiple counts or charges, the prosecutor may agree to drop some counts in the case against the accused in return for pleas of guilty to one or more of the other counts. This occurs when multiple offenses or violations arise from one criminal transaction or transactional series, and all are filed in a single charging document, whether by indictment or information. A variation on this theme occurs when multiple cases are filed against a single defendant because he or she committed a string of separate crimes. Prosecutors will drop some cases (or decline to file them in the first place) in return for pleas to others. The dropping, either of counts within cases or of whole cases already filed, involves the prosecutor's use of the power to enter a *nolle prosequi*, or "nol pros," of any charge—that is, to file "an interest not to pursue."

Prosecutors often justify this approach on the grounds that the offender "took the plea on the important charges." Sometimes this is true where the pleas were to the most serious charges. Most judges will not sentence the offender to any more time—or to stiffer conditions—for the additional offenses anyway, since there is in most states a presumption toward what is called *concurrent sentencing*. This means that all terms will be served simultaneously. Often the accused winds up with an impression that he or she has been let off with a less severe sentence than might have been handed down on all charges, but this impression is false; the state really gives up nothing in the bargain. But where more serious charges are dropped in return for a plea to the lessers, then we have a vertical lowering of the case as well as a horizontal reduction in numbers, and the potential for a truly less severe sentence is great.

Probably the most common situation in this category is that involving the young burglar or thief with a dozen or more offenses, all of which carry a maximum of, say, fifteen years. But this sentence potential can be reached by filing only one or two of the cases; the others can be kept unfiled as leverage to induce pleas to the original charges. There are, of course, astute offenders who see through all this and recognize the prosecutor's ploy for exactly what it is.

Sentence Bargains

A *sentence bargain* is one in which the accused agrees to plead to charges as filed in order to obtain a lesser sentence. The prosecutor agrees not to oppose the defense counsel's efforts to mitigate the sentence, and may even join defense counsel in assuring the defendant of a certain sentence. From the defendant's perspective, the sentence is the important matter anyway, and many defendants become less apprehensive about pleading guilty if they are confident they will not be incarcerated, or at least not given a substantial prison term. Most cases in this category are relatively simple, single-transaction crimes of lesser seriousness to begin with, so there is often little or no room for reduction in the number or the seriousness of the charges. The sentence is the only issue at stake.

Critics of sentence bargaining—and there are many—often point out that all discretion is removed from the court when this process is utilized. They argue that sentencing should be at the discretion of a neutral, detached person, the judge. Sentencing, they assert, is designed to serve the interests of society, and a sentence that represents a bargain struck by lawyers on the basis of the relative strengths or weaknesses of their cases or of their desire to move on to other cases does not reflect a concern for the proper goals of punishment.

Some prosecutors' offices decline to sentence bargain, both for the philosophical reasons just stated and for reasons having to do with their responsibilities to the victims and their families. As we discussed earlier, there are, on the other hand, many prosecutors who sentence bargain routinely after they have become comfortable with their role in determining penal policy in their jurisdiction and have established a set of informal guidelines for themselves covering "serious," "nonserious," and "junk" cases.

JUDICIAL REVIEW AND ACCEPTANCE OF PLEAS

Pleas of guilty are subject to review and acceptance by the trial judge. This means, of course, that the judge can refuse to accept the plea and can hold the case over for trial.

ABA Standards

In 1968 the American Bar Association published a copyrighted set of standards for pleas of guilty. The standards are nonbinding, but they provide a guide for a judge's conduct when handling cases in which plea agreements have been reached. The portion appropriate for consideration is as follows:

Consideration of Plea in Final Disposition

(a) It is proper for the court to grant charge and sentence concessions to defendants who enter a plea of guilty or nolo contendere when the interest of the public in the effective administration of criminal justice would thereby be served. Among the considerations which are appropriate in determining this question are:

(i) that the defendant by his plea has aided in ensuring the prompt and certain application of correctional measures to him;

(ii) that the defendant has acknowledged his guilt and shown a willingness to assume responsibility for his conduct;

(iii) that the concessions will make possible alternative correctional measure, which are better adapted to achieving rehabilitative, protective, deterrent or other purposes of correctional treatment, or will prevent undue harm to the defendant from the form or conviction;

(iv) that the defendant has made public trial unnecessary when there are good reasons for not having the case dealt with in a public trial;

(v) that the defendant has given or offered cooperation when such cooperation has resulted or may result in the successful prosecution of other offenders engaged in equally serious or more serious criminal conduct;

(vi) that the defendant by his plea has aided in avoiding delay (including delay due to crowded dockets) in the disposition of other cases and thereby has increased the probability of prompt and certain application of correctional measures to other offenders.

(b) The court should not impose upon a defendant any sentence in excess of that which would be justified by way of the rehabilitative, protective, deterrent or other purposes of the criminal law because the defendant has chosen to require the prosecution to prove his guilt at trial rather than to enter a plea of guilty or nolo contendere.[17]

A Plea-Taking Checklist

Judges are supposed to be assured that the guilty pleas they accept from defendants are offered voluntarily, with full knowledge of the consequences of a conviction, and that the offense being pleaded to is based on the evidence presented—that is, that the plea is "accurate." Part of the *voluntariness* issue revolves around whether the accused was improperly coerced or was made improper promises by the attorneys. The irony is, of course, that the whole process is inherently coercive—a matter we shall take up later—and that defendants are usually bending to pressure, if not to actual threats.

A prudent judge will engage in a structured dialogue with the defendant that not only inquires into all aspects of the plea agreement but that also preserves the questions and answers for the record. This is to head off possible appeals later.

An excellent illustration of the duties of a judge and of a checklist that might be used in the acceptance of guilty pleas is provided by the recently updated Rule 3.172 of the *Florida Rules of Criminal Procedure*:[18]

Acceptance of Guilty or Nolo Contendere Plea

(a) Before accepting a plea of guilty or nolo contendere the trial judge shall satisfy himself that the plea is voluntarily entered and that there is a factual basis for it. Counsel for the prosecution and the defense shall assist the trial judge in this function.

(b) All pleas shall be taken in open court, except that where good cause is shown a plea may be taken in camera.

(c) Except where a defendant is not present for a plea, pursuant to the provisions of Rule 3.180(c), the trial judge should, when determining voluntariness, place the defendant under oath and shall address the defendant personally and shall determine that he understands the following:

(i) The nature of the charge to which the plea is offered, the mandatory minimum penalty provided by law, if any, and the maximum possible penalty provided by law; and

(ii) If the defendant is not represented by an attorney, that he has the right to be represented by an attorney at every stage of the proceeding against him and, if necessary, one will be appointed to represent him; and

(iii) That he has the right to plead not guilty or to persist in that plea if it has already been made, and that he has the right to be tried by a jury and at that trial has the right to the assistance of counsel, the right to compel attendance of witnesses on his behalf, the right to confront and cross-examine witnesses against him, and the right not to be compelled to incriminate himself.

(iv) That if he pleads guilty, or nolo contendere without express reservation of right to appeal, he gives up his right to appeal all matters relating to the judgment, including the issue of guilt or innocence, but he does not impair his right to review by appropriate collateral attack.

(v) That if he pleads guilty or is adjudged guilty after a plea of nolo contendere there will not be a further trial of any kind, so that by pleading guilty or nolo contendere he waives the right to a trial; and

(vi) That if he pleads guilty or nolo contendere, the trial judge may ask him questions about the offense to which he has pleaded, and if he answers these questions under oath, on the record, and in the presence of counsel, his answers may later be used against him in a prosecution for perjury; and

(vii) The complete terms of any plea agreement, including specifically all obligations the defendant will incur as a result.

(viii) That if he or she pleads guilty or nolo contendere the trial judge must inform him or her that, if he or she is not a United States citizen, the plea may subject him or her to deportation pursuant to the laws and regulations governing the United States Naturalization and Immigration Service. It shall not be necessary for the trial judge to inquire as to whether the defendant is a United States citizen, as this admonition shall be given to all defendants in all cases.

(d) Before the trial judge accepts a guilty or nolo contendere plea, he must determine that the defendant either 1) acknowledges his guilt, or 2) acknowledges that he feels the plea to be in his best interest, while maintaining his innocence.

(e) The proceedings at which a defendant pleads guilty or nolo contendere shall be of record.

(f) No plea offer or negotiation is binding until it is accepted by the trial judge formally after making all the inquiries, advisements and determinations required by this Rule. Until that time, it may be withdrawn by either party without any necessary justification.

(g) Should the trial judge not concur in a tendered plea of guilty or nolo contendere arising from negotiations, the plea may be withdrawn.

(h) Except as otherwise provided in this Rule, evidence of an offer or a plea of guilty or nolo contendere, later withdrawn, or of statements made in connection therewith, is not admissible in any civil or criminal proceeding against the person who made the plea or offer.

(i) Failure to follow any of the procedures in this Rule shall not render a plea void absent a showing of prejudice.

The Issue of Voluntariness

It should be perfectly obvious that one should not give up one's constitutional right to a full trial—with attendant rights to confront the accused, to force the state to prove its case, and to judgment by a jury, as well as the subsequent right to appeal—without full advisement and understanding of what one is surrendering. At the same time, it is also obvious that in many cases the court winks at provisions regarding the voluntariness of pleas and that many defendants receive less than the best and most vigorous representation by their counsel. The pressure to plead guilty, even in the absence of threats or explicit promises, is enormous.

Many pleas are tendered out of fear of "doing time," even where the accused asserts that he or she is absolutely innocent of any crime. The authors are aware of more than one case in which an accused has decided to plead guilty rather than contest charges because the case has been scheduled before a punitive judge, and the fear of possible jail time, with its personal and family consequences, outweighs considerations of establishing innocence.

Even more serious are cases in which the defendant pleads guilty in a capital case after receiving the prosecutor's assurance that, in return for the plea, the state will not seek the death penalty. Such a case reached the Supreme Court in 1970.[19] It involved a defendant named Harry Alford who was charged with first-degree murder in North Carolina. (This case occurred prior to the *Furman* case of 1972, which forced all states to redraft their death penalty statutes.) North Carolina's law stipulated that following conviction at trial for first-degree murder, the death penalty was mandatory unless the jury specifically recommended against it.

The prosecutor offered to allow the accused to plead guilty to second-degree murder and thus remove the possibility of the death sentence. After submission and acceptance of the plea, Alford changed his mind and requested a trial. He argued that the combination of the law and the prosecutor's deal had pressured him into the plea—that it had not been a voluntary or rational choice. Alford pointed out that even during the plea acceptance hearing before the judge he had stated that he was innocent of the crime, that he had pleaded guilty only to escape death, and that he had not been adequately represented by counsel.

The Supreme Court ruled that the plea deal was constitutional. Justice White argued for the court that Alford and the trial judge were responding to overwhelming independent evidence of his guilt. Alford's choice was, therefore, a free and rational one in light of a high likelihood that trial would have resulted in conviction and imposition of the death penalty. Because of the importance of the case, we excerpt the majority and dissenting opinions here.

North Carolina v. Alford

400 U.S. 25 (1970)

FROM THE OPINION

By Justice White

On December 2, 1963, Alford was indicted for first-degree murder, a capital offense under North Carolina law. The court appointed an attorney to represent him, and this attorney questioned all but one of the various witnesses who appellee said would substantiate his claim of innocence. The witnesses, however, did not support Alford's story but gave statements that strongly indicated his guilt. Faced with strong evidence of guilt and no substantial evidentiary support for the claim of innocence, Alford's attorney recommended that he plead guilty, but left the ultimate decision to Alford himself. The prosecutor agreed to accept a plea of guilty to a charge of second-degree murder, and on December 10, 1963, Alford pleaded guilty to the reduced charge.

Before the plea was finally accepted by the trial court, the court heard the sworn testimony of a police officer who summarized the State's case. Two other witnesses besides Alford were also heard. Although there was no eyewitness to the crime, the testimony indicated that shortly before the killing Alford took his gun from his house, stated his intention to kill the victim, and returned home with the declaration that he had carried out the killing. After the summary presentation of the State's case, Alford took the stand and testified that he had not committed the murder but that he was pleading guilty because he faced the threat of the death penalty if he did not do so. In response to the questions of his counsel, he acknowledged that his counsel had informed him of the difference between second- and first-degree murder and of his rights in case he chose to go to trial. The trial court then asked appellee if, in light of his denial of guilt, he still desired to plead guilty to second-degree murder and appellee answered, "Yes, sir. I plead guilty on—from the circumstances that he [Alford's attorney] told me." After eliciting information about Alford's prior criminal record, which was a long one, the trial court sentenced him to 30 years' imprisonment, the maximum penalty for second-degree murder. . . .

We held in Brady v United States . . . that a plea of guilty which would not have been entered except for the defendant's desire to avoid a possible death penalty and to limit the maximum penalty to life imprisonment or a term of years was not for that reason compelled within the meaning of the Fifth Amendment. Jackson established no new test for determining the validity of guilty pleas. The standard was and remains whether the plea represents a voluntary and intelligent choice among the alternative courses of action open to the defendant. . . . That he would not have pleaded except for the opportunity to limit the possible penalty does not necessarily demonstrate that the plea of guilty was not the product of a free and rational choice, especially where the defendant was represented by competent counsel whose advice was that the plea would be to the defendant's advantage. The standard fashioned and applied by the Court of Appeals was therefore erroneous and we would, without more, vacate and remand the case for further proceedings with respect to any other claims of Alford which are properly before that court, if it were not for other circumstances appearing in the record which might seem to warrant an affirmance of the Court of Appeals.

As previously recounted, after Alford's plea of guilty was offered and the State's case was placed before the judge, Alford denied that he had committed the murder but reaffirmed his desire to plead guilty to avoid a possible death sentence and to limit the penalty to the 30-year maximum provided for second-degree murder. Ordinarily, a judgment of conviction resting on a plea of guilty is justified by the defendant's admission that he committed the crime charged against him and his consent that judgment be entered without a trial of any kind. The plea usually subsumes both elements, and justifiably so, even though there is no separate, express admission by the defendant that he committed the particular acts claimed to constitute the crime charged in the indictment. . . . Alford entered his plea but accompanied it with the statement that he had not shot the victim.

If Alford's statements were to be credited as sincere assertions of his innocence, there obviously existed a factual and legal dispute between him and the State. Without more, it might be argued that the conviction entered on his guilty plea was invalid, since his assertion of innocence negatived any admission of guilt, which, as we observed last Term in Brady, is normally "[c]entral to the plea and the foundation for entering judgment against the defendant." . . .

In addition to Alford's statement, however, the court had heard an account of the events on the night of the murder, including information from Alford's acquaintances that he had departed from his home with his gun stating his intention to kill and that he had later declared that he had carried out his intention. Nor had Alford wavered in his desire to have the trial court determine his guilt without a jury trial. Although denying the charge against him, he nevertheless preferred the dispute between him and the State to be settled by the judge in the context of a guilty plea proceeding rather than by a formal trial. Thereupon, with the State's telling evidence and Alford's denial before it, the trial court proceeded to convict and sentence Alford for second-degree murder.

State and lower federal courts are divided upon whether a guilty plea can be accepted when it is accompanied by protestations of innocence and hence contains only a waiver of trial but no admission of guilt. This Court has not confronted this precise issue, but prior decisions do yield relevant principles. . . .

These cases would be directly in point if Alford had simply insisted on this plea but refused to admit the crime. The fact that his plea was denominated a plea of guilty rather than a plea of nolo contendere is of no constitutional significance with respect to the issue now before us, for the Constitution is concerned with the practical consequences, not the formal categorizations of state law. Thus, while most pleas of guilty consist of both a waiver of trial and an express admission of guilt, the latter element is not a constitutional requisite to the imposition of criminal penalty. An individual accused of crime may voluntarily, knowingly, and understandingly consent to the imposition of a prison sentence even if he is unwilling or unable to admit his participation in the acts constituting the crime.

Nor can we perceive any material difference between a plea that refuses to admit commission of the criminal act and a plea containing a protestation of innocence when, as in the instant case, a defendant intelligently concludes that his interests require entry of a guilty plea and the record before the judge contains strong evidence of actual guilt. Here the State had a strong case of first-degree murder against Alford. Whether he realized or disbelieved his guilt, he insisted on his plea because in his view he had absolutely nothing to gain by a trial and much to gain by pleading. Because of the overwhelming evidence against him, a trial was precisely what neither Alford nor his attorney desired. Confronted with the choice between a trial for first-degree murder, on the one hand, and a plea of guilty to second-degree murder, on the other, Alford quite reasonably chose the latter and thereby limited the maximum penalty to a 30-year term. When his plea is viewed in light of the evidence against him, which substantially negated his claim of innocence and which further provided a means by which the judge could test whether the plea was being intelligently entered, see McCarthy v United States, . . . its validity cannot be seriously questioned. In view of the strong factual basis for the plea demonstrated by the State and Alford's clearly expressed desire to enter it despite his professed belief in his innocence, we hold that the trial judge did not commit constitutional error in accepting it.

Relying on United States v Jackson, supra, Alford now argues in effect that the State should not have allowed him this choice but should have insisted on proving him guilty of murder in the first degree. The States in their wisdom may take this course by statute or otherwise and may prohibit the practice of accepting pleas to lesser included offenses under any circumstances. But this is not the mandate of the Fourteenth Amendment and the Bill of Rights. The prohibitions against involuntary or unintelligent pleas should not be relaxed, but neither should an exercise in arid logic render those constitutional guarantees counterproductive and put in jeopardy the very human values they were meant to preserve.

The Court of Appeals for the Fourth Circuit was in error to find Alford's plea of guilty invalid because it was made to avoid the possibility of the death penalty. That court's judgment directing the issuance of the writ of habeas corpus is vacated and the case is remanded to the Court of Appeals for further proceedings consistent with this opinion.

It is so ordered.

FROM THE DISSENT

By Justice Brennan

Last Term, this Court held, over my dissent, that a plea of guilty may validly be induced by an unconstitutional threat to subject the defendant to the risk of death, so long as the plea is entered in open court and the defendant is represented by competent counsel who is aware of the threat, albeit not of its unconstitutionality. . . . Today the Court makes clear that its previous holding was intended to apply even when the record demonstrates that the actual effect of the unconstitutional threat was to induce a guilty plea from a defendant who was unwilling to admit his guilt.

I adhere to the view that, in any given case, the influence of such an unconstitutional threat "must necessarily be given weight in determining the voluntariness of a plea."... And, without reaching the question whether due process permits the entry of judgment upon a plea of guilty accompanied by a contemporaneous denial of acts constituting the crime, I believe that at the very least such a denial of guilt is also a relevant factor in determining whether the plea was voluntarily and intelligently made. With these factors in mind, it is sufficient in my view to state that the facts set out in the majority opinion demonstrate that Alford was "so gripped by fear of the death penalty" that his decision to plead guilty was not voluntary but was "the product of duress as much so as choice reflecting physical constraint." Accordingly, I would affirm the judgment of the Court of Appeals.

ACQUIESCENCE AND SEVERITY

As we have observed, it is painfully obvious that many judges impose severer sentences on defendants who exercise their constitutional right to a trial, especially where evidence of guilt is overwhelming. There are four factors to be considered here.

The first factor is the time and energy of everyone associated with a trial. Judges are sensitive to the need to keep dockets moving and prevent backlogs. Some of them are also cognizant of the fact that trials lasting into late afternoons interfere with golf games, sailing, or other socially acceptable leisure activities. It is of no help that most trials are dreary recitations of depressingly similar facts and issues.

A second matter concerns trials in which defendants testify in their own defense, are convicted anyway, and can therefore be suspected of having perjured themselves on the stand. Even where perjury is not charged, nor a contempt citation issued, judges are still offended that the suspect testimony was given in their courtrooms and are likely to consider the implied perjury worth punishing.

Where the defense case itself is frivolous, it strains the court's patience and, in the judge's mind, warrants some punishment. Some clients refuse to listen to the advice of their attorneys and insist on trials, hoping for a prosecutorial error or for a gullible jury. Where the lawyer is the one responsible, the punishment may be aimed as much at him or her as at the accused.

Finally there is the strong feeling on the part of many judges that defendants who admit to their offenses and seem ready and willing to accept the consequences of their behavior qualify for a rehabilitative approach in sentencing. On the other hand, defendants who insist on their innocence, especially in the face of overwhelming evidence, are the ones who are seemingly in need of a strong dose of retribution and incapacitation. Incapacitation is even more appropriate if the accused comes to trial with a considerable record of prior crimes. Because the stakes are already so high, the only hope such people generally hold for themselves is to take a chance on acquittal in a trial, as slim a chance as it may be.

To sum up, if the trial is a "waste" of everyone's time, if the defendant is deemed an incorrigible offender, or if the judge would have preferred either to deal with other business or to take the afternoon off, that judge is likely to entertain whatever sentence the prosecutor deems appropriate. Without doubt, the sentence will be steeper than the defendant might have received if he or she had pleaded guilty. In the judgment of the court, the sentence will not necessarily constitute punishment for going to trial per se, but punishment deserved for the offender's overall behavior.

Perhaps no treatment of the issues of acquiescence and severity is better than that provided by criminologists Arthur Rosett and Donald Cressy in a book published some years ago.[20] They found that guilty pleas tend to fall into four categories: (1) defendants are eager to confess and accept responsibility; (2) essentially professional thieves accept occasional convictions and jailings as a cost of doing business; (3) defendants feel justified in their crimes though freely pleading guilty; and (4) "the huge majority of defendants submit to the painful consequences of conviction but do not know for certain whether they have committed any of the crimes of which they are accused." Only the first group of accused truly confess and repent, but officials insist on acquiescence even in the absence of repentance. They do so, write the authors, because it keeps the system running smoothly, seems to justify the therapeutic treatment of offenders, and it "eases any doubts about whether a defendant is guilty and about whether the sentence is just." Thus pleas do more than increase efficiency; they "have important social control functions, and, at the same time, great psychological value."

As to the issue of severity, Rosett and Cressy argue that the system "makes life painfully unpleasant for a person arrested" before any disposition, especially for a person kept in jail who thus loses job, property, friends, and family ties. Meanwhile the defendant's case is shuffled along as though it is of minor importance, defense counsel spends brief periods of time with the accused, speaking a strange jargon, and the vague threat of something really bad—a prison term—hangs over the head of the accused. The long prison terms most laws provide enhance the severity of the treatment of the defendant and provide officials with great leverage to obtain acquiescence in a guilty plea.

Rosett and Cressy view all this as fundamentally illegitimate abuse of power—an assault on any due process perspective and unwise even from the crime control standpoint. The only offenders really deterred are those in the first category, the true repenters. On the other hand, Rosett and Cressy recognize, as do Heumann and others, that bargains struck usually mitigate the harshness of statutory provisions and produce more realistic and sometimes even humane results. They urge not the abolition of plea bargaining, but its reform—through reductions in statutory penal terms, that is, reduced severity, and open procedures designed to secure "genuine acquiescence."

PLEA BARGAINING IN PERSPECTIVE

Specific reforms will be discussed in a later chapter. For now we want to return to the themes of crime control and due process, and to the question of whether plea bargaining serves either model. It seems clear on the face of it that due process is a casualty of plea bargaining, since a plea is used in part to circumvent the obstacles the rules are designed to erect. It can also be argued, as Rosett and Cressy and other critics do, that crime control too is ill served. If defendants feel cheated, they are hardly deterred; nor are they deterred if they feel like they've "beaten the rap." On the other hand, prosecutors argue that getting convictions in some cases ("half a loaf") serves crime control better than having an offender who can't be convicted at trial go scot-free. Even some defense attorneys will agree on this point.

Perhaps it comes down to how the process is conducted rather than whether it should take place at all. Few reformers any longer call for abolition of plea bargaining. Most call for changes in the way it is done, preferring to see open, formal proceedings governed by clearer rules of conduct.

SUMMARY AND CONCLUSIONS

This has necessarily been a very long and substantive chapter. It has examined plea bargaining in terms of the kinds of pleas available, the motivations of and factors considered by each of the major actors, the types of agreements that are reached, the role of the judge in deciding whether guilty pleas should be accepted, and the issues involved from both the crime control and due process perspectives.

There is ample evidence that the process can be abusive, both of defendants and society. Victims have historically had little to say about it. There seem to be few legitimate reasons to preserve it, much less use it so widely. Yet plea bargaining not only goes on, it has become the means by which all but a few criminal cases are disposed. Plea bargaining continues because of practical considerations and because there is a widespread sense that justice can often be better served through negotiated pleas than through trials. Anyone planning a career in the criminal justice system must understand the philosophy of the plea bargain as well as the process.

QUESTIONS FOR DISCUSSION

1. Do you believe that plea bargaining is extensive in your local courthouse? If so, do you think that it diminishes the quality of justice? Why or why not?
2. Which model, Crime Control or Due Process, is best served by plea bargaining? Are both models served concurrently? Which model is most damaged by plea bargaining? How?
3. With the current level of staffing in your community's courthouse, is plea bargaining essential to cope with the case load? If not, why does plea bargaining take place? If so, what would it—other than emphasis on plea bargaining—take to remedy the situation?
4. If you were on the bench, in what kinds of cases might you reject plea agreements arrived at by prosecutors and defense attorneys? Why? What reactions to your rejections would you expect from the attorneys, and how would you deal with those reactions?

NOTES

1. Milton Heumann, *Plea Bargaining: The Experiences of Prosecutors, Judges, and Defense Attorneys,* University of Chicago Press, Chicago, 1978, p. 32.
2. Ibid., pp. 27–32.
3. See, for example, James Eisenstein and Herbert Jacob, *Felony Justice: An Organizational Analysis of Criminal Courts,* Little, Brown, Boston, 1977; and Peter Nardulli, *The Courtroom Elite: An Organizational Perspective,* Ballinger, Cambridge, Mass., 1978.
4. J. Michael Thompson, "Caseload Pressure Theory," unpublished paper, 1985.
5. Heumann,, p. 103.
6. Ibid., p. 104.
7. Arthur Rosett and Donald C. Cressy, *Justice by Consent,* Lippincott, Philadelphia, 1976, pp. 85–86 and 133–134.

8. Heumann, p. 109.
9. Ibid., pp. 116, 118–119.
10. Ibid., p. 62.
11. Rosett and Cressy, p. 122.
12. Heumann, p. 81.
13. Ibid., p. 84.
14. Ibid., p. 134.
15. Rosett and Cressy, p. 71.
16. Ibid., pp. 80, 81.
17. ABA Commission on Minimum Standards for Criminal Justice, *Standards Related to Pleas of Guilty,* ABA, Chicago, 1968, pp. 36–37.
18. *Florida Rules of Criminal Procedure,* Rule 3.172.
19. *North Carolina v. Alford,* 400 U.S. 25 (1970).
20. Rosett and Cressy, pp. 146–159.

CHAPTER 11

ADJUDICATION BY TRIAL

After reading this chapter, students should be able to define and explain the importance of each of the following terms or phrases:

competency to stand trial
bench trial
hung jury
jury pardons
eligibility requirements
the voir dire
challenge for cause
peremptory challenge
scientific jury selection
discovery
liberal discovery
trial by ambush
deposition of witnesses
speedy trial rules
testimonial evidence
real evidence
direct evidence
circumstantial evidence
competency of witness
relevancy of evidence

opinion testimony
expert witness
judicial notice
evidentiary presumptions
hearsay evidence
exceptions to the hearsay evidence
 rule
admissions against interest
dying declaration
objections
alibi defense
insanity defense
M'Naughten rule
irresistible impulse test
Durham rule
involuntary intoxication defense
entrapment defense
duress defense
consent defense

The trial of a criminal case is the climax of the criminal justice process and the test of all elements of the case. If the police and the prosecutor have done their jobs and the defense its, a true verdict will allow justice to be done. Few human endeavors are so clearly decided in the public view. The prosecutor has the burden of proving each and every allegation beyond and to the exclusion of reasonable doubt. And he or she must do this with legally admissible evidence and do it convincingly.

The defendant is pitted against the powers of the state or federal government and is therefore frequently at a disadvantage because of limited resources. The defense's task of raising reasonable doubt by the end of the trial is also complicated by the very real belief on the part of many jurors that the accused wouldn't even be sitting in the courtroom unless he or she was, in fact, guilty. The role of being a defendant in a criminal case is at best uncomfortable and is very uncertain.

COMPETENCY OF THE ACCUSED

The accused must be competent to stand trial. He or she must be sane to the extent of understanding the nature of the proceedings and of being able to assist the defense lawyer in preparing and presenting the case. A defendant who is not sane to that degree cannot stand trial until the court adjudges him or her to be sane, a decision based upon the testimony of psychiatrists. The judge, the defense counsel, or the prosecutor may raise the issue of sanity; if the issue is raised, the judge will appoint experts, usually psychiatrists, to examine the defendant.

It is important to note that the issue of sanity as it relates to the defendant's *competency to stand trial* should not be confused with the defense of insanity at the time of commission of the crime. The latter is a question of fact for the jury to determine. In this case, the defense must raise the issue and introduce testimony to try to convince the jury that the defendant is not guilty because of legal insanity at the time the offense was actually committed. A defense based on insanity, which is independent of the issue of competency to stand trial, will be treated later in this chapter.

If the court—the judge—finds the accused unfit to stand trial, the accused will typically be committed to a mental hospital until such time as he or she can understand the nature of the proceedings and can assist the defense lawyer in the preparation and presentation of the case. A mere reluctance of the defendant to work with the lawyer will not, in and of itself, demonstrate legal incompetency to stand trial. Commitment to a mental institution does not preclude future prosecution. The defendant must, within a reasonable time, be brought to trial or a permanent commitment to the institution must be sought. This procedure is regulated by statute and varies greatly from state to state.

THE TRIAL JURY

The defendant, except in very minor cases with little or no potential for incarceration, is entitled to a trial by a jury of peers unless the defendant specifically waives that right. The Sixth Amendment states that "In all criminal prosecutions, the accused shall enjoy the right to a speedy and public trial, by an impartial jury of the State and district wherein the crime shall have been committed, which district shall have been previously ascertained by law, and to be informed of the nature and cause of the accusation; to be confronted with the witnesses against him; to have compulsory process for obtaining witnesses in his favor, and to have the Assistance of Counsel for his defense." The defendant's option to waive trial by jury and request a trial by the court—usually referred to as a *bench trial*—is sometimes restricted by rules that vary by jurisdiction. The federal courts and some states require approval by the prosecutor.

We Americans tend to take trial by jury for granted and do not appreciate the fact that our country places more value on jury trial than any other nation. Some persons look upon a jury as the ultimate in fact-finding mechanisms. This is simply not true. Juries are composed of persons selected by the opposing attorneys from the general public; juries are not a "blue-ribbon" group of experts, trained analysts, or persons with very special fact-finding skills. The value of the jury is that ordinary citizens are used to measure the behavior of their peers against the word of the law as it is stated by the judge. This provides some measure of citizen control over the processes of the courts. It thus allows an expression of our democratic ideals.

It can also result in some inexplicable outcomes. Cases of so-called *jury pardons,* in which jurors acquit because they feel a person should not be punished even though he or she is technically guilty, are not rare. There are also frequent cases of jury compromises in which jurors desiring the conviction of the defendant as charged reach agreement with jurors desiring acquittal, that agreement resulting in a verdict of guilty of a lesser included offense that the evidence clearly does not support. Examples can be found in controversial cases involving multiple deaths or the planned killing of a spouse abuser in which divided juries find the defendant guilty of manslaughter. Such verdicts often send prosecutors away muttering and place the guilty defendants back on the streets. They may also, however, serve to keep the written rules of law from causing oppression by unfair or overzealous application.

Not all defendants have a right to a trial by jury despite the brave words of the Sixth Amendment. An exception has been found in cases of "petty offenses." *Petty offenses* are generally those for which one cannot receive over six months in jail. The Supreme Court has not defined a "petty offense," but it has ruled that a petty offense is not to be punished by more than six months in jail.[1]

Size and Unanimity

Trial juries vary in size, though most states use a twelve-person jury for felony cases. (Some people say that the number stems from the number of Jesus' apostles.) Many jurisdictions use smaller juries for misdemeanor cases. Florida, Louisiana, South Carolina, Texas, and Utah use less than twelve for noncapital felony cases. The drafters of the Sixth Amendment did not require that a jury be composed of any specific number, and the Supreme Court upheld the use of six-person juries in the case of *Williams v. Florida* in 1970.[2] In *Williams* the Court required, among other things, that juries be "large enough to promote group deliberation . . . and . . . to provide a fair possibility for obtaining a representative cross section of the community."

Four states allow nonunanimous verdicts. Two—Louisiana and Oregon—permit such verdicts in felony cases, while Oklahoma and Texas limit nonunanimous verdicts to misdemeanor cases. The Supreme Court has always required the majority to be "substantial" in these cases, say five out of six. The advantage of allowing less than unanimous verdicts to convict is that they prevent stubborn, stupid, or "bought" single jurors from causing a so-called *hung jury*—a jury that cannot reach a decision—and the expense of retrial. The Court has intimated that convictions predicated upon less than 75 percent of the jurors' votes will likely be held unconstitutional.

Eligibility for Jury Service

Almost every state has legislation on the books that requires that jurors meet certain *eligibility requirements*. The requirements generally call for jurors who speak and understand English, are citizens of the United States, and reside in the locality in which they will sit. Typically excluded as ineligible by law are the insane and convicted felons. Often exempted, or entitled to decline to serve, are persons from certain walks of life such as lawyers, doctors, clergy, and teachers. Others, such as mothers with small children, who can convince the judge that jury service would constitute a real hardship may be excused. Judges vary considerably in what constitutes a hardship. "Hardship" may run the gamut from what is a mere inconvenience to something that is threatening to the health or safety of the party seeking to be excused. The authors know a judge who has never granted any excuses related to business or occupational hardships. On the other hand, they have seen judges excuse people about to go on a planned vacation trip with the proviso that they report for jury duty when they return.

The actual list from which the clerk or jury commissioner draws names for possible jury service varies from place to place. Since the 1960s the most commonly used list is that of registered voters. The coverage of the 18-and-over population found on voters rolls can vary from 60 to 80 percent. Lists of registered drivers, on the other hand, cover between 80 and 95 percent of the 18-and-older population. The federal government and some states use combined lists to broaden representation. Some courts have even turned to lists of high school graduates, hunting licensees, welfare recipients, utility customers, and even dog licensees.[3]

Whatever list or combination of lists is used, a percentage of all those listed needed for possible jury duty is determined, and the required number is randomly selected from among those listed. Those selected are then sent a summons to appear.

Discrimination by Race or Class

Various appeals to a higher court have been made by defendants who claim to have lost their cases because certain groups or classes of persons—usually persons of the same race, class, or ethnic group to which the defendant belongs—were improperly excluded from potential participation on their juries. Such discrimination has been ruled constitutionally impermissible.

This has not meant, however, that anyone has the right to have a jury composed only of those the defendant believes to be his or her peers, or even a jury in which each segment of the population is represented.[4] Therefore a black defendant has no right to an all-black jury, or even to a jury on which blacks are included. Is this not unfair to many blacks? Imagine the fear of a black defendant facing an all-white jury—an all-too-common occurrence in our criminal courts.

In 1979 the Supreme Court defined a three-pronged test for determining whether a jury pool was drawn from a fair cross section of any community: First, the group allegedly excluded must be a "distinctive" group in the community, not some tiny and irrelevant group such as blue-eyed college graduates; second, the group excluded from jury pools must be fairly and reasonably represented in the population of the community at large; and third, the underrepresentation of the group in the jury pool must be shown to be due to systematic exclusion in the selection process.[5] In other words, as Munsterman and Munsterman point out, any disparities in group representation must "be inherent in the process used and not a temporary aberration."[6]

JURY SELECTION

The process by which those eligible for jury service are examined by the judge and attorneys and a jury actually selected and seated is a complex and extremely important one.

The Voir Dire

Voir dire (in French, "to speak the truth") is the preliminary examination of prospective jurors. The group is known as a *venire*, or an array. In most states it is the attorneys who question the venire. Prevailing practice in three-quarters of the districts in the federal system and in some states is for judges to ask the questions, usually after obtaining input from the attorneys about subjects to be covered.

Valerie Hans has pointed out the arguments offered for and against attorney involvement in the voir dire. Attorneys are convinced judges do a poor job of detecting prejudice on the part of panel members because they do not ask probing questions, or they ask leading questions, with appropriate answers already indicated. (An extreme example of such a leading question might be: "You will be fair, won't you?") On the other hand, judges argue that attorneys ask unnecessary questions, which sometimes include attempts to make points, sometimes invade jurors' privacy, and usually cause the voir dire to take far longer than needed.[7]

There are two matters to be determined by the voir dire: (1) whether the prospective jurors are qualified to serve both legally and in terms of their capacity to hear, understand, and express themselves in English; and (2) whether they are capable of approaching the case without prejudice. Those believed to be prejudiced are subject to challenge by the attorneys.

Challenges for Cause

Lawyers can challenge the selection of any juror they think should not sit in judgment of the facts of the case. If the judge agrees that juror should not participate, he or she may allow the *challenge for cause* and excuse the juror from sitting on the case. A valid challenge for cause can be entered on the basis that the potential juror has a diminished ability to observe the proceedings, to understand the proceedings, or to make an unbiased determination after having observed and understood the proceedings. A person with, for example, a serious hearing loss or one who is very worried about a sick child at home is obviously unable to fully function as a juror. A venireman who is a friend of one of the parties or who hates one of the attorneys will probably be unable to exclude his prejudices from the deliberative processes. Persons who, because of familiarity with the case, have already formed an opinion as to guilt or innocence are excusable for cause. There is no limit to the number of persons who may be unqualified to sit in impartial and well-reasoned judgment of the defendant's innocence or guilt. The mere fact that a member of the venire is challenged for cause does not remove that potential juror; the judge must agree with the attorney and excuse the person.

Peremptory Challenges

Each side has a right to make what is known as a *peremptory challenge*. A peremptory challenge is one in which the challenging litigant does not have to state any reason for the challenge. Unless the challenge exceeds the number allowed by statute or rule, the judge must then allow the challenge and excuse the potential juror. Each state sets limits on the number of peremptory challenges; the number set is usually greatest for capital cases and least for misdemeanors. Sometimes the number of challenges allowed in a case involving multiple counts against the defendant is the sum of challenges that would be allowed for each count separately. If the number of counts or the number of codefendants creates the potential for a high number of peremptory challenges, the judge will sometimes pressure the attorneys to agree to a lesser number, thus shortening the time required to select the jury.

Peremptory challenges are used by the litigants to eliminate jurors they do not like only if they cannot utilize challenge for cause or if the judge has declined to excuse for cause. Remember, challenges for cause are limited in number only by the judge's discretion. Peremptory challenges are strictly limited, with six a typical allowance for a noncapital felony.

The use of the peremptory challenge is one test of lawyerly skill. The ability to identify jurors who might be against one's own interest is a subtle skill. Some lawyers seem to do this much better than others. Prosecutors typically look for conservative, hard-line, hardworking people for their jurors and avoid liberals, musicians, social workers, and unemployed and underprivileged persons. Defense lawyers usually want persons with a compassionate philosophy of life and those who would identify with oppressed persons. If the defendant is a prominent figure accused of fraud, these selection preferences might be reversed.

Of course, it is possible for attorneys to use peremptory challenges to exclude persons on the basis of race or religion—a practice that is hardly ethical, but has probably been all too common. A blow to this practice was struck, however, by the Supreme Court in 1986 in the case of *Batson v. Kentucky*. This case resulted in the overturning of a conviction of a black defendant obtained after the prosecutor used peremptory challenges to remove all four black veniremen. The Court ruled that prosecutors may not challenge potential jurors solely on account of their race; one cannot assume, that is, that black jurors as a group will be unable to consider impartially the evidence against a black defendant. The Court set forth means by which a defendant may make a prima facie case that racial or other illegal form of discrimination has occurred; the Court also provided that the prosecutor would have the burden of providing a "neutral explanation" for the challenges.[8] *Batson v. Kentucky* represents the first attempt to limit use of peremptory challenges by any standards other than the number permitted; Justices Burger and Rehnquist asserted in their dissent that the majority opinion effectively meant the end of the practice of peremptory challenges.

Since the venire is randomly selected, a lawyer can easily use all of his or her peremptory challenges and still not be satisfied with the jury. In jurisdictions known for conservative, hard-line citizens, prosecutors are apt to be left with unused peremptory challenges while defense attorneys exhaust theirs. In liberal jurisdictions the effect will, of course, usually be the reverse.

The Scientific Method of Jury Selection

The manner in which peremptory challenges are utilized is often intuitive and is guided by an attorney's instinct after voir dire is completed. Recently, more and more attorneys have begun to use psychological and sociological techniques to probe the attitudes of potential jurors toward their clients' cases. Questions meant to reveal certain personality characteristics and/or mental attitudes are asked during voir dire. Sometimes the potential juror's neighbors are even interrogated in an attempt to establish the leanings of the member of the venire.

Such *scientific jury selection* is of most value in highly publicized matters where public opinion is a factor, but the costs inherent in the technique can prohibit the ordinary defendant from utilizing it. And its value to an experienced and intelligent trial lawyer is questionable. The traditional intuitive and experientially guided methods of jury selection will probably long endure.

After the jury is accepted by both lawyers, it is sworn and can begin to hear evidence in the matter. The jury is considered complete only when each side has made all the challenges for cause and all the peremptory challenges it cares to make—or has perhaps exhausted all its peremptory challenges, though some lawyers like to retain one peremptory challenge as if they were soldiers saving the last bullet!

DISCOVERY

The system that allows the defense to "discover" the contents of the prosecution's case and, to a lesser extent, allows the prosecutor to learn about the defense's case prior to trial is called *discovery*. Philosophically, there are a number of arguments for and against full discovery, especially as it relates to the prosecutor's release of extensive data to the accused.

Variations in Discovery Schemes

Among the fifty-one jurisdictions in the United States, there is great variation as to just what is discoverable. Discovery runs the gamut from very limited to "liberal." The limited-discovery jurisdictions allow the trial court to enter an order only when defense shows a need for such things as the defendant's own statement and certain physical evidence. Other jurisdictions follow a moderate course and allow almost automatic approval of defense requests for such things as the defendant's own statement and documents and items of physical evidence.

The New Trend: "Liberal" Discovery

Several states have moved away from the moderate position and have modeled their discovery procedures after the American Bar Association standards entitled *Discovery and Procedure before Trial*.[9] The distinguishing characteristic of the ABA standards is that they allow the defense to discover virtually everything about the prosecution's case. These standards generally *require* the prosecutor to furnish the defense the names and addresses of all persons the prosecutor intends to call at trial or, in some jurisdictions, all persons the prosecutor knows to have knowledge of the case even if he or she does not intend to call them at trial. The standards also mandate that the prosecution produce such matters as statements by the accused; reports and statements of experts; results of scientific tests; books, papers, tangible items, and photographs that the prosecutor intends to use in the case; and any criminal records of persons the prosecutor intends to call as witnesses.

The defense, usually reciprocally, may be required to furnish the prosecutor with witness lists and medical and scientific reports. The defen-

News of Note

JURY EXPERT ADVISES HYNES IN HOWARD BEACH CASE

By E. R. Shipp

He is not expected to be in the courtroom during the jury selection in the Howard Beach case. But Jay Schulman, a sociologist, could nevertheless be a powerful influence on who is chosen to hear the emotional case.

Using skills developed in the early 1970's to help antiwar activists and prison inmates involved in uprisings obtain juries more sympathetic to their cases, Mr. Schulman has spent six months working with the prosecution team led by Charles J. Hynes.

Their goal is to coax from prospective jurors, with a minimum of questions, any deep-seated feelings they might have about race and racism.

That a prosecutor would use the services of Mr. Schulman or any jury consultant is unusual. But that Mr. Schulman is involved in this case is, perhaps, not so surprising.

'I reached out to him'

Something of a maverick who describes himself as being committed to "social justice," Mr. Schulman, who is 60 years old, said he was dismissed from a teaching position at Cornell in 1967, after he had become involved in antiwar activities. In 1969, he was dismissed by City College, after he had supported black and Puerto Rican students agitating for admissions changes.

"I reached out to him," Mr. Schulman said of how he and Mr. Hynes met last March." In my view, the prosecution was on the right side."

In the last 15 years, Mr. Schulman has worked on behalf of clients as diverse as Attica inmates; Claus von Bülow; Kathy Boudin, a Weather underground radical who was a defendant in the Brink's robbery and murder case; Gen. William C. Westmoreland; Wall Street figures charged with insider trading; battered women, and Larry Flynt and Al Goldstein, publishers of magazines with sexual content. He has rarely, if ever, worked with the prosecution.

He concedes that his work on behalf of corporations and affluent people helps finance the work he does free or at a reduced fee for those with whom he identifies politically and socially.

Reasons for volunteering

He was prompted to offer his services to Mr. Hynes, he said in an interview, "because I was deeply offended by the failure of the criminal-justice system to punish whites for assailing or killing blacks."

"More importantly," Mr. Schulman added, "I volunteered because I believe unless the city can solve its racial problems, unless blacks and minority and majority groups can work together, it's going to be a lousy city to live in. Blacks have to be sure they can get justice when it is their right."

The jury selection in the Howard Beach case is in several stages. Mr. Schulman said the judge's prescreening of prospective jurors through individual interviews had been influenced by Mr. Schulman's findings that there had been unusually heavy pretrial publicity in the case.

The selection began yesterday. The judge questioned 32 of 150 prospective jurors after telling them they had been summoned to a case that has "generated a great deal of publicity—national publicity, if not worldwide publicity."

No jurors were seated by the end of the day because the questioning was still in an early stage.

Mr. Schulman's added work will become evident as the selection proceeds to the voir dire. During the in-depth questioning by the lawyers,

Mr. Hynes is planning to use neighborhood profiles Mr. Schulman has developed, as well as questions devised during mock jury selections.

For the 1,000 or so hours he estimates he has put in on the trial preparation, Mr. Schulman said, he is waiving his normal criminal-case fee of $75 an hour. He will be reimbursed, however, for expenses that he estimates will reach $7,500.

That he is good at what he does is well known. A prominent New York trial lawyer, Herald Price Fahringer, said of Mr. Schulman, "Jay Schulman is to jury selection what Darwin was to evolution."

It all began in the winter of 1971, when Mr. Schulman, then unemployed after having been dismissed from his job as an assistant professor of sociology at City College, decided to use his skills to help his friends, including Philip Berrigan and other activists on trial as the Harrisburg 7, come up with what they thought would be a favorable jury.

His work since then has evolved—and been adapted by scores of others, including social scientists and market researchers, who have set up jury research concerns—to include several strategies. They measure the attitudes of communities from which the juries are to be chosen and develop profiles of what type of juror is good or bad for a particular client, help lawyers frame the questions they will ask prospective jurors and sit in the courtroom to help the lawyers analyze the responses.

One technique that Mr. Schulman is given some credit in refining is the open question. Rather than asking, for instance, whether a person is married and eliciting merely a yes or no, he would ask, "What is your marital status?"

Instead of asking whether the juror attended college, he would ask, "How far did you go in school?"

In each instance, the juror would probably give a lot more information about himself that could help the lawyers determine whether he was appropriate for that jury.

An aspect of Mr. Schulman's work that Mr. Fahringer said he had found particularly useful was what is known as the "alpha," or "authority," factor. Using a set of criteria, the lawyers determine whether a prospective juror is likely to be a dominant force in the jury room and whether that is helpful or harmful for their side.

Mr. Fahringer recalled how, despite the objections of a co-defense counsel in an obscenity case in Cleveland, he chose to keep a woman on the jury because of the alpha factor. The woman, he later found out, had singlehandedly persuaded the other 11 jurors to acquit his client.

That does not always work, as Mr. Schulman conceded. He totally misjudged two jurors in the case of Michael A. Nussbaum, a public-relations consultant tied to the late Donald R. Manes. After a short deliberation, the jurors convicted Mr. Nussbaum last August of soliciting a bribe of $250,000.

Some critics have accused Mr. Schulman of seeking publicity, a charge he denies. A friend said:

"It's not that he wants to get publicity for himself, because he frequently doesn't. But he likes to be where the action is, on the cutting edge of cases involving social justice."

Even some of Mr. Schulman's friends questioned his motives for taking the Westmoreland case, he recalled. Leonard I. Weinglass, the lawyer, stopped speaking to him for a while.

But Mr. Schulman said he was convinced that the general had been maligned by CBS News.

"He is, to my mind," Mr. Schulman said, "an extraordinarily decent man."

Source: The New York Times, September 9, 1987.

dant may also be ordered to stand in a lineup; be photographed and fingerprinted; and give blood, hair, handwriting, and voice samples.

The *liberal discovery* provided by the American Bar Association standards are prescribed for "serious criminal cases." Some states limit discovery to felony cases, and some other states extend discovery to misdemeanor cases as well as felonies.

The Prosecutor's View of Discovery

Liberal discovery works to the disadvantage of the prosecutor for a number of reasons. For example, if a defendant tells the truth when making a statement to police during the investigation, he or she has no need to examine the statement prior to trial because the truth will serve the case and is not difficult to remember. If, however, the accused lied to the officers in making the original statement, he or she may have trouble remembering the lies and needs liberal discovery in order to have the opportunity to inspect the earlier lies and weave testimony in such a manner as not to allow the lies to trap him or her.

Defendants who intend to lie at the trial need to know what evidence the prosecutor can produce at trial in order to design lies that will be believed by the jury. In jurisdictions that do not have significant discovery, the defendant is forced to wait until the prosecution has put forth its case at trial to decide which lies can be told within the credibility matrix created by the prosecution's case. In this situation, the decision-making process is difficult because the defendant has no leisure time in which to devise and refine his or her lies. It is far easier to lie if you have access to all the prosecution's secrets before trial.

An important feature of all the so-called liberal discovery systems is the right of the defendant to *depose,* or take the sworn statements, of the witnesses. This right is important for various reasons. The first is that the defense can thereby discover what the state or federal government can, if it wishes, prove at trial. This allows the defense to prepare its case, and if it is so inclined, to design perjury that will be plausible, at least to the point of creating reasonable doubt in the minds of the jurors. The statements will also provide the defense a guide in the search for evidence that can protect an innocent client. Statements from witnesses can also allow the opposing counsel to discredit trial testimony, since any differences between deposition testimony and trial testimony will be obvious, and a change in sworn testimony from the deposition to the trial can cause jurors to place less weight upon the credibility of the witness. It will appear to the jurors that witnesses are either perjuring themselves or just can't remember clearly. In either case, the testimony is rendered less valuable.

Discovery depositions not only allow defendants to better plan defenses—and even lies—for trial but also serve other, more subtle purposes. Witnesses are sometimes intimidated by the aggressive behavior of some defense attorneys at depositions and even by the presence of the defendant, who may just sit and stare while the witness, often the victim, gives his or her testimony. Intimidation is especially a factor in cases where the defendant is violent or appears physically formidable.

Minor inconsistencies in nonessential details are sometimes developed between pretrial deposition and the trial, which can be held months after the deposition. These inconsistencies are often pointed out by the defense with the intent of demonstrating that the witness is not to be believed. An experienced police officer will look over field notes and reports prior to the deposition in order to ensure accuracy and minimize the chances of having the testimony impeached. Likewise, immediately prior to trial, the experienced officer will review notes, reports, and the deposition given earlier in order to refresh his or her memory.

The Defense Lawyer's View of Discovery

On the other side of the equation, the defendant should not be *tried by ambush,* and full and liberal discovery will allow a proper investigation of the case against him or her so that all the truth, not just the part favorable to prosecution, will be brought out at trial. Apprised of the prosecution's case prior to trial, a defendant will know who to talk to and where to look to find the unbiased truth. Defense advocates are quick to point out that because the defendant is facing the might of the state, he or she has the right not to be surprised at trial and the right to prepare the case using witnesses and evidence that might raise reasonable doubt about the state's case.

Defendants rely on the right to impeach witnesses because of variations between the deposition testimony and trial testimony. Such variations form a valid basis for discrediting the state's witnesses. The criminal defense bar is also quick to point out that none of their procedures involving discovery and discovery depositions in and of themselves lead to lies and inconsistencies on the part of government witnesses; they merely reveal such defects so that the jurors, as triers of fact, can weigh the value of the testimony.

The reader should by now be correctly convinced that "liberal" discovery enhances the administration of justice and protects the rights of the accused, even though at the same time it allows some defendants a golden opportunity to beat the system simply by committing one more dishonest act—that is, perjury or the manufacture of evidence.

SPEEDY TRIAL

The Sixth Amendment to the Constitution states in part, "in all criminal prosecutions the accused shall enjoy the right to a speedy... trial," and many state constitutions have similar declarations of the right to a speedy trial. The most often cited federal case on constitutional speedy trial is *Barker v. Wingo,* which was decided by the Supreme Court in 1972.[10] Barker was charged with murder, but the state wished to prosecute his codefendant first in order to obtain that man's testimony against Barker, against whom the evidence was not particularly strong. This and other problems, including hung juries and appeals, caused the defendant to be tried five times before he was finally convicted. Barker himself was in turn finally tried and convicted *five years* after his arrest! The Court, in a long opinion, made a careful analysis of the right of speedy trial and declined to set a specific time as the outer limit after which the defendant ought not be brought to trial.

The *Barker* court adopted "a balancing test, in which the conduct of both the prosecution and the defendant are weighed"; four matters were to be considered in the "balancing test": (1) the length of the delay, with a seeming threshold of a year or so before anyone should become greatly concerned; (2) whether the defendant was indeed prejudiced by the delay, since defendants are sometimes benefited by a late trial; (3) whether the defendant actually objected to the delay; and (4) the cause of the delay.

If the delay exceeds a reasonable period the other three factors are to be examined. The issue of prejudice by delay occasionally cuts both ways, in that defense as well as state witnesses can move away, die, or forget just what actually did happen. One must remember that, unlike police officers and prosecution witnesses, defense witnesses rarely memorialize their observations in the form of statements and reports made almost contemporaneously with the criminal episode. It would seem that for this, if for no other reason, they would be more subject to forgetting their testimony. In looking at prejudice, the Court noted that oppressive pretrial confinement where the defendant is unable to make bail is an area where attention should be directed. The anxiety and concern of the accused are a valid consideration in making the judgment as to whether the case for the accused has been prejudiced.

If a long delay occurs and the defendant's ability to prepare or present a defense is diminished because of the delay, the court will look to whether the defendant actually objected to the delay, keeping always in mind that the defense often benefits from and desires delays, only complaining when the delays cease to benefit their cause. A failure to object diminishes the chances of getting the case dismissed. If the prosecution has a valid reason for delay, that in itself will influence the court to allow the prosecution to proceed over defense objections.

Speedy Trial under State Rules

Some states have adopted rules by which rights to a speedy trial are pinned to specific time limits, regardless of a showing of prejudice. These speedy trial rules are often very simple, requiring discharge of defendants who have not been brought to trial within set time periods after arrest—say 90 days for a misdemeanor and 180 days for a felony.[11] Numerous variations typically exist for prisoners out of state, prisoners already incarcerated for other charges, and other situations. Naturally, delays caused by the defendant—including his or her not being present for the trial—are not chargeable against the state. This rule has stopped the localized practice of keeping defendants in pretrial detention for excessive periods of time.

The rule has also resulted in the release of some guilty persons when, without malice, the state has failed to get the case set for trial on a timely basis. Defendants have been known, almost as a rule, to do nothing to draw attention to the fact that their trial dates are not yet set as the 90th—or 180th—day approaches. A busy prosecutor's office in which thousands of cases are processed each year is apt to lose an occasional case on speedy trial through oversight.

The Federal Speedy Trial Act

The Federal Speedy Trial Act of 1974 requires that cases be brought to trial within ninety days of arraignment (where the indictment of information is read to the defendant) unless circumstances exist that justify a longer delay.[12] A number of specific reasons can allow delay beyond ninety days.

The act has prevented some accused persons in the federal courts from having to suffer the lengthy delays that were often the rule rather than the exception before the passage of the act. The act has tended to lengthen some civil dockets because of the need to process criminal cases first. Still another view of this act was provided by a federal clerk of courts, who asserted that motions for delay of trial beyond the mandated period were so common that the increase in paperwork and hearings created an even greater jam in his jurisdiction than existed prior to the enactment of the Speedy Trial Act.

THE RULES OF EVIDENCE

Having determined whether the accused is competent to stand trial, whether the trial is to be by jury and, if so, of what size and composition, what portion of the state's case should be revealed to the defendant (and perhaps how much of the defense case the prosecutor can discover), and how soon after arrest the defendant's trial must be held, we are ready to examine the question of what kinds and forms of evidence may be used in such a trial.

As we have said, trials are adversary proceedings, and each party to litigation should, within the bounds of ethics, do its very best to win. With this in mind, we can see that rules governing the presentation of evidence must obviously exist if the trial is not to turn into a verbal brawl, with all sorts of unreliable and irrelevant testimony and physical exhibits coming to the attention of the jury. The rules of evidence are designed to ensure that the jurors in their fact-finding role are not exposed to that which is unreliable or does not logically bear upon the issues to be decided.

Rules of evidence are found in case law and, in some states, in evidence codes. The basic mission of the rules of evidence is to enable the fact finder—the jury in a jury trial or the court in a bench trial—to come to an accurate conclusion on the basis of reliable and nonprejudicial facts. From time to time, other interests bear upon the process, such as the exclusion of perfectly reliable evidence that was secured as a result or an illegal search and seizure. This sort of rule of evidence is designed not to ensure reliable and relevant evidence but to punish the police if they collect evidence in violation of a constitutional right of the accused.

We will not attempt to treat the rules of evidence thoroughly in this text, since such a treatment requires several academic hours in a college of law. Rather, we will briefly explain the basic rules so that the reader will at least be familiar with the vocabulary and a few basic points.

Kinds of Evidence

Admissible evidence encompasses whatever sort of proof can be legally placed before the trier of fact at trial. It is generally referred to by several terms, and knowledge of these terms will help us in our examination of the subject. The first two terms are easily distinguished: testimonial and real evidence. *Testimonial evidence* is obviously oral or written accounts of observations. *Real evidence* comprises finite and tangible objects such as guns and fingerprints.

Direct evidence is that which is usually provided by eyewitnesses and goes directly to prove the existence of the fact in question without the intervention of much deductive or inductive reasoning. An example would be a witness's testimony that he saw the accused shoot the victim. On the other hand, *circumstantial evidence* affords proof only by and through the application of logic that leads the fact finder from the circumstances to the truth of the facts in dispute. Thus the witness may testify that she heard a shot, saw the accused leave the scene in a hurry, and then found the victim at the spot from which the accused fled.

Competency of the Witness

A threshold question that must be answered before evidence is solicited is whether the witness is competent to testify; the judge decides on the *competency of the witness*. The judge's decision that the witness is competent to present to the jury is entirely different from and does not affect the jury's evaluation of the testimony. The jury can, in its entirely appropriate discretion, choose to attach great importance, moderate importance, or no importance at all to the testimony. Jurors are the ones who weigh the probative value of the evidence. They are apt to weigh heavily the testimony of a busload of nuns who happened to see the robbery and to disregard the testimony of the perpetrator who claims that someone else committed the crime while he, the accused, was alone in the forest.

A minor child, usually referred to at law an "an infant," may be incompetent to testify unless that child can demonstrate to the court that he or she understands the duty to tell the truth. Such understanding is determined by having the child take the stand and explain what the truth is and what a lie is and aver that it is wrong to lie. The decision to allow or disallow such testimony is the judge's and can be a difficult one to make.

Besides age, mental health and a prior criminal record are examples of bases upon which competency can be challenged. The modern approach to disqualifying a witness is generally predicated on two factors: (1) Is the witness capable of expressing himself or herself concerning the matter in such a manner as to be understood? (2) Is the witness able to understand the duty to tell the truth?

Relevancy of the Evidence

Relevant evidence is evidence that tends to prove or disprove a fact at issue. Facts at issue are usually referred to as *material facts*. Relevancy is the result of a relationship between the evidence and a material fact—a relationship that relies on logic, either inductive or deductive. The principles of logic involved are based either on science or on human experience. Relevant evidence is admissible except in specific instances; for example, some relevant evidence may not be admissible because it would cause prejudice against the defendant to a degree that the harmful effect of the prejudice would outweigh the helpful effect of the evidence. After argument by the lawyers who wish to admit the evidence and by the lawyers who wish to exclude the evidence, the issue is a matter for the court to decide. In making this decision, the court is guided in most states by case law, though in some states the court decides on the basis of an evidence code.

Opinion Testimony

Witnesses are generally called upon to testify as to what they saw, heard, or felt rather than as to their opinions about what that experience meant. Generally the jury is supposed to interpret the importance of testimony after hearing a rather sterile rendition of what was seen, heard, or felt. But sometimes a mere recitation of observations will not aid the trier of fact nearly as much as the opinion of the observer. If this is the case, the preferred method of conduct of trial is to allow the opinions and inferences of the nonexpert person—the lay witness—to be given if a person does not need special training, skill, experience, or knowledge to render such opinions. Examples of this type of permissible *opinion testimony* include judgments as to speed, distance, identity, emotional state, and the like.

Expert Testimony

If properly admissible evidence requires the testimony of an expert in order to give the evidence relevancy, *expert testimony* is called for. An *expert* is one who the court feels is especially knowledgeable in the subject area in which the testimony is sought. Factors that the court will consider in determining whether a person is an expert include special training, education, and experience. Examples of testimony that can be rendered by experts include testimony pertaining to firearm and fingerprint analysis, chemistry, serology, and accident reconstruction. Experts need not be degreed persons in every case. A person experienced in photography but without any formal training in the subject might be accepted by the court as a photographic expert if the court is impressed enough with the person's skills. A landowner can give opinion testimony as to the value of his or her own land; a property appraiser can give testimony as to the value of another's property.

Juries are not required to agree with expert testimony any more than they are required to believe or agree with any other witness. It is the sole province of the jury to decide ultimate fact issues and weight the testimony of all witnesses. It is not unusual for different experts called by opposing counsel at trial to express differing "expert" testimony as to the same basic evidence, a situation that can cause difficulty for the laypeople on the jury.

Judicial Notice

Judicial notice is the term that describes the court's acceptance as fact of certain things that are in general knowledge. For example, no one needs to prove the fact that a foot contains twelve inches, that gasoline burns, and that a certain town is within the county in which the jurors reside. If the judge takes judicial notice of such a fact, he or she will so instruct the jury and the jury is to consider the matter proven.

Evidentiary Presumptions

Evidentiary presumptions are presumptions provided by law that establish the proof of a fact or facts on the basis of proof of a second fact that is necessary to the case. For example, proof of entering with criminal intent is required to establish burglary. The burglary statute of one state provides that a proof of stealthy entry without the owner's permission provides the proof of criminal intent. This legally provided presumption allows a logical inference to be elevated to proof, but not to the level of conclusive proof. An evidentiary presumption is a rebuttable presumption. That means that the presumption is sufficient to defeat the defense's motion for a directed verdict of acquittal made after the presentation of the state's case, and the defendant is placed in the position of having to rebut the presumption by presenting some evidence and/or logical argument to convince the jury that the presumption is invalid. A rebuttable presumption of a simple, noncriminal nature is the presumption that a man who has been missing for seven years is dead. Evidence of his being alive will rebut the presumption. Most presumptions are rebuttable, but if no logical rebuttal is presented to the jury, the jury is supposed to accept the presumption.

Hearsay Evidence

"Hearsay" is one of the most commonly understood evidentiary terms. It refers to testimony wherein the declarant is not testifying to what he or she actually observed (saw, heard, felt, etc.) but to what another person told him or her. Generally, though with a great many exceptions, hearsay evidence is not admissible at trial. The Sixth Amendment to the Constitution guarantees that the defendant should have the opportunity to confront the witnesses against him. Trial practice also requires that witnesses be placed in jeopardy of perjury should they lie as to any material matter, and this requires that witnesses swear an oath or affirmation. Notice that the prohibition against hearsay testimony enforces these guarantees in the sense that it disallows the testimony of the out-of-court witness who cannot be confronted and cross-examined and who cannot be placed under oath or affirmation as a means of trying to guarantee the truthfulness of the testimony.

We give here one example of hearsay testimony: "I was told by the old man standing on the corner that he saw Dan Defendant take out a pistol and shoot Virginia Victim in the head." First, it is obvious that the man standing on the corner was not under oath when he made the statement as to who shot Virginia. Second, the defendant does not have an opportunity to cross-examine and determine if the man has poor eyesight, was drunk when he made the observation, has an ongoing feud with Dan Defendant, or the myriad of other factors that might show him to be an unreliable, incompetent, or prejudiced witness.

Exceptions to the Hearsay Evidence Rule

The rule against the presentation of hearsay testimony has numerous exceptions, some of which are rather complicated. We will treat only a couple of them here.

Admissions against Interest *Admissions against interest* actually include both confessions and admissions. A *confession* is a statement by the accused that he or she is guilty of the act in question. An *admission* is a statement harmful to the defendant in which he or she admits to doing something that might infer guilt but declines to accept responsibility for a crime. "I was in the room where Joe was robbed, I had my gun out, and I got some of Joe's money, but I didn't rob him" is an admission. Both a confession and an admission are admissible at trial for two logical reasons. One, the maker of the confession or admission, the defendant, is present for potential cross-examination. Two, the maker of a statement "against interest" is presumed, in theory at least, to be telling the truth. The reasoning is that one would hardly tell lies that would implicate oneself in a crime, but the validity of that assumption is, in the opinion of the authors, based upon questionable logic.

Dying Declaration Another exception to the rule against hearsay is the *dying declaration,* a statement made by a person who is dying. The dying declaration is admitted for two basic reasons, both supposedly grounded in logic. One is that a dying person is not motivated to tell lies. The other is that the hearsay evidence should be admitted since impending death obviously will prevent the witness from attending the trial and testifying.

Typically, such testimony is admissible only if the declarant acknowledges the fact that death is near and if death does in fact follow relatively soon after the declaration. Dying declarations are usually only usable in homicide cases and then only against the accused killer.

Other Testimony of Deceased   Still another exception to the admissibility of hearsay testimony was recently made by a New York trial judge who admitted the grand jury testimony of a witness to a murder who was himself subsequently murdered. The trial judge's reasoning raised an intriguing question regarding the conflict between the right to confront witnesses against oneself and the state's duty to bring murderers to justice. (See accompanying box.)

The Use of Objections

If an attorney asks for evidence from a witness, either testimonial or real, that the opposing attorney believes to be contrary to the rules of evidence, it is the opposing attorney's duty to object to the introduction of that evidence. Raising *objections* to the use of improper evidence is one of the main duties of trial counsel. Opposing counsel will state ''I object; that is hearsay,'' or ''Objection, your honor, that's irrelevant,'' or whatever other objection is appropriate. The requester of the evidence will often argue to the court that the question should be answered, stating the legal grounds that allow the answer. The court will then sustain or deny the objection, and the witness will be instructed to answer or not answer the question, to answer without reference to hearsay, or to respond in whatever way is required to proceed with the case without violating the rules of evidence. If counsel fails to object to evidence that should have been objected to, the party against whom the objectionable evidence was used cannot raise the point on appeal. The rule is that objections must be made in a timely fashion or not at all.

THEORIES OF DEFENSE

There are several ways of defending the accused in a criminal trial. The facts of the case and skills of the defense attorney dictate which of these will be employed in an effort to gain an acquittal. Each of these methods of defense carries with it particular rules or principles established in case law. We shall examine a few of the major defenses.

The Defense of Alibi

An *alibi* is a claim by the defendant that he or she was somewhere else when the crime took place. It is supportable by the testimony of witnesses for the defense who swear they were with or saw the defendant in a place removed from the scene of the crime at the time of its occurrence or so close to that time that the defendant could not have covered the distance and committed the crime in the time frame allowed.

News of Note

ACCOUNT OF A SLAIN WITNESS ALLOWED IN A MANHATTAN MURDER TRIAL

By Philip Shenon

A Manhattan man on trial for murder was involved in the slaying of a key witness against him, a judge ruled yesterday.

For that reason, the judge, Acting Justice Myriam J. Altman of State Supreme Court in Manhattan, said grand jury testimony by the witness could be used as evidence in a new trial for the defendant.

The witness, Bobby Edmonds, was shot to death several hours after his name was made public last Nov. 14. He had been scheduled to testify the next day against the defendant, Nathaniel Sweeper. After Mr. Edmonds's death, a mistrial was declared.

"I find by clear and convincing evidence that the defendant was involved in the homicide of Edmonds and that the murder was committed by individuals acting on his behalf," Acting Justice Altman said in a 10-page decision. "Sweeper's motive to harm Edmonds was clear."

This was the first time the testimony of a murdered witness has been ruled admissible in a New York State court, according to the Manhattan District Attorney's office. The prosecutors would not say whether they planned to charge Mr. Sweeper with involvement in Mr. Edmonds's death.

The ruling was made after six weeks of debate over what to do with the grand jury testimony. In it, Mr. Edmonds, a 38-year-old heroin addict who lived in Harlem, said that he saw Mr. Sweeper, 23, kill a man in October 1982.

Mr. Sweeper's lawyer, James Merberg, said he was surprised by the rul-ing. "There's clearly no evidence" to support the decision, he said. He said he was not sure he could appeal it before Mr. Sweeper's new trial began, on Jan. 30.

Mr. Merberg had argued that introducing Mr. Edmonds's testimony in court would deprive his client of the constitutional right to confront a witness. Acting Justice Altman said Mr. Sweeper gave up that right when he helped arrange the "execution" of Mr. Edmonds. Because of information provided in court, Mr. Sweeper discovered four days before the murder of Mr. Edmonds that he was to testify, the judge said.

In the decision, Acting Justice Altman said the murder had been carried out by a group called the Vigilantes, which sells narcotics and has a policy "to kill potential witnesses who cooperate with the police against them." Mr. Sweeper, she said, was an "active and high-ranking Vigilante."

Police officials have said the 40-member group was tied to at least 15 murders.

The release of Mr. Edmonds's name "only confirmed" what Mr. Sweeper already knew, she said.

"The defendant had ample opportunity to contact his people to 'finalize' plans for the elimination of the witness," she said. "The defendant was the only one who had anything to gain from the murder of a destitute and dying heroin addict."

She also said the timing and manner of Mr. Edmonds's death were "strong and persuasive evidence of the defendant's involvement."

Source: The New York Times, January 6, 1984.

Some jurisdictions require defendants who intend to employ an alibi to so inform the prosecutor prior to trial. This is only fair from the prosecutor's standpoint, since it allows him or her to check out the alibi to see if it seems to be truthful and to subpoena witnesses to show its untruthfulness if it can be shown. An alibi presented as a surprise at trial may have the effect of perpetrating a fraud upon the jury, since the prosecutor has not been forewarned and is not able to meet the defense with sworn testimony. Alibi defenses presented by family members or friends are usually not believed if the prosecutor's case is reasonably strong.

The Defense of Insanity

The *defense of insanity* is a claim that the defendant should be excused from criminal responsibility for his or her acts because of diminished mental capacity. Long ago, jurists agreed that if small children were to be excused from criminal responsibility because of an inability to form the requisite criminal intent, then persons with diminished mental capacity or severe mental illness should also be excused. The problem has been in deciding what constitutes a mental condition that would excuse one's acts. The definition of the point where criminal acts are to be excused is a legal concept, even though it is described by a medical term, "insanity." The law has sought to find an easily understood definition of the term for juries, a definition that would comport with the theory of free will yet not necessarily fit the nomenclature of mental illness utilized in psychiatry. Defense lawyers who urge juries to acquit their clients by reason of insanity make much of the fact that some diagnosis has been made that labels their client with a term approved by the American Psychiatric Association—such as "schizophrenic" or "depressed"—hoping that the process of labeling will convince the jury that the defendant should be excused from responsibility for his or her acts. It should be noted that the process of diagnosing mental illness and attaching labels to the diagnoses has only an indirect relationship to the legal standards enunciated below.

The M'Naughten Rule   In 1843 a man named M'Naughten, who suffered from a delusional psychosis, thought Sir Robert Peel was persecuting him. (Readers will recall that Sir Robert Peel established the modern police system in England and that English policemen are referred to as "bobbies" in memory of his name.) M'Naughten thought that he was shooting Peel when he mistakenly shot and killed Peel's assistant, a man named Drummond. M'Naughten was apprehended and eventually brought to trial; the jury acquitted him. Peel and Drummond were popular persons, the trial received much publicity, and public indignation was aroused by the verdict. In reaction, the judges of the Queen's Bench developed the so-called M'Naughten rule.

The rule requires that the accused, to be excused from criminal responsibility, must have met the following standard at the time of the commission of the crime: "It must be clearly proved that, at the time of committing the act, the party accused was laboring under such a defect of reason, from disease of the mind, as not to know that nature and quality of the act he was doing, or, if he did know it, that he did not know it was wrong."[13] Many lawyers refer to the rule as the "right from wrong test" and describe its effect as requiring a defendant to be able to "distinguish that which is wrong from that which is right" with respect to the act alleged.

The Irresistible Impulse Test The M'Naughten rule is often criticized by those who point out that the ability to distinguish that which is right from that which is wrong does not excuse those persons who meet the responsibility standard but are driven by irresistible impulses resulting from mental disease. Some states apply a rule that is essentially the same as M'Naughten, with the addition of an excuse from criminal responsibility if the defendant "has lost the power to choose between right and wrong."

The Durham Test The case of *Durham v. United States* set a standard for excusability by insanity that is preferred by many psychiatrists.[14] The *Durham* case allows defendants to be excused for their otherwise criminally punishable acts if the act "was a product of mental disease or defect." This standard was used for a time in the District of Columbia, but it was noted that juries too often put undue emphasis on the fact that some psychiatrist had said that the defendant was legally insane. For this and other reasons, the Durham test has been generally rejected.

Different states use the above-stated rules or variations thereof that are difficult to catalog. Here we have only tried to make the reader aware of some of the variations upon the theme of excuse by reason of insanity. It is interesting to note that the juries, as the official embodiment of the conscience of the community, are the ultimate deciders as to whether the defense of insanity is to be honored. The citizens who sit as jurors, without formal psychological training in most cases, listen to expert testimony and the arguments of counsel and decide what is to be done. It is their prerogative to decide between conflicting psychological and psychiatric testimony or to reject all such testimony and be guided by common sense and the testimony of lay witnesses. Juries faced with conflicting expert medical testimony often predicate their decisions on a commonsense evaluation of the complexity and cunning of the defendant's acts in relation to the commission of the crime, often concluding that defendants who are able to plan and carry out complex crimes should not be excused from criminal responsibility for their acts.

The Defense of Intoxication

Intoxication by alcoholic drink or drugs is only a defense when the intoxication is involuntary and is so severe that it prevents the defendant from having the criminal intent necessary. An example of *involuntary intoxication* might be a situation in which a person unaccustomed to alcoholic beverages is tricked into consuming alcohol by a misrepresentation that the drink is, for example, cranberry juice. In these exceedingly rare cases of involuntary intoxication, the defendant is subject to being excused for his or her acts if the jury is convinced that the involuntary intoxication substantially caused the defendant to meet the standards of the insanity defense. This is not to say that intoxication causes legal insanity but rather that the standard is approximately the same.

Even if the intoxication is voluntary, the actor may have a defense if the intoxication prevented him or her from being able to form the criminal intent—known as *mens rea*—necessary for the crime in issue. For instance, first-degree murder usually requires premeditated intent; if the actor was so intoxicated as to have been unable to form the intent to kill but does in fact kill, the chargeable crime will drop to a level of homicide that does not require specific criminal intent. If the crime has for its *mens rea* recklessness or negligence, voluntary intoxication will not remove criminal intent under the theory that the ingestion of intoxicating substances is the recklessness that is ultimately provable, such ingestion being inherently reckless.

The Defense of Entrapment

Entrapment is another defense that the defendant must affirmatively assert if he or she is to take advantage of its protection. Entrapment is only effective where the defendant is able to establish that he or she committed the criminal deed as a result of being encouraged in the act by any agent of law enforcement.

Defendants often are confused as to what the legal defense of entrapment is. They confuse the "setting of a trap" with entrapment. It is perfectly legal for a police officer to set a trap where the intended fruits of crime are easily attacked by the criminal. In these situations, the police only provide the opportunity for the criminal to strike. In a true case of entrapment, the police must actually cause the defendant to be coaxed or coerced into committing a crime that he or she ordinarily would not have committed. The theory behind the defense of entrapment is that it is wrong for the government to cause persons to commit crimes. A classic case of entrapment is the situation in which an undercover agent makes friends with a narcotics user who has never sold narcotics, yet the agent pressures the user to make the sale. If the jury believes that the defendant would not have sold the drugs without the urging of the agent, the defendant must be found not guilty by the defense theory of entrapment. This defense actually admits the crime and blames it on the agent, a risky course for the defendant to take at trial, for if the jury is not sympathetic to the defendant's claim of being coerced into the crime, that defendant is almost certain to be found guilty.

An example of a trap that does not constitute entrapment is the situation in which a police officer leaves a car, with the keys in it, parked in a neighborhood that has been plagued with car theft. The subsequent arrest of the thief is not entrapment, since no one coerced or cajoled the thief into stealing the car; the police merely provided an opportunity to steal a car that was under surveillance.

Other Defenses

Occasionally defendants will present one of several other possible defenses. Two that appear with some frequency are the defense of duress and the defense of consent.

Duress   The defense of *duress* is based on a defendant's claim that some other person "made me do it." Such a defense is risky since, like that of entrapment, it begins with the defendant admitting he or she committed the act. The jury is asked to believe, however, that the defendant had no way of avoiding the criminal act or of refusing to commit it because of coercion by another individual. A defendant may claim, for example, that he or she was threatened with the loss of life, of great bodily harm, or of loss of a loved one. The authors' own experience suggests that juries rarely believe such claims or, at least, do not excuse the crime because of them.

Consent   Another claim often appears in cases concerning sexual battery or forcible rape, though it is also used in cases of embezzlement and theft. This is the defense of *consent,* which simply says, "She let me do it." The victim, in other words, is said to have volunteered to be victimized by the accused. Again, there is substantial risk in saying to the jury, "I did the act, but I'm not guilty of any crime."

SUMMARY AND CONCLUSION

In this chapter we have tried to provide the reader with some understanding of the basic rules under which criminal trials are conducted in the United States. We have discussed the importance of determining the competence of the accused to stand trial. We have examined the importance, composition, and selection of trial, or petit, juries. We have discussed the principles of discovery and presented some arguments for and against this procedure. The importance of, and the qualifications surrounding, the concept of "speedy trial" have been examined. We have reviewed some of the major rules concerning the nature, types, and forms of evidence that are presentable in a criminal trial. Finally, we have explained some of the major theories of defense that may be employed on behalf of the accused.

This background in fundamental principles and rules of adjudication by trial should help even the most casual observer of courtroom proceedings to better understand the drama (or the "game," as it is sometimes referred to) that is being played out. It should certainly provide a sound basis for moving on to the subject of the conduct of criminal trials, which we take up next.

QUESTIONS FOR DISCUSSION

1. A major case, which would have brought to trial an accused child molester and murderer against whom the evidence appeared to be overwhelming, is lost because of the failure to begin trial by the speedy trial date. Is this fair? Does this serve the goals of the Due Process Model?
2. If you were a prosecutor selecting a jury for the trial of an accused child molester and murderer, on what grounds might you peremptorily challenge members of the venire? What challenges for cause might you expect to see? Would you be agreeable to a change of venue?
3. If you were the defense attorney for an accused child molester and murderer, on what grounds might you peremptorily challenge members of the venire? What challenges for cause might you expect to see? Would you be agreeable to a change of venue?
4. What are the primary reasons for the "rules of evidence" as provided by common law and by statute? Do these rules promote or defeat the subgoal of the "search for truth"?
5. If you were a defense attorney with a confessed satanic-torture-multiple murderer for a client, what theories of defense would you be most likely to employ? What factors could determine your chances—slim as they might be—of success?

NOTES

1. *Baldwin v. New York,* 399 U.S. 66, 90 S. Ct. 1886, 26 L. Ed. 2d 437 (1970).
2. *Williams v. Florida,* 399 U.S. 78, 90 S. Ct. 1893, 26 L. Ed. 2d 446 (1970).

3. G. Thomas Munsterman and Janice T. Munsterman, "The Search for Jury Representativeness," *Justice System Journal,* vol. 11, no. 1, 1986, p. 65.
4. Ibid., p. 61.
5. *Duren v. Missouri,* 439 U.S. 357, 99 S. Ct. 664 (1979).
6. Munsterman and Munsterman, p. 62.
7. Valerie Hans, "The Conduct of the Voir Dire: A Psychological Analysis," *Justice System Journal,* vol. 11, no. 1, 1986, p. 46.
8. *Batson v. Kentucky,* 54 L.W. 4425 (1986).
9. American Bar Association Standards, *Discovery and Procedures before Trial,* approved draft, 1970 (§ 1.5).
10. *Barker v. Wingo,* 407 U.S. 514, 92 S. Ct. 2182, 33 L. Ed. 2d 101 (1972).
11. *Florida Rules of Criminal Procedure,* Rule 3.220.
12. The Federal Speedy Trial Act of 1974, 18 U.S.C. §§ 3161–3174.
13. M'Naughten's Case, 10 Clark and Fin. 200 (1843).
14. *Durham v. United States,* 214 F. 2d 826 (D. C. Cir. 1954).

CHAPTER 12

THE CONDUCT
OF THE TRIAL

*After reading this chapter, students should be able to define and explain
the importance of each of the following terms or phrases:*

presumption of innocence

courtroom demeanor

impeachment of witnesses

sequestered jury

pretrial jury instructions

opening statements

order of proof

directed verdict of acquittal

cross-examination

rebuttal case

surrebuttal case

closing arguments

charging the jury

charge conference

dynamite charge

verdict

polling of the jury

formal adjudication

withholding adjudication of guilt

extralegal factors

jury group dynamics

appeals

issues not raised in time

plain error

The steps in the criminal trial and the specific roles played by each of the
major actors are matters long settled in the Anglo-American tradition.
Recall that the traditional principles of the adversary process were established in the early English trial by battle. This adversarial process is quite
different from the practice on the continent of Europe, where judges—
often laypersons—act as direct participants in a process essentially
accusatorial in nature.

THE ROLES OF MAJOR PARTICIPANTS

In other chapters we have described the duties of court officials in regard to matters other than the trial proper. Here we shall concern ourselves with the roles played by the prosecutor, the defense attorney, the defendant, the witnesses, the jurors, and the judge during the conduct of a criminal trial. Keep in mind that the two attorneys and the judge are members of a "work group" having some common interests and objectives but that here we shall be emphasizing their differentiated and adversarial roles.

The Prosecutor

As you will remember, most cases are disposed of by a plea of guilt or *nolo contendere*. But cases can go to trial for various reasons. The defendant may be innocent and desire to exercise his or her rights to a trial in which the prosecutor must meet the burden of proving each and every element of the offense beyond and to the exclusion of every reasonable doubt; confident that the system will function as intended, the innocent defendant feels the trial will bring acquittal. More often, the defendant is guilty but hopes, with a hope sometimes fed by the facts provided by liberal discovery, that the prosecutor does not have a case that will dispel each and every reasonable doubt. Some defendants elect to go to trial because they are burdened with criminal records that will ensure maximum incarceration whether they plead guilty or lose at trial. They decide that they might just as well "roll the dice"; while they cannot hope for a favorable plea bargain from the prosecutor nor a lighter sentence from the court by pleading, they can hope against hope for an acquittal in a trial.

As we have seen, the strongest cases from the state's point of view are generally adjudicated by plea, and the weakest are adjudicated by trial. This puts the prosecutor in the position of going to a jury with the weakest cases.

In many of the roles, the prosecutor functions more like a judge than an advocate. The prosecutor's duty is to "do justice," which often requires that he or she make a judgment not to prosecute.[1] But after the prosecutor has decided to proceed with a case, that prosecutor is then cast in the role of the advocate of the state's case, aborting an effort to win only if he or she decides that the defendant is not guilty or that justice is not served by continuing prosecution. This advocacy is a primary feature of the adversary system, where the sides are clearly drawn and each side battles to convince the jury that the facts are in its favor. The attorneys are cast in the roles of champions for their clients, for at least in theory, they are in the best position to present the facts for their clients. If the attorneys competently present these facts, the jury is expected to be able to reach a fair and true decision as to guilt or innocence.

The prosecuting attorney has the so-called *burden of proof* or the *burden of going forward with the proof*. These terms describe the fact that the defendant is cloaked with a "mantle of innocence" that must be stripped away by facts provided by the prosecution. This *presumption of innocence* is provided by law for every defendant, regardless of guilt, and remains with the defendant until the prosecution has removed every reasonable doubt as to its existence. Legally, the defendant has no burden of proof at all. The accused can be acquitted by simply sitting in silence without calling a single witness or testifying in his or her own behalf. Such an acquittal will be gained if the prosecutor fails to meet the burden of proof. Jury instructions in all jurisdictions point out to the jury that the defendant is presumed innocent and that no inference of guilt is to be drawn from the fact that he or she chooses not to testify.

It is in this context that the prosecutor arrives in court on the day of trial. The prosecutor is expected to present the case against the defendant in a convincing yet ethical and gracious manner. Later in this chapter we will trace the steps in the performance of the prosecutor's task.

The Defense Attorney

The prosecutor is virtually *always* referred to as an officer of the court, while the defense attorney is only *sometimes* referred to that way. You have seen the quasi-judicial functions of the prosecutor, noted that the prosecutor's duty is to do justice, and realized that that duty frequently but not always requires the prosecutor to be an adversary. The role of the defense attorney is very different. Defense attorneys frequently try to utilize any type of technical loophole in the law to gain freedom for their clients. This may have nothing to do with justice or truth or equity; it is quite simply an effort to defeat the protective laws that society provides. But it can also be thought of as bringing justice to a person unfairly persecuted by a powerful state.

The defense attorney, like the prosecutor, is forbidden to proceed unethically or to use evidence that is perjured. Unlike the prosecutor, however, the defense counsel's duty is not to preserve the system but to free a client by any means short of unethical conduct.[2] The defense attorney must portray the client in the light most likely to lead to acquittal. Defense counsel must exploit any weakness in the prosecution's case and draw the jury's attention to that weakness. In so doing, the defense attorney will often point out inconsistencies that bear on the issues and weaken the impact of the case against the client.

Defense attorneys, like prosecutors, vary in their skills, personalities, and ethics. Most defense attorneys will not knowingly use perjured testimony. They will also not commit the crime of *subornation,* that is, they will not seek to induce perjury. Rarely, some defense attorneys, for whatever reason, perhaps from too close a continuing association with the morally bankrupt, tend to lie and cheat. Some few of the worst defense attorneys actually criminalize, that is, take part in the creation of criminal schemes and advise their clients on how not to be caught or on how to avoid conviction if caught. These lawyers are not only acting unethically but are committing crimes themselves by so assisting in the perpetration of crimes by their clients.[3]

The defendant, regardless of the heinousness of the crime, is entitled to a competent attorney who makes every effort to seek acquittal. An attorney can ethically seek acquittal even if he or she knows the client is guilty. But the attorney must not knowingly ask questions that will elicit lies from the client. If the client is determined to testify to what the defense lawyer knows to be lies, that lawyer should either withdraw from the case or state to the jury that the client wishes to make a statement and allow the client to make the statement without the benefit of questioning by counsel.[4]

At trial, defense lawyers must make every effort, by use of the rules of evidence, to keep all possibly harmful testimony from the jury. Some defense attorneys raise objections so frequently that the jurors develop the clear feeling that the defendant has something to hide. The defense lawyer has a dilemma then when the prosecutor persists in presenting objectionable evidence: Defense counsel has a duty to keep harmful evidence out of court, but frequent objections are apt to offend the jury. This is an area where improperly zealous prosecutors can force defense lawyers to risk alienating the jury. Such gamesmanship on the part of a prosecutor is unfair but does occur.

The Defendant

The defendant has a definite role at trial. The first, though not immediately apparent, role is to appear innocent. No matter how the defendant might ordinarily look, he or she is almost certainly going to be cleaned up for the jury and dressed in a socially acceptable manner. *Courtroom demeanor* is critical to a defendant's case, and a competent defense lawyer will coach the defendant on how to behave so as not to appear hostile or dishonest. A surly defendant can easily tip the scales toward conviction.

Defendants are expected to keep their lawyers informed as to how they believe the testimony of prosecution witnesses comports with the

News of Note

ACTRESS TEACHES ASPIRING LAWYERS
THE 'RIGHTS' OF COURTROOM BEHAVIOR

MIAMI (AP)—To win a case before a trial jury, an attorney needs something that isn't taught in law school, says veteran actress and television producer Iris Acker.

She calls it "courtroom demeanor."

For years, Mrs. Acker has been coaching lawyers on how to speak, dress and establish credibility with jury panels.

"In law schools, attorneys are helped with everything except their bad habits," said Mrs. Acker, who began her show business career at 11 in her native Bronx, N.Y.

"An attorney must have believability so no matter what you say no one will doubt you," she added enthusiastically.

Teachers, Mrs. Acker explained, rarely correct students for choppy sentences, cutting off words, swaying from side to side when they speak or not looking at the person they address.

"If you don't look a jury in the eye, they won't trust you," said Mrs. Acker, who produced a 13-week series called "The Jury Box" at WLRN during her five-year tenure at the public television station here.

A lengthy career in the theater has given her the wherewithal to teach voice projection and modulation, not only to attorneys, but to celebrities who are to be interviewed on television.

At her studio in North Miami, Mrs. Acker, who gives her age as 50-plus, also advises attorneys on courtroom attire.

"They should wear nothing that's disconcerting—avoid stripes, polka dots and wild ties," she said. "Nothing should detract from what you're saying."

Mrs. Acker also teaches aspiring actors how to audition for commercial work. She's made a video cassette and written a book on the subject.

She became involved with attorneys when, several years ago, she was invited to a seminar at Nova University in Fort Lauderdale.

"It was for attorneys who wanted career changes and get back to courtroom work," she recalled.

"I was to critique attorneys on how they handled themselves—physically and verbally—in court."

Mrs. Acker also believes her expertise would be useful to campaigning politicians.

After watching the recent vice presidential debate, she said, "If I had (Dan) Quayle, what a job I could do with him. He was politically coached, but not dramatically coached. He needed me."

Source: Daytona Beach Sunday News-Journal, November 6, 1988.

---

truth as they themselves know it. This will assist defense lawyers in the formulation of questions for cross-examination.

The defendant may be called to testify. If the defendant does take the witness stand, he or she must have at least the appearance of veracity. The defendant must tell a story that falls within the bounds of believability, bounds established largely by the prosecution's case and common sense. The defendant's testimony must be factually strong enough to withstand cross-examination by a determined prosecutor. If the story or the defendant or both are weak, the defendant can lose the case during cross-examination. It takes considerable skill to prepare a defendant for cross-examination. Some defendants are so obviously guilty that the defense attorney should keep them off the stand at all costs. It must be remembered that defense attorneys work for their clients, no matter how guilty or ignorant those clients may be. Some clients will go against counsel's best advice and take the stand when they should not. The clients' wishes, though, short of a desire to commit perjury, must be considered by their lawyers, and clients should be allowed to make major decisions in their own defense after being advised of all alternatives by their lawyers.

The Witnesses

All testimony must come from sworn witnesses. Their testimony, plus any real evidence, is all that the jury can rely on for factual evidence. In this context the defendant is obviously one of the witnesses that the jury can consider as a source of fact.

Witnesses are presumed to be telling the truth. But juries are composed of persons who have experience at living in the real world, and as such they are not so naive as to believe that all witnesses invariably tell the truth. They, as jurors, are supposed to resolve conflicts in testimony using common sense. They are expected to look to why a witness might testify in a particular manner. Does the witness have any motivation to lie? The motivation of the defendant and the defendant's family is obvious, but it is sometimes difficult for the jury to reconcile divergent testimony when the witnesses for each side seem to have nothing to lose or gain.

In popular idiom, impeachment is the process for removing a public officer, usually for corruption or other misconduct in office. In a trial, the term "impeachment" has a very different meaning; the *impeachment of a witness* is the technique of demonstrating to the jury that a particular witness is not worthy of being believed. The opposing lawyer is the person responsible for creating impeachment, with the goal of discrediting any testimony damaging to the client.

The manner and means of impeachment are governed by the rules of evidence and case law. Generally, the party calling the witness is not permitted to impeach that witness. Several means of impeachment are typically available and include: (1) introducing statements made earlier by the witness that are not consistent with his or her statements made in court (depositions are often used for this purpose); (2) showing that the witness is biased; (3) demonstrating that the testimony of the witness is in conflict with the testimony of other witnesses; and (4) attacking the char-

acter of the witness by showing that he or she has been previously convicted of a crime.

Most jurisdictions allow judges to comment on the evidence that has
been presented and remark as to the weight to be accorded certain portions of a witness's testimony. Other states absolutely forbid the court to
comment on the evidence; these jurisdictions even afford the defendant a
new trial if the comment is significant. In those jurisdictions that allow
comment on the testimony, the judge will usually point out conflicts and
pinpoint testimony that is of doubtful veracity.

The authors have noted that absolutely impartial and honest witnesses
can sometimes testify to differing facts. This is a result of human imper-
fection in the ability to observe, remember, and relate. Attorneys often
try to get witnesses to reflect carefully and thoroughly on the facts of a
case and articulate them prior to trial. This will often lead to clearer and
more accurate testimony. Some attorneys get carried away and actually
"coach" the witnesses to testify in a manner that is not completely truthful but that best serves the client. A fine line often separates refreshing
the memory of a witness and "coaching."

The Defendant as Witness

The Fifth Amendment of the Constitution clearly provides that "No person ... shall be compelled in any criminal case to be a witness against
himself." The effect of this provision is much more sweeping than one
would first imagine. Its effect stretches across the width and breadth of
the criminal process. At trial, the privilege means that defendants cannot
be forced to testify and the fact that they take the stand, if they do,
means that they are taking it of their own accord. Prosecutors sometimes
put on such a good case that defendants are put in a very bad light if they
do nothing to explain away their criminal involvement. The situation can
become very difficult for defendants who see the prosecution build a
tight case. They must then decide whether to risk the prosecutor's cross-
examination, which follows the defendants' testimony—if they have the
courage to take the stand. Of course, a truthful defendant should not fear
cross-examination. We will have more to say on cross-examination later
in this chapter.

Defense lawyers often use voir dire not just to ask questions of the
prospective jurors but also to explain, in a light most favorable to the defendant, various aspects of the trial, including the defendant's right not to
take the stand. Such instructions are usually presented in the form of rhetorical questions: "Do you understand fully that my client sits there
cloaked with the presumption of innocence and is not required to testify
and that he has the right to sit back and require the State to prove its case

fully and may choose not to say anything at all?'' Prosecutors, of course, indulge in jury instruction by rhetorical question as often as defense lawyers do and try just as hard to condition the jury to their way of thinking.

The decision as to whether a defendant will take the stand is often one of the most critical decisions faced by the defense in the trial. The impression that the defendant makes on the jury is vital. The defendant's apparent credibility can often make or break the case for the defense. The skill of the prosecutor at cross-examination and the ability of the defendant to withstand the cross-examination are crucial factors if the defendant decides to testify. Better defense lawyers usually have a good feel for all factors that help determine whether the defendant should take the stand.

Any comment on the part of the prosecutor to the jury as to the fact that a defendant did not take the stand is considered—and rightly so—to be tantamount to a deprivation of the right to remain silent and results in a mistrial. This principle was established in the case of *Griffin v. California,* which was decided by the Supreme Court in 1965.[5] Justice William O. Douglas wrote the Court's majority opinion, which states that the Fifth Amendment guarantee against self-incrimination requires that prosecutors be forbidden to make any comment on the silence of the defendant. The majority and dissenting opinions in that case are excerpted here.

Griffin v. California

380 U.S. 609 (1965)

FROM THE OPINION

By Justice Douglas

If this were a federal trial, reversible error would have been committed, *Wilson v United States,* ... so holds. It is said, however, that the Wilson decision rested not on the Fifth Amendment, but on an Act of Congress, now 18 U.S.C. §3481. That indeed is the fact, as the opinion of the Court in the Wilson case states.... But that is the beginning, not the end, of our inquiry. The question remains whether, statute or not, the comment rule, approved by California, violates the Fifth Amendment.

We think it does. It is in substance a rule of evidence that allows the state the privilege of tendering to the jury for its consideration the failure of the accused to testify. No formal offer of proof is made as in other situations; but the prosecutor's comment and the court's acquiescence are the equivalent of an offer of evidence and its acceptance. ...

If the words ''Fifth Amendment'' are substituted for ''act'' and for ''statute,'' the spirit of the Self-Incrimination Clause is reflected. For comment on the refusal to testify is a remnant of the "inquisitorial system of criminal justice," *Murphy v. Waterfront Comm.,...* which the Fifth Amendment outlaws. It is a penalty imposed by courts for exercising a constitutional privilege. It cuts down on the privilege by making its assertion costly. It is said, however, that the inference of guilt for failure to testify as to facts peculiarly within the accused's knowledge is in any event natural and irresistible, and that comment on the failure does not magnify that inference into a penalty for asserting a constitutional privilege.... What the jury may infer, given no help from the court, is one thing. What it may infer when the court solemnizes the silence of the accused into evidence against him is quite another. That the inference of guilt is not always so natural or irresistible is brought out in the *Modesto* opinion itself:

> Defendant contends that the reason a defendant refuses to testify is that his prior convictions will be introduced in evidence to impeach him ([Cal.] Code Civ. Proc. §2051) and not that he is unable to deny the accusations. It is true that the defendant might fear that his prior convictions will prejudice the jury, and therefore another possible inference can be drawn form his refusal to take the stand....

We said in *Malloy v Hogan,...* that "the same standards must determine whether an accused's silence in either a federal or state proceeding is justified." We take that in its literal sense and hold that the Fifth Amendment, in its direct application to the federal government and in its bearing on the states by reason of the Fourteenth Amendment, forbids either comment by the prosecution on the accused's silence or instructions by the court that such silence is evidence of guilt.

Judgment reversed.

By Justice Harlan

I agree with the Court that within the federal judicial system the Fifth Amendment bars adverse comment by federal prosecutors and judges on a defendant's failure to take the stand in a criminal trial, a right accorded him by that amendment. And given last Term's decision in *Malloy v Hogan,* 378 U.S. 1, 84... that the Fifth Amendment applies to the state in all its refinements, I see no legitimate escape from today's decision and therefore concur in it. I do so, however, with great reluctance, since for me the decision exemplifies the creeping paralysis with which this Court's recent adoption of the "incorporation" doctrine is infecting the operation of the federal system.

FROM THE DISSENT

By Justice Stewart, with whom Justice White joins, dissenting

... Moreover, no one can say where the balance of advantage might lie as a result of attorneys' discussion of the matter. No doubt the prosecution's argument will seek to encourage the drawing of inferences unfavorable to the defendant. However, the defendant's counsel equally has an opportunity to explain the various other reasons why a defendant may not wish to take the stand, and thus rebut the natural if uneducated assumption that it is because the defendant cannot truthfully deny the accusations made.

I think the California comment rule is not a coercive device which impairs the right against self-incrimination, but rather a means of articulating and bringing into the light of rational discussion a fact inescapably impressed on the jury's consciousness. The California procedure is not only designed to protect the defendant against unwarranted inferences which might be drawn by an uninformed jury; it is also an attempt by the state to recognize and articulate what it believes to be the natural probative force of certain facts. Surely no one would deny that the state has an important interest in throwing the light of rational discussion on that which transpires in the course of a trial, both to protect the defendant from the very real dangers of silence and to shape a legal process designed to ascertain the truth.

The California rule allowing comment by counsel and instruction by the judge on the defendant's failure to take the stand is hardly an idiosyncratic aberration. The Model Code of Evidence, and the Uniform Rules of Evidence both sanction the use of such procedures. The practice has been endorsed by resolution of the American Bar Association and the American Law Institute, and has the support of the weight of scholarly opinion.

Despite the constitutional guarantee, prosecutors will often try to make a subtle point of the fact that a defendant has not testified. They will try by implication to bring the jury to the conclusion that the defendant would have taken the stand if he or she had been innocent; they do this by making statements in the closing argument that point out the fact without actually commenting on it. Such a statement might typically take this form in closing argument: "Ladies and Gentlemen of the jury, I told you that I would prove Mr. Dan Defendant guilty of burglary and you saw me do it; you watched all the State's witnesses come forward and take the oath and testify fully. We gave you full sworn testimony as to each and every element of the case and let Ms. Defense Lawyer cross-examine our witnesses and you saw how they were unshaken by her cross-examination." Such argument is not too unusual and may serve to cause the jury to wonder why the defense did not call a certain credible witness who did not fear cross-examination.

The Jury

If the trial is not a so-called bench trial, where the judge sits as the trier of fact, the jury sits in the role of fact finder and must decide upon guilt or innocence. The jury is sworn to do its duty, is cautioned not to read or watch or listen to media accounts of the proceedings, is ordered not to discuss the case with anyone else and not to visit the scene of the crime unless taken there on court order, and so on. In highly publicized cases, the jury may be *sequestered,* or kept away from the public and isolated from media accounts of the crime. The usual method for sequestration is to board the jurors at a hotel convenient to the courthouse. This may be done during the entire trial or only during jury deliberation.

Jurors pick their own leader, commonly referred to as a *foreman,* from among themselves. Experienced court personnel can often guess the identity of the foreman before the jurors retire to the jury room to choose him or her. They are able to do so by recalling the behavior of the jurors during voir dire.

Jurors, if they are to perform their duties well, must be attentive not only to what is said but to how it is said. It is an unfortunate fact that many lies are told under oath in court. Jurors are charged with resolving the conflicts in testimony by deciding who is telling the truth and who is not. Often the jury instructions give specific instructions to the jurors as to factors they should weigh when they find conflicts in testimony. They are told to look for such things as motive to lie, demeanor on the stand, and discrepancies in testimony.

Before they retire to consider their verdict, jurors are also instructed in the law they are to apply to the case. This instruction comes during the so-called *jury charge* that the judge gives the jury before it retires to consider the verdict.

In a few jurisdictions the jury has a sentencing role in noncapital cases. In five states the jury has the authority to impose sentences for all offenses; two states allow juries to sentence only in certain specified crimes; and two other states allow the defendant to choose whether to be sentenced by the judge or by the jury.

The Judge

The role and status of the judge are unique in American government. At trial the judge is expected to be absolutely impartial and to lead the persons involved in the courtroom process effectively, efficiently, and fairly through the trial. The judge is charged with the sometimes difficult duty of seeing that all parties receive a fair trial.[6] But trials are almost never perfect, and the appellate courts will allow small errors at trial to go by without retrial. This is the doctrine of *harmless error,* and judges do not become, in most cases, overly concerned with small errors at trial. Judges do, however, become most concerned when errors are serious enough to cause mistrial or reversal upon appeal, especially where defendants are on trial for their lives or are liable to long prison terms.

The judge's concern for an errorless trial is based on pride in the fact that he or she can effectively lead the courtroom team through trial; but the concern is also based on the fact that it is embarrassing to have one's case reversed by the appellate court, and such occurrences fuel judge-level gossip.

Judges, who were, after all, real people before they donned their judicial robes, have widely differing styles of courtroom leadership. Some are activists, setting the cadence and tone of the proceedings. Others let the participants do all of the leading, interrupting only when they discern impending error. Some judges are energetic and hardworking and pay close attention to all the proceedings before them. Others are lazy and indolent, even to the point of sleeping at the bench. (When queried about this judicial napping, most are quick to point out that they were "just resting their eyes.")

The judges who manifest these different styles will explain their roles in a fashion that justifies their behavior. The activists will point out the need for strong leadership and direction and will cite the need to proactively anticipate problems and move the participants in the proper direction. These activists tend to require deference from courtroom personnel; less active judges will place less importance on a showing of lawyerly submission to their authority. Passive judges will remind others that a judge is charged with ensuring the fairness of the proceedings, not with leading the participants down a path of the judge's choosing. After all, the passive judge might state, judges are the referees and not the combatants.

THE STEPS IN A TRIAL

The process of a criminal trial is divisible into any number of steps or phases; we have chosen, not altogether arbitrarily, to treat a trial in terms of ten steps. As the reader will see, we shall include those steps necessary to a trial by jury, though defendants may opt for a bench trial. In outlining the ten steps, we pick up the process following the empaneling of a jury, since that topic was covered in the previous chapter.

Pretrial Jury Instructions

Prior to the opening statements by the lawyer(s), the jury is instructed by the court. In most jurisdictions the *pretrial jury instructions* are written and published as a sort of manual that the court reads from when and as appropriate. The text is usually so divided that the appropriate portions are severable. The instructions are designed to be impartial and simple to understand. The portions read prior to trial typically caution the jury that it is the sole trier of the facts, that the court is the legal authority, that the arguments of counsel are not evidence but are persuasive in nature, and that the only evidence to be considered is that which is sworn and given from the witness stand or is tangible and admitted into evidence by the court. The jury is ordinarily cautioned not to read or listen to news accounts of the trial and not to visit the scene or discuss the case with any-one. The judge will also caution the jury that the indictment or information is not evidence, that it is only an accusatory instrument with no value as evidence, and that the defendant is presumed innocent unless and until proven guilty.

The Opening Statements

The prosecutor invariably makes some sort of an opening statement prior to the presentation of the state's (or federal government's) "case in chief." The defense lawyer (or lawyers, if there are multiple defendants) will sometimes make an opening statement after the prosecutor's statement, but may put off making an opening statement until the case for the defense is actually begun. This gives the defense attorney a chance to evaluate the state's case and tailor the defense case and the statement describing it to evidence that the prosecutor has produced. Many defense lawyers like the flexibility they gain in waiting.

The *opening statement* is intended to assist the jury in understanding the testimony and the arguments that are to be presented. An opening statement draws the jury's attention to the relevant portions of the testimony and, at least in theory, assists the jury in its role as fact finder. Testimony at trial is frequently complex and burdened with much verbiage. Without an opening statement, the jurors could become confused by testimony that is really not helpful in determining guilt or innocence.

Lawyerly skill is required to make an effective opening statement. It can be reversible error to state that certain testimony will be presented and then not to present the promised evidence. The reason is obvious. The lawyer ought not to create the illusion of testimony that, for one reason or another, will not be or cannot be presented. The opening statement is technically not evidence but often is as effective as the actual sworn evidence. If the lawyer is convincing as to the content and importance of the testimony that is about to be adduced, the initial impression on the jury is going to be in favor of his or her cause—and initial impressions are difficult to dispel.

A classic opening statement will tell the jury the "story" of the crime as it happened and will outline the testimony of the witnesses in the sequence in which they will appear. The prosecutor will thus be able to sensitize jurors to those items of proof that are important. The jurors will be assisted in knowing what to listen for in the testimony as the case develops and will be more likely to properly appreciate the testimony as it is given. Without the preview given in the opening statement, the jurors might be faced with a great deal of testimony that does not become relevant until well into the trial; this pertains especially in those cases containing proof by circumstantial evidence. If the jurors are not told what to watch for prior to the beginning of testimony, they will have to try to discern the relevant testimony from among all the testimony that they heard during the trial. Not only is the jury's job made easier by the opening statement but the likelihood of a decision based on all the relevant facts is increased.

If the defense counsel elects to make an opening statement before the prosecution's case is begun, he or she has the opportunity to point out the potentially weak areas of the case so that the prosecution's witnesses can be seen in a critical light and the fact pattern that the prosecutor promises to develop can be critically analyzed. In most jurisdictions the defense counsel has the option of not making an opening statement until the prosecution has rested its case and the case for the defense is begun. In delaying an opening statement, the defense loses the advantage of previewing for the jury the potential flaws in the prosecution's case but gains the advantage of delivering an opening statement based on what the prosecutor has proved or failed to prove. A delayed opening statement by the defense also has the advantage of being much safer than one given before the prosecutor has shown proof that could only have been anticipated in the opening moments of the trial.

The Case for the Prosecution

The prosecutor must initially present a *case in chief,* which must prove, beyond and to the exclusion of a reasonable doubt, each and every element of the crime charged, including, of course, the identity of the defendant as the perpetrator.

The lawyerly duties of the prosecutor, beyond the obvious superficial difference in mission to convict or acquit, are very different from the duties of the defense lawyer. Keep in mind that the prosecutor has the burden of proof and must, through legally admissible testimony, prove each element of the case. While the prosecution is presenting the case, the role of the defense lawyer is to exclude as much testimony as possible that would be damaging to the client and to discredit that which cannot be excluded. It is immediately obvious that a skilled prosecutor will have a plan whereby he or she can put on enough evidence to demonstrate to the jury that the defendant has committed the crime(s) charged and leave no reasonable doubt as to the guilt of the defendant.

Prosecutors, if they have the time and if the case is important, go to considerable effort to plan their *order of proof,* the sequence of presentation of evidence. In a complex case this is often very involved. Some items of proof, such as latent fingerprints, inked fingerprints, and the expert comparison of latent and inked prints, may require bringing in several witnesses to identify the exhibits before the expert witness testifies that the prints do indeed belong to the defendant. One witness may testify only to the "lifting," or recovery, of the latent prints at the crime scene. Another might testify that he took known, inked fingerprints from the defendant whom he identifies as being in the courtroom. Still another may testify that he examined both sets of fingerprints and finds them to match conclusively.

It takes some degree of lawyerly skill to decide upon the sequence in which witnesses will testify and evidence will be placed before the court. For example, it can be difficult to develop a logical sequence of proof when it is necessary to have an eyewitness take the stand early in the trial to set the scene and identify a piece of evidence that as yet has no significance since it has not yet been testified to by an expert. The testimony of the eyewitness would probably be more valuable in that it would have more impact on the jurors if that witness could also testify to the relevance of the evidence, but only the expert can do this. The decision-making process as to which witnesses are called, and when, and by whom particular pieces of physical evidence should be admitted is a critical one. The logic of proof, which is influenced by the order of proof, is what will ultimately convince or fail to convince the jury beyond a reasonable doubt that the crime has been committed.

The prosecutor must be ever mindful of the fact that *all* the elements of the crime have to be proved in order to achieve a verdict of guilty from the jury. Most prosecutors keep some sort of written inventory of what they must prove. An example of such an inventory of proof in a hypothetical first-degree murder case follows:

1. That Virgil Victim is, in fact, dead
2. That he died by a criminal instrumentality, a gunshot wound to the head
3. That he was shot in the county where the court's venue lies
4. That he died when and where specified in the indictment
5. That Dan Defendant killed Virgil
6. That Dan acted with premeditation and malice aforethought

Such an inventory or checklist is a simple trial aid to ensure that the prosecutor does not omit some essential piece of proof during the heat of trial. In the intensity of the effort to be thorough and convincing, many prosecutors have failed to take stock before resting a case and have found that, much to their horror and chagrin, they had failed to prove a simple but essential element.

The reader is urged to observe different prosecutors in action in criminal trials. This is usually easy to arrange in a town of any appreciable size. The contrast in styles and effectiveness is instructive. Much about prosecution can also be learned from observing the defense and the court in action. Note the ways in which the defense attempts to limit the parameters of what is admitted for the jury to consider.

When prosecutors have completed the presentation of the case in chief, they will announce that "the State (or Government) rests." If enough evidence to make a prima facie case has not been put forth, the prosecution faces an immediate challenge: the defendant's motion for a directed verdict of acquittal.

Motion for a Directed Verdict of Acquittal

At the close of the prosecution's case in chief, it is typical, even obligatory by custom, for the defense to move the court to "direct a verdict of acquittal" or, in other jurisdictions, enter a "summary judgment of acquittal." Such a verdict or judgment in effect says, "The prosecution has failed to make an adequate case for the jury to debate and the Court hereby acquits the defendant of the crime charged." The acquittal is final and obviously occurs after jeopardy has attached, so the defendant is free from ever facing the charges again.

The defense usually argues all sorts of issues in its motion for a directed verdict of acquittal or motion for judgment of acquittal so that those issues will be recorded by the court reporter; as a part of the record of trial then they can form the basis for appeal if the prosecution wins. Courts do not often grant these defense motions, preferring to allow the jury to decide on the issues. The granting of a directed verdict means that the prosecutor just did not prove the case; this can be a point of considerable embarrassment to a prosecutor, unless it is rendered by the occurrence of something unforeseeable during the trial. Once in a great while a victim who identified the defendant at a lineup will not identify the defendant at trial, whether through fear of retaliation or loss of memory. Such a failure to identify is the sort of defect that will lead to a directed verdict or judgment of acquittal. In a situation in which the one witness is the victim, this lack of ability to identify can be fatal to the prosecutor's case; so too can the suppression of pretrial identification because of police error. Other deficiencies in the prosecution's case can also give the judge cause to direct a loss.

The Case for the Defense

In a strict sense the defendant is never required to put on any case at all, since the accused is always presumed to be innocent. But it is obvious that if the defense believes that the "cloak of innocence" has been stripped away by the prosecutor's case in chief, then counsel had better do something in the way of presenting a case, if possible, that will at least leave the jurors with a feeling that the prosecutor has not dispelled *all* reasonable doubt as to each and every element of the offense alleged.

Recall that the prosecutor must prove each and every element beyond and to the exclusion of reasonable doubt. This, taken from the defense's viewpoint, means that the defendant will be acquitted if there remains reasonable doubt as to any essential element of the crime. Thus the defendant's actual burden of proof (though in the strict sense there is none) is to ensure that reasonable doubt remains in one or more areas. How the defendant creates or preserves this doubt depends on the facts of the case and defense counsel's lawyerly skill.

Defense technique is dependent on an infinitely variable set of factors, including but not limited to:

1. The strength and quality of the prosecution's case
2. The actual facts that the defendant is able to introduce
3. The nonfactual testimony that a defendant disposed toward perjury can produce in court, either by his or her own statements or by those of others
4. The exclusionary rules that the defense can successfully exert

Defense will put on that testimony that they believe will most effectively convince the jury of reasonable doubt. Remember, the defendant is presumed to be innocent, but practicality requires presentation of a case to dispel, at least partially, the prosecution's proof. The most effective way to do this is through the use of the testimony of witnesses who would have no apparent motive to lie. Juries look with a jaundiced eye on the self-serving testimony of the defendant and with only a slightly less jaundiced eye upon the testimony of the defendant's family and friends. Far preferable is the testimony of persons with no motive to lie.

As we have already stated, the decision as to whether the defendant will take the witness stand and testify in his or her own behalf is often crucial. Juries seem to expect defendants to take the stand and state their innocence—or at least make some excuse for their behavior. Recall that the right to silence that springs from the Fifth Amendment allows a defendant not only not to be called to the stand by the prosecutor but also mandates that the prosecutor never comment on the fact that the defendant has not taken the stand. Mention of the lack of testimony by the accused is an almost automatic reason for mistrial.

Defendants who are guilty and who do not wish to commit perjury will obviously have to stay off the stand. Likewise defendants who are willing to commit perjury, but who are not skillful liars, are well advised to avoid testifying. Skilled prosecutors can have a fine time with untruthful defendants and expose them for what they are. On the other hand, truthful defendants at least in theory, will be unshaken in their testimony by even the most rigorous and skillful *cross-examination*. Yet in real life, some truthful defendants are so frightened by the experience of cross-examination that they appear to be untruthful and harm their own case.

At the conclusion of the defendant's case in chief, the defense counsel will announce, "The defense rests," and renew the motion for a directed verdict or summary judgment of acquittal, a motion that is routinely denied unless the defense has brought out virtually irrefutable evidence of innocence and has so destroyed the state's case that it clearly should not go to the jury. This is exceedingly rare.

The Rebuttal Case and the Surrebuttal Case

If the defense has brought out new issues that were not addressed in the prosecution's case in chief, the prosecutor has the opportunity to present witnesses for the purpose of dealing with the new matters in issue.

A typical example of a rebuttal is seen in the case in which the prosecutor has indeed proved murder, but the defense in its case in chief brings in expert and lay testimony to the effect that the defendant meets the M'Naughten standards for insanity and is therefore entitled to acquittal. The assertion of this defense and the supporting testimony allows the prosecutor to make a case in rebuttal. In the *rebuttal case,* the prosecutor can call whatever witnesses are available to meet the defendant's insanity defense.

Whenever the state puts on a rebuttal case, the defense is presented with the opportunity of responding with a *surrebuttal case* so long as it presents testimony that responds to issues raised in the state's rebuttal case.

Closing Arguments

An elderly attorney was heard to advise a young lawyer that "an opening statement is where you tell them [the jury] what you are going to tell them, the proof is what you tell them, and the closing argument is where you tell them what they have already been told." This is essentially true. The *closing argument* is the final sales pitch by the attorneys to convince the jurors that reasonable doubt does or does not exist and that the defendant should therefore be acquitted or convicted.

Lawyerly skill in constructing and delivering a closing argument is particularly critical in that it is the last representation of the party's case that the jurors will hear and last impressions are important.

At the beginning of closing argument, it is altogether typical for the attorneys to remind the jury that their arguments are not evidence, and that if the jurors remember the facts differently, they are to utilize their own recollection and not the recitation of the attorney. The prosecutor will then summarize his or her case, citing important pieces of testimony, and try to convince the jury that no reasonable doubt remains as to the guilt of the accused. The prosecutor will call upon the jurors to do their sworn civic duty as jurors and return a verdict of guilty so that the law can punish the evildoer for such crimes against society. The defense attorney will point out the flaws in the prosecutor's proof and remind the jurors of conflict in the state's testimony. Defense will argue as eloquently as possible and urge acquittal.

Most courtroom observers feel that the closing arguments are the climax of the trial and the best examples of a lawyer's ability. It is not unusual for the people who work in a courthouse to suddenly materialize in a courtroom where closing arguments are about to be given in an exciting case.

The sequence of giving closing argument varies somewhat among the states, but it is not unusual for the prosecution to make an initial closing argument, followed by the defendant's close, and then a rebuttal summary by the prosecutor. In some states, if the defense has put on no witnesses other than the accused himself, then the defense goes first *and* last, a valuable privilege.

Instructions to the Jury

Instructing the jury is often referred to as *charging the jury* and is done before closing arguments in some states and after closing arguments in others. The judge decides what instructions are to be given during a *charge conference,* which is held with opposing counsel, usually in the judge's chambers.

The instructions are important because they contain the rules of law that the jurors are to utilize in gauging the evidence. Remember, jurors are laypersons, most of whom would be hopelessly confused by a reading of the applicable statutes. Jury instructions are devised to state the law, concisely and accurately, in plain, everyday English. This is not a simple task. Many states have books of jury instructions, typically proposed by a bar committee and approved by the state supreme court. These instructions embody both the statutes and case law in relatively simple instructions, which are generally so artfully drawn that a layperson or a law enforcement officer in search of the true meaning of the criminal law is well advised to consult them.

Even though the jury instructions are designed to be as simple as possible, the very complexity of the law can make the instructions unwieldy. Many trials have several counts and/or counts with lesser included offenses, all of which require the reading of very lengthy jury instructions.

The jury is also instructed in things other than the definitions of the possible crimes.

Jurors are instructed as to the burden of proof and as to what "reasonable doubt" is. They are also instructed on how to deliberate, how to ask questions of the court, and how to reach a verdict. They are cautioned not to communicate with nonjurors. They are then provided verdict forms to be signed by the person they elect foreman. The verdict forms will be of "guilty as charged," "guilty of lesser included offenses," and "not guilty." If an insanity defense has been made, the jury will also receive a "not guilty by reason of insanity" verdict form.

Juries frequently sequestered, isolated from all persons except the court and the bailiffs, during their deliberations. Whether or not they are sequestered, they are almost always ordered not to read any newspaper accounts of the trial or listen to or view any news of the trial. This is a precaution designed to protect them from inferences of the media and opinions of friends and neighbors.

Jury Deliberations

After the closing arguments and instructions are completed, the jury retires to the jury room. Its first order of business is to elect a foreman except in those states where the first juror selected is automatically foreman. The foreman will usually take a preliminary vote to see where the jury stands. Only rarely is the first vote unanimous. Generally the first vote is followed by discussion, debate, and later votes. Usually a unanimous decision is eventually reached and, with the decision, a *verdict.* If the jury is unable to reach a verdict, the judge will usually bring the jurors back into the courtroom and read them a so-called *dynamite charge,* an instruction to the jury that it is their duty to reach a verdict and that they should go back to the jury room and reach a verdict if they can. Ultimately, if the jurors are unable to reach a unanimous decision, they communicate this fact to the court and the court will declare a mistrial.

After a mistrial, the prosecutor will reevaluate the case and decide whether to proceed with a fresh trial. If the prosecutor is convinced that it is folly to proceed, he or she will enter a *nolle prosequi* and abandon the case.

Announcement of the Verdict

When the jury has reached a verdict of guilty or not guilty, it returns to the courtroom, and the foreman passes the signed verdict form to the judge, who reads it silently and passes it to the clerk for public reading. If the verdict is "guilty," the defense may ask the judge for a *polling of the jury,* which means that each juror will be asked whether his or her verdict was indeed "guilty." This sometimes causes a wavering juror to recant a vote of guilty and "hang the jury," which is, of course, the very reason that the defense requests the poll.

If the verdict is "guilty," the judge will probably remand the defendant to custody, but if no presentence investigation is to be held, the court will sometimes impose its sentence immediately. This topic is reserved for the next chapter. If the verdict is "not guilty," the defendant is immediately released unless other charges are still pending and bail has not been posted on them.

Formal Adjudication

In some places the jury's verdict closes the trial, since it acts as the court in determining the guilt or innocence of the accused. In other states, however, the judge acts as the court in the rendering of *formal adjudication.* Judges may not adjudicate a defendant guilty in the face of a verdict of acquittal, but they are permitted to decline to adjudicate a defendant guilty in spite of a jury verdict to that effect. Is is not at all unusual for judges to announce that they are *withholding adjudication of guilt,* a means of suspending adjudication. Generally this is followed by a sentence of probation, a matter to be taken up later. If the judge withholds adjudication of guilt, the defendant does not obtain a record of conviction.

It is highly unusual, but permissible, for a judge to decline to accept the jury's verdict of guilty and to enter an adjudication of acquittal of the defendant. This is similar to the directed verdict of acquittal discussed earlier, but follows the verdict and directly overturns it. When this unusual event occurs, it dumbfounds the jurors, infuriates the prosecutor, and even surprises defense counsel.

EXTRALEGAL INFLUENCES ON JURY VERDICTS

It has already been established that jurors can be prejudiced or biased going into a trial. Jury verdicts can be influenced by these biases—indeed by many factors unrelated to the evidence itself. Marilyn Chandler Ford has reviewed the literature on studies done on these *extralegal factors* and what follows is a brief summary of what her review found.[7]

Influence of the Juror's Personal Characteristics

Personal characteristics of jurors include gender, race, age, and socioeconomic status. Despite the widespread feeling throughout the legal pro-

News of Note

WHEN JURORS ARE ORDERED TO IGNORE TESTIMONY, THEY IGNORE THE ORDER

By Michael Allen

Two police officers burst through James Duncan's door without a warrant, punch him in the stomach and then handcuff him to a radiator while they ransack his apartment. Mr. Duncan sues them for conducting an illegal search.

A big damage award seems likely—that is, until the officers' attorney casually mentions to the jury that the search revealed evidence of heroin trafficking. The judge sternly orders the jurors to disregard the statement.

But do they? A new study by the American Bar Foundation and Northwestern University, using this and other fictional cases, suggests not. In the study, mock jurors who didn't hear about the heroin were nearly twice as likely to award punitive damages to Mr. Duncan as those who did, and typically assigned over $10,000 more in total damages.

The results, says New York University law professor Stephen Gillers, tend to confirm what many trial lawyers have long suspected: "You can never unring the bell."

Forbidden information

This study, and others like it, [is] adding new fuel to an old debate over just how good jurors are at filtering out forbidden information from their deliberations. For example, how is one to ignore the pregnant wife of a defendant who sits in the front row every day? Or the blockbuster newspaper article that exposes massive fraud in city hall the week before the mayor goes on trial? Or hints that a doctor being sued for malpractice has a huge insurance policy that will cover any losses?

The issue becomes crucial when highly prejudicial material, such as a criminal defendant's arrest history, comes out in open court. Although judges have the option of declaring a mistrial, they rarely do because of the high cost of starting over. So they must rely on judicial instructions to force the jurors to filter out the legally irrelevant information.

Some courtroom observers say that's sometimes asking too much. "The bottom line is, most jurors, because they're human beings, find it difficult to ignore what they consider important," says Donald Vinson, chief executive officer of Litigation Sciences Inc., a Los Angeles consulting firm that advises lawyers on the psychology of trials. "The problem is, what they think is important and what lawyers and judges think is important may be quite different."

Mr. Vinson learned that lesson the hard way a few years ago when one of his clients, a large pharmaceutical maker, was sued for product liability. The plaintiff's lawyer, ignoring a pretrial agreement, asked a witness if it wasn't true that the company had been sued before. The judge immediately cut off the answer, reprimanded the lawyer and instructed the jury to ignore the question as irrelevant.

But at the end of the trial, jurors awarded $12 million to the plaintiff. Mr. Vinson says that in post-trial interviews, every juror admitted to having considered the stricken statement. "It sure as hell was (relevant) to the jurors," he says.

Jury manipulation isn't usually so overt, say attorneys, and disciplinary actions by the bar are extremely rare. However, lawyers often use subtle—and perfectly legal—tricks to present taboo subjects to jurors.

For example, prosecutors delight in getting a criminal defendant on the witness stand, because it gives them a chance to parade his criminal record before jurors. Such volatile evidence is permitted in this situation because it goes to the issue of the witness' credibility. Judges caution jurors to weigh the record only in determining whether to believe the defendant, not to gauge the probability that he's committed yet another crime.

Many researchers call that a fiction. "It's laughable, because juries don't disregard it," says Michael Saks, a law professor at the University of Iowa. "They do the rational thing instead of the just thing."

The American Bar Foundation experiment is one of the latest in a growing body of research by social scientists suggesting the limits of judicial admonishments. In the experiment, 536 subjects were shown a videotape of closing arguments in a mock trial of police officers accused of improperly searching the house of a suspected criminal, the fictional Mr. Duncan. About a third of the viewers were told the search turned up incriminating evidence, which the judge instructed them to ignore since it wasn't relevant to determining the reasonableness of the police conduct.

But researchers found that, far from disregarding the results of the search, jurors tended to use them to make sense of preceding events, a phenomenon psychologists call "hindsight bias." When evidence of criminality was found, for example, jurors remembered evidence that supported the officers' story. They even remembered the policemen to be experienced—a fact not mentioned in the trial. Such findings could be particularly bad news for doctors facing malpractice suits or companies defending against product-liability claims, since jurors are often told to disregard the injury and focus on what the defendants should have known beforehand.

Other research includes a landmark 1973 study at the University of Washington that found that inadmissible evidence has its greatest effect on jurors when the rest of the evidence is inconclusive, and a later experiment showing that jurors are affected by pretrial publicity even when they swear in jury selection that they aren't.

Pretrial publicity

Students of the courtroom disagree over whether jurors can successfully weed out pretrial publicity from their deliberations. Most judges tend to play down the effects of publicity, and successful appeals based on prejudicial articles are rare. "Most people care a lot more about sitcoms they watch than news they might hear about," says William Schwarzer, a federal judge in San Francisco. He adds that jurors are generally good about listening to instructions from the bench.

But John Carroll, an associate professor of behavioral and policy sciences at Massachusetts Institute of Technology, says preliminary results of a study he's working on indicate that not only are jurors significantly influenced by pretrial publicity, but a judge's instructions may actually exacerbate the effects. "By telling people to disregard this, the judge is drawing attention to it," he says.

This points up a dilemma that often faces attorneys when the opposing counsel brings out prejudicial evidence—for example, mentioning that a plaintiff in a rape case has a history of wrongfully accusing men. In order to lay the groundwork for an appeal, the plaintiff's attorney must register an objection. But by making a big deal about it, the attorney might stamp the incident indelibly in the minds of jurors. "It's almost a no-win situation," says Saul Kassin, an associate professor of psychology at Williams College.

One judge claims he's solved the problem. James L. McCrystal, a common-pleas judge from Erie County, Ohio, has for years been videotaping witness testimony before showing it to jurors. That way, he says, he can edit out anything untoward before it is used in deliberations. Otherwise, he says, "it's like spitting in milk—(afterward) you can't separate it out."

Source: The Wall Street Journal, January 25, 1988.

fession that women are more lenient (thus more pro-defense) than men, most studies find them to be more conviction-prone than men. The record is mixed, however, and several studies show no relationship between gender and verdicts. Ford states that "the data do suggest that there may be interaction between crime type, gender and willingness to convict. There also may be interaction between race, gender and verdict."[8]

There seems to be some tendency for younger jurors to be more lenient than older ones, but this, too, is mediated by other factors, specifically crime type and gender. As for race, almost all studies that exist focus on the race of the defendant and the victim; few focus on the influence of the juror's race, but there is one study that found black females more likely to convict than black males or whites of either sex.[9]

Studies on the effects of socioeconomic factors and educational levels of jurors are also ambiguous in results, with case type and gender complicating the results. Ford concludes that "the influence of social and demographic factors on juror behavior is unclear."[10]

As has already been made clear, personality factors and attitudes have always been important to the experienced trial attorney in jury selection. Much of the work in this area has established links between political conservatism and authoritarian personalities on the one hand and willingness to convict on the other. This is particularly relevant in death-penalty cases, where the Supreme Court still upholds the practice of excluding persons opposed to capital punishment from juries. Ford cites studies that indicate that not only are death-qualified jurors more likely to be advocates of the Crime Control Model than excluded jurors but that they are likely to rate the prosecutor and state witnesses highly and to use a lower threshold of reasonable doubt necessary for a conviction.

As for the trait of empathy, it has been found to yield mixed results since it can be extended to victims as well as to defendants and is thus seemingly conditioned by factors of case type and gender. Confirmed, for example, is the lawyers' experience that female jurors identify with rape victims and express greater certainty of defendants' guilt.[11]

Effects of Trial Processes and Participants

Ford's survey of the effects of processes and participants lends support to the judgments of experienced attorneys on some key points. For example, stories have greater impact on juries than dry recitations of facts or logic. Visual media, especially videotapes, increase realism for jurors.

Ford finds that defendant characteristics and appearance are important. Attractiveness generally works in favor of defendants, but female defendants may suffer if their good looks were used to facilitate the crime. Data on the effect of social attractiveness are mixed, though some studies indicate that a higher socioeconomic status of the defendant is associated with leniency. (Of course, our experience is that defendants placed higher on the socioeconomic scale are more likely to retain attorneys and thus obtain a better quality of defense.) Defendant race appears to be an important factor. Minorities appear to be treated more harshly than whites. Jurors, both black and white, are more likely to penalize other-race than same-race defendants, especially if the victim is of the same race as jurors. Jurors penalize interracial crimes more heavily than crimes in which victim and defendant are of the same race. Studies regarding the impact on the juror of the personal characteristics of witnesses, judges, and attorneys produce varied and inconclusive results.

Pretrial publicity, even general crime news not related to the specific case pending seems to enhance already established juror biases. Rape and capital cases are especially sensitive to such influence, and extra lawyerly care during voir dire in these cases seems well placed.

Effects of Jury Group Dynamics

Studies of *jury group dynamics* and decision making are terribly difficult to do since we are forbidden from studying the behavior of real juries deliberating real cases. We are forced to rely on mock trials, using students or volunteers, not real jurors. So conclusions often have to be taken with the proverbial grain of salt.

What is indicated is that small (less than twelve-member) juries behave somewhat differently from large juries, and it has largely to do with the balance of minority versus majority views and the degree to which jurors are persuaded to change their verdicts. Neither prosecution nor defense necessarily gains from smaller as opposed to larger juries, but majorities for acquittal seem to win converts more easily than majorities for conviction.

Females and lower-status persons are less likely to debate or to be selected as foremen, but they are not necessarily likely to have less influence on the outcome of the debate. Style of deliberation varies. Some deliberations are verdict-driven; an early ballot is taken and active consideration of the evidence is limited. Other deliberations are evidence-driven; balloting is delayed until discussion has taken place and the evidence fully analyzed. Group deliberations were also found to mute juror biases and to moderate jurors' use of inadmissible or irrelevant evidence. None of this was found to favor state over defense or vice versa.

Conclusions

After her review of the studies, Ford states that "Clear positive finds were few and often attenuated by juror or case characteristics. . . . Interestingly," she continues, "despite all the potential influences discussed, one gains the sense that juries rely primarily upon legal evidence.... It is likely that extralegal factors intrude most prominently in truly close cases."

She adds: "[W]hile close cases may occur only infrequently, we nonetheless should consider measures to reduce the effects of extralegal factors."[12] Ford proposes two measures: more careful scrutiny of those exposed to pretrial publicity and a reexamination of the practice of barring anti-death-penalty jurors from capital-case juries.

It is interesting to note the degree of support given the jury system by social science findings. As has already been pointed out, much of what has been reported here has long been known on an experiential basis by members of the legal profession, and few if any surprises emerge from Ford's review. If anything, it is refreshing to discover that jurors and juries may not be as manipulable as some more cynical types would have them. We are cheered to find that Ford comments that "scientific jury selection procedures (jurimetrics), heralded by some,... appear highly questionable."[13]

APPEALS

Appeals Initiated by the Defense

The vast majority of criminal appeals are initiated by the defendant, unhappy with the results of the case and hoping that some superior court will make a more suitable decision. All fifty states provide some form of *appeal* or review of criminal convictions, even though some of them do not refer to the process as appeal, instead calling the vehicle for a review a *writ of error*. Federal case law seems to hold that there is no absolute constitutional right to an appeal. *McKane v. Durston* is a late-nineteenth-century case in which the Supreme Court of the United States said that the states were not required to provide a right to appellate review or even appellate courts![14] A lot of time has passed since that case was decided, and one could probably predict that if the question were to be readdressed today, the court would, in view of the widespread availability of criminal review, find the availability of some form of appellate review to be part and parcel of due process.

Cost-Free Appeals for Indigents

The due process clause of the Fifth Amendment does not directly address the availability of appeal for one who cannot afford a lawyer and court costs. Yet the quality of appeal available to a person cannot be predicated on the amount of money he or she has. That is no less true of the appellate process than of the trial process. Here, too, an indigent defendant can often end up with a better appeal than a person of modest but not indigent means.

The Supreme Court spoke to the issue of free counsel on appeal for indigents in *Douglas v. California* when Justice Douglas delivered the majority opinion, stating: "Here the issue is whether or not an indigent shall be denied the assistance of counsel on appeal. The evil is the same, discrimination against the indigent. For there can be no equal justice where the kind of an appeal a man enjoys depends on the amount of money he has."[15]

The Supreme Court in *United States v. MacCollom* made reference to *Douglas v. California,* supra, and made the issue of free appeals for indigents somewhat more clear:

> In *Douglas v. California,* supra, the Court held that the State must provide counsel for an indigent on his first appeal as of right. But in *Ross v. Moffitt* ... we declined to extend that holding to a discretionary second appeal from an intermediate appellate court to the Supreme Court of North Carolina. We think the distinction between these two holdings of the Court is of considerable assistance in resolving respondent's equal protection claim.[16]

The Court went on to say that if the respondent had taken his direct appeal soon after his trial he would have been entitled to free assistance. But because of his tardiness, MacCollom lost the right to his first appeal by several years, and the Court considered his late request discretionary and not deserving of free assistance.

Bail Pending Appeal

In both the state and federal systems, bail pending the disposition of appeal is at least possible. The issue gives rise to debate, and the opponents of allowing a convicted person access to bail cite several logical objections. A convicted defendant is far more apt to flee than one who still works under the "presumption of innocence." Another objection is that such appeals are often resorted to as a means of delaying proceedings, while the defendant can remain at liberty on bail to commit more crimes, even crimes resorted to as a means to raise money to pay the appellate lawyer. A third objection is that many appeals are totally without merit and release pending such an appeal merely puts off the process so long that the system is made less effective, especially from a standpoint of deterrence.

Section 3148 of the Federal Bail Reform Act specifically addresses the issue of bail after conviction in a federal court. The section provides that such release be available under the same rules and guidelines as ordinary pretrial release as provided in Section 3146, unless the court finds that other factors are present. The rule instructs the court to proceed under the aforementioned release criteria unless "the court or Judge has reason to believe that no one or more conditions of release will reasonably assure that the person will not flee or pose a danger to any other person or to the community. If such a risk of flight or danger is believed to exist, or if it appears that an appeal is frivolous or taken for delay, the person may be ordered detained."[17]

Appeals Initiated by the Prosecution

This entire area of consideration is fraught with problems that basically stem from the constitutional prohibition against double jeopardy. Most states avoid the problems of double jeopardy by allowing the prosecutor to appeal only pretrial or postconviction rulings. Appeals by the prosecution are most often directed at pretrial matters—such as the court's granting of a defense motion to dismiss for lack of speedy trial, technical dismissals involving indictment or information, and pleadings on the basic constitutionality of a criminal law. Such matters as the court's grant of a pretrial motion to suppress an item of evidence frequently give rise to interlocutory appeals. Only a few states will allow an appeal from rulings at trial if the prosecution brings the appeal. Recall that once an acquittal is recorded, it cannot be overturned.

Many prosecutors believe that trial judges should make decisions in close or unclear matters in favor of the prosecution and not in favor of the accused since the accused can appeal and the prosecution cannot. Defense lawyers reply to this assertion by noting that the defendant should not be required to bear the cost and annoyance of an appeal just to give an appellate court the opportunity to make a decision that the trial judge should have made in the first place.

Issues Not Raised in Time

As a general rule, appellate courts will not consider issues that were not raised at time of trial. The reason for this rule is rather simple: It keeps the defense from purposely ignoring a point that the court could address at trial with the intent to let the issue remain hidden unless the trial is won by the prosecution, whereupon it becomes a basis for appeal. This rule keeps the defense more honest and imposes some degree of finality at the trial level.

It is obvious that the defense at trial must be both well educated in the law and very alert if important points for appeal are to be preserved. If no objection by the defense and subsequent overruling of that objection appear upon the record, the point will not be addressed by the appellate court. The rule seems harsh but the system would be even more unwieldy and potentially unfair to the government without it.

As with most rules, this one has its exception. Appellate courts will occasionally afford an appeal based on a matter not objected to at the trial level and therefore not articulated in the record of trial. Normally this sort of appeal claims to raise matters that are *plain error,* affecting substantial rights of the defendant. No really satisfactory definition of what is or is not "plain error" is available, and the courts are not too convincing in their explanations, much less their ability to recognize plain error in any sort of a consistent manner.

One other basis for appeal on an issue not brought up at trial is the claim that the defense attorney was incompetent. This is often a "last-resort" issue in capital cases where execution is imminent.

SUMMARY AND CONCLUSION

This chapter has dealt with the way in which a criminal trial is conducted, with an examination of the roles of the major participants and of the specific steps involved. The expectations of the prosecutor, defense counsel, defendant, witnesses, jury, and judge have been described, and some attention has been given to the practical realities of the situation each participant encounters. We have provided observations about the likely attitudes and reactions of jurors to certain developments, observations based on considerable trial experience.

The basic steps of the trial process have been analyzed. Readers should remember that some steps are essential. These are pretrial jury instructions, opening statements by attorneys, the case in chief offered by the prosecution, closing arguments, instructions to the jury, jury deliberations, and a verdict. Other steps are optional, depending on the strategies of the attorneys and the requirements of the situation. These optional phases of trial are the motions for a directed verdict of acquittal, the presentation of a case for the defense, and the presentation of a rebuttal case by the state.

It should be abundantly clear by now that the burden of proof rests on the doubt about an essential element of the state's case. On the other hand, jurors generally expect some attempt by the defense to counter evidence presented by the prosecution, which tends to create some burden for the defense, whether one legally belongs there or not.

The appellate process has also been discussed in this chapter—including the defendant's rights to appeal at no cost and to bail during appeal. But whether a notice of appeal is filed or not, with the verdict entered into the record, the trial court is ready to order the release of the defendant who is acquitted or to begin the process of sentencing the defendant who is convicted. The next chapter examines this aspect of the court's work.

QUESTIONS FOR DISCUSSION

1. If you were defense counsel under what circumstances might you advise your client to waive the Fifth Amendment protection and take the stand? Under what circumstances would you advise strongly against it?
2. Why would a defense attorney delay an opening statement to the jury until after the state's case has been presented? Would requiring the defense to present the statement at the opening of trial inhibit the defendant's rights under the Due Process Model and promote the Crime Control Model? Why or why not?
3. Given the jury selection process used in your community, do you think juries are competent to decide the issues presented in criminal trials? Why or why not?
4. Do you think jurors should be allowed to take notes during trials? Explain your answer.
5. Do you think jurors should be given written copies of jury instructions? Explain your answer. If your answers to the previous question and to this one are not either both affirmative or both negative, how can you reconcile the difference?

NOTES

1. See "ABA Standards Related to the Prosecution Function," Part I, Section I.I, as reprinted in *Comparative Analysis of Standards and Goals of the National Advisory Commission on Criminal Justice Standards and Goals with Standards for Criminal Justice of the American Bar Association,* Washington, D.C., 1974, p. 274.
2. Ibid., Part I, Section I.I, p. 316.
3. Ibid., Part III, Section 3.7, p. 328.
4. Ibid., Part IV, Section 7.7, p. 338.
5. *Griffin v. California,* 380 U.S. 609, 85 S. Ct. 229, 4 L. Ed. 2d 06 (1965).
6. Hazel Kerper and Jerold H. Israel, *Introduction to the Criminal Justice System,* 2d ed., West, St. Paul, Minn., 1979, pp. 332–333.
7. Marilyn Chandler Ford, "The Role of Extralegal Factors in Jury Verdicts," *The Justice System Journal,* vol. 11, no. 1, 1986, pp. 16–39.
8. Ibid., p. 18.
9. Carol J. Mills and Wayne E. Bohannon, "Juror Characteristics: To What Extent Are They Related to Jury Verdicts?" *Judicature,* vol. 64, no. 1, pp. 22–31.
10. Ford, p. 19.

11. Sheila R. Deitz et al., "Measurement of Empathy toward Victims and Rapists," *Journal of Personality and Social Psychology,* vol. 43, 1982,
12. Ford, p. 30.
13. Ibid., p. 32.
14. *McKane v. Durston,* 153 U.S. 684, 14 S. Ct. 913, 38 L. Ed. 864 (1894).
15. *Douglas v. California,* 372 U.S. 353, 365, 9 L. Ed. 2d 811, 83 S. Ct. 814 (1963).
16. *United States v. MacCollom,* 426 U.S. 317, 48 L. Ed. 2d 666, 96 S. Ct. 2086 (1976).
17. Public Law 89-465, 89th Congress 5.1357, 80 Stat. 214.

CHAPTER 13

SENTENCING

After reading this chapter, students should be able to define and explain the importance of each of the following terms or phrases:

restitution
reintegration
fines
probation
shock probation
conditions on probation
incarceration
mandatory minimum terms
determinate sentencing

indeterminate sentencing
sentencing disparities
presentence investigation
suspended sentence
concurrent sentences
consecutive sentences
aggravating circumstances
mitigating circumstances
victim impact statement

From the viewpoint of the defendant, no decision made by officials of the criminal justice system is more important than that made by the judge (or, in a few states, the jury) at sentencing. So too from the perspective of the lawmakers, provisions regarding what penalties ought to be imposed on convicted criminals are of paramount importance since the penalties embody the very purpose of the criminal code.

Despite (or perhaps because of) the crucial nature of sentencing, there is no step in the criminal justice process over which there is less agreement and in the practice of which there appears to be less consistency. Many observers speak or write of the "anarchy" of sentencing.

We shall survey some of the goals of sentencing here, then describe the laws under which, and the process by which, convicted persons are sentenced. Finally we shall examine the controversy over disparities in sentencing.

THE GOALS OF SENTENCING

Traditional Goals

In Chapter 1 we discussed the various notions about and approaches to justice, particularly to criminal justice. Under the heading of the substantive aspect of criminal justice, we gave considerable attention to the various, and sometimes conflicting, goals or purposes of penal sanctions: retribution, deterrence—both specific and general—incapacitation, and rehabilitation. Recall that the goal of retribution is that of imposing a form of punishment on the offender as a means of demonstrating the community's strong disapproval of his or her act. Deterrence, you will remember, is the goal of convincing the offender (specific deterrence) or other potential lawbreakers (general deterrence) of the folly of committing further crimes. Incapacitation is simply the goal of isolating the offender from those who can be victimized or otherwise rendering the offender incapable of committing further crimes. Finally, rehabilitation, you recall, is the goal of "curing" the offender of the illness or correcting the social maladjustment that is assumed to have caused or contributed significantly to the commission of criminal acts.

Emerging Goals

In addition to the traditional goals just reviewed, two other identifiable goals have emerged in the sentencing of some selected offenders.

Restitution In the past few years, restitution has arisen—or, perhaps more accurately, been resurrected—as a goal of a system of justice. *Restitution* is based on the desire to do something for the victim while, at the same time, attempting to show the offender that he or she has some direct responsibility for the harm done. Thus, under restitution, stolen property is to be returned or replaced, damaged property repaired or replaced, and possibly even medical bills paid directly by offenders. This approach is generally limited to small property offenses by younger offenders, but recently restitution has been a part of sentences handed down in some large-scale embezzlements and frauds. But restitution implies that the offender has the ability to pay or to earn the sums necessary, and most convicted offenders will probably remain unqualified for this approach.

Reintegration Depending upon how one defines rehabilitation, reintegration of offenders into productive roles in the community may be a distinct goal of a system of justice. Certainly there has been a trend toward the view that rehabilitation cannot be accomplished within an artificial or confining environment. But while rehabilitation as a goal focuses upon the mental health or attitudes of the individual offender, *reintegration* is concerned with the offender's interactions with others. Officials are concerned with the offender's ability to hold down a job, perform well in school, keep a family together, or otherwise demonstrate an ability to function productively in society. The shift in emphasis from treatment of the offender's own condition to his or her actual performance is reflected in the shift of the role of probation officers and other corrections personnel from acting as "therapists" to acting as "community resource managers." In this role, officials refer their clients to employers, school officials, welfare departments, and other agencies—both public and private—that can offer the specialized treatment or services the particular offender seems to require.

This review of the goals of sentencing is important for two reasons. The legislators who enact penal codes obviously have some goals in mind and try to convey to the public, to the offenders, to criminal justice officials, and especially to the judges what these goals are and how they should be ranked in order of importance. Secondly, the judges also obviously have their own ideas about the goals and use their sentencing authority to try to realize those ideas. The more leeway or ambiguity that exists in the code, the more the sentencing process is based on the diverse goals of individual judges. The more precise or restrictive the code, the less opportunity there is for judges to impose their own notions through their sentences.

PENAL CODES: TYPES OF PENALTIES

This brings us to a consideration of penal codes and the extent to which they variously limit or permit discretionary sentencing in the courtrooms of the land. The penal codes of the states and the federal government address two specific questions. What type of penalty should be imposed? How severe should that penalty be? Types of penalties possible include fines, probation, terms in local jails, incarceration in prisons or other secure institutions, and, of course, death.

Fines

The right of the state to impose *fines* on those convicted of offenses goes back to antiquity. Recall the discussion of bots in Saxon England, especially the fact that they were imposed for even the most serious of violent crimes and were tied to the extent of injury done the victim. In current practice, fines are used primarily in cases of minor offenses, even noncriminal infractions and ordinance violations. The codes of virtually every state provide, however, for fines in all but the highest categories of felony crimes, those of capital or life felonies. Fines are generally authorized for use as supplements to substitutions for jail or prison terms.

The codes contain upper, but not lower, limits on what fines can be imposed for specific offenses or for category of offense. One state, for example, provides that fines for designated crimes should not exceed $15,000 for life felonies, $10,000 for felonies of the first and second degrees, $5,000 for felonies of the third degree, $1,000 for misdemeanors of the first degree, and $500 for second-degree misdemeanors, the lowest classification of crimes in the state penal code. The statute also makes clear that these fines may be imposed in addition to or in lieu of any term of incarceration.[1]

It was once a common practice to sentence a person guilty of a minor offense to "thirty days or thirty dollars," in other words, to pay a fine or be jailed for refusal or inability to pay. Some years ago, however, the U.S. Supreme Court ruled that sentencing those who could not afford to pay fines to jail terms was a violation of the equal protection of the laws doctrine found in the Fourteenth Amendment of the Constitution.[2] Since this decision, states have had to rely on other means of collecting fines. Some have even set up installment plans for those found indigent.

Probation

Probation is a status the judge may impose upon those found guilty, but it is not one the defendant need accept. Probation is an alternative to incarceration in a jail or other institution, and the individual may prefer to serve time rather than accept or be bound by the conditions that the court may attach to the probation. Far more often, however, those convicted of crimes would rather be at large and take their chances of being caught in some violation of the conditions of probation. Newman has observed that "probation is seen as a lenient sentence," but points out that "it *is* a sentence and not simply a dismissal of the case."[3]

The sentencing judge usually has the choice of either suspending a jail or prison sentence and substituting the probationary sentence or of sentencing the individual directly to a term of probation. The judge also enjoys considerable latitude in setting forth the period of time to be served on probation. The period of probation may even be longer than the jail or prison term that would otherwise have been appropriate. The judge also sets the *conditions of probation* under which the offender must live. The judge may even begin the probation with a condition that requires the offender to serve a period of time in jail. This approach is sometimes called *shock probation*, since the idea is to shock the offender into good behavior by providing a taste of what it's like to have a cell door slam shut behind him.

There are, to be sure, conditions that go beyond the bounds of reason and the law. Kerper and Kerper have noted a decision made some years ago by a California appellate court in a case involving a female convicted of robbery who was ordered as a condition of probation not to become pregnant until she was married. After she violated this condition, she was sent to prison. But the revocation of probation was overturned by the appellate court, which then prohibited trial court judges from imposing conditions for probation that have no relationship to the offender's original crime, that relate to conduct that is not in itself criminal, or that forbid conduct not reasonably related to future criminal conduct by the offender.[4] David Jones has summarized the state of the law as follows: "Conditions of probation may not be enforced if they are unreasonable such as if they violate the offender's freedom of speech, endanger the offender's welfare, or enjoin the offender from engaging in an innocuous activity."[5]

On the other hand, probationers may lose a good deal of the privacy and protection enjoyed by other citizens. Probation officers and police may be permitted to search a probationer's person and property without a warrant in most states, and the waiver of Fourth Amendment protections against a warrantless search may be used as a condition of probation. In general, therefore, a probationer is no longer covered by the requirements inherent in the notion of due process, but is instead subject to a degree of supervision and action more in keeping with crime control values.

Kerper and Kerper have recorded some cases in which rather unusual conditions were imposed under probation and later upheld on appeal. Among these were requiring a rapist to undergo a vasectomy, forbidding a bookie to have a telephone in his home or under his control, and forbidding a person convicted for offenses arising out of an antiwar demonstration from participating in future demonstrations.[6]

Probation may be offered to any criminal defendant. David Jones points out that technically probation consists of either suspension of sentence or suspension of administration of sentence.[7] In any case, probationary status is not a right but a privilege, and the judge may revoke it and resentence the offender to jail or prison or order that the original prison sentence be carried out. In such a situation, the probationer receives a hearing on allegations brought by his or her probation officer. The revocation hearing is held before the court that retained jurisdiction over the probationer. We will cover the revocation hearing in the section on sentencing procedures.

Incarceration

Of the three basic options open to the judge—fine, probation, and incarceration—the latter raises the most difficult issues and questions. Whether a judge chooses this option depends upon many factors, including the following:

1. The provisions of state law regarding:
   a. The freedom granted the judge to decide whether to incarcerate or not
   b. The freedom granted the judge to set the term of incarceration
   c. The authority given the parole board to release offenders prior to completion of their sentence
2. The attitudes of the judge regarding:
   a. The goal or goals to strive for—retribution, incapacitation, deterrence, or rehabilitation
   b. The extent to which justice requires uniformity or individualization of sentence
   c. The character of the offender in terms of attitude and behavior, previous record, and the danger the offender's release would pose to the community
   d. The political, legal, and social culture prevailing in the community
   e. The relationship of the judge with other members of the courtroom work group and their recommendations
   f. The traditional means by which cases or defendants of this type have been dealt with in the past

To be sure, few if any judges analyze each case in terms of all the items just mentioned, but these items all play some role in determining the pattern of a judge's choices. Studies of judicial behavior in sentencing generally indicate that, beyond what the law requires or permits, the two most relied-upon factors are the seriousness of the immediate crime and the past record of the person to be sentenced.

Code provisions differ vastly from jurisdiction to jurisdiction. An increasing number of states have adopted laws carrying *mandatory minimum terms* in jail or prison for certain types of offenses, for the use of a firearm or other "deadly weapon" in the commission of a felony, and for inflicting certain injuries on victims in the commission of crimes. In these situations, the judge has no choice but to sentence the offender to at least the stated minimum. Whether the offender will actually serve all of that term depends on whether the law requires a minimum term of service of sentence or only a minimum sentence. In the latter case, a parole authority may release the offender before the term of service is completed.

Apart from mandatory minimum terms, penal codes permit judges freedom to choose between incarceration and other means of punishment. But the codes differ considerably on the matter of lengths of prison terms once incarceration is chosen. Code differences show up in two areas: the degree of freedom provided the judge in setting the minimum and/or maximum periods of sentence and the degree of authority given corrections and/or parole officials to set the actual term of service or to release inmates before they finish service of sentence.

PENAL CODES: DETERMINATE VERSUS INDETERMINATE SENTENCING

In a very general sense, state penal codes can be placed along a spectrum representing the extent to which prison terms are fixed on the one hand and subject to being shortened by prison and parole authorities on the other. On one end of this spectrum is the *determinate,* or fixed, *sentence* of a given period of months or years. A determinate sentence is pronounced by the judge and must be served to the exact day of completion. This is also called *flat-time sentencing.* At the other end of the spectrum is the *indeterminate sentence* under which the judge sets no term. The parole authority may release the offender at any time up to the completion of the legal maximum for the particular crime committed.

All existing schemes lie between the extremes of determinate and indeterminate sentencing. Most states permit the judge to set both a maximum and a minimum sentence, with the parole authority permitted to grant parole only within the specified range. Some states require that the minimum sentence be a certain percentage (say, 30 percent) of the maximum, and provide therefore that the minimum be set by whatever maximum the judge pronounces. Figure 13.1 illustrates the range of possibilities we are discussing.

Of course, there are other factors that further complicate this picture. There is the matter of "good time," or reduction of service of sentence for good behavior. In some states inmates automatically earn a set amount of good time (say, one day per week), which is deducted from the sentence unless the inmate is subject to disciplinary action for specific acts of violations of prison rules. In other states good time must be earned, and the extent to which an inmate's sentence may be shortened depends on the policies and practices of the particular prison. From an inmate's standpoint, the definiteness of the sentence depends heavily upon this factor—in other words, can he or she count on a specified reduction of sentence or is release subject to the will of prison administrators?

Then there is the difference between states that provide parole for inmates released before completion of sentence and states that permit early release with no parole. In effect, the latter constitutes early termination

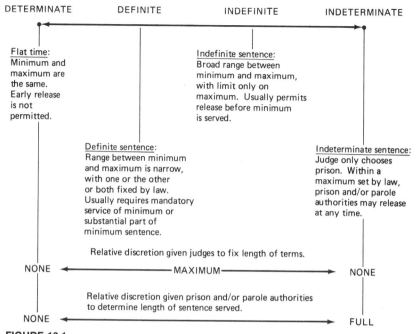

DETERMINATE   DEFINITE   INDEFINITE   INDETERMINATE

Flat time:
Minimum and
maximum are
the same.
Early release
is not
permitted.

Indefinite sentence:
Broad range between
minimum and maximum,
with limit only on
maximum. Usually permits
release before minimum
is served.

Definite sentence:
Range between minimum
and maximum is narrow,
with one or the other
or both fixed by law.
Usually requires mandatory
service of minimum or
substantial part of
minimum sentence.

Indeterminate sentence:
Judge only chooses
prison. Within a
maximum set by law,
prison and/or parole
authorities may release
at any time.

Relative discretion given judges to fix length of terms.

NONE ◄——————— MAXIMUM ———————► NONE

Relative discretion given prison and/or parole authorities
to determine length of sentence served.

NONE ◄—————————————————————————► FULL

FIGURE 13.1
Range of Sentencing Codes

of sentence, and neither parole board nor parole supervisors exist. Maine now uses this approach. It is not to be confused with flat time, however, in which there is no early release.

In the current debates over determinate versus indeterminate sentencing and legislative considerations of proposals to reduce a judge's discretion to fix sentence, it must be remembered that "good-time" provisions and the authority of parole boards are crucial factors. There cannot be any real reduction of *sentencing disparities*—irrational and unjustifiable differences between sentences from offender to offender—unless all factors are taken into account. Discretion is like a balloon, some have pointed out, and squeezing it at one point—say, at judicial sentencing—will cause it to bulge elsewhere—say, in release decisions. That is why some states, as part of sentencing reform laws, have restricted the authority of parole boards or eliminated such boards entirely. We shall discuss this topic in Chapter 15.

THE PROCESS OF SENTENCING

The process that results in pronouncement of sentence on a person adjudged guilty of a crime may actually begin as soon as formal charges are filed with the trial court and may continue, at least technically, through the service of the terms of a sentence. But it is more frequently treated as a process that begins with a presentence investigation, usually performed by a probation officer, and ends when the trial judge relinquishes jurisdiction over the offender. In the case of probationary sentence, that relinquishment does not occur until the terms of the probation have been met, or until probation has been revoked and the offender sentenced (more accurately, resentenced) to a jail or prison term. Even in cases of incarceration, judges can—and often do—retain jurisdiction over offenders so that they may prevent his or her parole or otherwise alter the length of sentence. In short, sentencing is not a one-shot affair.

Presentence Investigations

In most jurisdictions the judges are able (in some they are required) to order the preparation of *presentence investigation (PSI)* reports. These reports vary considerably from place to place—or even from preparer to preparer in one place—but they represent an attempt to find out as much as is necessary or possible about the offenders. Typically these reports deal with such matters as prior criminal records; family histories; and educational, employment, and military experience. Data are obtained from public records, but also, where feasible, from interviews with people who know the subject. Neighbors, friends, teachers, and employers may be contacted.

Presentence investigations may also contain assessments of the attitudes and potential for rehabilitation of their subjects. All this information is supposed to assist trial judges in their efforts to individualize justice and pronounce the appropriate sentence for the person in question. If judges are to sentence wisely, PSI reports must be thorough and insightful. In fact, some reports are woefully inadequate in either or both regards.

How much insight the preparers can be expected to have into the psyche of each and every offender on whom they write a report is open to real question. The PSI preparers are generally probation officers, who are, for the most part, terribly overworked and grossly underpaid. As dedicated as they might be (and many of them are amazingly dedicated), probation officers are usually swamped with cases on which to perform PSIs, and most also carry a case load of probationers to be supervised and assisted. In fairness, it must be said that despite all these limitations some excellent PSIs are conducted and reports written.

Judges vary, too, in the degree to which they pay serious attention to the information contained in the PSI reports. Many judges find the reports extremely helpful. Some, in fact, lean on them too heavily, and routinely sentence in accordance with the recommendations contained in the reports; hence in many cases the probation officer is really the person determining the sentence. Some judges, on the other hand, pay little or no attention to PSI reports, relying instead on the suggestions of attorneys or on their own ability to judge human nature and character by observing a defendant's behavior in the courtroom. Of course, there are some judges who base sentence almost solely on the seriousness of the crime and the prior criminal record, if any, of the offender, and who consider that they have little need for the additional sociological, psychological, and perhaps "irrelevant" information of the report. But most of the judges with whom the authors have spoken claim to put great stock in PSIs and assert that they carefully study them before imposing sentences.

One final note regarding PSIs: States vary in the extent to which they make the contents of the reports available to defendants or even to the public. Kerper and Israel have noted that California, among others, makes the reports public record, while some states disclose the entire contents to defendants and defense attorneys only. Still other states withhold portions of the reports that deal with sentence recommendations or portions that could jeopardize the rehabilitation of the offender or that could result in danger to the offender or other persons. Kerper and Israel note that most states leave the matter of disclosure to the courts, but that full disclosure is required in cases where the sentence is death.[8]

Sentence Hearings

Defendants are given the right to make a statement—the *right of allocution*—before sentence is pronounced, and the defense attorney is permitted to address the court. Most courts permit the prosecutor to offer comments or recommendations. Many states are using more substantial hearings, however, some going so far as to entertain briefs and affidavits from opposing sides as to the veracity of information contained in the PSIs. Proposals have been made by some, including the American Bar Association, that such hearings include examination and cross-examination of witnesses in proceedings much like those of the adversarial preliminary hearing.

Thirty-seven states have enacted capital punishment statutes for specific types of murder—for example, murder for hire, kidnapping resulting in death, murder during the commission of a felony, and murder of a law enforcement officer. These statutes, passed in the wake of *Furman v. Georgia,* all require either the judge or the jury to examine specific guidelines to assist in weighing aggravating or mitigating circumstances of the crime. Rulings since *Furman* have established that the capital prisoner is to be afforded every possible legal right, such as the right to have *all* mitigating circumstances to the crime considered at the time of sentencing.

With the formalities out of the way, the trial judge pronounces sentence. The judge may make some remarks for the record as to how he or she feels about the defendant, the crime, and the evidence; then the defendant and the defense attorney stand before the bench while sentence is pronounced.

If the sentence is to probation, the judge will state the conditions of that probation and its length for the record. If the sentence is to the local jail or other facility, the judge will specify the length of sentence. If the sentence is to imprisonment in a state institution, the judge will stipulate the term—or the minimum or maximum term or whatever reference to length the law of the state permits or requires.

In most states, the judge may pronounce sentence, then announce that it is *suspended,* that is, put on hold. The offender is then either put into a probationary status (with or without formal adjudication of guilt) or released outright, with the understanding that violation of any stated conditions or the commission of any further crimes will result in the reimposition of the sentence just suspended. In some places, the judge may suspend sentence without pronouncing any particular terms, thus allowing the court, in the case of later revocation, the leeway to pronounce a sentence stiffer than the one originally imposed. Since conditions can be—and generally are—placed on those who receive a suspended sentence, many states now refer to this as a "conditional discharge" rather than a "suspended sentence."

There is one other variable that must be mentioned. Where defendants have been convicted of multiple crimes, the judge may choose between having the sentences run concurrently or having them served consecutively. Thus an offender who is sentenced to three to five years for burglary and one to three for larceny, with the sentences to be served *concurrently,* will in effect serve the stiffest of the two sentences: three to five years. The same offender sentenced to *consecutive terms* will have to serve a minimum of four years (one year plus three) and could serve a maximum of eight years (three years plus five). Most states provide that the sentences will be concurrent unless the judge specifies they are to be consecutive. Many also provide that a sentence for a new crime be made concurrent with a sentence for a previous crime that remains to be finished, or even that sentences pronounced in different jurisdictions be served concurrently.

Imposing the Death Penalty

Sentencing convicted persons to death obviously involves unique and justifiably difficult steps in the process. In 1972 the U.S. Supreme Court established a virtual moratorium on the death penalty with its decision in the case of *Furman v. Georgia*.[9] In that case a deeply divided Court ruled that the death penalty had been imposed "so wantonly and freakishly" that it was cruel and unusual and therefore in violation of the Eighth Amendment.

Many states enacted new capital punishment statutes in the wake of the Court's ruling, and in 1976 a still-divided Supreme Court accepted those that had several built-in checks on unbridled discretion, but rejected those that attempted to avoid capriciousness by making the death penalty mandatory for certain classes of crimes.[10] Among the features that the Court accepted as essential to a constitutional process of sentencing a person to death were (1) the requirement that there be a separate sentencing hearing before the trial jury; (2) the requirement that the jury hear evidence concerning the presence of specific statutory *aggravating* and *mitigating circumstances*; (3) the requirement that the jury must find that at least one aggravating circumstance is proven beyond a reasonable doubt; (4) the requirement that there be automatic appeal and consideration of the penalty by the state's highest court; and (5) the requirement that this review result in rejection of death if the court finds it was imposed as a result of prejudice or if the death penalty is disproportionate in terms of penalties imposed in comparable cases.

States that have acceptable capital punishment statutes have what are known as *bifurcated* (two-part) *processes,* with the first part concerning the issue of whether the evidence proves the accused guilty of capital murder beyond a reasonable doubt and the second part concerning the issue of the death penalty itself. In the penalty phase, an adversarial hearing takes place before the jury in which statutory aggravating and mitigating circumstances concerning both the offender and the offense are considered. Evidence not admissible in trial, especially that involving the background and criminal record of the defendant, are now pertinent. The jury is required to reach a decision by majority vote. In Georgia and other states, this decision as to life or death is binding on the judge, whereas in Florida the decision is merely advisory, and the trial judge may reject a jury's recommendation for either life or death and impose the opposite. In the case of rejection of a recommendation for life, however, the judge bears an extraordinary burden to prove the existence of aggravating circumstances the jury apparently ignored or the nonexistence of mitigating circumstances the jury reported finding.

In 1987 the Supreme Court ruled that personal characteristics of the victims could not be used as part of the consideration of aggravating factors in death penalty cases.[11] The Court, by a vote of 5 to 4, struck down a Maryland law that permitted use of so-called *victim impact statements* during sentencing hearings. Justice Lewis Powell joined the more liberal, or the Due Process Model–oriented, justices and wrote the opinion for the Court. He stated that the process must focus on the "moral blame-worthiness" of the offender and that the age and character of victims and the feelings of family members about their loss is irrelevant to such a finding. Consideration of evidence on such matters may inflame a jury to decide in favor of death for the convicted killer, thus reintroducing prejudice and capriciousness into the process.

Still another major 1987 decision saw Powell join the more conservative, or Crime Control–oriented justices and, in an opinion that met with bitter dissent, refuse to reverse death sentences on the grounds that a large study demonstrated that, in Georgia at least, persons who kill whites are much more likely to be sentenced to death than persons who kill blacks.[12] Powell wrote that since discretion is exercised in death cases, disparities are going to result. But in order to overturn a particular death sentence on grounds of racial discrimination, Powell wrote, the defendant "must prove that the decision makers in *his* case acted with a discriminatory purpose." This decision provoked an especially bitter dissent from Justice Brennan and three colleagues, and excerpts from the opinions in this case are presented here to illustrate just how deep and intensely felt are the divisions between the justices on the matter of capital punishment, a division that obviously goes beyond due process versus crime control principles.

McCleskey v. Kemp

95 L. Ed. 2d 262 (1987)

FROM THE OPINION

By Justice Powell

This case presents the question whether a complex statistical study that indicates a risk that racial considerations enter into capital sentencing determinations proves that petitioner McCleskey's capital sentence is unconstitutional under the Eighth or 14th Amendment.

McCleskey, a black man, was convicted of two counts of armed robbery and one count of murder in the Superior Court of Fulton County, Ga., on Oct. 12, 1978. McCleskey's convictions arose out of the robbery of a furniture store and the killing of a white police officer during the course of the robbery.

The evidence at trial indicated that McCleskey and three accomplices planned and carried out the robbery. All four were armed. McCleskey entered the front of the store while the other three entered the rear. McCleskey secured the front of the store by rounding up the customers and forcing them to lie face down on the floor. The other three rounded up the employees in the rear and tied them up with tape. The manager was forced at gunpoint to turn over the store receipts, his watch, and $6.

During the course of the robbery, a police officer, answering a silent alarm, entered the store through the front door. As he was walking down the center aisle of the store, two shots were fired. Both struck the officer. One hit him in the face and killed him.

Several weeks later, McCleskey was arrested in connection with an unrelated offense. He confessed that he had participated in the furniture store robbery, but denied that he had shot the police officer. At trial, the state introduced evidence that at least one of the bullets that struck the officer was fired from a .38-caliber Rossi revolver. This description matched the description of the gun that McCleskey had carried during the robbery. The state also introduced the testimony of two witnesses who had heard McCleskey admit to the shooting.

Conviction and Sentence

The jury convicted McCleskey of murder. At the penalty hearing, the jury heard arguments as to the appropriate sentence....

The jury recommended that he be sentenced to death on the murder charge and to consecutive life sentences on the armed robbery charges. The court followed the jury's recommendation and sentenced McCleskey to death.

On appeal, the Supreme Court of Georgia affirmed the convictions and the sentences....This Court denied a petition for a writ of certiorari....The Superior Court of Fulton County denied McCleskey's extraordinary motion for a new trial. McCleskey then filed a petition for a writ of habeas corpus in the Superior Court of Butts County. After holding an evidentiary hearing, the Superior Court denied relief.... The Supreme Court of Georgia denied McCleskey's application for a certificate of probable cause to appeal the Superior Court's denial of his petition and this Court again denied certiorari....

McCleskey next filed a petition for a writ of habeas corpus in the Federal District Court of the Northern District of Georgia. His petition raised 18 claims, one of which was that the Georgia capital sentencing process is administered in a racially discriminatory manner in violation of the Eighth and 14th Amendments to the United States Constitution.

Statistical Survey

In support of his claim, McCleskey proffered a statistical study performed by Professors David C. Baldus, George Woodworth and Charles Pulanski, (the Baldus study) that purports to show a disparity in the imposition of the death sentence in Georgia based on the race of the murder victim and, to a lesser extent, the race of the defendant.

The Baldus study is actually two sophisticated statistical studies that examine over 2,000 murder cases that occurred in Georgia during the 1970's. The raw numbers collected by Professor Baldus indicate that defendants charged with killing white persons received the death penalty in 11 percent of the cases, but defendants charged with killing blacks received the death penalty in only 1 percent of the cases. The raw numbers also indicate a reverse racial disparity according to the race of the defendant: 4 percent of the black defendants received the death penalty, as opposed to 7 percent of the white defendants.

Baldus also divided the cases according to the combination of the race of the defendant and the race of the victim. He found that the death penalty was assessed in 22 percent of the cases involving black defendants and white victims; 8 percent of the cases involving white defendants and white victims; 1 percent of the cases involving black defendants and black victims; and 3 percent of the cases involving white defendants and black victims.

Similarly, Baldus found that prosecutors sought the death penalty in 70 percent of the cases involving black defendants and white victims; 32 percent of the cases involving white defendants and white victims; 15 percent of the cases involving black defendants and black victims; and 19 percent of the cases involving white defendants and black victims.

Baldus subjected his data to an extensive analysis, taking account of 230 variables that could have explained the disparities on nonracial grounds. One of his models concludes that, even after taking account of 39 nonracial variables, defendants charged with killing white victims were 4.3 times as likely to receive a death sentence as defendants charged with killing blacks. According to this model, black defendants were 1.1 times as likely to receive a death sentence as other defendants. Thus, the Baldus study indicates that black defendants, such as McCleskey, who kill white victims have the greatest likelihood of receiving the death penalty.

District Court Action

The District Court... concluded that McCleskey's "statistics do not demonstrate a prima facie case in support of the contention that the death penalty was imposed upon him because of his race, because of the race of the victim, or because of any Eighth Amendment concern."... As to McCleskey's 14th Amendment claim, the court found that the methodology of the Baldus study was flawed in several respects. ... Accordingly, the Court dismissed the petition.

The Court of Appeals for the 11th Circuit, sitting en banc,... assumed the validity of the study itself and addressed the merits of McCleskey's Eighth and 14th Amendment claims. That is, the court assumed that the study "showed that systematic and substantial disparities existed in the penalties imposed upon homicide defendants in Georgia based on race of the homicide victim, that the disparities existed at a less substantial rate in death sentencing based on race of defendants, and that the factors of race of the victim and defendant were at work in Fulton County."

Even assuming the study's validity, the Court of Appeals found the statistics "insufficient to demonstrate discriminatory intent or unconstitutional discrimination in the 14th Amendment context, [and] insufficient to show irrationality, arbitrariness and capriciousness under any kind of Eighth Amendment analysis."...

The Court of Appeals affirmed the dismissal by the District Court of McCleskey's petition for a writ of habeas corpus, with three judges dissenting as to McCleskey's claims based on the Baldus study. We granted certiorari... and now affirm.

McCleskey's first claim is that the Georgia capital punishment statute violates the Equal Protection Clause of the 14th Amendment. He argues that race has infected the administration of Georgia's statute in two ways: persons who murder whites are more likely to be sentenced to death than persons who murder blacks, and black murderers are more likely to be sentenced to death than white murderers.

As a black defendant who killed a white victim, McCleskey claims that the Baldus study demonstrates that he was discriminated against because of his race and because of the race of his victim. . . .

Equal Protection Principle

Our analysis begins with the basic principle that a defendant who alleges an equal protection violation has the burden of proving "the existence of purposeful discrimination." . . . A corollary to this principle is that a criminal defendant must prove that the purposeful discrimination "had a discriminatory effect" on him. . . . Thus, to prevail under the Equal Protection Clause, McCleskey must prove that the decision makers in his case acted with discriminatory purpose. . . . McCleskey's claim that these statistics are sufficient proof of discrimination, without regard to the facts of a particular case, would extend to all capital cases in Georgia, at least where the victim was white and the defendant is black.

The Court has accepted statistics as proof of intent to discriminate in certain limited contexts. . . .

But . . . the application of an inference drawn from the general statistics to a specific decision in a trial and sentencing simply is not comparable to the application of an inference drawn from general statistics to a specific venire selection or Title VII case. In those cases, the statistics relate to fewer entities, and fewer variables are relevant to the challenged decisions. . . .

McCleskey's statistical proffer must be viewed in the context of his challenge. McCleskey challenges decisions at the heart of the state's criminal justice system. "[O]ne of the society's most basic tasks is that of protecting the lives of its citizens and one of the most basic ways in which it achieves the task is through criminal laws against murder." . . . Implementation of these laws necessarily requires discretionary judgments.

Because discretion is essential to the criminal justice process, we would demand exceptionally clear proof before we would infer that the discretion has been abused. The unique nature of the decisions at issue in this case also counsel against adopting such an inference from the disparities indicated by the Baldus study. Accordingly, we hold that the Baldus study is clearly insufficient to support an inference that any of the decision makers in McCleskey's case acted with discriminatory purpose. . . .

McCleskey also argues that the Baldus study demonstrates that the Georgia capital sentencing system violates the Eighth Amendment. . . .

In light of our precedents under the Eighth Amendment, McCleskey cannot argue successfully that his sentence is "disproportionate to the crime in the traditional sense." . . . He does not deny that he committed a murder in the course of a planned robbery, a crime for which this court has determined that the death penalty constitutionally may be imposed. . . . McCleskey argues that the sentence in his case is disproportionate to the sentences in other murder cases. . . .

Although our decision in Gregg as to the facial validity of the Georgia capital punishment statute appears to foreclose McCleskey's disproportionality argument, he further contends that the Georgia capital punishment system is arbitrary and capricious in application, and therefore his sentence is excessive, because racial considerations may influence capital sentencing decisions in Georgia. We now address this claim.

Evaluation of Challenge

To evaluate McCleskey's challenge, we must examine exactly what the Baldus study may show. Even Professor Baldus does not contend that his statistics prove that race enters into any capital sentencing decisions or that race was a factor in McCleskey's particular case. Statistics at most may show only a likelihood that a particular factor entered into some decisions. There is, of course, some risk of racial prejudice influencing a jury's decision in a criminal case....

Because of the risk that the factor of race may enter the criminal justice process, we have engaged in "unceasing efforts" to eradicate racial prejudice from our criminal justice system.... It is the jury that is a criminal defendant's fundamental "protection of life and liberty against race or color prejudice." ...

The capital sentencing decision requires the individual jurors to focus their collective judgment on the unique characteristics of a particular criminal defendant. It is not surprising that such collective judgments often are difficult to explain. But the inherent lack of predictability of jury decisions does not justify their condemnation. On the contrary, it is the jury's function to make the difficult and uniquely human judgments that defy codification and that "buil[d] discretion, equity, and flexibility into a legal system." ...

McCleskey's argument that the Constitution condemns the discretion allowed decision makers in the Georgia capital-sentencing system is antithetical to the fundamental role of discretion in our criminal justice system....

Process of Sentencing

At most, the Baldus study indicates a discrepancy that appears to correlate with race. Apparent disparities in sentencing are an inevitable part of our criminal justice system.... Any mode for determining guilt or punishment "has its weaknesses and the potential for misuse." ... Despite these imperfections, our consistent rule has been that constitutional guarantees are met when "the mode [for determining guilt or punishment] itself has been surrounded with safeguards to make it as fair as possible." ... Where the discretion that is fundamental to our criminal process is involved, we decline to assume that what is unexplained is invidious.

In light of the safeguards designed to minimize racial bias in the process, the fundamental value of jury trial in our criminal justice system, and the benefits that discretion provides to criminal defendants, we hold that the Baldus study does not demonstrate a constitutionally significant risk of racial bias affecting the Georgia capital-sentencing process.

Two additional concerns inform our decision in this case. First, McCleskey's claim, taken to its logical conclusion, throws into serious question the principles that underlie our entire criminal justice system. The Eighth Amendment is not limited in application to capital punishment, but applies to all penalties.... Thus, if we accepted McCleskey's claim that racial bias has impermissibly tainted the capital-sentencing decision, we could soon be faced with similar claims as to other types of penalty.

Moreover, the claim that his sentence rests on the irrelevant factor of race easily could be extended to apply to claims based on unexplained discrepancies that correlate to membership in other minority groups, and even to gender.... Also, there is no logical reason that such a claim need be limited to racial or sexual bias.

If arbitrary and capricious punishment is the touchstone under the Eighth Amendment, such a claim could—at least in theory—be based upon any arbitrary variable, such as the defendant's facial characteristics, or the physical attractiveness of the defendant or the victim, that some statistical study indicates may be influential in jury decision making. As these examples illustrate, there is no limiting principle to the type of challenge brought by McCleskey.

The Constitution does not require that a state eliminate any demonstrable disparity that correlates with a potentially irrelevant factor in order to operate a criminal justice system that includes capital punishment. As we have stated specifically in the context of capital punishment, the Constitution does not "plac[e] totally unrealistic conditions on its use."...

Second, McCleskey's arguments are best presented to the legislative bodies. It is not the responsibility—or indeed even the right—of this Court to determine the appropriate punishment for particular crimes. It is the legislatures, the elected representatives of the people, that are "constituted to respond to the will and consequently the moral values of the people."... Capital punishment is now the law in more than two-thirds of our states.

It is the ultimate duty of courts to determine on a case-by-case basis whether these laws are applied consistently with the Constitution. Despite McCleskey's wide-ranging arguments that basically challenge the validity of capital punishment in our multiracial society, the only question before us is whether in his case.... the law of Georgia was properly applied. We agree with the District Court and the Court of Appeals for the 11th Circuit that this was carefully and correctly done in this case.

FROM THE DISSENT

By Justice Brennan

Adhering to my view that the death penalty is in all circumstances cruel and unusual punishment forbidden by the Eighth and 14th Amendment, I would vacate the decision... insofar as it left undisturbed the death sentence imposed in this case.... Murder defendants in Georgia with white victims are more than four times as likely to receive the death sentence as are defendants with black victims.... Nothing could convey more powerfully the intractable reality of the death penalty: "that the effort to eliminate arbitrariness in the infliction of that ultimate sanction is so plainly doomed to failure that it—and the death penalty—must be abandoned altogether."...

Even if I did not hold this position, however, I would reverse the Court of Appeals, for petitioner McCleskey has clearly demonstrated that his death sentence was imposed in violation of the Eighth and 14th Amendments.... McCleskey has demonstrated precisely the type of risk of irrationality in sentencing that we have consistently condemned in our Eighth Amendment jurisprudence.

At some point in this case, Warren McCleskey doubtless asked his lawyer whether a jury was likely to sentence him to die. A candid reply to this question would have been disturbing. First, counsel would have to tell McCleskey that few of the details of the crime or of McCleskey's past criminal conduct were more important than the fact that his victim was white.... Furthermore, counsel would feel bound to tell McCleskey that defendants charged with killing white victims in Georgia are 4.3 times as likely to be sentenced to death as defendants charged with killing blacks.... In addition, frankness would compel the disclosure that it was more likely than not that the race of McCleskey's victim would determine whether he received a death sentence: 6 of every 11 defendants convicted of killing a white person would not have received the death penalty if their victims had been black.... Finally, the assessment would not be complete without the information that cases involving black defendants and white victims are more likely to result in a death sentence than cases featuring any other racial combination of defendant and victim. The story could be told in a variety of ways, but McCleskey could not fail to grasp its essential narrative line: There was a significant chance that race would play a prominent role in determining if he lived or died.

Race and Sentencing Process

The Court today holds that Warren McCleskey's sentence was constitutionally imposed. It finds no fault in a system in which lawyers must tell their clients that race casts a large shadow on the capital-sentencing process. The Court arrives at this conclusion by stating that the Baldus study cannot "prove that race enters into any capital-sentencing decisions or that race was a factor in McCleskey's particular case."... The Court's evaluation of the significance of petitioner's evidence is fundamentally at odds with our consistent concern for rationality in capital sentencing, and the considerations that the majority invokes to discount that evidence cannot justify ignoring its force.

It is important to emphasize at the outset that the Court's observation that McCleskey cannot prove the influence of race on any particular sentencing decision is irrelevant in evaluating his Eighth Amendment claim. Since Furman v. Georgia (1971), the Court has been concerned with the risk of the imposition of an arbitrary sentence, rather than the proven fact of one.

Defendants challenging their death sentences thus never have had to prove that impermissible considerations have actually infected sentencing decisions. We have required instead that they establish that the system under which they were sentenced posed a significant risk of such an occurrence. McCleskey's claim does differ, however, in one respect from these earlier cases: It is the first to base a challenge not on speculation about how a system might operate, but on empirical documentation of how it does operate.

Risk Held Intolerable

... Close analysis of the Baldus study, however, in light of both statistical principles and human experience, reveals that the risk that race influenced McCleskey's sentence is intolerable by any imaginable standard.

The Baldus study indicates that, after taking into account some 230 nonracial factors that might legitimately influence a sentencer, the jury more likely than not would have spared McCleskey's life had his victim been black. The study distinguishes between those cases in which (1) the jury exercises virtually no discretion because the strength or weakness of aggravating factors usually suggests that only one outcome is appropriate; and (2) cases reflecting an "intermediate" level of aggravation, in which the jury has considerable discretion in choosing a sentence. McCleskey's case falls into the intermediate range. In such cases, death is imposed in 34 percent of white-victim crimes and 14 percent of black-victim crimes, a difference of 139 percent in the rate of imposition of the death penalty. In other words, just under 59 percent—almost 6 in 10—defendants comparable to McCleskey would not have received the death penalty if their victims had been black.

... Over half—55 percent—of defendants in white-victim crimes in Georgia would not have been sentenced to die if their victims had been black. Of the more than 200 variables potentially relevant to a sentencing decision, race of the victim is a powerful explanation for variation in death sentence rates—as powerful as nonracial aggravating factors such as a prior murder conviction or acting as the principal planner of the homicide.

These adjusted figures are only the most conservative indication of the risk that race will influence the death sentences of defendants in Georgia. Data unadjusted for the mitigating or aggravating effect of other factors show an even more pronounced disparity by race.

A final case: In 1988 the Court unanimously ruled that death cannot be imposed in cases where reliance is made on the grounds the murder in question was "especially heinous, atrocious and cruel."[13] This language was ruled unconstitutionally vague and thus provided juries and judges with insufficient guidance in the exercise of their discretion in sentencing. Even the most conservative justices agreed that the interests of due process for defendants were not met by so vague a standard, which permitted "unfettered discretion of the jury" in violation of the Eighth Amendment.

SUMMARY AND CONCLUSION

This chapter has examined sentencing in terms of its objectives (retribution, deterrence, incapacitation, rehabilitation, restitution, and reintegration), its types (fines, probation, and incarceration), and the factors that shape a judge's decision. We have covered the role played by statutes, judicial attitudes, and environmental factors in sentencing decisions. We have paid particular attention to the differences between determinate, definite, indefinite, and indeterminate sentencing. In this we have emphasized the differences between these types of sentencing systems in terms of the degree of discretion given both the judge and the parole authority in determining the actual time the offender serves. Finally, we have given special attention to the presentence hearing, which is, of course, especially important in capital cases where the decision is between life and death.

We began this chapter by saying that no decision made in the judicial process is more important to the defendant than the sentencing decision. Many people agree that this decision is of utmost importance and that it is often made without due regard for the interests of the victims or protection of the public. It is too important a matter, these critics say, to be left to the judges. In Chapter 15 we shall study various proposals—and the actions of some states—to restrict or curtail the discretion of judges in sentencing.

QUESTIONS FOR DISCUSSION

1. If you were a trial judge, which goal or goals would you emphasize at sentencing? Why? Would it change from case to case depending on circumstances?
2. Again, if you were the judge, how would you decide which offenders before you belonged in prison and which should be placed on probation or in some other alternative program? What specific factors would determine which offenders deserved some leniency and which should receive the stiffest penalties permissible?
3. Is your own state's system essentially determinate or indeterminate in character? What factors limit a judge's discretion?
4. What is the condition of your state's prison system, especially in terms of population size and growth versus capacity? How, if at all, should this factor be taken into account by judges in sentencing?
5. If your state has no death penalty, what arguments can you make for establishing one? What arguments can you make for keeping the death penalty outlawed? How would you employ principles from the Crime Control and Due Process Models in either of the arguments?
6. If your state has the death penalty, how is it being applied? What persons, if any, have been executed? Are death sentences imposed fairly, in your view, or are they products of bias? If you would abolish the penalty, what arguments would you use?

NOTES

1. Florida Statute No. 775.083.
2. *Tate v. Short,* 401 U.S. 395 (1971).
3. Donald J. Newman, *Introduction to Criminal Justice,* 2d ed., Lippincott, Philadelphia, 1978, p. 281.
4. Hazel B. Kerper and Jansen Kerper, *Legal Rights of the Convicted,* West, St. Paul, Minn., 1974, p. 250.
5. David A. Jones, *The Law of Criminal Procedure: An Analysis and Critique,* Little, Brown, Boston, 1981, p. 540.

6. Kerper and Kerper, p. 257.

7. Jones, p. 538.

8. Hazel B. Kerper and Jerold H. Israel, *Introduction to the Criminal Justice System,* 2d ed., West, St. Paul, Minn., 1979.

9. *Furman v. Georgia,* 408 U.S. 238 (1972).

10. *Gregg v. Georgia,* 428 U.S. 153 (1976).

11. *Booth v. Maryland,* 96 L. Ed. 2d 440 (1987).

12. *McCleskey v. Kemp,* 95 L. Ed. 2d 262 (1987).

13. *Maynard v. Cartwright,* 100 L. Ed. 2d 372 (1988).

CHAPTER 14

COURT EFFICIENCY
AND MANAGEMENT

After reading this chapter, students should be able to define and explain the importance of each of the following terms or phrases:

structural unification
centralized management
centralized budgeting
delay reduction
management information
date-certain scheduling
individual calendaring

master calendaring
alternative dispute resolution
mediation
arbitration
multidoor courthouse
closed-circuit television

In 1906 Roscoe Pound, a renowned jurist and later dean of the Harvard Law School, delivered an address to the annual convention of the American Bar Association that inspired a movement that continues to the present day, a movement dedicated to reform of the judiciary. In his famous speech, Pound said that a judicial system designed to serve a rural, small-town America was inadequate in an urban, industrialized society. He pointed to several features of our judicial system that cause great dissatisfaction, among them the existence of many different kinds of courts, jurisdictions that overlap and create additional confusion, and the lack of efficiency in the way personnel are used.[1] It is unfortunate, but true, that many of the weaknesses noted by Pound are still with us almost a century later.

ELEMENTS OF THE REFORM MOVEMENT

The reform movement was actually organized in 1913 with the incorporation of the American Judicature Society in Chicago. That organization has sponsored and worked for several key changes in judicial structure, procedures, and administration ever since its founding. Its journal, now called *Judicature,* has provided a forum for advancing, debating, and analyzing reform activities and programs for over seventy years.[2]

The American Bar Association became involved in reform in 1937, with the drafting of standards of judicial administration under the leadership of ABA president Arthur T. Vanderbilt and Fourth Circuit Chief Judge John J. Parker. The ABA's involvement in the development of precise standards for all aspects of judicial work and administration is reflected in the adoption of *Standards Related to Court Organization* in the mid-1970s and *Standards Related to Court Delay Reduction* in the mid-1980s.[3]

National commissions have studied and recommended changes in the court system on at least three occasions. The 1931 Wickersham Commission, the President's Commission on Law Enforcement and the Administration of Justice of 1965–1967, and the National Advisory Commission on Criminal Justice Standards and Goals, which opened for business in 1971, have all addressed themselves to defects in the courts and have proposed a variety of changes. Many of these proposed changes dealt with matters really external to the operation of courts, such as decriminalizing certain offenses and making available wider opportunities for nonincarcerative sentences. Some of the proposed changes dealt with court processes such as plea bargaining and sentencing. Others dealt with matters consistently central to court reform: unification and simplification of court structure, procedural and managerial reforms to speed up the disposition of cases, and technological changes aimed at promoting efficiency.

UNIFICATION AND CENTRALIZATION

The five essential elements of court unification are structural consolidation and simplification, centralized rule making, centralized management, state financing, and centralized budgeting. Most of the states have adopted one or more of these elements since the early 1970s. Many have adopted the entire package.

Structural unification, as mentioned in Chapter 3, has taken various forms, but it generally involves the consolidation or elimination of courts with limited jurisdiction, especially the elimination of justice of the peace courts. It also has involved the consolidation of general jurisdiction trial courts into a single tier of courts and the unification of all these courts under the administration of the chief justice of the highest appellate court, thus creating a single hierarchy. The hierarchy usually consists of trial court administrative or presiding judges in each judicial district, circuit, or county, who are responsible to the chief justice for matters of administration and case management.

A structurally unified court system is generally also one in which procedural and administrative rule making is centralized in the body of the highest court or in a conference or council of judges chaired by the chief justice. Varying degrees of rule-making authority may be delegated to local court systems as part of this arrangement; in some cases, local rules may require approval, in other cases they are simply permitted to stand unless found to be contrary to the statewide rules. The idea, of course, is to control the degree to which local courts can depart from statewide standards regarding due process of law. It is possible, of course, to centralize rule making without structurally overhauling the courts themselves.

Centralized management of courts is apart from, but generally dependent upon, structural unification. It calls for the chief justice and the state court administrator who works for him or her to do systemwide planning and to operate a personnel system for the courts. This approach also permits the chief justice to reassign judges as well as support personnel from areas with lighter case loads to locales with heavy loads and backlogs of cases.

Usually related to structural unification, but still separate elements of judicial structure, are state-level financing and centralized budgeting for courts. These items are usually linked together, of course, but need not be. States can provide most or all the funds for courts on the basis of requests from the courts and/or some formula for distribution. *Centralized budgeting,* on the other hand, calls for the head of the judicial branch of government to prepare and administer a single budget covering all operations of the entire judiciary. Ronald Stout observes that unified budgeting "has consistently been identified as a key element in improving the administration of state judicial systems."[4] Centralized budget making facilitates adoption of other administrative changes and the development of data about court needs and expenditures. Then the administrative head can use the power of the purse to ensure implementation of program directives.[5]

Ted Rubin summarizes the benefits said to be derived from combining all five of the reforms into a single package, thus creating a monolithic court system:

> The central, hierarchical approach suggests greater efficiency, more flexibility in manpower assignment, greater uniformity in the administration of justice

throughout a state, a central spokesman for improving the court system (increasingly chief justices deliver a biennial "state of the courts" address to state legislative bodies . . .), and certain benefits through central oversight . . . central service assistance . . . central training programs . . . and central research and development functions.[6]

But while many perceive only benefits from unification, and many states have adopted all or significant parts of the package, there are bureaucratic pitfalls and drawbacks to centralization that some enthusiastic reformers are likely to overlook or play down. Rubin points out the following:

• Standardization and conformity to centrally dictated rules and methods ignores the uniqueness of communities in which the trial courts operate and their capacity to innovate and deal effectively with their own problems.
• Organizations and groups with which trial courts interact and upon which they depend greatly—such as the police department, the sheriff's office, the prosecutor's office, defense firms, and the court clerk's office—are generally local in nature, and courts need flexibility in working with them.
• Centralized administration may not only be impractical, it may be resented as infringement on the prerogatives of local authorities.
• Those court systems that are well endowed in terms of finances, staff, and administrative ability may be penalized by being taken into a statewide system that intends to spread the wealth more "equitably" among all courts.
• Job satisfaction of employees tends to be higher in organizations that are locally controlled and more susceptible to employee desires than in a larger, essentially faceless bureaucracy.
• Central administration tends to deal with matters through orders and directives, while local administrators tend to rely more on negotiation and consultation to resolve problems.[7]

Consequences of State Funding and Budgeting

John Hudzik examined state financing and budgeting in particular detail.[8] He reviews the claims that proponents have made in citing increased funding for local courts and improvements in efficiency, effectiveness, and equity in court operations. Hudzik asserts that these claims are not supported by evidence or by logic, but seem to be based on a general acceptance of the alleged virtues of centralization in government. He goes on:

A plausible case, arising in part out of organizational theory, can be argued for negative consequences to occur as well. So, too, some empirical evidence is now emerging which is contradictory to earlier assertions concerning the benefits of state financing.[9]

Hudzik argues that the drive for court unification and administrative centralization in the 1970s was in the classical organizational theory mold: "Rational planning, hierarchy, chain of command, and coordination were offered as the cardinal virtues." Three other articles of faith also influenced the movement: (1) inequities and inefficiencies are due to the political fragmentation and overlapping powers at the local level; (2) budget planning requires sophisticated program budgeting, with its emphasis on goals and objectives; and (3) increased funding can solve problems.

Dealing with levels of expenditure, Hudzik found that in 1979 per capita judicial expenditure in state-financed systems was $14.47 (excluding Alaska with its extraordinary cost of living, the figure was $13.50) and averaged $11.92 in non-state-financed systems. He found that average shares of the total criminal justice budget going to the judiciary was somewhat higher in state-financed systems as well. But Hudzik points out that changes in accounting procedures, and the fact that several states had relatively high court expenditures before adopting state financing, weaken the notion that state financing causes increased funding for courts.

Hudzik also examined the increases that did occur in some states upon a shift to state financing and found that in many of them there were enormous jumps in judicial personnel. This included the shifting of existing personnel and programs from nonjudicial into the judicial category as the state assumed budgetary authority. In short, the increases were not entirely real, but largely illusory. When adding the feature of centralized budgeting to the mix, Hudzik found "some evidence to suggest that judicial systems with centralized budgeting receive slightly better treatment than those with state financing alone." But, he notes, important controls—work loads and changes in program efficiencies, for example— which would help clear up the question of whether state funding and state budgeting are good for courts, cannot be added to the analysis.

Hudzik also considered nonfinancial consequences of state financing and budgeting. Proponents' claims for greater efficiency, effectiveness, and equity "remain unsubstantiated," he says, while there are other outcomes that proponents of state financing do not mention. Among these are the fact that links between courts and local governments, particularly with other criminal justice agencies, are weakened and that trial courts are no longer tied to their communities. Breaking the hold of local politics may be desirable, but the politics of state bureaucracy is substituted for it. Besides, the state may not really promote higher and better standards of justice and efficiency.

In fact, this leads to Hudzik's next point: The concern for effectiveness and for service may be replaced with a concern for efficiency and productivity measured in quantitative terms. "The focus is likely to be on operations instead of on the operation's effects, the former being more easily measured from the distance of the state capital than is the latter."

Hudzik also argues that more standardization and red tape, thus less innovation and variety of efforts, also result from a state takeover of funding. If local courts seek to circumvent state rules or policies, more effort is put into monitoring compliance than planning new changes. Funding tends to shift to a formula basis, which holds every court to common criteria and ignores local differences in task allocation.

Finally, Hudzik suggests that state funding does not guarantee fiscal stability. State revenue sources tend to be highly responsive to business cycles of boom and bust, plus the courts wind up competing with a large number and variety of state agencies and programs for the available revenue.

Hudzik is not necessarily opposed to state financing or state budgeting for trial courts. He wants it understood, however, that claims of benefits, in the absence of evidence, remain merely claims, and there are several possible negative consequences that need to be considered.

The present authors have considerable experience in state agencies (a university and a state attorney's office), and our own personal experience leads us to agree strongly with Hudzik's concerns about bureaucratization, less flexibility, preoccupation with formulas and so-called objective measures of performance, and the need to submit to often silly reporting and auditing requirements to justify even the most obviously sensible actions. At the same time, we recognize that local control of agencies often has negative consequences related to local politics, vast differences in tax bases, intense parochialism, and other factors that can undermine the quality of justice offered by the courts.

Striking an Appropriate Balance

Ted Rubin has noted that significant problems can be associated with either too little or too much centralized state administration of courts. He writes:

> A wise balance suggests, in general, a higher share of state funding to local courts, but the retention of a sufficient local funding provision to afford a legitimacy to local court management; a judicial council structure representative of all courts so as to provide trial judge input into state court system administrative rules and policies, and a stronger interest in implementing [them]; state court system powers and functions agreed to as needed by the represen-

tative judicial council; probably trial judge appointment of their own presiding judge in accordance with a state rule that this position should be filled by judges with the keenest administrative skills rather than by seniority; appointment of trial court administrators by trial judges rather than by state court administrator.[10]

Rubin argues that it may make more sense to unify all trial courts into district units, with divisions of the court assigned to the various jurisdictional specialties such as juvenile, probate, criminal, and civil. Such an approach would deal with the vast majority of problems associated with fragmentation of courts, and yet preserve local control. It would create a unit large enough to employ managerial and technological innovations, mix the trial judges in a more generalist practice of law and yet—except in those major urban areas with 200 or 300 judges—avoid the worst aspects of bureaucratization usually associated with statewide systems.[11]

Florida's court system comes close to what Rubin has suggested. Its trial courts are in two tiers (county and circuit), but all judges are members of circuit councils presided over by circuit presiding judges, and trial court administrators work for each of the twenty presiding judges. Thus the trial courts achieve the essential advantages of consolidation while remaining somewhat autonomous from state control. The state funds judges' salaries, as well as those of other court personnel, and covers most expenses. Counties, however, still provide courthouse and office space, telephone service, postage, and furniture. There also is considerable flexibility in the rules of procedure promulgated by the supreme court to allow for local rules on many key matters. Furthermore, the clerks remain elected officials at the county level, and provision of probation services is divided between the state in the circuit or felony courts and the counties in the county courts.

Dale Good reports that a similar balance was achieved in Minnesota's court reorganization of 1977. The plan was produced by the Select Committee on the State Judicial System, chaired by an associate justice of the supreme court and staffed by representatives of various interest groups. Good writes:

> The Committee's sensitivity to the political ramifications of reforms is apparent from its continuous reference to maintaining a decentralized, participatory management structure for the courts. A close reading of the committee's report . . . reveals that the reform measures were intended to establish such a scheme.
>
> • Operational control of the courts was made the responsibility of the local bench, the chief judges of the district, and the trial court administrators.
> • The state-level management responsibilities of the chief justice and state court administrator were focused on those areas where statewide uniformity

(personnel standards, records, information and statistics) or statewide purview (temporary judicial assignments) was necessary.[12]

DELAY REDUCTION

One of the most persistent complaints about the courts is that they take far too long to dispose of cases. This complaint is directed as much at civil as at criminal processing, and the complaint is hardly recent in origin. An attorney speaking at an annual meeting of the American Bar Association said:

> The public impatience with delay and uncertainty is at present, perhaps, more pronounced than ever. The modern inventions that have so greatly quickened the transportation of persons and property, the transmission of intelligence and all business operations, inspire the public with the belief that movements of lawyers and judges can and should be hastened.[13]

William Falsgraf, 1985 president of the ABA, comments that this "sounds like something" he himself could have said, though the words were spoken in 1891. Falsgraf continues, that delay "signals a failure of justice and subjects the court system to a loss of confidence in its fairness and utility as a public institution."

It is difficult to specify, of course, what constitutes a "reasonable" period of time from arrest to disposition of a case, or, conversely, what constitutes an "unreasonable" delay that jeopardizes justice. Even the U.S. Supreme Court has not established a firm period beyond which the right to a speedy trial has been denied. Most observers agree that a median disposition time of half a year or more represents "excessive" delay.

The difficulty from a legal standpoint of setting firm disposition times is that, more often than not, delay serves the interests of the defendant in criminal cases, and it is defendants who are entitled to speedy trials, not victims, witnesses, or other interested parties. Continuances and other attempts to postpone disposition are regularly employed as tactics by defense attorneys, though in some places and in some types of cases (usually those in which the defendant is awaiting trial in jail), prosecutors seek to put off the matter until they win a concession or plea of guilty.

The point is, however, that time should not be so useful a tactical weapon for either side. Justice would seem to require the passage of only enough time to assess adequately the evidence and prepare for trial. Courts should have adequate resources and mechanisms to manage their dockets and dispose of cases without either "railroading" defendants or aggravating victims and witnesses to the point they withdraw or tell officials they will not cooperate in any future case.

Studies of Delay and Its Reduction

The National Center for State Courts, along with forty-three other court-related organizations, sponsored a national conference on delay and its reduction in the fall of 1985. At that conference, research results were presented that included the following principal findings:

1. Trial court delay is not inevitable and some high-volume courts handle their cases expeditiously.

2. It is possible for courts to reduce delays significantly.

3. State-level leadership is important, but local leadership and commitments are critical to institutionalizing effective case-flow management.

4. There is no single model or technique; a variety are being used and adapted to local conditions.

5. There are, however, several key elements common to successful delay-reduction programs.

6. Backlog must first be reduced before case-processing times can be brought under control.

7. Alternative dispute-resolution programs can be an effective part of an overall case-load management system, but are not a "quick fix" in and of themselves.

8. Many state trial courts still have serious backlogs and delay problems.

9. A most critical factor in delay reduction or prevention is the "local legal culture."[14]

The National Center conducted a study of upper criminal court processing times in nineteen urban centers in 1978 and was able to compare 1976 or comparable base-year cases used in that study with 1983 cases used for the 1985 study. Table 14.1 summarizes the findings and indicates that not only are processing times widely disparate, but that the courts fell into three categories: those that affected significant reductions in delay, those that held their own with reasonably good records, and those whose records deteriorated. The worst record is obviously that of Boston, while Jersey City apparently deserves kudos for its efforts.

Key Elements of Successful Delay Reduction

Participants in the delay-reduction conference discussed elements that presenters listed as contributing to effective delay reduction in a variety of courts.[15] Some of these are surveyed here.

Time Standards It is very important to the success of any program aimed at reducing delays to set time standards. Such standards—usually

TABLE 14.1

CHANGES IN UPPER COURT CRIMINAL CASE PROCESSING TIMES, 1976–1983

	Median (in days)			Third quartile (in days)			Percent cases over 150 days		
	Base year*	1983	Change	Base year*	1983	Change	Base year*	1983	Change
Jersey City, NJ	376†	121	−255	639†	371	−268	84	44	−40
Bronx, NY	328	230	−98	499	420	−79	79	65	−14
Providence, RI	277‡	182	−95	573‡	453	−120	§	54	§
Phoenix, AZ	98	44	−54	134	82	−52	18	9	−9
Oakland, CA	58	17	−41	116	110	−6	19	20	+1
Dayton, OH	69‡	64	−5	104‡	119	+15	§	18	§
San Diego, CA	45	43	−2	64	61	−3	4	4	0
New Orleans, LA	50	49	−1	115	98	−17	16	14	−2
Portland, OR	51	52	+1	81	90	+9	4	7	+3
Detroit Recorder's Court, MI	40‡	43	+3	170‡	117	−53	§	17	§
Miami, FL	81	93	+12	148	207	+58	24	34	+10
Wayne County, MI	33	49	+16	70	92	+22	7	15	+8
Cleveland, OH	71	88	+17	150	168	+18	25	29	+4
Minneapolis, MN	60	84	+24	139	132	−7	24	19	−5
Boston, MA	281	307	+26	487	478	−9	75	80	+5
Wichita, KS	76†	108	+32	§	140	§	§	18	§
Pittsburgh, PA	58	90	+32	91	161	+70	9	27	+18
Newark, NJ	99	146	+47	179	356	+177	34	49	+15

*Unless otherwise indicated, data for the base year are derived from Tables 2.4 and 2.5 in *Justice Delayed* (pp. 14–17).
†*Source:* Sample of cases terminated in 1979.
‡*Source:* David W. Neubauer et al., *Managing the Pace of Justice,* National Institute of Justice, Washington, D.C., 1981. For these three courts, the "baseline" data are based on a sample of cases *filed* prior to the start of a delay-reduction program. In Detroit Recorder's Court, the base period is April–October 1976; in Providence, it is all of 1976; and in Dayton it is July 1977–October 1978.
§Data unavailable or not applicable.
Source: State Court Journal, vol. 9, no. 4, Fall 1985, p. 19.

in the form of outside limits on how long cases should take—set goals for the system, give attorneys a sense of unacceptable time lengths, provide yardsticks for measuring performance, prompt attorneys and others to prepare their cases or settle them in a timely manner, and help change assumptions about the duration of litigation.

Management Information   In order for goals to be set, baseline data are needed. So, too, are operational support (calendars, notices, and subpoenas), the monitoring of all stages of all cases, identification of exceptional cases, a "tickler" to let judges and staff know about upcoming events, and key reports for managers to use in assessing how well things are going. All this means a management information system. But, conferees noted, such a system need not be computerized. There are excellent manual systems. Computers, however, if properly programmed and used, can supply needed information instantaneously. (We shall address the subject of the use of computers in courts later in this chapter.)

Management Control of Cases   Several conferees noted the need for court officials to gain quick control of cases and ride herd on them. Devices mentioned by various judges include (1) holding a conference on the status of each case within a certain number of days of filing, (2) using such conferences to set firm dates for all future events, (3) setting time limits on the voir dire, (4) starting trial at 8 A.M. and taking short lunch breaks, and (5) controlling attorneys' questions by not letting them repeat questions in altered forms.

Date-Certain Scheduling   A critical aspect of delay reduction is establishing a practice of scheduling the next event or events for a certain date. Firm dates encourage more disciplined lawyer behavior and contribute to earlier settlements or plea bargains. This is particularly true of trial dates, since nothing so inspires efforts to settle as an imminent trial. In order to hold to these dates, it may be necessary to use retired judges or attorneys as pro tem judges or to shift cases among judges on date of trial.

Control of Continuances   A corollary to the above is reduction of continuances by making it tougher to obtain them. Requiring written motions and the approval of all parties are sample tools. Some experimentation may be in order to arrive at an approach that does away with continuances for convenience of counsel while preserving those that are truly necessary.

Effectively Used Calendaring Systems   There are two approaches to establishing the calendar for a trial court. *Individual calendaring* involves assigning a case to a particular judge at its inception and having that judge responsible for every event in the life of that case. *Master calendaring* was developed presumably to make more efficient use of resources in multijudge courts by having each event in a case handled by whatever judge was available at the time the event took place.

Conferees disagreed as to whether master calendaring or individual calendaring or some hybrid best served promotion of delay reduction. The key is to make the system work by setting firm trial dates and controlling continuances.

It should be noted here that, as of January 1986, New York state shifted from master calendaring to an individual calendaring system. Judicial officials in that state were convinced that the master calendar system lent itself to frequent postponements and lengthy delays because each judge who handled a phase of a case had to familiarize himself or herself with the record. This was not the sole reason for the shift, however.[16]

Bar Association Involvement The full participation of state and local bar associations is important to delay-reduction programs. Since the lawyers know how the system works and have a vested interest in it, they must be involved in planning and implementing solutions.

Commitment of the Judges Finally, conferees agreed that a clear commitment by judges themselves is a *sine qua non* of delay reduction. The involvement of judges, like the involvement of attorneys, is a simple recognition of the fact that no workable reform can be imposed from outside the system.

Alternative Methods of Dispute Resolution

Other than by simply speeding up the process, there are two other approaches to reducing delay in case disposition. One is to reduce the scope of the law by abolishing statutes and the other is to divert more and more disputes out of the judicial system into alternative dispute-resolution forums.

The first option would involve the decriminalization of certain so-called victimless crimes and, on the civil side, would bar cases involving "heart-balm" actions (suits for breach of promise to marry, alienation of affection, adultery, etc.), bar the defense of contributory negligence or impose liability without fault, and bar judicial appeals of some administrative actions.[17]

The second option is to provide various alternative means for disputes and potential criminal cases to be resolved without taking them to court

News of Note

1-JUDGE, 1-CASE SYSTEM CUTS BACKLOG IN NEW YORK

By Kirk Johnson

A new system of one-judge, one-case justice has cut the backlog of pending felony cases in New York City more than 16 percent since it was introduced last January, court administrators announced yesterday.

The decline—from nearly 13,000 in early January to just under 11,000 as of last week—was the sharpest in that key indicator in at least three years, they said.

The new system, which involves both civil and criminal cases, calls for each case to be handled by a single judge, from the moment the cases enter the court system until they are settled by a verdict, a plea or a dismissal.

In addition to the drop in pending felony cases, the new system has also increased the number of cases disposed of, and the rate at which they are finished, according to the court figures.

Drop in lead time

For example, in the first seven months of the new method, the average length of time between a defendant's arraignment in a felony case and the settling of the case in the city's courts has dropped by more than three full weeks, to an average of 178 days, compared with 201 days in the same period last year.

But court administrators, led by the state's Chief Judge, Sol Wachtler, stressed that the purpose of the new system was to improve justice in more ways than simply making it swifter. Thus, they said, the success of the new system was still unclear.

"The numbers are very exciting, but they don't show it all," said Judge Wachtler, who has been the prime mover behind the new system. "We've changed, in a very traumatic and dramatic way, an entire court system—one of the largest in the world."

"I'm not quite ready to go out and proclaim victory after seven months," he said.

Still, most court administrators and legal officials said they were heartened by the figures released yesterday.

"Taking all these figure together, it shows that we're moving in the right direction," said Justice Milton L. Williams, deputy chief administrative judge of the New York City courts.

According to Justice Williams, the speed and volume that has come with the individual assigning of cases has also brought considerable administrative headaches, both for his staff and for the individual courtroom personnel.

Under the old master-calendar system, for example, judges received cases one at a time, after they had passed through a panel that disposed of as many cases as possible. Under the new individual assignment system, he said, a judge used to one-at-a-time justice might have 800 cases to worry about.

"It might seem like a lot, but many of them might never reach the point of a trial," said Justice Williams, who has been responsible for putting the new system into effect in New York City. "What we've had to do is educate the judges as to what those numbers really mean."

Source: The New York Times, August 1, 1986.

News of Note

A TIME BOMB IN NEW YORK COURTS

By Raoul Lionel Felder

A time bomb is ticking in New York State's judicial system. Its explosive ingredients are two well-intentioned reforms that promised speedier, fairer justice but are delivering delay and chaos. Those reforms are the six-year-old divorce law and a new system of assigning judges to cases.

Unless action is taken quickly, the overburdened court system will collapse. Its victims will not be criminals but rather ordinary citizens seeking only to end a painful period and put their lives in order.

At present, litigants in a matrimonial matter must wait up to nine months for cases to go to trial. For some parents, that means waiting nine months for the right to see their child. Such legal limbo prolongs pain and instills cynicism about the system's ability to dispense effective, timely justice. It undermines public confidence in the courts.

This crisis has its roots in the 1980 divorce law's vast expansion of mechanisms for financial discovery. Intended to protect all parties, the process has been perverted and obfuscates and delays. As a result, routine cases may become long-running, unbearably cumbersome matters.

When each side stakes its claim, individual and joint property (including such intangibles as business good will and homemakers' services, and prospective rights such as pension and co-op conversions) must be identified and valued. The use of an expert by one spouse inevitably requires the other party to counterthrust with another expert. Because each case is unique, simple solutions like relying on precedent are not available. Miscalculation abounds. Justice creeps, when it moves at all.

Complicating this morass is the state's nearly year-old individual assignment system under which one judge handles a case from start to finish. It is modeled after a similar one that works superbly in the Federal court system. But Federal courts are not comparable to our creaking, overburdened state system.

State judges in Manhattan alone handle more civil cases than the entire Federal system in all 50 states. The Federal courts effectively handle manageable caseloads with appointed, carefully screened judges and adequately trained support personnel. The state system struggles in perpetual turmoil with more than 1,000 cases assigned to one judge.

The state Office of Court Administration has published statistics to show that its system of assigning one judge to a case is working. That rosy picture is distorted by the large pool of older, virtually completed cases concluded in the early weeks of the system but credited to it.

Any lawyer or candid judge will admit that the system is tottering. Each month, a huge number of new cases is poured into the mouth of the system's funnel; only a tiny few trickle out. Each judge controls his or her court as a fiefdom. Woe to the parties who find themselves before a judge who lacks the talent and administrative skill needed to prod cases through to the end. It's not unheard of for a trial to consist of two hours in November, three hours the following January and two more in March.

Steps can be taken to avert collapse. Some can be accomplished administratively, others will require legislation. Here's what must be done—now.

Have all marital assets valued by court appointed experts under court mandate. Eliminate all distinctions between classes of property subject to equitable distribution. Eliminate as marital property the value of any personal service, business or profession that does not have true value or marketability.

Further, mandate use of arbitration procedures in all cases, using retired judges and lawyers who would supervise all discovery procedures at either party's request. Tax or levy a charge in matrimonial cases to pay for court appointed appraisers, arbitrators, etc.

In addition, assign judges to matrimonial cases from the entire panel of judges on a rotation basis. Let judges be judges, not administrators. Hire professional administrators and personnel to supervise the court system on a local level. Finally, appoint an independent monitoring panel (not under the control of the courts composed of judges) to review the system and to make midcourse corrections.

We all have a stake in efficiency and fairness in the judicial system. We need to defuse this bomb.

Raoul Lionel Felder is a lawyer.

Source: The New York Times, November 22, 1986.

for formal adjudication. These alternatives include (1) *mediation,* a process in which a third party listens to and promotes negotiations between disputants that lead to a settlement; (2) *arbitration,* a process in which the third party hears the arguments of the parties and renders a decision as to how the dispute is to be resolved; (3) so-called minitrials, often conducted before lawyers acting as judges; and (4) referral to any number of other social service, consumer, or governmental agencies.

Mediation versus Arbitration   Mediation and arbitration have been used by government agencies in dealing with labor relations for years. There is widespread confusion about the difference between the two approaches, however, and John Cooley explains the sources of the confusion as well as detailing the differences between the two processes. He points out:

> The most basic difference between the two is that arbitration involves a *decision* by an intervening third party or "neutral"; mediation does not.
>
> Another way to distinguish the two is by describing the processes in terms of the neutral's mental functions. In arbitration, the neutral employs mostly "left brain" or "rational" mental processes—analytical, mathematical, logical, technical, administrative; in mediation, the neutral employs mostly "right brain" or "creative" mental processes—conceptual, intuitive, artistic, holistic, symbolic, emotional.
>
> The arbitrator deals largely with the objective; the mediator, the subjective. The arbitrator is generally a passive functionary who determines right or wrong; the mediator is generally an active functionary who attempts to move the parties to reconciliation and agreement, regardless of who or what is right or wrong.[18]

Though arbitration and mediation are most clearly applicable to civil disputes, they can be applied in situations that could otherwise result in prosecution. Many areas have citizen dispute settlement (mediation-type) programs sponsored by bar associations to which a wide variety of cases—including simple assaults, consumer fraud, bad check charges, and other potentially criminal matters—are referred. Arbitration is widely used in cases of juvenile thefts, vandalism, drug possession, and other nonviolent offenses. Pretrial diversion of those accused in misdemeanor, and even felony, cases is formalized in many parts of the country, and such diversion often takes the form of, or involves, arbitration in which a prosecutor, probation officer, or other official orders a settlement between disputing parties.

The Multidoor Courthouse Professor Frank Sander of Harvard is credited with creating a concept that became known as the *multidoor courthouse*. In a 1976 address to the Conference on the Causes of Popular Dissatisfaction with the Administration of Justice, Sander proposed a "dispute-resolution center" where a screening clerk would direct each grievant to a process appropriate for his or her case. Sander imagined a building with many rooms, each containing a different process for resolving disputes.[19]

Professor Sander's views inspired the ABA to develop a three-stage process for creating multidoor centers, with the first stage to be creation of a centralized intake and referral service. Three project sites—Tulsa, Oklahoma; Houston, Texas; and Washington, D.C.—were chosen, and the intake offices were opened between April of 1984 and January of 1985. The Houston program handles a considerable number of infractions and misdemeanor matters, with the prosecutor's staff sending 40 to 50 percent of its cases to the multidoor center. Most of these, in turn, are referred to neighborhood justice centers for resolution.[20] Washington's program director has indicated that among its added referral points there will soon be a mediation service for minor crimes, delinquency, and "persons in need of supervision" cases.[21]

Though formal pretrial diversion programs for those accused of crimes have been around for many years, these attempts to establish comprehensive systems to divert civil as well as criminal matters away from the courts are new. They represent another effort to reduce the time and energy courts spend on relatively minor matters, thus presumably freeing up resources to more efficiently handle those cases that must be formally adjudicated.

The Question of Justice

The efforts to reduce delays and backlogs in criminal cases raises the question of whether justice is better served by a speedier process. We already know that judges, prosecutors, and defense attorneys have notions about how long cases should take and that each actor has some interest in promoting a certain amount of delay. There are critics among them of "overly speedy" processing, which they view as jeopardizing justice. If the system is trying merely to dispose of cases as rapidly as possible, with little concern about procedural rights and substantive outcomes, then justice is not necessarily served. A team that studied successful programs in delay reduction found most court participants thought that justice was being better served with the new system, but that some dissenters thought that things were moving too fast. One public defender was quoted as saying that the program amounted to "One, two, three, you're in jail."[22] In particular, he complained that the really tough cases were being rushed through. In Detroit, a court administrator spoke of "pressure cooker" tactics and "squeezing pleas."[23] One Detroit judge, a regular on the city's bench, spoke to the researchers about one of the visiting judges used in a crash program to clear the backlog:

> There was this sitting judge who had outstanding statistics for anyone who was crash-program oriented. He might have disposed of more cases than anyone else. And the irony of it all is his real attitudes in terms of criminal defendants are incredibly harsh.... But when he came aboard during the crash program, he saw his mission to get rid of cases.... So you have a right-wing Judge X, hostile as hell to criminally accused people, coming over and literally giving the store away.[24]

The researchers concluded:

> In sum, the old saying that "justice delayed is justice denied" may be something of a half-truth.... The delay-reduction programs that we studied visibly contributed to the more efficient *administration* of justice. But the programs' impacts on justice, a commodity influenced by the lens of the beholder, are necessarily more uncertain.[25]

The above discussion can also be related to the crime control versus due process theme. Generally, as was indicated by the public defender, speed works on behalf of crime control objectives and is the antithesis of due process values. But it is possible for courts to be so jammed and slow that due process is not accorded the defendant either. It is also possible, as was pointed out in the example of the visiting judge, for efforts to expedite disposition and rush to judgment to work against the interests of crime control. As we have already said, the ideal is some process that permits for complete investigation and full consideration of the facts and protection of the defendant's rights but does not permit dragging cases out for the convenience of attorneys or to give either side tactical advantages over the other.

COMPUTER TECHNOLOGY

Court reformers have long pointed out that the judiciary seems wedded to nineteenth- or even eighteenth-century ways of doing things. This seems especially true with regard to matters of modern management and technology. The situation is changing radically, however, especially in urban areas and unified state systems. Among the technologies being increasingly employed in courts are those related to computers and audiovisual equipment.

Computers have been around for sometime now, but in recent years, major breakthroughs in the development of microchips and resultant miniaturization of equipment and its cost have brought application within the reach of virtually every court in the land. Computers are nothing more nor less than electronic devices that can store, retrieve, manipulate, and present data. They can be used in several ways: as simple data storage and retrieval instruments for various aspects of court operations and business; as devices that "automate" certain routine operations in the court or clerk's office; and as tools for doing research into court operations, with a view to either doing scholarly analysis of how things are done or to testing the potential impact of changes on the system.

Types of Court Data

There are essentially two types of data needed by courts, though many data elements cross over this distinction: data related to specific cases being processed by the courts and data related to the resources being used by the court. The first type would include such items as names and other identifiers of the parties before the court; classifiers of the type of case; data regarding which courtroom and judge are assigned the case and which attorneys are representing each side; data on witnesses subpoenaed; a schedule of dates on which key events are to take place or have been completed; data on actions already taken, such as decisions about bail, discovery, suppression, and so on; and even transcripts of court proceedings. As to resource utilization, the data include all the records on court personnel; inventory and property records; accounting and budgeting figures; records of juror utilization and fees; records of witness utilization and fees; bonds, fines, fees, forfeitures, and other income or transfer accounts; and records of courtroom and other space assignments and utilization.

There are two overlapping spheres of application of these data: Case-specific data can be used to expedite events in the processing of the case itself, and case-specific data and resource data can be used in the management of the court as an organization. The latter application includes management of the records themselves, jury management, and witness management, as well as the traditional concerns of any organization.

Management Information Systems

Broadly speaking, a *management information system* is one that brings all the essential data about the operations and resource utilization of an organization to its manager or managers in a useful and timely manner. A court-related management information system would have to include the data elements already mentioned and, because of the nature of court organization, data about or from key supporting and collaborative offices such as the prosecutor's and public defender's offices, the sheriff's department, and the probation office.

The system also would have to be capable of producing statistical reports about all phases of court operations. Such statistical reports should lend themselves to measuring the efficiency of the operations, pinpointing key needs or bottlenecks, and projecting future case loads for planning purposes. Any management system capable of doing all this in a multijudge courthouse or multicourthouse judicial district or circuit would almost certainly have to be computerized.

There are key issues to be resolved in designing a management information system for courts. They include the issue of the scope of the system: Beyond the court itself and the clerks' office, should the prosecutor, the sheriff, the probation department, the public defender, and/or the juvenile service agency be involved in a single system? If the system is multiagency in scope, which should be the host agency and what should be the responsibilities of each participant in terms of program design, data input, and financial support? If member agencies already have operating systems, can they be integrated into the new system or should the new one be added on top, thus duplicating many functions? How can the system ensure the security of information on individuals while providing access to data to all those who need it? Finally, and perhaps most importantly to some if not all agencies, how can the capacity of the statistical component for comparing the production of one agency against another be utilized in a productive rather than destructive fashion? The effort to create a criminal justice information system has often been undermined by these issues.

To Computerize or Not to Computerize?

A question distinct from that of what kind of information system to establish is the question of whether a court using a manual records system should computerize. Many courts, like other organizations, have jumped into computerization without carefully considering all the issues and ramifications of doing so. Considering the problems encountered in many states, Thomas Schrinel has outlined a series of steps courts should take in evaluating the matter:[26]

1. Examine the nature of the "problem" computerization is expected to solve. Is it many problems or one? How many court officials see the problem? Is there a consensus among them on its definition?

2. Examine all possible solutions. What will automation accomplish that a manual system cannot? Is there an alternative using existing resources? Are there less expensive alternatives? Are the alternatives practical? What are the costs of an automated system? Will the expenditure result in a significant improvement without disrupting the integrity of the courts? How will implementation of a new system impact on current operations?

3. If automation seems the desirable choice, there are still other questions, including: Are qualified consultants involved or are vendors being relied on? Is the current manual system being properly maintained? (Schrinel warns that the manual system must be fine-tuned and functioning during the changeover.) Is the new system expandable and flexible in response to changes? Will the system fit the specific court or is it an effort to duplicate what works somewhere else? Has the impact on court personnel been fully considered? Can the staff assume the new work load and adjust to the new procedures? Have all related costs been included? Is there space sufficient to house the equipment? What are the possibilities of sharing the computer system with other agencies? At this point, one has to consider the matters discussed above regarding multiagency systems, and bring in a true systems analyst.

Schrinel's warning and questions should not be taken as debunking the value of computerization of court records. He is, however, raising many legitimate issues that all too often have not been thought through. The result is that some courts are resistant to change because of the bad experiences of others.

The Computerized Courtroom

Prototype "courtrooms of the future" have been set up in the federal district courts for northern Illinois and Arizona and in Wayne County Circuit Court in Detroit.[27] In Chicago, three personal computers are stationed on the bench of Judge Prentice H. Marshall and at each counsel's table. The officials can read transcript within seconds of the actual testimony, and this has proven a boon to the attorneys in checking on who has testified to what while the trial is in session as well as to deaf participants and to translators who have to interpret testimony to those who don't understand or speak English. The project is sponsored by the National Shorthand Reporters Association, and it enables court reporters to provide a day's transcript in printed form within a half hour of the conclusion of proceedings.

Court reporters have used computers since the mid-1970s to help produce transcripts, but the old system uses cassette tapes taken from the stenotype machine, and the tapes have to be run through the computer. The new, so-called real-time system bypasses this step, feeding the impulses from the typing directly into the computer in the reporter's office. There a person called a scopist, who works off a monitor, edits and cleans up the draft and prints the transcript, which is made available to the attorneys before the end of the day and can be used by jurors during deliberations.

As is often the case, a major obstacle to quick adoption by others is the cost, which can run as high as $75,000 per judge or courtroom, a large bill for a multijudge court. Another obstacle is the attitude of lawyers. Attorney Paul Bernstein, president of the Chicago Bar Association's Microcomputer Users Group, points out that most lawyers resist any change in the way they are accustomed to doing things. But, he observes, because this test is being conducted in a federal court, it will have a nationwide impact. "You will be seeing more lawyers bringing computers into courtrooms," he observes. "[W]ithin a decade, the great majority will have them. Once a critical mass develops, all lawyers will realize they better participate. Lawyers that don't computerize will be at a significant disadvantage. A lot are now."[28]

AUDIOVISUAL SYSTEMS

Another source of change in the courts is audiovisual technology. Amplification of the voices of participants in the courtroom is the simplest application of this technology, but uses multiply as the equipment and the product improve and become less and less expensive.

There are three general uses of audiovisual technology: (1) as a means of bringing evidence before the court, as seen in videotaped testimony, confessions, and drunkenness tests; (2) as a means of preserving a record of what goes on in the court; and (3) most recently, as a means of staging hearings via closed-circuit video conference calls.

Presentation of Evidence

Use of videotape to present testimony or other forms of evidence is becoming commonplace in many states. The late Bronx District Attorney Mario Merola used videotaped confessions in murder and other serious felony cases since the mid-1970s. Placing a clock within camera range to demonstrate that there had been no editing or erasures, Merola claimed, "we get a conviction in virtually every case." He indicated that the use of videotaped confessions also reduced the number of trials. "The defendant might say, the police beat me up. But then the defendant's lawyer views the taped confession. He sees it didn't happen. The lawyer takes a plea the next day."[29]

The same effect follows from taping the behavior of motorists arrested for drunk driving. They are usually so embarrassed at the visual evidence of their condition that they plead quickly.

Another application of this technology is to take the depositions or complete testimony of witnesses who cannot, for whatever reason, appear at the hearing or trial personally. President Nixon's testimony in the trial of his top White House aides, President Ford's testimony against would-be assassin Lynette Alice Fromme, President Reagan's testimony in the trial of Admiral Poindexter, and actress Jodie Foster's testimony in the trial of John Hinckley were all presented by videotape.[30] The technique permits questions or answers to which objections are sustained to be edited out entirely. It has also been used to obtain testimony from children in cases of alleged sexual abuse. Even very small children who would be silent in the environment of a courtroom can be persuaded to testify in a more comfortable setting.

Still another evidence-preserving and -presenting application is the videotaping (in addition to standard photographing) of crime scenes at the time of the initial investigation to illustrate conditions and to give a better perspective on physical arrangement and distances. The tape preserves the images obtained at the crime scene for later replay in court. Videotape has also been used in connection with a new laser technology for lifting fingerprints from surfaces—including human skin—from which it had once been impossible to get prints.

Finally there are cases in which an entire trial has been videotaped, and the edited tape then presented to a jury to watch on monitors. This obviously saves considerably on jury time and expense. Experiments have even demonstrated that jurors are more attentive if the image is in color rather than black and white. But this use of video has its limitations and problems. The most obvious is that jurors can only see what the camera was focused on and cannot observe the reactions of defendants or others to what witnesses are saying unless split screens or quick cross-switching between cameras is employed.

Record of the Trial

An even more controversial use of audiotape and videotape is as the official record of the trial for purposes of review and appeal. Use of audiotaping has been standard in some courts, especially courts of limited jurisdiction, for over a decade.

Predictably a battle of sorts has developed between traditional court stenographers and those championing audiotaping systems. A few years ago experiments were conducted in which the traditional and the technological systems were pitted against one another in selected federal district courts. The General Accounting Office found that taping would save money, as much as $10 million per year. A study by the Federal Judicial Center in twelve courtrooms found that not only were taping systems less expensive, they produced transcripts that had far fewer errors than those done by stenographers.[31] It is probably in response to these findings that the court reporters are sponsoring tests of the computerized reporting system described earlier.

Videotapes have been used in Ohio and Tennessee as records of trials as a substitute for transcripts. Justices have generally found, however, that it takes them much longer to review a videotape record than to read a printed transcript, so this application is not likely to become widespread.[32]

Closed-Circuit Television Hookups

The latest application of audiovisual technology is in the *closed-circuit television* hookup for two-way sound and image transmission between a judge, clerk, reporter, and prosecuting attorney in one location—usually the courthouse—and an incarcerated defendant and his or her attorney in a room set up for televising within the jail.

In Miami, Florida, the judicial circuit instituted such a system for misdemeanant arraignments in 1982.[33] The chapel of the jail is linked to the arraignment courtroom, and each has 45-inch rear-projection monitors. A specially trained bailiff acts as technical director at a control panel in the courthouse, and corrections officers operate the equipment at the jail. The system has arraigned tens of thousands of defendants without transporting them across the street to the courthouse and jamming the small holding cells. Interviews with all participants indicate that only defense attorneys are unhappy with the system. Some of their comments are instructive:

> The video system presents only an image of the accused. The personal confrontation which is essential is effectively removed.
>
> By having the arraignment in the chapel, judges can "turn us off." The state attorney, however, is five feet from the judge. It makes our positions very unequal.
>
> It puts the judge and prosecutor on the same side and the public defender and the defendants on the other—the good guys versus the bad guys.[34]

Defendants themselves, however, were largely supportive, and judges want to expand the system into other jail facilities and to include hearings on other motions. Orange County (Orlando), Florida, is one of several other areas that have installed a similar system, and other uses are being explored—such as taking children's testimony in abuse trials via live hookups instead of using tape as described earlier.

Critique of Audiovisual Technology

Kathy Stuart and Lynae Olson have set forth four questions courts should examine before jumping into audiovisual technology:[35]

1. Will time expenditures be reduced or increased?
2. Will the system handle a significant amount of court business?
3. What administrative and procedural changes will be required?
4. Are the equipment and operational requirements, including costs, reasonable and practical?

Stuart and Olson found that closed-circuit television hookups perform well but that equipment costs are high. They found that frequent use of videotape enhanced its acceptance by personnel, while systems infrequently used only increased a court's resistance to the technology. Stuart and Olson concluded that the spread of the technology has been hampered largely by the demands it makes on personnel time and on a court's budget. But as costs continue to come down and equipment becomes easier to operate, audiovisual technology—video technology in particular—should have a rosy future in the courts. It is not inconceivable that closed-circuit hookups using satellites will make it possible to hold hearings or trials that involve parties thousands of miles apart.

COMMENTARY ON COURT REFORM

Several years ago, Geoff Gallas wrote a piece for *Judicature* in which he reviewed the major recommendations of court reformers.[36] He listed seven such recommendations:

- Centrally administered state judicial systems
- Merit selection of judges
- Judicial discipline and removal commissions
- Unitary state financing and budgeting
- Unified merit personnel systems for all court employees
- Central rule-making authority
- Modern technology and professional court administrators

Gallas labeled these principles "the conventional wisdom" and reviewed the literature on these reform measures, writing:

> Taken together, these critics underline what every objective reform advocate must admit: there is *little or no empirical evidence or experience* which shows conclusively that unified court systems and unified trial courts produce better or even more justice; that judicial merit selection means better judges; [or] that judicial administrators and the introduction of modern technology positively affect judicial administration.... This is not to argue that the promised and desired outcomes do not occur, but rather to highlight how much of the conventional wisdom remains problematic.[37]

Gallas pointed out that the concept of equity carried to its logical extreme would dictate a unitary national court system with equal and identical resource allocation, a prospect that would create a conflict with federalism, a conflict not addressed "in any systematic way by reformers." Furthermore, he stated that a "detached perspective" suggests "four interrelated consequences of court reform":

- An increase in the quantity of services with no absolute guarantee that the services will be better
- An increase in costs borne by taxpayers
- An increase in "standardization"
- [I]ncremental, not comprehensive, systematic change

Gallas supported these assertions with evidence of an increase in court staffs, a dramatic increase in budgets (over 100 percent in one six-year period), the failure of the Federal Speedy Trial Act of 1974 to bring ninety-four federal districts into conformity in standardization of case time (much less into conformity in standardization of qualitative justice), and the piecemeal approach that states have taken to adopting elements of the reform package.

Gallas urged the undertaking of academic research aimed at "practical relevance and comprehension of the simplest sorts of operational realities." He proposed that such research be designed to account for and pinpoint the political outcomes of specific reforms, to deal with ends (justice) rather than just means, to allow for the dynamism of problems and the unanticipated consequences of change, and to be specific about the level of system or problem being analyzed, whether statewide or within a specific courthouse, whether related to a specific judge or to a courtroom team.

Some months after the appearance of the Gallas article, Dale W. Good responded with a piece in which he chastised Gallas for expecting too much too soon and for treating the reform measures as though they were aimed at attaining a universal standard that was never in the plans of the reformers.[38]

Good noted "two fundamental flaws" in Gallas's analysis. The first is that Gallas "may be testing the foundation of court reform before it has been given a chance to temper." The second flaw is that Gallas faults research done by particular institutions for focusing only on the particular jurisdiction or problem the reform addressed and for being, therefore, devoid of generalizations that are applicable or testable elsewhere. Good claimed, "[T]hat may not be so unusual a problem," and pointed out that the "meaning of reform, the impetus for reform, and therefore, the evaluation of its success, are *inherently* context-specific." For example, he argued that the impetus for reduction of delay in criminal cases may vary from jurisdiction to jurisdiction from a libertarian desire for equity to a conservative desire to cut costs. Thus, not only is the application of reform measures context-specific, but so must be the evaluation of the reform measures, especially since there is no monolithic goal, as Gallas implied there was.

Good also asserted that Gallas confused the ends and the means of reforms. Specific reforms are not intended to achieve some predetermined absolute concept of equity that cuts across jurisdictions and states; the reforms instead are aimed at making tools by which policymakers other than administrators may measure progress toward differing standards and concepts of what qualitative justice is. Thus merit selection is a tool by which judges may be selected in accordance with a standard of "merit" that is not monolithic but varies from community to community. Centralized funding of courts is not aimed at some absolute equity or sameness of courts, but is again a device by which policymakers can determine how to achieve approximations of equal justice that are impossible to even gauge with localized and widely disparate funding.

Good set forth the Minnesota system, of which he is part, as an example of the sensitivity that reformers have to qualitative considerations in reallocating political power and authority. While the Minnesota courts have been unified in several key respects, there is flexibility for local and regional variations in determining budget levels and achieving the general goal of delay reduction. The state operates a single case-tracking management information system and conducts an ongoing weighted case-load study of work loads in the courts—not to enforce a single standard in management information systems and work loads, but to provide data by which decisions can be made about resource allocation on an informed basis.

SUMMARY AND CONCLUSION

This chapter has examined court reform in specific areas not covered in previous chapters. We have discussed the unification of courts, the remedies aimed at reducing delay in case processing, and the applicability of computer and audiovideo technology. In each area, we have attempted to outline the thrust of the reform and to present a discussion of the issues that reform creates for those concerned about the courts. Particular attention has been paid to potential or real problems accompanying each of these reforms.

The highlights of a debate in *Judicature* have been presented as a means of focusing the reader's attention on the lack of agreement over the thrust and purpose of the reform movement. Both Geoff Gallas and Dale Good obviously care about achieving justice in the courts, and their disagreements over the aims and achievements of reformers only serve to illustrate the dynamism that now exists in a field where tradition held sway for so long.

Much, in fact, of what these writers say applies to the discussion that follows in the next, and last, chapter of this volume, where we deal with the more obviously political and social issue of discretion, its use, and its abuse. We also look at whether the efforts of policymakers to limit the discretion of court officers—especially the prosecutor and judge—are attempts to achieve greater equity for citizens or to reallocate power and restrict the independence of the judiciary.

QUESTIONS FOR DISCUSSION

1. Does your community's judicial system have a serious problem with delays in the processing of cases? If not, why not? If so, what factors seems to contribute to the problem?
2. Examine the consequences of long delays for (a) the accused person, (b) the victim, (c) the local jail, and (d) other criminal justice agencies. What are some of the things that can be done to attack the problem?
3. What uses does your court system make of computer technology? Are various criminal justice agencies sharing in a common criminal justice information system (CJIS), or are they each operating independently?
4. What applications of video technology are made in your community's courts? Has the technology resulted in substantial improvements in court operations? Has it resulted in cost savings?

NOTES

1. Roscoe Pound, as cited in H. Ted Rubin, *The Courts: Fulcrum of the Justice System,* Goodyear, Santa Monica, Calif., 1976, p. 208.
2. See Herbert Harley, "Concerning the American Judicature Society," as reprinted in Russell R. Wheeler and Howard R. Whitcomb (eds.), *Judicial Administration: Text and Readings,* Prentice-Hall, Englewood Cliffs, N.J., 1977, pp. 56–63.

3. American Bar Association, *Standards Relating to Court Organization* ABA, Chicago, 1974, and *Standards Relating to Court Delay Reduction,* ABA, Chicago, 1985.

4. Ronald Stout, "Planning for Unified Court Budgeting," *Judicature,* vol. 69, no. 4, January–February 1986, p. 205.

5. G. Alan Tarr, "Court Unification and Court Performance: A Preliminary Assessment," *Judicature,* vol. 64, no. 8, March 1981, p. 363.

6. Ted Rubin, *The Courts: Fulcrum of the Justice System,* 2d ed., Random House, New York, 1984, p. 235.

7. Ibid., p. 235.

8. John K. Hudzik, "Rethinking the Consequences of State Financing," *The Justice System Journal,* vol. 10, no. 2, Summer 1985, pp. 135–137.

9. Ibid., p. 135.

10. Rubin, p. 236.

11. Ibid., p. 236.

12. Dale W. Good, "Court Reform: Do Critics Understand the Issues?" *Judicature,* vol. 8, no. 63, p. 371.

13. Alfred Russell, as quoted in William W. Falsgraf, "The Quest for Justice," *State Court Journal,* vol. 9, no. 4, Fall 1985, p. 6.

14. Ibid., p. 17. The findings are summarized from Barry Mahoney, Larry L. Sipes, and Jeanne A. Ito, "Implementing Delay Reduction and Delay Prevention Programs in Urban Trial Courts: Preliminary Findings from Current Research," National Center for State Courts, Williamsburg, Va., 1985.

15. The following passage draws upon "What Are the Key Elements of Successful Programs?" *State Court Journal,* vol. 9, no. 4, Fall 1985, pp. 20–26.

16. Sam Roberts, "State to Adopt One-Case, One-Judge System," *The New York Times,* October 12, 1985, pp. 1 and 30.

17. Maurice Rosenberg, "Can Court-Related Alternatives Improve Our Dispute Resolution System?" *Judicature,* vol. 69, no. 5, February–March 1986, p. 254.

18. John W. Cooley, "Arbitration vs. Mediation: Explaining the Differences," *Judicature,* vol. 69, no. 5, February–March 1986, pp. 263–264.

19. Linda J. Finkelstein, "The D.C. Multidoor Courthouse," *Judicature,* vol. 64, no. 5, February–March 1986, p. 305.

20. "Toward the Multi-door Courthouse: Dispute Resolution Intake and Referral," *NIJ Reports/SNI* 198, July 1986, pp. 2–7. The article is based on reports by Janice Roehl and Larry Ray.

21. Finkelstein, p. 306.

22. See John Paul Ryan, Marcia J. Lipetz, Mary Lee Luskin, and David W. Neubauer, "Analyzing Court Delay Programs: Why Do Some Succeed?" *Judicature,* vol. 65, no. 2, August 1981, p. 68.

23. Ibid., pp. 68–69.

24. Ibid., p. 69.

25. Ibid., p. 69.

26. Thomas Schrinel, "Court Records Management: Evaluate before You Automate," *Justice System Journal,* vol. 8, no. 1, 1983, pp. 102–117.

27. June Altman, "Court Goes High-Tech," *Management Information Systems Week,* July 21, 1986, pp. 1 and 8; and Chris Tlustos, "Courts Show Transcripts in Real Time," *Government Computer News,* August 1, 1986, pp. 1 and 22.

28. Altman, p. 8.
29. Marcia Chambers, "Videotaped Confessions Increase Conviction Rate," *The New York Times,* June 5, 1983, p. 30.
30. Tamar Levin, "Judges Learn the Virtues of Videotape," *The New York Times,* July 22, 1984, p. 22E.
31. David Lauter, "Tape Recorders Still Top Reporters after the Latest Battle on Transcripts," *The National Law Journal,* July 18, 1983, p. 17.
32. Merlin Lewis, Warren Bundy, and James L. Hague, *An Introduction to the Courts and Judicial Process,* Prentice-Hall, Englewood Cliffs, 1978, p. 300.
33. W. Clinton Terry III and Ray Surette, "Video in the Misdemeanor Court: The South Florida Experience," *Judicature,* vol. 69, no. 1, June–July 1985, pp. 13–19.
34. Ibid., p. 18.
35. Kathy Stuart and Lynae K. E. Olson, "Audio and Video Technologies in Court: Will Their Time Ever Come?" *Justice System Journal,* vol. 8, no. 3, 1983, pp. 287–306.
36. Geoff Gallas, "Court Reform: Has It Been Built on an Adequate Foundation?" *Judicature,* vol. 63, no. 1, June–July 1979, pp. 29–36.
37. Ibid., p. 30.
38. Good, pp. 367–375.

15

DISCRETION, DISPARITY, AND JUSTICE

After reading this chapter, students should be able to define and explain the importance of each of the following terms or phrases:

disparities

appellate review of sentences

sentencing councils

mandatory minimum sentences

presumptive sentences

sentencing guidelines

By now the reader should be well aware of the extent to which discretionary authority is vested in each of the major officials of the criminal justice system, but in particular, as it concerns us here, in the prosecuting attorney and the judge. The former exercises his or her discretion with regard to charges to be filed, withdrawn, or amended during the process. The judge's major area of discretion is, of course, at sentencing. These officials may use their discretion to accomplish objectives consistent with either crime control or due process values. They must, however, confine themselves within limits set forth by law. If they do not so confine themselves, they are guilty of illegal as well as unethical behavior.

DISCRETION AND DISPARITIES

The Uses of Discretion

A pioneer commentator on the subject of discretion, Kenneth Culp Davis, wrote that an official exercises discretion "whenever the effective limits of his power leave him free to make a choice among possible courses of action or inaction."[1] Burton Atkins and Mark Pogrebin observe that this "suggests latitude of decision-making rather than formality or certainty. It suggests that, unlike the symbolic idea of due process, idiosyncrasy rather than rules may guide decision-making within the administration of criminal justice."[2]

Prosecutorial Discretion   Recall that prosecuting attorneys have almost total control over the question of who is to face what criminal charges in a court of law. Prosecutors can, in effect, determine law enforcement policies for their districts by selection of persons to be prosecuted and by prioritization of criminal laws to be employed in such prosecutions. This discretion extends beyond the matter of original filings or referrals to grand juries to the whole business of plea bargaining and pretrial settlement of cases. Few checks exist upon this power. Grand juries can decline to indict, but they rarely do when prosecutors make it clear that charges are warranted in the cases before them. Judges can dismiss charges not adequately grounded in facts demonstrated by evidence, but most judges take the attitude that this is a matter to be left to the trial. These negative checks are not terribly potent. It is even more rare for a judge to command that charges be activated against someone. Most states prohibit such judicial "interference" with the prosecutorial function. The only remaining weapons in the hands of other authorities is removal of prosecutors from office by impeachment, recall, or some other rarely used device, or the prosecutor's temporary replacement by a substitute named by a court or governor for the duration of a particular case or period.

Judicial Discretion   Judges exercise discretion over several points in the criminal process, but the impact of their decisions varies from place to place. Judges set bail or other conditions of pretrial status for the accused. They dismiss unfounded charges; they rule on motions including those to suppress key evidence or to exclude key testimony or witnesses; and, most importantly, they sentence. In most of these matters, however, the judge is limited by law and further bound to some degree by courthouse traditions and work group expectations. Still, judges are to a considerable extent the masters of their own courtrooms and dockets, and, as has already been discussed, they are rarely removed or otherwise sanctioned for official behavior.

As an aside to this point, let us point out that trial court judges are also guaranteed virtual immunity from civil suits by damaged parties. This was most recently affirmed by the U.S. Supreme Court in the case of *Stump v. Sparkman*.[3] The Court, through Justice Byron White, has said in another case that appellate processes and other forms of discipline make civil liability of judges unnecessary and that "Absolute immunity is . . . necessary to assure that judges, advocates, and witnesses can perform their respective functions without harassment or intimidation."[4]

Resultant Disparities

The problems associated with discretionary authority are not limited to those of principle. It is not simply that discretion belies the notion that we are a nation ruled by laws rather than by humans. It is that the exercise of discretion results in disparities of treatment of criminal cases and, more importantly, of people by the system. These disparities appear to be so vast and pervasive that they undermine the confidence citizens have in the officials most directly responsible for their protection. The disparities undermine any effort to convince offenders, victims, law enforcement officials, or anyone else for that matter, that "crime does not pay" in this country. To the contrary, many observers are by now convinced that crime pays rather handsomely, thank you. It is especially rewarding for persons with sufficient skills, intelligence, or wealth to avoid capture or prosecution, to "beat the rap," or to serve little or no sentence if convicted.

Part of the problem with the above generalizations—other than the fact that they are only partially true—is that the results cited are often due to the law itself (or its drafters) rather than to the actions of its enforcers and administrators. We cannot address disparities in the statutory classifications of crimes or in the impact of rulings on evidence and procedural questions that have a differential impact on different levels of criminal activities. We can deal here only with disparities that arise solely from the differential manner in which actual cases are handled.

As our discussion in Chapter 1 pointed out, there are two essentially contradictory approaches to what justice demands in terms of processing cases and defendants. One calls for similar if not identical treatment of all those who commit similar crimes or crimes of equal seriousness—in other words, the "legal justice" approach. The other calls for distinctions to be made among and between defendants of varying backgrounds, criminal records, motivations, and propensities for rehabilitation—in other words, the "justice of dispensation." The argument over whether the punishment should fit the crime or the criminal is centuries old. We shall not resolve it here. It is central, however, to any attempt to define what is meant by "disparity." The proponents of legal justice view the individualization of treatment as automatically disparate, while those who believe in fitting the treatment to individual offenders are convinced that disparities would result from identical punishments. It is important to note that disparities result when similar situations are treated very differently, but disparities also result when very different situations are treated in a similar manner.

Such disparities can only be explained by reference to the operating penal philosophy; hence we should look for evidence of disparities only within states or within the federal system. Comparing states with one another or with the federal system is inappropriate since differing penal philosophies and statutory provisions are at work. We can study disparity then, only in looking at how armed robbers are treated in various counties in Texas or how corporate executives convicted of price fixing are treated in the federal district courts of different regions of the country. The fact that professional burglars may serve an average of five years in maximum security in one state and eighteen months in community treatment centers in another does not indicate a disparity as we have defined it.

Studies of Disparities

Disparities in sentencing became a national issue with the publication of federal district court Judge Marvin Frankel's book, *Criminal Sentences: Law Without Order*.[5] The judge wrote that, at least in the federal courts, the defendant in most cases "has no way of knowing or reliably predicting whether he will walk out of the courtroom on probation, or be locked up for a term of years that may consume the rest of his life, or something in between."[6] Frankel went on to observe that judges' sentencing powers are:

> ... so far unconfined that, except for frequently monstrous maximum limits, they are effectively subject to no law at all. Everyone with the least training in the law would be prompt to denounce a statute that merely said the penalty for crimes "shall be any term the judge sees fit to impose." A regime of such arbitrary fiat would be intolerable in a supposedly free society, to say nothing of being invalid under the due process clause. But the fact is that we have accepted unthinkingly a criminal code creating in effect precisely that degree of unbridled power.[7]

Federal Studies A study done some years ago of federal district court sentencing points out that disparities appear at four different levels. There are disparities in sentences between offenses (bank embezzlers get fines and probation while bank robbers go to prison); between individual judges on the same bench; between judicial districts within the same judicial system; and between individual cases or offenders which have no basis in the seriousness of the offenses or prior records of the offenders. This early study illustrated the problem of disparities by contrasting the pattern of sentencing in the federal court of the Southern District of New York in 1972 with the national averages for all federal courts for the same year in eighteen categories of federal offenses. The likelihood of going to prison in the SDNY was substantially lower in some categories and higher in others. The average length of prison sentences was considerably shorter than the national averages in most categories (actually less than half in some) but very much higher in two of them: narcotics and rackets/extortion cases.[8]

Judges usually respond to such analyses by saying that statistics cover up the true differences between cases and offenders—that what appears to be disparity is really the "individualization" of justice to fit the particular circumstances of each situation. In response to this criticism, another approach to the study of disparities was developed. Judges attending workshops and institutes were each asked to read presentence reports on hypothetical offenders and state the sentence they would impose. The results again pointed to apparent disparities.

One study involved judges from three midwestern federal judicial circuits. An income tax evader would have been sentenced to a fine by three judges, to probation by twenty-three judges, and to prison terms by twenty-three others, with those terms running between one and five years. A bank robber would have received diagnostic commitment from twenty-eight judges, straight prison terms of up to twenty years from fourteen judges, indeterminate terms for up to twenty years from six judges, and probation with psychiatric care from three judges.[9]

In another study, fifty judges drawn from the Second Federal Circuit (New York, Connecticut, and Vermont) proposed sentences in twenty cases covering twenty different crimes. An extortionist and tax evader would have gotten anywhere from three to twenty years in prison; a thief, from four years' probation to 7½ years in prison; a heroin possessor, from a year's probation to two years in prison; a briber, from a $2,500 fine to six months behind bars plus six months probation plus a $5,000 fine; a bank robber, from five to eighteen years in prison; a bank embezzler, from two years' unsupervised probation to an indeterminate term under the Youth Corrections Act; and a conspirator to commit securities fraud, from a $2,500 fine to a year in prison plus a $1,000 fine.[10] These results not only showed disparity among judges dealing with the same offender and offense, but illustrated the tendency to deal harshly with crimes involving violence or its threat and leniently with white-collar crime. Some observers, including the authors of the Second Circuit study, declined to include this tendency within their definition of disparity and limited their concern to differences among judges in dealing with defendants "similarly situated."[11]

Studies of Local and State Courts   Another early study that focused on the criminal courts of three major American cities—Baltimore, Chicago, and Detroit—found that there may be significant disparities within them in terms of who goes to prison and who gets probation or a suspended sentence, but there is little disparity in the length of prison terms, once factors such as seriousness of offense and characteristics of the offenders are accounted for. James Eisenstein and Herbert Jacob report that differences among the decisions over who goes to prison and who does not, insofar as they could be explained at all, were due to a mix of the seriousness of the original offenses, the characteristics of the offenders, and the "identity of the courtroom," or, in other words, the particular judges making the decision.[12] But they were unable to explain most of the variances. (See Figure 15.1.) The implication is that up to 85 percent of the variance in these decisions in Chicago could not be explained, or could be explained only by the preferences of individual judges, and that 75 percent of the variance for Baltimore and 66 percent for Detroit were also unexplained.

As for variations in sentence lengths, Eisenstein and Jacob found that there was far less variance within these courts on that point, that most of the variances could be explained by measurable factors, and that of these factors the seriousness of the offenses was the most potent explanation.[13] (See Figure 15.2) Eisenstein and Jacob comment that "much of the sentencing disparity [regarding sentence lengths] that other studies emphasize was apparently absent from these three cities."[14]

This study has thus indicated that the major disparity problem may be focused on the decision as to whether to imprison convicted felons and not on the length of prison terms. Of course, the study was done within specific cities and did not compare various cities or counties within specific states.

Commenting on research into disparities, Alfred Blumstein and his colleagues write:

> In studying the determinants of sentences, it is not sufficient to consider only factors relating to offense, the offender, and case processing variable. Although some statistical studies have included as many as thirty explanatory variables relating to case attributes, two-thirds or more of the variation in sentence outcomes [is] unexplained. Many researchers have looked to elements of the decision making process, especially differences among judges, for the sources of that remaining variation.[15]

Charles E. Frazier and E. Wilbur Boch studied sentences in a six-county Florida circuit and focused on differences among judges in terms of their ages, their years of judicial experience, and whether they had been prosecutors prior to serving on the bench. They found that these variables had no impact on variances in sentencing. On the other hand, the identity of the probation officers did, in fact, have an impact,

FIGURE 15.1
Relationship between the Decision to Sentence Convicted Defendants to Prison and Selected Characteristics*

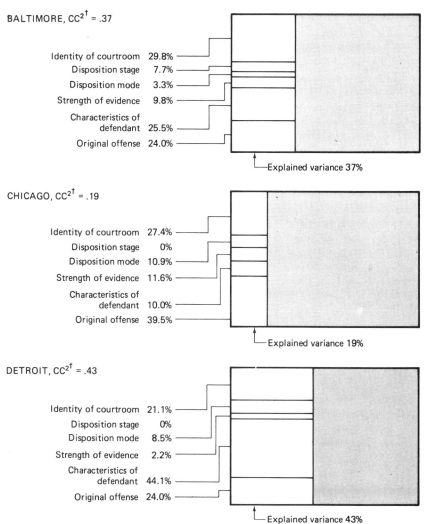

BALTIMORE, $CC^{2\dagger}$ = .37

Identity of courtroom	29.8%
Disposition stage	7.7%
Disposition mode	3.3%
Strength of evidence	9.8%
Characteristics of defendant	25.5%
Original offense	24.0%

Explained variance 37%

CHICAGO, $CC^{2\dagger}$ = .19

Identity of courtroom	27.4%
Disposition stage	0%
Disposition mode	10.9%
Strength of evidence	11.6%
Characteristics of defendant	10.0%
Original offense	39.5%

Explained variance 19%

DETROIT, $CC^{2\dagger}$ = .43

Identity of courtroom	21.1%
Disposition stage	0%
Disposition mode	8.5%
Strength of evidence	2.2%
Characteristics of defendant	44.1%
Original offense	24.0%

Explained variance 43%

*Multiple discriminant function analysis with variables forced in reverse order of presentation above. Weighted file sample used in Baltimore; random indictment sample plus observational trial courtroom sample used in Chicago; and observational sample used in Detroit. Improvement in predictive ability (Tau) was 57 percent in Baltimore, 45 percent in Chicago, and 63 percent in Detroit.

†Canonical Correlation Squared.

Source: James Eisenstein and Herbert Jacob, *Felony Justice: An Organizational Analysis of Criminal Justice,* Little, Brown, Boston, 1977, p. 277.

FIGURE 15.2
Relationship of Length of Sentence to Selected Characteristics*

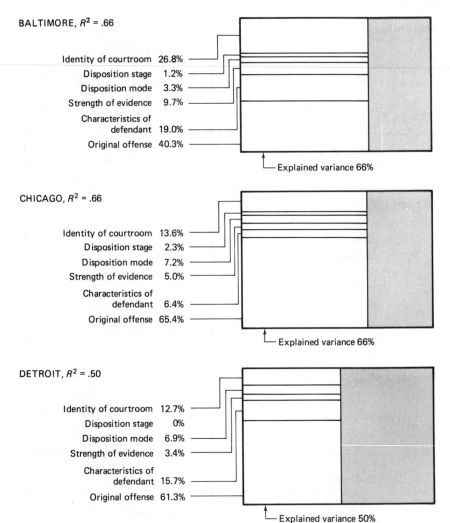

BALTIMORE, R^2 = .66

Identity of courtroom	26.8%
Disposition stage	1.2%
Disposition mode	3.3%
Strength of evidence	9.7%
Characteristics of defendant	19.0%
Original offense	40.3%

Explained variance 66%

CHICAGO, R^2 = .66

Identity of courtroom	13.6%
Disposition stage	2.3%
Disposition mode	7.2%
Strength of evidence	5.0%
Characteristics of defendant	6.4%
Original offense	65.4%

Explained variance 66%

DETROIT, R^2 = .50

Identity of courtroom	12.7%
Disposition stage	0%
Disposition mode	6.9%
Strength of evidence	3.4%
Characteristics of defendant	15.7%
Original offense	61.3%

Explained variance 50%

*Stepwise multiple regression was used, forcing variables in reverse order of presentation above. The Baltimore analysis was based on a file sample of defendants sent to prison (N = 191); the Chicago analysis was based on weighted indictment and informational samples of defendants sent to prison (N = 173); in Detroit we used the entire sample of defendants sent to prison (N = 256). Life sentences were excluded. Sentence length (in months) was transformed by taking the natural logarithm.

Source: James Eisenstein and Herbert Jacob, *Felony Justice: An Organizational Analysis of Criminal Justice,* Little, Brown, Boston, 1977, p. 283.

increasing by 10 percent the amount of variance that could be explained. Their conclusion was that future research should pay more attention to judicial subcultures: "Jurisdictions with similar social, economic, and political environments may develop similar subcultures of justice and, in turn, they may manifest sentencing patterns that are not greatly different."[16]

Belinda McCarthy and Charles Lindquist have reviewed the literature and found that there has been great inconsistency in research findings about disparity and the factors that enter into it. Their own research, using cases from Birmingham, Alabama, involved dividing the cases into three specific crime categories: murder, assault, and robbery. Factors lost when studying crimes in the aggregate became important in explaining sentence variances among cases in each category. An example was the race of the defendant. This factor was related to sentence severity in robbery cases, but did not relate as much in other categories or in the aggregate. On the other hand, they found that a few variables (for example, type of counsel) that were significant factors in sentence variances in the sum total of cases disappeared as a factor when each crime category was looked at separately.[17]

As Blumstein et al. have put it, "The evidence for sentence disparity is extensive, but data on the sources of that disparity are scarce." They suggest exploring how judges develop and then apply their own goals in sentencing. The authors also explain that sentencing decisions may not be the end product of a linear process, but of a complex and multistage process in which cases are assigned to different categories by each of the actors, including prosecutors and probation officers. One category is of those cases in which rehabilitation is seen as the appropriate goal, another contains those cases in which criminal records indicate defendants require incapacitation, and still another is composed of cases in which the crimes are so heinous that only severe punishment will suffice. Each category may thus have entirely different "sentencing rules."[18] This goes back to what we were saying earlier about defining disparity in terms of the very different sentences imposed in similar cases. The trick is to identify all the criteria and apply them correctly so that truly similar cases are being compared with one another. Only then can researchers hope to pin down the reasons for whatever disparities appear.

DEALING WITH DISCRETION AND DISPARITIES

If one assumes that disparities are the inevitable result of unbridled discretion, then it would appear necessary to find and implement methods of limiting or controlling discretion. Kenneth Culp Davis some years ago pointed out that there were two approaches to this. One is to confine discretion—that is, to set up boundaries within which discretion is permitted but outside of which, it is not. Another is to impose supervisory controls of one decision maker over another—in other words, establish a formal check, with one official having to answer to another for any act that either falls short of or exceeds some standards of justice.[19]

In the case of prosecutors and judges, there are generally maximums established by law to limit the charges that may be filed and the sentences that may be imposed. But there are no laws or rules requiring the prosecutor to file anything or to take a specific action in any given case, and the sentencing laws of most states permit judges to withhold or suspend sentence. In short, there are upper-limit boundaries in law, but few if any minimum-level boundaries. As for supervisory checking, we have already made it clear that judges may dismiss prosecutorial actions deemed excessive but may do nothing about prosecutorial inaction, while judges may be checked in a few states by appellate courts that review sentences that are deemed too harsh but are rarely if ever answerable for leniency.

On this last point, the supervisory pressure in many places, especially those with very heavy case loads, may be to keep charges and sentences to the bare minimum. New York police have complained for years about what they consider the wholesale reductions of felony arrests to misdemeanor charges, district attorneys complain that they are under pressure from judges to bring only the most dangerous or notorious defendants to trial, and judges complain that their chief administrator pushes for docket clearance at any cost. One judge even told a reporter that the only way he could meet these demands was "by letting people walk." When asked what would happen if he bucked the system and "started dishing out real justice," the judge replied: "They wouldn't give me an air-conditioned courtroom this summer. . . . You don't know what it is to work in a courtroom that's not air-conditioned."[20]

The question of how we establish stricter standards, or set up supervisory systems that encourage officials to observe basic standards, runs into the question of whether such actions require the allocation of vastly increased resources to handle the overload on the existing system.

Still another question is whether any attempt to control discretionary power at any one point in the criminal justice system will simply cause that power to appear at another point. Candace McCoy states that the "often used simile likens the discretion-ridden criminal justice system to a set of hydraulic brakes. If you push down on one point," she continues, "the displaced volume of fluid will exert pressure and 'bulge out,' reappearing elsewhere in the mechanism." Thus it is "probably a fruitless strategy" to try to concentrate on any one component when attempting to deal with abuses of discretion.[21]

DEALING WITH PROSECUTORIAL DISCRETION

In looking at prosecutorial discretion, we find two phases of the operation of the office requiring attention: the screening of cases and filing of original charges and, of course, plea bargaining. Can prosecutors be required to take some action against every accused or at least be called to answer to some other authority such as a judge for every instance in which they decide not to file? Can plea bargaining be abolished? If not, can it be controlled by specific standards or can its review by the courts be made more effective?

In looking at these questions, we shall consider both of the approaches to controlling discretion already mentioned: the establishment of standards or rules that set limits and the use of supervisory authority to check the behavior of prosecutors.

Control of Filing of Charges

Davis points out that there are models one can look to for limiting the discretion of prosecutors in the filing of charges. One is the West German system, in which the prosecutor is not free to withhold prosecution if the evidence is clear and the law is not in doubt. If the German prosecutor questions the wisdom of prosecution, he or she is supposed to defer to a judge who reviews the case and rules on its prosecutability. If a case raises the matter of whether a prosecution is wise from a policy standpoint, any decision by a prosecutor not to file is reviewed by superiors in the Ministry of Justice. Victims also have to resort to legal procedures to compel prosecution in cases where it is withheld.[22]

Another model, this one American, is the system used by the National Labor Relations Board; this system makes use of a set of procedural rules that call for notification of accusing parties as to (1) reasons for not taking action, (2) the possibility of appeal to the Office of Appeals, and (3) actions taken by the General Counsel of the NLRB in response to decisions made by the Office of Appeals. The General Counsel also provides opinions on pending cases to regional offices on request, and the combination of advisory opinions and actions on appeals is published in a "book of digests."[23] Thus the regional officers have an evolving set of guidelines and policies to follow as well as supervisory authority to answer to for their decisions.

Law professors Charles Bubany and Frank Skillern have proposed a specific set of guidelines and rules for prosecutors that would take into consideration three levels of concern: the strength of the evidence; the benefits versus the costs of prosecution, including the impact on victims, on other cases the defendant might be involved in, and on the police; and the probable effect on the defendant, including a consideration of more productive alternatives.[24] But while many prosecutors already employ such guidelines internally, Bubany and Skillern would make them the basis for review of the prosecutor's decisions. Such review could be initiated by either defendants or "aggrieved citizens" by means of a complaint to which the prosecutor would have to respond to a central prosecutorial agency. That administrative agency could presumably order a prosecution activated or withdrawn. If the complainant was not satisfied with the agency's actions, the case could be taken to court for a judicial review that could result in a court order. The authors comment that such "administrative and judicial review serve a useful function of validating prosecutorial policies and practices," especially since most are already "reasonable and defensible."[25] But the reviews will end the suspicions and secrecy, they argue, as well as bring the few errant prosecutors or cases into line.

Whether this proposal would have the intended effect or merely add to the work load remains to be seen. In any case, only a handful of states and the federal system have anything like such a centralized administrative agency in place. Either such agencies would have to be created or state attorneys general would have to be more powerful and active, and the status of prosecutors as constitutional officers or agents solely of the county would be significantly altered.

Control of Plea Bargaining

Perhaps it serves to recall that there is, of course, judicial review of guilty pleas, and thus of plea bargains. True, judges in most places cannot order prosecutors to withdraw their offers or reinstate charges they have dropped, but they can refuse to accept the pleas and order defendants to prepare for trial. Nevertheless, most judges rarely do this and claim to be compelled to accept whatever pleas come in; and prosecutors regularly state that it is judges who apply the most pressure to settle cases without trials. We cannot, therefore, look to judicial review for relief here.

Banning the Plea Bargain　What about abolishing plea bargains altogether? The National Advisory Commission recommended just such action almost two decades ago. Then, in 1975, the attorney general of Alaska, for whom all prosecutors in that state work, issued an order that all bargaining involving the promise of leniency in sentence was to be ended. Charges were to be reduced only if lack of evidence or the interests of justice required it.

The effect of this virtual ban was studied in 1979 by a research team funded by the National Institute of Justice. Analyses were performed of court processes and actions prior to and following the ban. The results were instructive:[26]

• Court processing of cases actually speeded up.
• Defendants pleaded guilty at about the same rate after the ban as they had before.
• The number of trials increased (up 97 percent in Anchorage) but did not become unmanageable.
• Sentences became more severe for some classes of offenders, especially those committing minor and drug-related offenses and those with little or no previous criminal record.
• There was virtually no change in convictions or sentences for violent offenders.

The researchers found that prosecutors were generally pleased to get away from sentence bargaining and that they had not sought to circumvent the order by entering into negotiations with defense counsel prior to filing charges. As to the effect on dispositions, the study comments that relatively "clean" offenders and property crime offenders found their avenue to a good deal cut off, while repeat and violent offenders had not really had such an avenue prior to the ban anyway. The team concluded that "the motive for most pleas of guilty in Alaska lay more in the intrinsic realities of the cases than in any prosecutorial concessions or guarantees offered to defendants in the form of plea bargains."[27]

As to the impact—or lack of it—on the system and the disposition of its case load, the team wrote that "Most of our original hypotheses were disproven, and we were frequently surprised by the discrepancies between our expectations and the actual effects. . . . Perhaps some of these unanticipated findings will serve to open minds and lead to a reexamination of old beliefs about plea bargaining.[28]

Banning as a Ploy How about a "ban" on plea bargaining that actually enhanced the power of prosecutors to bargain on their terms? For an example of this, we look to California, where voters approved Proposition 8 (a so-called victims' bill of rights) that bans plea bargaining in the superior courts of the state in twenty-five serious felony categories. This action is part of a strong shift within California away from due process and rehabilitation-oriented policies toward a strong crime control approach. The proposition, with its elimination of a state exclusionary rule and other such "get-tough" provisions, was a logical follow-up to the earlier (1976) adoption of a determinate sentencing law—an act we shall discuss later.

The plea bargaining ban demonstrates the hydraulic or displacement effect about which McCoy and others warned. Since the ban covers only the superior courts, and since California law permits felonies to be disposed of at the municipal court level, the "bulge" has appeared at this lower-court level. McCoy reports that the municipal courts can take a plea, pronounce a sentence, then certify the case up to superior court for approval. Superior court judges are reluctant to overturn the dispositions and try the cases, so in the first two years of operation of the new ban, the share of "serious" felonies settled in municipal courts and certified upward went from 18.8 percent to 27.8 percent.[29]

The irony of this situation is that, according to McCoy, rather than being an unexpected consequence, this is exactly what the framers of Proposition 8 intended. They knew that lower-court judges are less independent, more loaded with cases, and therefore more likely to go along with prosecutor's recommendations than superior court judges. This is supported by the fact that sentences have gotten somewhat harsher. Specifically, McCoy reports, probation rates dropped and average sentence length increased in certain crime categories.[30]

So here is an attempt to limit the discretion of one component (general trial court judges) and permit expanded discretion at another level (really with the prosecutors), seeking the end result of harsher sentences.

Restricting the Plea Bargain Even prior to the Alaskan ban, Manhattan district attorney Richard H. Kuh attracted a lot of attention when he issued a set of restrictive guidelines to his assistants. First, he virtually banned participation by assistants in sentence bargaining in March of 1974. Then in August of that year he issued detailed rules concerning plea bargains, which he grounded in a desire to "assure a considerable degree of consistency" and to resist judicial or case-load pressures for cheap deals. The rules are too involved to reproduce here, but they called upon assistants to avoid overcharging, to reduce charges from felonies to misdemeanors as early in the proceedings as possible, to avoid misstatements (threats) to defense counsel, and to hold scheduled in-office conferences with defense counsel rather than behind-the-scene meetings. Kuh stipulated special rules for multiple-crime offenders and in cases involving homicide, larceny, narcotics, and rackets. He also placed specific limitations on other cases, though he recognized that bargaining was essential in a system as overloaded as Manhattan's.[31]

It is difficult to say what the impact of Kuh's rules would have been on case processing, since he was replaced in late 1974 by Robert Morgenthau, who dispensed with the rules. But prosecutors throughout the country have followed Kuh's lead and placed restrictions of varying types and degrees on plea bargaining. Examples of such rules are given below:

1. There must be no agreement without consultation with, or the approval of, the investigating officer and/or the victim.

2. Agreements must be approved by the chief prosecutor or a reviewer specifically designated by the chief prosecutor.

3. Agreements must not be used to circumvent mandatory punishment provisions; so, for example, prosecutors cannot "eat" the gun where the law specifies a minimum punishment for using firearms.

4. Agreements cannot be made to reduce felonies by more than one level or to reduce any felony case to a misdemeanor.

5. Agreements cannot be made with defendants with serious prior convictions.

In general, a tough line on plea bargaining necessitates an equally tough line on filings. The police in New York, Alaska, and New Orleans have all complained about prosecutorial charging policies in the wake of bans or restrictions on plea bargains.[32] Judges have also complained that it forces them to bargain with defense attorneys in disposing of cases rather than to wait for deals to come for their blessing. But if judges want to bargain with the defense over sentences, this is clearly within their scope of authority and is quite properly removed from the hands of prosecutors.

Any attempt to ban or strictly limit plea bargains requires not only clear statements of policy and rules, but administrative supervision to ensure compliance. As noted, in Alaska this comes from the attorney general. In most places, however, it is left to the chief prosecutor of each office and may, in large offices, be delegated to division chiefs. But there is no review of these matters by outside agencies. Prosecutors may, as Kuh did, make their policies public, thus inviting public scrutiny as well as the scrutiny of other justice officials. But seasoned criminals learn the ropes anyway. Revealing the rules of the game only serves to enlighten the public and to "demystify" the process a bit, while introducing an element of accountability that has been too long missing. Whether an outside agency or a centralized office of prosecution should be given the authority to enforce the rules is another matter entirely. At the very least, this would require a fundamental change in established beliefs about the independence of the prosecutor.

DEALING WITH JUDICIAL DISCRETION IN SENTENCING

There have been few attempts in recent years to wrestle with the matter of prosecutorial discretion but many attempts to deal with the discretion given judges to decide what sentence offenders should serve. These efforts involve a number of social and political forces and several alternative approaches.

There are four major approaches. One is to institutionalize *appellate review of sentences* as a matter entirely apart from review of convictions. Another is to set up *sentencing councils* through which judicial peers may influence one another. A third is to change the laws themselves to provide for *mandatory minimum* sentences, for what are called *presumptive sentences,* or for other more structured statutory alternatives. A fourth is to have a commission, usually answerable to the judiciary, design *sentencing guidelines* to standardize sentences without changing the law.

Appellate Review of Sentences

If there is to be meaningful appellate review of sentences, there must be specific statutory or constitutional provisions regarding the standards for sentencing. The Eighth Amendment standard of "cruel and unusual punishment" is of little or no help in challenging an overly harsh sentence unless there is a dramatic change in the philosophy of the Supreme Court on the subject. A recent case involved a forty-year sentence given a black man by a Virginia court for possession and distribution of nine ounces (about $200 worth) of marijuana. The federal district court and U.S. Court of Appeals both ruled that the sentence was an unconstitutional violation of the Eighth Amendment, but this result was overturned 6 to 3 by the Supreme Court. The Court held that sentence lengths were "purely a matter of legislative prerogative"; in the opinion written by Justice William H. Rehnquist, the Court warned that a successful challenge to a prison term would be "exceedingly rare," that such a challenge would probably only succeed in a case where a life term was given for a parking violation.[33]

Yet some states have provided for appellate review of sentences for some time. They have allowed the appellate courts to design standards of harshness, and two states (Connecticut and Massachusetts) have even established separate special courts to review sentences.[34]

Still, in the absence of specific statutory or constitutional provisions, these appellate courts have been very reluctant to overturn sentences imposed by trial judges. Only in legislation or through a guidelines system is it possible for prosecutors to seek review of sentences deemed too lenient. Thus appellate review of sentencing does not in and of itself offer real opportunities to restrict judicial discretion and/or reduce sentencing disparities.

Sentencing Councils

Another approach is to set up councils of judges operating in criminal trial courts to preview cases pending sentencing and make recommendations as to appropriate sentences to the judges handling the cases. This has been tried over the past two decades, especially in a few federal district courts. The councils may reduce the extremes of disparity, but they do not impose any effective limits on the discretion of sentencing judges nor result in an articulated policy or set of guidelines for sentencing throughout any particular jurisdiction.[35]

Legislated Limits or Controls

In recent years various legislatures have voted to impose limits on sentencing discretion. Most states have debated changes in their penal codes and some have passed significant legislation. In 1984 the U.S. Congress adopted a major overhaul of the federal criminal code that included proposals for a fundamental restructuring of sentencing. The new laws generally provide for sentences that fall into one of two categories, mandatory minimum sentences or presumptive sentences, but other approaches have also been tried.

Mandatory Minimum Sentences   Laws that require judges to sentence convicted persons to a minimum number of days, months, or years in jail or prison for specified offenses have been widely adopted. These laws generally reflect a desire to "get tough" and reflect an approach based on retribution, deterrence, or incapacitation as a proper goal in sentencing. Some of these laws cover specific, usually violent, crimes. Others cover any crime committed with the use of firearms or involving serious threats to life. Still others are known as "recidivist," or repeat offender, statutes, since they invoke the mandatory time or provide for specified additional terms to be added to regular sentences in cases where the offender has a previous record of similar crimes.

Many states have opted for the mandatory minimum approach because it is obviously both simple and attractive. But these laws are generally so broad-brush in their approach that severe injustices can result in specific cases. Florida's three-year mandatory minimum for use of a firearm in the commission of any of a list of felony crimes, for example, can result in imprisonment for three years with no earlier parole possible for a wife, who, during a heated fight with her husband, grabs the family pistol and fires it in his general direction. Her punishment would be the same as that for the intended target of the law—armed robbers and burglars.

Recidivist statutes are somewhat more reasonable in that they require the offender to have a record as a true criminal, and they address the very real problem of the large numbers of offenses committed by a relatively small number of offenders. Recidivist statutes generally require separate prosecution of the recidivism itself following the disposition of the current case.

Presumptive Sentences   More sophisticated than the mandatory minimum is the presumptive sentence approach. Basically this involves establishing a benchmark sentence for each class or type of offense and then providing for reductions from or additions to that presumed sentence if specific mitigating or aggravating circumstances are found to be present. Judges are required to use the presumed sentence or justify in writing their deviation from it by citing specific distinguishing circumstances.

There are variations on this theme. In California, for example, in addition to reductions in sentence linked to mitigating circumstances and increases linked to aggravating circumstances, there are "enhancements" for such specific matters as use of a firearm, great pecuniary loss to victims, previous record of imprisonment, and multiple offenses.[36] But the law does not require that imprisonment be used by judges except in situations covered by specific provisions. Nevertheless, prison (and, for that matter, jail) sentences have increased in proportion to nonincarcerative sentences, although this trend began before the new law went into effect.[37] The California statute also takes one other step toward determinacy: It eliminates the authority of the parole board to decide when convicts should be released. Terms are reduced only by good-time provisions, and there is one year of parole supervision for offenders when they are released.

The state of Indiana has a presumptive sentencing plan that carries longer presumptive terms than that of California and provides for more adjustment in the face of either aggravating or mitigating circumstances. The Indiana plan also has a longer list of offenses for which probation may not be selected and provides for mandatory additions of thirty years to the terms of those with two previous felony convictions. The Indiana parole board does not decide early releases—these are matters of earned good time as in California—but can decide whether to rerelease an offender whose parole it has revoked.[38] Indiana has clearly opted for a tough crime control approach.

Other Determinate Schemes   Illinois and Maine have sentencing schemes that do not involve presumptive sentences but do permit the judge to choose a specific length of time from a wide range of terms. The major difference between the two states is that Maine provides no minimum for crimes less than murder, whereas Illinois provides minimums for each crime listed. The determinate character of both plans rests on the fact that, once the judge has pronounced a term, no other authority may alter it. Maine, in fact, has abolished its parole board, while Illinois has limited its board to cases dealing with revocation, release from prison, and early release from parole.

What all these legislatively dictated schemes have done is to introduce more determinacy into sentencing—that is, they enable inmates to predict more reliably their release dates. Some schemes reduce the discretion of judges; others actually increase judicial discretion in some regards while eliminating or severely limiting the discretion of parole boards to shorten terms of imprisonment. Whether any of the schemes has significantly reduced disparities in terms of actual sentences served by felons who commit similar crimes is subject to much analysis and debate.

Judicial Sentencing Guidelines

A very different approach to achieving more determinacy and reducing disparity is found in the development of guidelines by the courts or their designated administrators or study teams. The guideline approach does not assume changes in the law regarding the terms or conditions of sentence or the authority of either courts or parole boards. It is essentially an attempt on the part of courts to clean up their own house and provide a scheme whereby laws do not become necessarily harsher nor do prison populations explode.

Sentencing guidelines of one sort or another have been implemented by several states and are in process of being drafted for the federal government. Guidelines generally grant more flexibility to judges than do legislatively adopted presumptive sentencing schemes. Some guidelines systems, such as those of Denver and Chicago, are entirely voluntary—that is, judges are allowed to ignore the guidelines completely or to use them only to calculate the extent to which the actual sentence conforms to or departs from the guideline. Other, more meaningful guideline schemes require the computation to be performed first and permit judges to depart from the recommended sentence only if they state their reasons for doing so.

According to Michael and Don Gottfredson, there are nine aspects of a meaningful sentencing-guideline system:

1. The guidelines must provide an explicit general policy to guide decisions in individual cases.

2. They must employ explicit weights and criteria.

3. They must employ charts or a grid.

4. They must structure but not eliminate discretion.

5. Judges must provide reasons for any departures.

6. There must be a monitoring and feedback system.

7. Authorities must have the power to modify the guidelines whenever circumstances make modification desirable.

8. There must be some allowance for modifying the general policy "in response to experience, resultant learning and to social change."

9. The guidelines must be open to the public.[39]

Guidelines are intended to reduce disparities, but they do not necessarily dictate that all sentences have a common purpose. Minnesota's guidelines have the dominant but not exclusive goal of retribution. While Florida's guidelines state that retribution is the primary goal of the penal sanction, they allow for other goals to be utilized in determining sentences, especially in those cases in which the scores fall below those indicating prison terms. Pennsylvania's system maintains the requirements of that state's statutory and case law that the diverse goals of rehabilitation, deterrence, incapacitation, and retribution all have their place in determining appropriate sentences. John H. Kramer and Robin L. Lubitz assess the Pennsylvania system this way:

> The commission's guidelines balance the various rationales for sentencing with respect to the individual offender and the circumstances of the offense. Although the underlying structure of the guidelines is generally retributive, other principles of sentencing are emphasized in different areas of the guidelines. For example, for violent offenders with a serious prior record, incapacitation is an important goal; for moderately serious offenders, specific and general deterrence is stressed through short but certain incarceration; and for less serious offenders, rehabilitation considerations may come into play.[40]

Sentencing-guideline systems have generally been developed only after empirical studies have been made of past sentencing practices and outcomes. A large sample of old cases is analyzed to see what factors account for the sentences pronounced, those factors are given weights, and a set of guidelines is drafted to make explicit and formal policy out of what was once only implicit. Such an approach does not directly address questions of what is just or best, but simply formalizes existing practices. On the other hand, if it is shown that factors such as race or sex have been significant in past sentencing practices, this approach allows for change; the factors given weight in the new guidelines are those that are legally defensible.

Another step in sentencing reform was taken in Maryland and Florida where multijurisdictional experiments were conducted in 1981 and 1982 under the sponsorship of the National Institute of Justice. Those experiments were intended to test the guidelines sentences against prior sentences to see if guidelines did in fact alter case processing and if disparities were reduced. Both states went on to develop permanent sets of guidelines; but whereas Florida stuck by its empirical analysis of over

200 variables in over 5,000 real cases, Maryland used normative factors to set guidelines and then tested them in hypothetical cases.[41]

In Florida a sentencing guidelines commission was authorized by the legislature and placed under the supreme court of the state. Its fifteen members examined the results of the study; considered many modifications and adopted some on the basis of normative and policy considerations; and produced a set of guidelines that was adopted as part of the criminal rules of procedure by the supreme court and as part of the statute on sentencing by the legislature. Effective in October 1983, the use of guideline scoresheets has been required for every felony sentencing.

Most systems use a single matrix for determining sentences. The matrix permits calculation of an offense-seriousness score using factors determined to be the most salient—such as felony level, victim injury, weapon use, and so on—and the calculation of an offender score based primarily on past criminal record. The simplest system then provides a matrix with horizontal and vertical axes on which the intersection of the two scores provides the recommended sentence. The Minnesota system is shown in Figure 15.3.

Pennsylvania's system permits consideration of aggravating or mitigating circumstances and provides three ranges for judges to employ. It also permits a "weapon enhancement," by which one to two years of prison time can be added to the guideline sentence. Only where a judge departs entirely from these ranges must the sentence be justified and is it subject to appeal. (See Figure 15.4.)

Florida's system is the most complex, having separate scoresheets for nine different categories of crimes and precise tables for calculating offense scores relative to both the "primary" and related offenses. Scores are calculated on the basis of degree of physical injury to the victim, the offender's prior record, and whether he or she was under legal restraint (on bail, probation, parole, or "wanted") at the time of the offense. All scores are added and then placed on a table of sanctions. An example scoresheet is provided in Figure 15.5.

In Florida there was, at first, general acceptance of these guidelines by judges, prosecutors, and defense attorneys. Sentences were found to be within the guidelines about 80 percent of the time. A study of the impact of the guidelines revealed that judicial circuits with disparate records moved closer together in distributing probationary, jail, and prison sentences among their convicted felons; that prior record became a much more important factor in separating prison from nonprison sentences; that very long prison sentences virtually disappeared while the mean length of sentences declined only slightly; and that, for scoring purposes, prosecutors seemed to alter their charging and bargaining practices to some degree to obtain convictions on more counts. In general, sentenc-

FIGURE 15.3 Minnesota Sentencing Grid

Seriousness Levels of Conviction Offense	Criminal History Score						
	0	1	2	3	4	5	6 or more
1 Unauthorized use of motor vehicle / Possession of marijuana	N	N	N	N	N	N	19 / 18–20
2 Theft-related crimes ($250–$2500) / Aggravated forgery ($250–$2500)	N	N	N	N	N	N	21 / 20–22
3 Theft crimes ($250–$2500)	N	N	N	N	19 / 18–20	22 / 21–23	25 / 24–26
4 Nonresidential burglary / Theft crimes (over $2500)	N	N	N	N	25 / 24–26	32 / 30–34	41 / 37–45
5 Residential burglary / Simple robbery	N	N	N	30 / 29–31	38 / 36–40	46 / 43–49	54 / 50–58
6 Criminal sexual conduct, 2nd degree	N	N	N	34 / 33–35	44 / 42–46	54 / 50–58	65 / 60–70
7 Aggravated robbery	24 / 23–25	32 / 30–34	41 / 38–44	49 / 45–53	65 / 60–70	81 / 75–87	97 / 90–104
8 Criminal sexual conduct, 1st degree / Assault, 1st degree	43 / 41–45	54 / 50–58	65 / 60–70	76 / 71–81	95 / 89–101	113 / 106–120	132 / 124–140
9 Murder, 3rd degree / Murder, 2nd degree (felony murder)	105 / 102–108	119 / 116–122	127 / 124–130	149 / 143–155	176 / 168–184	205 / 195–215	230 / 218–242
10 Murder, 2nd degree (with intent)	120 / 116–124	140 / 133–147	162 / 153–171	203 / 192–214	243 / 231–255	284 / 270–298	324 / 309–339

Note: "N" denotes a presumption of a nonimprisonment sentence.

Source: Andrew von Hirsch, Kay A. Knapp, and Michael Tonry, *The Sentencing Commission and Its Guidelines,* Northeastern University Press, Boston, 1987, p. 179.

ing seemed to become more uniform but not very different in overall severity.

However, recent interviews with judges and attorneys reveal a mixed but increasingly hostile response to the guidelines. Complaints focus on the rigidity of the guidelines, denial of discretion, and too much leniency, especially in the burglary category. Critics also discount the system as a legislative effort to accomplish control of prison populations and budgets through the guise of guidelines supposedly dedicated to uniformity and "truth in sentencing."[42]

A study in Minnesota revealed that sentences became somewhat more uniform there and conformed to intended guidelines policies in the first year of implementation. However, subsequent increases in prison commitments led to adjustments in the guidelines aimed more at reducing prison commitments than at promoting further uniformity and equity in sentencing.[43]

Certainly guidelines can be used to accomplish goals other than reducing disparities. They can be used to increase certainty of incarceration for some crimes or, even more ambitiously, to try to control crime. They can also be used to control prison population, overtly in Minnesota's case and covertly, say some, in Florida's.

The experiences of different states vary according to the goals the guidelines were designed to accomplish and to the degree of agreement on the worthiness of those goals. On the whole, the guidelines approach is less likely to be resisted by judicial officials than is legislative change, since the guidelines approach involves these officials in the process and therefore produces a system more in tune with the legal culture.

Parole Reform

Many attempts at sentencing reform include the elimination of, or the imposition of severe restriction on, a parole board's authority to modify sentences. The parole boards of many states have acted as moderators of the extremes of sentencing by reducing the length of some sentences, though they can do nothing about the disparities that exist between those receiving prison terms and those not. Some parole boards have even pointed the way for the courts by adopting guidelines based on risk scales that give weighted values to various characteristics of offenders and their crimes. Others, however, act without much attention to criteria, seeming to be arbitrary and capricious in their decisions and thus adding to the disparities that already exist in the system. In any case, there is widespread belief that even where parole decisions are reasonable and reflect a concern for equity, they should not be seen as substitutes for sentencing decisions.

FIGURE 15.4 Pennsylvania Sentencing Grid

Offense Gravity Score	Prior Record Score	Minimum Range	Aggravated Minimum Range	Mitigated Minimum Range
10	0	48–120	statutory limit	36–48
Third degree murder	1	54–120	statutory limit	40–54
	2	60–120	statutory limit	45–60
	3	72–120	statutory limit	54–72
	4	84–120	statutory limit	63–84
	5	96–120	statutory limit	72–96
	6	102–120	statutory limit	76–102
9	0	36–60	60–75	27–36
e.g.: rape;	1	42–66	66–82	31–42
robbery inflicting	2	48–72	72–90	36–48
serious bodily injury	3	54–78	78–97	40–54
	4	66–84	84–105	49–66
	5	72–90	90–112	54–72
	6	78–102	102–120	58–78
8	0	24–48	48–60	18–24
e.g.: kidnapping;	1	30–54	54–68	22–30
arson (Felony 1)	2	36–60	60–75	27–36
voluntary	3	42–66	66–82	32–42
manslaughter	4	54–72	72–90	40–54
	5	60–78	78–98	45–60
	6	66–90	90–112	50–66
7	0	8–12	12–18	4–8
e.g.: aggravated	1	12–29	29–36	9–12
assault causing serious	2	17–34	34–42	12–17
bodily injury; robbery	3	22–39	39–49	16–22
threatening serious	4	33–49	49–61	25–33
bodily injury	5	38–54	54–68	28–38
	6	43–64	64–80	32–43
6	0	4–12	12–18	2–4
e.g.: robbery	1	6–12	12–18	3–6
inflicting bodily	2	8–12	12–18	4–8
injury; theft by	3	12–29	29–36	9–12
extortion (Felony 3)	4	23–34	34–42	17–23
	5	28–44	44–55	21–28
	6	33–49	49–61	25–33
5	0	0–12	12–18	non-confinement
e.g.: criminal mischief	1	3–12	12–18	1½–3
(Felony 3); theft	2	5–12	12–18	2½–5
by unlawful taking	3	8–12	12–18	4–8
(Felony 3); theft	4	18–27	27–34	14–18
by receiving stolen	5	21–30	30–38	16–21
property (Felony 3)	6	24–36	36–45	18–24
bribery				

Offense Gravity Score	Prior Record Score	Minimum Range	Aggravated Minimum Range	Mitigated Minimum Range
4 e.g.: theft by receiving stolen property, less than $2,000, by force or threat of force, or in breach of fiduciary obligation	0	0–12	12–18	non-confinement
	1	0–12	12–18	non-confinement
	2	0–12	12–18	non-confinement
	3	5–12	12–18	2½–5
	4	8–12	12–18	4–8
	5	18–27	27–34	14–18
	6	21–30	30–38	16–21
3 Most misdemeanor 1's	0	0–12	12–18	non-confinement
	1	0–12	12–18	non-confinement
	2	0–12	12–18	non-confinement
	3	0–12	12–18	non-confinement
	4	3–12	12–18	1½–3
	5	5–12	12–18	2½–5
	6	8–12	12–18	4–8
2 Most misdemeanor 2's	0	0–12	statutory limit	non-confinement
	1	0–12	statutory limit	non-confinement
	2	0–12	statutory limit	non-confinement
	3	0–12	statutory limit	non-confinement
	4	0–12	statutory limit	non-confinement
	5	2–12	statutory limit	1–2
	6	5–12	statutory limit	2½–5
1 Most misdemeanor 3's	0	0–6	statutory limit	non-confinement
	1	0–6	statutory limit	non-confinement
	2	0–6	statutory limit	non-confinement
	3	0–6	statutory limit	non-confinement
	4	0–6	statutory limit	non-confinement
	5	0–6	statutory limit	non-confinement
	6	0–6	statutory limit	non-confinement

Source: Andrew von Hirsch, Kay A. Knapp, and Michael Tonry, *The Sentencing Commission and Its Guidelines,* Northeastern University Press, Boston, 1987, pp. 186–188.

FIGURE 15.5 Sentencing Guidelines Scoresheet

1. PRIMARY DOCKET NUMBER	2. ADDITIONAL DOCKET NUMBERS	3 OBTS NUMBER	4. CATEGORY:

1 _ 2 _ 3 _ 4 _ 5 _ 6 _ 7 _ 8 _ 9

5. NAME (LAST NAME FIRST)			
	6. DATE OF BIRTH	7. SEX: M _ F	8. RACE: _ B _ W _ OTHER

9. VIOLATION: _ PROB _ CC

10. COUNTY	11. JUDGE AT SENTENCING	12. DATE OF OFFENSE	13. DATE OF SENTENCE	14. _ PLEA _ TRIAL	15. DOC #

POINTS

I. PRIMARY OFFENSE AT CONVICTION

Counts   Degree   Statute   Description

I. _____

II. ADDITIONAL OFFENSES AT CONVICTION

Counts   Fel/Misd   Degree   Statute   Description

II. _____

(Continue on Reverse)

III. A.. PRIOR RECORD

Counts   Fel/Misd   Degree   Statute   Description

OFFICE USE ONLY

(Continue on Reverse)

III. A. _____ _____ _____

III. B. SAME CATEGORY PRIORS (categories 3, 5 and 6 only) III B. ____

III. C. PRIOR DUI CONVICTIONS (category 1 only) III C. ____

IV. LEGAL STATUS AT TIME OF OFFENSE IV. ____

_____ (1) no restrictions _____ (2) restrictions

V. VICTIM INJURY

Number of Victims/Occurrences   Injury

_____   none or no contact

_____   slight or contact but no penetration

_____   moderate or penetration

_____   severe or death

TOTAL POINTS V. ____

GUIDELINE SENTENCE _____   PERMITTED SENTENCE _____

TOTAL SENTENCE IMPOSED _____

REASONS FOR DEPARTURE _____

JUDGE _____   PREPARER _____

| OFFICE USE ONLY | T.S. ____ | COMP. ____ | S.P. ____ | PROB. ____ |
| | C.C ____ | C.J. ____ | E.F. ____ | |

Source: State Court Administrator's Office, Tallahassee, Florida.

SUMMARY AND CONCLUSION

This chapter has examined the issue of discretion and the disparities that result in the criminal process. We have looked briefly at evidence of disparities in the disposition of cases, especially in regard to what is of greatest concern to defendants: disparity in sentencing. Proposals and efforts to limit or regulate discretion in the hope that that in itself would reduce disparities have been studied. Particular attention has been paid to discretion in charging (though nothing is being done to limit prosecutors' control in this area), plea bargaining, and sentencing. We have looked at various schemes for establishing sentencing guidelines, the approach currently adopted by several states, and by the federal government. Guideline systems seem to offer the best chance for balancing a desire for increased equity with a desire to fit the punishment to the offender and the offense and the desire to maintain judicial independence.

Pressures to reduce disparities and ensure more evenhandedness and consistency come from both the crime control and due process camps. Ideologically, haphazard handling of defendants and cases defeats the purposes of both schools of thought. Deterrence based on some degree of certainty is not achieved, nor are the due process rights of defendants fairly realized in any system in which one's fate is determined so much by the luck of the draw.

There are no simple answers. No changes in law or procedure will work in the absence of intelligence, good sense, and the determination of all participants to achieve a better system of criminal justice. The outcome is still in doubt, but much being done now is encouraging to those who hope for that better system.

QUESTIONS FOR DISCUSSION

1. What do you consider the single largest problem in the courts in your community? What steps can or should be taken to solve it? How will such steps impact on the various agencies, including the prosecutor's and public defender's offices, the clerk of court, the sheriff's office, and the jail?
2. What, if any, limits have been placed on the exercise of discretion by judicial officials? If some limits have been adopted, are they effective? If none have been tried, should some be applied? If so, which limits, and how should they be imposed?
3. Does our judicial system, as currently structured and operating, give unfair advantage to the objectives of Packer's Due Process Model or to the Crime Control Model? Explain.

NOTES

1. Burton Atkins and Mark Pogrebin, *The Invisible Justice System: Discretion and the Law,* Anderson, Cincinnati, 1978, p. 2.
2. Ibid., p. 2.
3. *Stump v. Sparkman,* 435 U.S. 349 (1978).
4. *Butz v. Economou,* 98 S. Ct. 2894 (1978).
5. Marvin Frankel, *Criminal Sentences: Law without Order,* Hill and Wang, New York, 1972.
6. Ibid., p. 6.
7. Ibid., p. 8.
8. Whitney North Seymour, Jr., "Sentencing Study for the Southern District of New York," in Leonard Orland and Harold R. Tyler, Jr. (eds.), *Justice in Sentencing,* Foundation Press, Mineola, N.Y., 1974, p. 170.
9. Administrative Office of the United States Courts, *Federal Offenders in United States Courts, 1972,* in Pierce O'Donnell, Michael J. Churgin, and Dennis E. Curtis (eds.), *Toward a Just and Effective Sentencing System: Agenda for Reform,* Praeger, New York, 1977, p. 7.
10. Ibid., pp. 8 and 9.
11. Ibid., p. 10.
12. James Eisenstein and Herbert Jacob, *Felony Justice: An Organizational Analysis of Criminal Justice,* Little, Brown, Boston, 1977, pp. 276–279.
13. Ibid., p. 281.
14. Ibid., p. 285.
15. Alfred Blumstein et al. (eds.), *Research on Sentencing: The Search for Reform,* vol. 1, National Academy Press, Washington, D.C., 1983, pp. 118–119.
16. Charles E. Frazier and E. Wilbur Boch, "Effects of Court Officials on Sentence Severity," *Criminology,* vol. 20, no. 2, August 1982, p. 270.
17. Belinda R. McCarthy and Charles A. Lindquist, "Ambiguity and Conflict in Sentencing Research: Partial Resolution through Crime-Specific Analysis," *Journal of Criminal Justice,* vol. 13, 1985, pp. 155–169.
18. Blumstein et al., pp. 123–124.
19. Davis, as quoted in Atkins and Pogrebin, p. 2.
20. Arthur Browne, "Soft Judges, Hard-Core Crooks," *New York Daily News,* July 20, 1982, pp. 4 and 18.
21. Candace McCoy, "Determinate Sentencing, Plea Bargaining Bans, and Hydraulic Discretion in California," *Justice System Journal,* vol. 9, no. 3, 1984, p. 256.
22. Davis, as quoted in Atkins and Pogrebin, pp. 222–223.
23. Ibid., p. 225.
24. Charles P. Bubany and Frank F. Skillern, "Taming the Dragon: An Administrative Law for Prosecution Decision-Making," *American Criminal Law Review,* vol. 13, no. 3, Winter 1976, pp. 496–497.
25. Ibid., pp. 504–505.
26. Michael Rubenstein, Stevens H. Clarke, and Teresa J. White, *Alaska Bans Plea Bargaining,* U.S. Government Printing Office, Washington, D.C., 1980, pp. vii–viii.

27. Ibid., p. 224.
28. Ibid., p. viii.
29. McCoy, p. 269.
30. Ibid., p. 272.
31. For the full text of Kuh's memorandum, see *Criminal Law Bulletin,* vol. 11, no. 1, January–February 1975, pp. 48–65.
32. William F. McDonald, "The Prosecutor's Domain," in William McDonald (ed.), *The Prosecutor,* Sage, Beverly Hills, Calif., 1979, pp. 42–43.
33. *Huto v. Davis,* as reported in *The New York Times,* January 12, 1982.
34. Hazel B. Kerper and Jerold H. Israel, *Introduction to the Criminal Justice System,* 2d ed., West, St. Paul, Minn., 1979, p. 369.
35. Shari Diamond and Hans Zeisel, "Sentencing Councils: A Study of Sentence Disparity and Its Reduction," in Atkins and Pogrebin, pp. 300–314.
36. Stephen P. Lagoy, Frederick A. Hussey, and John H. Kramer, "The Prosecutorial Function and Its Relation to Determinate Sentencing Structures," in McDonald, pp. 220–221.
37. Jonathan Casper, "Implementation of the California Sentence Law," *Public Administration Times,* March 15, 1982, p. 5.
38. Lagoy et al., "The Prosecutorial Function and Its Relation to Determinate Sentencing Structures," pp. 222–223.
39. Michael Gottfredson and Don M. Gottfredson, "Guidelines for Incarceration Decisions: A Partisan View," *University of Illinois Law Review,* 1984, p. 293.
40. John H. Kramer and Robin L. Lubitz, "Pennsylvania's Sentencing Reform: The Impact of Commission-Established Guidelines," *Crime and Delinquency,* vol. 31, no. 4, October 1985, p. 486.
41. Deborah M. Carrow, "Judicial Sentencing Guidelines: Hazards of the Middle Ground," *Judicature,* vol. 68, nos. 4–5, October–November 1984, p. 164.
42. Roger Handberg and N. Gary Holten, "The Impact of Florida's Sentencing Guidelines on the Processing and Disposition of Criminal Cases," unpublished report, 1985.
43. Kay A. Knapp, "What Sentencing Reform in Minnesota Has and Has Not Accomplished," *Judicature,* vol. 68, nos. 4–5, October–November, 1984, pp. 181–189.

EPILOGUE:
THE PROGNOSIS FOR
CRIMINAL COURTS

As this text goes to press, the judicial system, and criminal courts in particular, appears to be under siege. The scourge of drugs and its spinoffs—youth gangs, murder, aggravated batteries, robberies, burglaries, thefts, tax evasion, money laundering, and so on—threatens to completely overwhelm systems that are already stressed. There seems to be an accompanying if not associated explosion of economic and environmental crimes as increasing numbers of people, unwilling or unable to act in a socially responsible way, succumb to greed or lust for power.

Drug trafficking and attendant street crimes have given increasing impetus to citizen action, with both productive and dangerous results. Neighborhood watches cooperating with authorities are one thing; citizen patrols that act in competition to the police are another; and outright vigilantism (as manifested in the burning of a "crack house" or the beating of drug addicts) is still another. Because some drug gangs are armed with automatic military weapons, other citizens are rapidly adding such weapons to what is already the largest civilian arsenal in the world. This all speaks to a growing loss of confidence in the legal system.

The demand for application of pure crime control techniques to address the more obvious manifestations of lawlessness has never been greater, and concern for the values of due process has never been less popular. Prisons and jails are jam-packed in most states, and many are undertaking unprecedented building programs to incarcerate an ever-growing share of offenders.

The U.S. Supreme Court has, as already indicated, become increasingly receptive to crime control arguments and has turned ever more sharply away from its earlier concern for the protection of due process values and the rights of accused persons. Most citizens welcome and heartily support this transformation. Capital punishment has steadily regained favor until over three-quarters of Americans now support it. Serial killer Ted Bundy's execution was met with cheers.

Prosecutors have begun to use relatively new laws, such as the RICO (racketeering influenced and corrupt organization) acts, and new techniques born of video and computer technologies to attack crime and alleged criminals. Former New York U.S. attorney for the Southern District, Rudolph Giuliani, scored spectacularly in gaining federal convictions and imprisonment of almost all the top Cosa Nostra family bosses. His very successes, however, demonstrate the intractibility of organized crime, since business continues as usual.

Then there are the seemingly unprecedented number of stories of persons being falsely accused, prosecuted, and imprisoned in the face of apparently overwhelming evidence of their innocence, and of cases where the convictions are much later reversed. Some of these are due to honest errors; others are due to prosecutorial zeal or misconduct; and a few involve outright conspiracy to frame someone to deflect public outrage or to cover up for the real offenders.

There are also more and more situations in which private attorneys are active members of the criminal conspiracies or gangs they are well paid to represent in court. Some of these attorneys avoid criminal defense work and confine themselves to setting up dummy corporations and otherwise aiding and abetting money-laundering schemes and related tax evasions.

Meanwhile, Operation Greylord in Chicago and other investigations elsewhere have pointed out the depth of corruption on some benches. Judges are under the strictest scrutiny in American history.

Despite all this, the judicial system may, overall, be more competent and fair than at any time in our history. It can reasonably be asserted that the vast majority of officials are honest and effective in their work, and their work is more visible and perhaps better understood by more citizens than ever before.

Certainly, scholarly studies of court personnel and operations have never been so numerous or varied. While there is as yet an absence of coherent theory about how courts work, the cumulative effect of the many books, articles, and papers is the establishment of a data base and the education of students in the basic facts about law, courts, attorneys, and the legal process.

We conclude this text by expressing the hope that a legal and judicial system that has evolved over hundreds of years will survive the current onslaught of troubles and emerge stronger and more evenhanded in its decision making than ever. For such a hope to be realized, bright young people must enter the professions of law enforcement, law, and corrections and work to serve the common good rather than focus on narrow self-interest. The law does not operate like some machine; it accomplishes only what people who occupy the positions of authority compel it to accomplish.

Toward that end we urge all readers of this text to consider involvement in the justice system—if not as professionals, then as citizens, for we all have a vital role to play in the promotion of justice through law. It is our hope that this text has not only informed the reader but also inspired in him or her a deeper curiosity about the system of laws and courts. The future of our criminal courts and prospects for enlightened developments in law, control of crime, individual rights, and domestic tranquility rest on the decisions our readers will make.

INDEX